ONLY CRY FOR THE LIVING

Only Cry for the Living is published as a joint publication between Jocko Publishing and Di Angelo Publications INC.

JOCKO PUBLISHING
Di Angelo Publications
4265 San Felipe #1100
Houston, Texas, 77027

Only Cry for the Living Copyright 2020 Hollie S. McKay. In digital and print distribution in the United States of America and worldwide.

www.jockopublishing.com
www.diangelopublications.com
www.holliemckay.com

Library of Congress cataloging-in-publications data
Only Cry for the Living. Downloadable via Kindle, iBooks, NOOK.

Library of Congress Registration

ISBN-13: 978-1-942549-63-5

Interior Layout Design By: Kimberly James
Dust Jacket Design by: Jon Bozak

First Edition

10 9 8 7 5 6 4 3 2

1. History --- Military --- Iraq War
2. History --- Military --- Afghan War
3. History --- Middle East --- Iraq
4. Travel --- Special Interest --- Military
5. Travel --- Middle East --- General
6. Political Science --- Human Rights
7. Political Science --- Terrorism

ONLY CRY FOR THE LIVING

Memos From Inside the ISIS Battlefield

HOLLIE S. MCKAY

FOREWORD BY JOCKO WILLINK

*For my Kurdish-Syrian goddaughter and namesake, Hollie,
the beautiful child of Mazloum and Parishan.*

You are so deeply loved.

If one were to tell an unborn child that outside the womb there is a glorious world with green fields and lush gardens, high mountains and vast seas, with a sky lit by the sun and the moon, the unborn would not believe such absurdity. Still in the dark womb how could he imagine the indescribable majesty of this world? In the same way, when the mystics speak of worlds beyond scent and color, the common man deafened by greed and blinded by self-interest cannot grasp their reality.

From *Rumi's Little Book of Life*
The Garden of the Soul, the Heart, and the Spirit

FOREWORD

War reveals the complex and often contradictory face of human nature. On one end of the spectrum, people make incredible sacrifices to care for others. They protect, they defend, and they nurture those who cannot take care of themselves. Some heroic people will do anything to safeguard their families and their friends; sometimes people even make valiant sacrifices for those they don't actually know at all. War can unveil these beautiful and moving sacrifices.

But war also exposes the most vile and despicable of behaviors. Torture. Rape. Murder. Genocide. The ability for human beings to commit abhorrent atrocities with wanton disregard for morality is sadly displayed over and over again. Evil does exist.

It is critical that, as human beings, we never forget our nature—and our potential—for both good and evil. We must remember that we are capable of glorious and benevolent actions—acts that will bring light, love and laughter into the world. We must also remember that, as human beings, we are capable of demonic and reprehensible behavior that propel the world toward darkness.

We must remember.

Only Cry for the Living serves a share of our memory—and thereby, our conscience. This book, written by the incredibly courageous Hollie McKay, takes us deep into the psyche of war. She achieves this not only by simply reporting on what happens during war, but also by interviewing and conversing with those who directly participated in or were personally impacted by war. Hollie has spent extensive time on the ground in the Middle East, including Afghanistan, Syria, Pakistan, and Iraq—where she witnessed first-hand the fight of Kurdish,

Syrian, Iraqi, and American forces against the sadistic rise of ISIS, also known as ISIL or Da'esh.

Through her detailed and intense writing, Hollie brings us onto the battlefield with her. We can feel the impact of explosions. We can hear sniper rounds being fired. We can see the rubbled buildings and war-torn streets. We can smell blood, fire and death.

She lets us listen in on her conversations. We talk with ISIS sympathizers who murdered on behalf of their twisted caliphate. Hollie introduces us to the vile miscreants that traveled from first-world countries to fight for this wretched nightmare of a state controlled by Islamic extremists. Hollie allows us to see the difference between those who willing volunteer as ISIS fighters and people––such as a fourteen-year-old child soldier––indoctrinated and brainwashed into doing ISIS's sinister bidding on the battlefield. Through her interviews, we see the face of evil.

But Hollie also introduces us to heroes. We meet the soldiers that take the fight to the enemy, including the "Black Devils," a name given by the opposition, who ruthlessly hunted down and killed ISIS fighters. Perhaps serving an even worse fate to ISIS are the female Kurdish soldiers who hunt and kill insurgents. Their efforts deliver the insult of an afterlife without paradise for the fanatical enemy fighters, who believe death at the hands of a woman precludes them from that so-called paradise. Moreover, Hollie brings us into heartfelt discussions with Yadizi women who were captured, tortured, starved, and raped, but who survived and show indomitable strength as they carry on with their lives.

These are just some of the examples of the views Hollie delivers in this book—views not only of war, but of human nature. While I do not wish war on anyone, I do wish a better understanding of war for all of us. That is what Hollie McKay does with this book: she gives us all a better understanding of war and human nature. It is not a comfortable read. It is not a pleasant read. It is an important read.

But don't just read it.

Remember it.

Jocko Willink
November 2020

INTRODUCTION
July, 2014

"When you hear the bomb sirens, we will stop," said the old Israeli cab driver ever-so-spiritedly as we sped through the West Bank. "Crouch down against the side of the road. Don't worry; there will be lots of us. It's like a big party!"

I had just ventured back over the Allenby/King Hussein Bridge land crossing after spending some time sipping tea and watching wild camels with the Bedouins in Jordan.

Operation Protective Edge — also known as the Israel and Gaza war — was just launching in early July 2014.

An ominous carillon pierced the air and lingered for minutes before standard procedures followed. Then, finally, the pursuit of a normal life resumed. I glanced at my driver and watched his cheery face collapse.

He explained casually, in a tone flushed with anguish, that these little procedures made him think of his father who had been killed in the Six-Day War of 1967, and of his brother who passed in the Yom Kippur War of 1973.

I had forgotten to ask his name, but knew I would not forget the deep agony in his eyes or his snow grey hair, which he said turned from a rich black within days of hearing the news — his son, too, had died inside his wife's womb amid the stress of the First Intifada of 1987.

In that series of slow-motion moments, I knew that, while I was soon to return to my comfortable Los Angeles life, I had opened a door and started to walk down a road from which I knew there was no retreat. My insides growled with curiosity and an intense longing to understand these conflicts; to understand how countries could continue to douse themselves in blood, decade after decade; to understand why it could not be stopped.

All this, and yet both friends and foes were cut from the same cloth of human existence. It seemed they were fighting each other for the same things: freedom, future, and their families. Only deep down, nobody really wanted to fight and be apart from those they loved night after night. Everyone I had spoken to during that trip insisted they wanted peace, but opined that they were caught in the middle and had to defend their own people, wrapped in a situation they could not control. Each had their own unique story to tell.

The everyday people had no control over the decisions made by their leadership — whether it was offense, defense, or a tactic of terror. And yet the decisions over which they had no control impacted every aspect of their lives. All they could do was watch from the grimy glass window until the glass shattered, waiting for the war to gush into their lives.

Nearby, brutality was tearing Iraq apart yet again.

Just a few weeks earlier, in late October, Iraq's second-largest city of Mosul had fallen out of Baghdad's government-controlled hands and come under the rule of a group known as Islamic State, ISIS, ISIL, or the Arabic derogatory term, Da'esh. We knew little about them other than that they were deemed "too brutal" even for their main insurgency predecessor, Al Qaeda.

I had felt an unexplainable obligation to that country, to its people, to the place we as a nation had left behind before it was ready to stand on its own. Or perhaps I was trying to make sense of something that made no sense.

As we journeyed to Jerusalem that day, I thought about myself as a little girl. I remembered one afternoon, dancing around the living room to Madonna and unexpectedly catching sight of footage of the Gulf War on television. I remember with clarity being shocked and appalled as hollowed buildings burned and children just like me ran unaccompanied for their lives. There was a flashing image of one little girl who looked my age, covered in blood and wailing, the foot of an armed soldier beside her.

I couldn't understand how, in 1991, given the modern and magical world my six-year-old self-thought we lived in, that it was possible for there to be war anywhere. I had been raised to believe that war was a bygone concept. After learning my grandfather fought in WWII, in some era lifetimes before I was born, I had simply thought that the world had learned its lesson and there was no way people needed to orchestrate mass killings anymore. I was convinced that surely everyone now valued life and talked through their problems.

I think in that precise moment of glancing at the television, my naiveté disappeared — but my idealism did not, and I hope it never will. Perhaps it was my childhood curiosity that drove me to the point of obsession; of needing to make sense of what went through my mind as my city fell to the earth and the entire country was doused in flames; of wondering what it must have felt like to have been trapped inside.

I sat in that backseat and scrawled in my little black notebook. Today, those little black books are many. Over time, they piled up in my California beachside kitchen and later filled the drawers of several tiny Manhattan apartments, all filled with references to small Iraqi villages like Wardak and Nasr and foods like tashreeb and dolma and names like Mohammed and Miriam and Saif — people who I met along the way, who I didn't know if I would ever meet again, and about whom I often wondered if they were still alive.

I had wanted to understand this plight, a plight I did not know when I started would become a full-blown genocide, and I had to be there in my own skin. I had to stand beside ordinary people thrust into extraordinary situations, whose lives and livelihoods had been ravished by something that was no fault of their own. I wanted to understand conflict from a micro-level — from the human level — through deeply personal stories, rather than through the big, brooding macro-level statistics and weapons.

Throughout the years of ISIS occupation, I made countless trips in and out of Iraq to investigate the onslaught as a writer. As time went on and the fight to free the embattled nation intensified, I spent more and more time in the region, determined to play whatever small role I could to deliver a rough draft of history through the lens of the ordinary people surviving it. As the years went forth and the battle intensified, I wrote more and more memos as exemplified in this collection.

While they may never be the ones to read this book, it is these ordinary people for whom this book is written — by capturing anecdotes of their lives and nuggets of their history, I had figured they would never disappear into the void that is the collateral damage of war. Somehow, they would stay alive forever. They would know that their presence, their stories, and their contribution to the world truly mattered.

MEMOS

FIRST YEAR OF ISIS: 2014
America, the Savior

AMONG THE FIRST TO FLEE
November, 2014

Tents swooshed across muddy fields as the arid summer heat softened into fall. The days grew shorter and the nights colder. Little feet in rainboots stampeded along the gated confines of the displacement camp just outside of the northern Kurdish city of Erbil, sheltering thousands of Muslims and Yazidis from the Mosul area.

A row of young boys sat along an old metal pipe, excitedly singing Arabic songs. The girls whizzed each other around in wheelbarrows and played with their dolls on patches of earth that had hardened from mud to crusty dirt.

"It is still like a playpen to them, like a big party," one frail father said absently, as if he was staring right through me. "Soon they will know."

Crevices of stress had been delicately carved into his tanned face. His party was one of torment as he paced in circles, as if slowly going mad. I did not know what had happened to him and his family, but it did not feel right to ask.

The children noticed the new cluster of outsiders and raced toward us, tiny arms open for an embrace. I was there with my good friend from California, Mylee Cardenas. Mylee was a U.S Army veteran, tough around the edges with tattooed sleeves and a forthright demeanor, contrasted with soft eyes and layers of wisdom. And Mohammad Huzaifa Muluki was a twenty-three-year-old student from Baghdad who had written to me about a campus campaign he had started with a handful of other students.

When I leave this world, I'll leave no regrets; leave something to remember so they won't forget, Beyonce had sung at the United Nations General Assembly in New York two years earlier. I was here.

Those lyrics had spawned the "I was here" campaign and hundreds were sweeping the Baghdad streets and rehabilitating archaeological sites, raising money for disabled students.

But since then, a new tragedy had been lumped into the pile.

At the camp, the sight of fresh faces brought with it a renewed belief that someone was coming to save them from ISIS, to tell them that everything was okay, to ensure that their situation was not forgotten; with a hope that it would all be fixed soon.

The first boy to introduce himself was a nine-year-old named Abdullah. He struck me with his light eyes, gap-toothed smile, and the spattering of freckles across his nose. There was gentleness in his demeanor — I wondered how such gentleness could come from a child that had been ripped from his home by war. Abdullah told us that he was a Muslim from Sinjar — or Shengal, as they say in Kurdish. He had been forced to flee two months earlier when ISIS invaded his village. He insisted on showing us around the camp, annotating like a proud tour guide. He explained the different people who lived there and where they were all from. He explained how they had all been confronted with the same vicious enemy, and how they coped in different ways.

"Some ISIS we knew," Abdullah said. "Some of our neighbors became ISIS, too."

I did not know then that such a phrase would be repeated time and time again as the years went on. I did not realize then the importance of that phrase, the clefts, and all the conspiracies that would come from it. That one phrase would come to represent the fissures of a country that I wasn't sure could ever be put back together.

"Our neighbors became ISIS, too."

ISIS took over large swaths of Iraq beginning in June 2014. Iraqi Army soldiers had abandoned their weapons and ran, igniting international condemnation and frustration. While President Obama had initially dismissed ISIS as the "JV team," it was evident that — as much as we all wanted to disregard the group as a bunch of thug wannabes — their potency could not be denied.

Now, in the heart of autumn, Abdullah boldly led the pack of young children, weaving through the tents. He commanded a certain respect from the other young ones: when he smiled, they smiled; when he laughed, they laughed. Abdullah had a kind of infectious energy that gave me a glimmer of hope for them and their future.

The afternoon passed and Abdullah and his camp friends still seemed to be such happy beings, oblivious to the darkness that reigned not so far away. The innocence was, in many ways, tragic. A day would come when they would grow up and realize the unfairness and all the things that terror had robbed from them, far beyond material things like clothes and possessions. They could no longer roam freely in the streets; they could no longer wrap themselves in the arms of a mother who was not stained by her trauma; they could no longer wander down their village road to seek an education.

Education is not viewed as a life and death matter when such conflicts arise — but often it gets lost altogether. *What is war?* War is children being sent off to work or made to stay home and fend for the family, even when the likes of the United Nations set up temporary schools. When a child loses everything, all they have left is their still-open minds. Education was as pertinent to their immediate survival as it was to their future.

Yet who was I to tell these people suffering from war what should be done? There were no happy endings or alternatives. The future was fantasy, and living day-by-day was all that mattered.

The children posed for pictures and their parents encouraged them to do so, pushing them into the frame. If their picture appeared in a newspaper or on the internet, maybe it would bring them the lifeline to be saved and hand-plucked to go to a better world. If the world knew their story and all they endured, surely help would arrive on their doorstep.

I could not bring myself to shatter such an illusion.

I asked one young mother for permission to take a photograph of her with her children and she nodded shyly in agreement, only for a man to charge over in anger and demand that I delete the photograph, insisting that I prove it had disappeared from my phone.

The woman did not know the man, but her eyes fell to the ground in subservience. He was not her husband, nor a distant relative, but his word stood for more than hers, and that photo had to be wiped.

BE GRATEFUL. BE ALIVE.
November, 2014

For many Christians caught in the crossfire, their possessions and homes were erased. Only their memories could not be wiped — not now, not ever.

In the immediate months after the ISIS assault, before the burns of those who had fled the area had scabbed over, I went to meet with a group of Christians camped inside a church. They were just beginning to grapple with what had happened.

The message on the whiteboard inside the Mar Elia Chaldean Catholic Church in Iraq's semi-autonomous Kurdish region bared a message for the hundreds of Christian families driven from their homes: "Be grateful. Be alive. Be happy. Be careful."

However, Christianity's central tenet of forgiveness was a hard sell for the children who, after living much of their lives in relative peace with Muslim neighbors, found themselves homeless and traumatized. Hundreds of families were living in limbo — a sprawling complex of tents outside a house of worship.

"It's hard to explain what is happening," Father Daniel Alkhory told me in the predominantly Christian district of Ankawa, a smile gracing his round face and youthful skin. "I was teaching them the parable of Ishmael and Lazarus, talking to them about Heaven and Hell, so I used that to bring up ISIS. I asked them where ISIS will go, and they said, 'Directly to Hell!'"

To help bring a sense of understanding and forgiveness to the madness, Father Daniel told the children a story of a Christian in Mosul who had lived next to a Muslim man for more than twenty years when one day the Muslim man suddenly threatened him, ordering him to leave Mosul within twenty-four hours simply because he was a Christian.

"So, the Christian man started to pack his things, but said he wouldn't leave without saying goodbye to that neighbor," he recounted. "His neighbor opened the door, and was really angry and shouting at him, 'Why are you here? I told you to leave Mosul!' The Christian man said he wouldn't leave without first saying goodbye. His Muslim neighbor started to cry and promised to protect him."

Throughout the land controlled by ISIS, the homes and churches of Christians had been looted and burned to the ground. Before, Christians in Iraq made up around 1.5 million — or five percent — of the population, but current estimates of their number hovered around 200,000, their people depreciated by murder, forced conversions, and flight — primarily at the hands of Islamic radicals. Those who remained refused to renounce their beliefs, even under the threat of death.

One Christian man living at Mar Elia brandished a large tattoo of Jesus' mother, Mary, on his arm. He wanted it photographed, insisting on pulling down his shirt and posing in an act of self-defiance, to inform the world that he would not let ISIS curtail his Christian devotion. The man's Christian faith was discovered by the invading militants; the crosses were ripped off the walls and his family was forced to flee to the Kurdish region.

More than 100,000 Christians had fled the clutches of the terrorist organization since its advance across the Nineveh Plains in Iraq, which was home to some of the world's most ancient Christian communities. The Kurdish region had already taken in more than 1.5 million displaced people, including Christians and other ethnic and religious minorities According to Father Daniel, the word "displaced" was crucial terminology.

"'Refugees' is a bad word and refers to people who don't know each other, but these people here are our family. They are displaced people. We want to take the negative energy out with the words we use," Father Daniel explained. "And we never call it a camp. It's a center."

In a gentle sing-song voice, he spoke of the children's trauma. He conversed in a way that made me think he was still childlike himself, cocooned in the perpetual cycle of trying to find the light in the darkest corner; of trying naively to believe, while Iraq had seen war for decades, that the end to their suffering would soon arrive.

"They've lost their hopes and dreams and we try to help them understand that life keeps going," he said. "A child is like a flower; we can shape them. We must take care of them now — otherwise, the next generation of ISIS could come from these children."

Father Daniel moved toward the sunlight sinking in the west. "Through all their sadness and depression, they wanted revenge," he continued. "I knew I needed to build a unique environment for them."

That environment consisted of time spent on artistic endeavors, such as drawing and creating shapes to express their feelings and frustrations, as well as dancing and outings to play in the park. The children had recently gone on an excursion to see their first-ever 3D movie, Teenage Mutant Ninja Turtles, at the local cinema.

"They wore the glasses and were just so happy," Father Daniel mused, illuminating all the activities he had orchestrated.

The center even hosted their very own "Got Talent" and "The Voice" competitions, modeled on the hit American versions, where the children could perform for friends and family and win prizes.

But, of course, Mass and Bible study made up critical components of every day.

The flashpoint of Mar Elia's crisis began at midnight on August 6, when Kurdish troops cautioned a local bishop in Qarakosh that the Christians had to leave as ISIS was closing in. Church leaders began knocking on doors, urging families to flee instantly.

"Fifteen families stayed, as they didn't wake up... Sadly, we don't have any contact with them anymore. At the beginning, they were describing the horrors and said they couldn't even turn on a light as ISIS would become suspicious," Father Daniel noted.

With no realistic prospect of returning to their homes anytime soon, the thousands of displaced families strewn across the Kurdish region had no choice but to start their lives from scratch in unfamiliar territory.

"Father, when can we go home? When can I see my friends?" one young boy quipped, having waited anxiously for a lull in our conversation to launch his omnipotent query. Refusing to allow doubt to fill the vacuum of delay, Father Daniel told the boy that he should make new friends at the center.

"And maybe one day you will go home and meet your old friends once again," Father Daniel enthused, forever drawing light from the darkest crevices. "And you will have double the friends you had before."

But home, as it was for hundreds of families from Christian villages, had quickly become a collection of tents donated by several organizations and placed on church grounds. The tents were divided into halves for each family, an average of four persons squishing into every half tent. Some organizations had even started donating caravans to families. But room on the grounds was running out, and the proliferation of caravans morphed into more of a curse than a blessing.

The children, screeching in playful delight, weaved between the tents and caravans, relishing the moments outside the stringent classroom.

Those old enough attended school from 9:00 A.M. to 4:00 P.M. during the week, with after-school activities running from 6:00 P.M. to 8:00 P.M. each night. Moving on with life meant structure and stability, even if the world outside was falling apart.

"We just want them to be happy and to keep smiling," Father Daniel hummed. "We just want the children to feel like they are at home." We want to make a party for them every day."

Father Daniel gathered the children together on the concrete block as the twilight swept the sky, and they sang hymns in both Arabic and English. The songs evolved from melancholy into upbeat jingles, and with it their energy levels ascended.

"I just keep telling the kids you have to forgive. Forgiveness will lead us to so many paths," Father Daniel emphasized, his eyes cast to the deep pink sky. "I don't want them to grow up and be after revenge and be angry."

FISH FROM MOSUL DAM
November, 2014

The sky was angry, and the late November rain mirrored the furor of conflict below.

Icy rain poured down on the frontline fighting position overlooking Mosul Dam, where sixteen Peshmerga fighters mustered around a small hut. Perched atop a small hill, the hut was the only visible means of protection from enemy fire, and just below it, a handful of other fighters hovered around a small campfire for warmth.

We had arrived at the frontline fighting position after a long, wet day on the road — longer than anticipated. It wasn't until we reached the entrance point to the Dam that we discovered it had been closed off due to heavy bombardment. The driver, a man known as Omar, was a cousin of a friend's friend. The friend had assured me that he spoke English and was a policeman in his main job. Only it wasn't until he came to collect us from the hotel that I realized he had no weapon for protection. His personal car seemed barely drivable, and he spoke very little English.

Idling at the road closure, Omar declared that the only way to get to the meeting point was to drive across an open field to reach another road. We barely entered the densely-muddied field before — sure enough — the car got stuck. The wheels spun and kicked up clumps of clay around the windows, yet we did not move, but rather sunk deeper into the earth with every passing moment. The feeling was one of mild discomfort, being stranded in open terrain with bombs falling just miles away. Eventually, in exasperation, I decided to trek to the lonely road and hope for help.

Fortunately, a Peshmerga vehicle soon came into sight and I flagged the soldiers down. Roughly twenty minutes more of sputtering and stalling as the soldiers worked magic on the car, and then we were again on our way.

The Peshmerga, the decades-old Kurdish rugged mountain militia whose name translates to "those who face death" had, in just a few months, galvanized the western world with their will and tenacity against the brutal enemy.

The soldiers at Mosul Dam greeted us warmly, and another Omar, a senior intelligence official who I had for weeks been emailing with and talking on the phone received me like a long-lost friend. It was not unusual for even high- ranking government officials to give up their cushy houses, dust off their rifles, and fight like any ordinary fighter. We climbed into their armored jeep and were transported into their little world — a world dominated by the ever-escalating war.

Just hours earlier, the road leading into that Kurdish army base was hit by artillery from ISIS — or Daesh, as it quickly became known in the Middle East — forcing some closures. The fighters were far from rattled, calmly sharing jokes, pita, and cigarettes ahead of another long and frosty night protecting their cherished land. The soldiers had recently cleaved control of the prized Dam from ISIS, who had held the area for a terrifying ten days in late summer, sending tremors through the international community. The fear was that ISIS at any moment could bust open the weak construct of the poorly-fashioned Dam and unleash a tirade of massive waves, which had the potential to flood all the way down to Baghdad and take out millions of people in its veracity.

"Now we know their key points and from where they try to attack us. It's weather like now — the fog — that allows them not to be seen by the planes," Omar explained about the war against the jihadist insurgency. "When it is raining, it is a good time for them to start attacking. In the beginning, the villages in Iraq were communicating and helping them attack. They shot at us from the front and back. But the villagers soon realized that these people were not good. They were not human."

Omar spoke about how they always raced with the rain, vying to prepare before the skies opened and chaos reigned. I wondered if they would always be racing the rain in one way or another; I wondered how long the peace would last, and whether they would ever breathe a real sigh of sunshine.

The Peshmerga fighters don a mishmash of camouflage clothes and wield whatever guns they can get their hands on. Their formal training is limited, and their best attributes are instinct and will.

"We have principles. We were brought up on those principles and an innate drive to serve. We treat Kurdistan like our second mother," Omar, who was a high-value target, explained. "If you do something day after day you learn, and we learn how to fight very fast."

The Peshmerga began as something of a mountain militia in the 1920s when the push for Kurdish independence began. In recent decades, they had faced unrelenting persecution from the Ba'ath loyalists of former Iraqi dictator Saddam Hussein. One Peshmerga fighter told me they don't suffer from "psychological issues" pertaining to combat because they have grown up around fighting and have developed an early understanding that it is "just what we have to do." To them, PTSD was something of a first-world phenomenon.

While the issue of possible psychological ramifications as a consequence of both shooting and being shot garners little — if any — mainstream attention, the daughter of a retired Peshmerga fighter told me that, in her experience growing up, she witnessed the mental anguishes of battle every day in her father's eyes — in the way he moved and the way he slept.

The Peshmerga soldiers range from around eighteen to more than seventy years old, with many coming out of retirement in the quest to defeat the ISIS threat. During days of intense conflict, the Peshmerga are lucky to return to their base for two or three hours of sleep and a quick bite to eat before venturing back to their fighting locus. As it stood, a prominent portion of fighters are not soldiers but what they call "security advisors," who don't take a salary and volunteered simply out of devotion.

"There are Special Forces that have been arranged for these people. They don't register their names and don't sign contracts. They just want to serve Kurdistan," Omar said.

Due to a limited supply of weapons, volunteers often have little choice but to bring their own firearms — usually a rudimentary AK-47 — with the M4 and M16 rifles, the BKC — an Iraqi clone of the Soviet PKM machine gun — and the DshK heavy machine gun — called the "doshka" in Iraq — being the staple weapons used in the battle against much better-equipped opponents.

Despite their lack of advanced technology and cutting-edge scopes, the Peshmerga remained acutely aware of how many Islamic State fighters they took out each night at battle. Although they were outgunned, the Kurdish fighters kept their wits about them, giving themselves a tactical advantage over the enemy. One Peshmerga soldier explained how ISIS commanders often drug young fighters with special tablets that leave them disoriented and shooting wildly into the night. Sometimes, they were able to keep going despite being shot several times, taking upwards of twenty bullets before they went down.

"For those who survive, when they realize what they have done, they sometimes regret it," Omar acknowledged.

The Peshmerga also rely on a growing intelligence-gathering network that supplies logistical support to those who battle in the field.

"We have secret service inside ISIS-controlled villages in Mosul and other places, passing information," Omar continued. "Some are even living with ISIS and they don't know."

U.S. airstrikes were said to have helped Kurdish and Iraqi government forces seize control of the critical Mosul Dam in late August after ISIS seized the area weeks earlier. Before Islamic State, the Tigris River dam was operated and controlled by around 1,200 Iraqi families. Roughly half of those families had returned home after the brief ISIS takeover. But the fear remained: the almost two-mile-long dam could be deliberately blown up in the evil quest to flood Mosul — which sat thirty miles downstream — and even torpedo down so far as to hurt the people of Baghdad.

Built exclusively for Saddam Hussein in the early 1980s, the dam, according to a 2006 U.S. Army Corps of Engineers report, was considered particularly dangerous and "constructed on a very poor foundation." U.S. taxpayers had subsequently spent tens of millions on interim fixes throughout their occupation, but little had been achieved and the dam was just one in an ever-bulging file of looming threats.

Much of the Kurdish population now views the United States of America as their only dependable ally in the developing war against the terrorist organization, and their desperation for American equipment was the eclipsing message.

"The airstrikes are good, but we need weapons," Omar italicized, dismissing the notion that U.S. ground troops are the ultimate answer. "We already have military on the ground, but we're fighting an enemy that has acquired all the sophisticated U.S. weapons that went to the Iraqis, and now ISIS has them. This isn't a balanced fight."

Due to the internal squabbling over oil exports between the semi-autonomous KRG and the Iraqi Central Government, the Kurds bemoaned that they had not received the billions of dollars in military supplies owed to them after the 2003 U.S. war. The Kurdish region was legally entitled to 17.5 percent of the Baghdad budget, but for almost a year, Kurdish leaders claimed they had not received their agreed-upon portion.

The Kurds, based on previous agreements between Erbil and Baghdad, were not allowed to purchase their own weapons without approval from the Central Government.

"We tried to buy weapons from the outside, from places like Russia and America, but the Foreign Ministry wouldn't allow it," Omar explained. "The Iraqi government hasn't given us one single bullet."

They were sure they could take ISIS out of Mosul very quickly — if only they possessed American weapons. To many, America was the ethereal superhero, with gizmos and gadgets that could perform the stuff of miracles. They were sure that Mosul could be fought and won any day now, and the sooner the better. The longer they waited, the worse it would become — ISIS would only prosper and dig its heels into the antiquated city.

They seemed so sure it would happen soon, that nobody would want to wait to take them out.

Western powers viewed the Kurdish people as a safeguard against further ISIS advances, but in order to take the offensive, the Peshmerga stressed that they needed more help.

"The United States needs to think about the message it is sending," Omar quipped, serving us fish from the glorious dam that just months earlier had been a sanctuary vacation spot for Iraqis far and wide. "If ISIS is an existential threat as the Iraqis claim, and if it threatens U.S. interests abroad and its security at home, then more must be done to arm the Peshmerga."

Almost every Kurd wants to share their history — history of their people and their oppression. But the string that could be weaved through and through was that they did not expect to be granted their freedom for nothing. They knew they would have to fight for it every step of the way. The succession of let-downs, of losses and gains, was all part of their rough climb up the rope of revolution.

At the top they would find their independence. When they referred to their soldiers killed on the battlefield, they sometimes said that they were martyred, and sometimes said they were murdered. I wondered how differently Americans would see wars if the press and the people spoke of our troops in the firing line as having died in a homicide rather than killed in action.

The rain fell harder, and bullets flew wildly into the growing darkness that hid the dead ISIS bodies nearby. Hungry, untamed dogs had gouged into the skeletons almost immediately. Some had been dead for days. Some had names and others had been left nameless. Some, maculated by the creatures howling at the moon, had no faces.

HAUNTED BY HALABJA
November, 2014

A little girl's picturesque porcelain face, lying face up in the mud — mouth open, eyes squeezed tightly shut. Stone cold. It was the first image I saw when I walked into the remembrance museum. It's the kind of picture that leaves you raw. That little girl, with soft black curls falling over her ashen face, would have been about my age now. Only she will forever be timeless, wrapped in the chilling history of what human beings can do to other human beings.

On March 17, 1988, the morning after Saddam Hussein's Ba'ath Party unleashed a tirade of chemical weapons and killed 5,000 Iraqi-Kurds in the city of Halabja, a few brave photojournalists ventured into the city to ensure the brutal dictator's atrocities would be documented and exposed to the world.

In the middle of all the death and destruction on the Iranian border, one photographer noticed a young boy on a truck in the street — a foot raised between cracks of debris and barely breathing. That glimmer of life in such a dire situation became a story cited in global newscasts over the ensuing week.

The little boy's entire family — three brothers, a father, and a pregnant mother —lay dead in the truck beside him. His name was Akram Muhammad Mahmud, a ten-year-old who would spend the next few years playing outside, longing to go back to school as soon as the Iraq-Iran war was over.

Akram looked at me shyly, extending his hand.

Nearly twenty-seven years later, he was working at the memorial site known as Halabja Monument and Peace Museum, constructed in 2003. On the anniversary of the attack in 2006, thousands of residents rioted at the site, protesting what was thought to be capitalizing on tragedy and misusing aid funds, destroying many of the archives.

The monument was rebuilt into a hub of reflection and solace, poised against the serene Iranian mountainside, with several abandoned Ba'ath party tanks sitting idly to one side. Inside, the iconic photographs taken in the pallid aftermath of the attacks have been recreated as life-sized images and statues: a mother clutching her dead baby, lifeless children strewn across pavements.

"We need to remind the new generation about what happened to this town, and we need to keep reminding them, so it doesn't happen again," Akram told me, standing beside the very truck in which his family died, now in a permanent fixture outside the museum. "Sometimes I can't stop crying. Every day I look at the pictures and am reminded that it is my family in those pictures."

There was such a depth of sadness in the way he shared his story, constantly reliving a cursed history.

Saddam had ordered the chemical attack amid the Iran-Iraq war following intel reports that Iranian soldiers had been implanted inside the Kurdish city.

Akram still didn't seem quite sure how or why his life was spared, or why he was the only survivor within the proximate area. He recalled having instinctively placed his mother's scarf around his mouth for protection the moment "something felt wrong." He recalled throwing up blood into the scarf, which still smelled of his mother even though she was dead beside him. He recalled the way his vision blurred slowly, fading into blackness. He remembered cars rolling over bodies as other victims, in their last few minutes on earth, vomited chunks of green. Some were visibly burning, their skin boiling with bubbles. Others laughed uncontrollably — an eerie side effect of the lethal chemical cocktail of VX, sarin, tabun, and mustard gas.

Then there were the scores of doomed civilians who rushed the moving vehicle in the mayhem following the attack, hauling themselves up only to fall off, prompting the driver to repeatedly stop and help them back on until he too, exhausted and over-exposed to the toxins, dropped down beside the car's door for the last time.

The photojournalists clamoring through the piles of lifelessness took Akram under their wing until he reached the Iranian border. There, he was hospitalized and later placed in a refugee camp before being reunited with his grandparents, to whom he broke the grim news of his family's fate.

"The tragedy was just so big that nobody felt like they were the only victim," he said. "What we can do now is understand the reasons why we have war outbreaks, and the slaughter of civilians must be stopped."

The mere mention of ISIS — the ghastly militant group that surrounded the semi-autonomous Kurdistan and kidnapped and slaughtered thousands — brought wincing pains to Akram's face.

Those pangs of persecution are ones any Halabja survivor knows all too well.

Before that day in 1988, Halabja was a thriving city of 80,000, known for its rich history and embrace of Kurdish culture. Its local politicians, artists, and intellectuals were notoriously outspoken in demanding basic rights for the Kurdish people who had long been oppressed by Saddam's regime. The chemical attack came in waning days of the Iran-Iraq war, as rumors circulated that Iranian forces hid in the besieged town.

With the passage of decades, even with all its wounds of history, Halabja had become a quiet, nostalgic place, forever haunted by the massacre that gutted its inhabitants. Never would it — never could it — return to what it had been. Beyond the thousands killed in the attack, another 10,000 were injured and, in the ensuing years, thousands more would succumb from subsequent complications and birth defects.

The impact of that fateful day still reverberates.

"All these years later, thank God I am much better, but the effects of the chemical weapons are still here," Akram said, staring off into the hilltops that defined a zigzagging border between Iran and Iraq. "Women's fertility has been largely affected; many miscarry their babies even all these years later."

The monument pays particular tribute to the journalists who dared enter the city, who had distributed the first images of the attack in Iranian newspapers and television newscasts worldwide. But, according to multiple Kurdish professionals and locals living just forty-five miles away in the Iraqi-Kurdistan city of Sulaymaniyah, Saddam's censorship laws prohibited them from finding out about the brutal attack until three years later.

"We knew nothing about it until 1991, after my family returned from having fled to Iran as refugees," my friend Jwan recollected, standing with us at the monument. She was a Kurdish local who had been eight years old when the incident took place.

There was a special breed of despondency that clung to the place. The sky cracked into a splinter of lightning, coupled with a gentle roll of thunder.

As it turned out, the Iraqi Special Tribunal did not charge Saddam for crimes against humanity in connection to Halabja. His cousin, Ali Hassan al-Majid, who commanded Iraqi forces in the country's north at that time, was finally executed in 2010 for his role in organizing the massacre.

Down the road from the monument sat a mass gravesite, the names of the victims etched across the thousands of headstones barely readable in the pouring November rain. There was no welcome sign, just one large and eerie reminder:

"Ba'ath's Members are not allowed to enter."

THE WAR STILL KILLS
November, 2014

Their wars, one bleeding into the next, trapped them on a treadmill that would not stop. The war from the 1980s, decades ago, was killing those who had not even been born when it began. The people of Iraq and Kurdistan battled a new war while an old one still attacked them out of nowhere.

Landmines and unexploded bombs have threatened lives and limbs in Iraq for generations, the vestiges of decades of intense conflict with a host of enemies. ISIS, however, had turned a crisis into a catastrophe.

Infamous for leaving explosive devices and sophisticated booby traps in villages as it retreated, the jihadist command had compounded a problem that left hundreds of square miles riddled with deadly, hidden bombs. With violence persisting and funds dwindling, Iraqis and aid workers were desperate to keep children safe as they tried to address the hidden threat.

"It's crucial now to talk about safe behaviors," said Chris Elliot — a community liaison manager with the international humanitarian de-mining organization, Mines Advisory Group (MAG) — during a village meeting at a refugee camp attended by young children who escaped from ISIS-controlled regions. "Firstly, we talk about different types of mines and IEDs (improvised explosive devices) and how to spot them when they go back to their homes. Then we talk about dangerous areas and what you would do if you saw a landmine."

The message, he underscored, was about trying to get the kids to stop, or at least run away, so they wouldn't be harmed and take other kids away and then report it to the police or a religious leader.

Danger lurked everywhere. In Jurf Al-Sakhar, a town of 80,000 sixty miles southwest of Baghdad reclaimed by the Iraqi army from the Islamic State in October, some 3,000 explosives had already been found after just a few months of occupation. Authorities faced the arduous task of preventing displaced families from returning to their homes, as the cleanup was expected to take months.

MAG was one of the few international humanitarian de-mining NGOs left doing clearance work in the ravished country and, as it stood, could only operate in the northern region of Iraqi-Kurdistan, which bore the brunt of the refugees. Kurdistan's furrowed military force, the Peshmerga, had also been attempting to defuse the threat, but were working with little equipment, skills, and money to do a guaranteed job.

"We aren't working in any areas that the Kurdish Regional Government (KRG) has taken from ISIS. That is where we desperately need funding," lamented Neil Arnold, the Iraqi technical operations manager for MAG. "Basically, we are a charity, so if we want to do something new, we have to come to the donors with proposals, and hopefully get the interest and money so we can mobilize and go into these areas too."

For now, they remained focused on clearing the calamities that had spawned the pre-ISIS brutality. The thought of what lay ahead was too much to fathom. But how long could they continue their lifesaving work in the northern parcel of the country? That had become a cause for concern.

The proposals that had been drafted just before the ISIS emergence now fell onto the chopping block. Both local and international donors had turned their attention to the urgent problem of internally displaced people (IDPs) and refugees filtering over borders.

Spare funds were becoming harder to come by. MAG's efforts in the Kurdish region were funded largely by the U.S. Department of State. But with winter on the periphery and an ascending number of refugees seeking the basic means to stay alive, priorities had changed. The outbreak of ISIS would leave greater patches of land that were otherwise scheduled to be cleaned of dirtied, old war remnants. The heinous terror group would sew more terror and claim more lives without having to lift a finger.

What is war? War turns our attention to the imminent and leaves the unfinished wars of the past taunting from the shadows.

MAG, which operates in over forty countries in an effort to secure the safety of civilians affected by armed violence and conflict, started work to clear landmines in Iraq in 1992. By 2014, they had cleared almost seventy-seven million square meters of mines and UXOs (unexploded ordnances), and handed the terrain back to authorities and communities for use. Almost two million UXOs had been detected and destroyed, and the organization had conducted 25,000 risk education sessions to teach civilians how to detect explosive remnants of war (ERW) and small arms light weapons (SALW) and determine the appropriate course of action.

To further illustrate that message, the children in the small refugee camp were issued coloring sheets with messages to help identify dangerous objects. The organization's long-term strategy in the region was to respond to the immediate humanitarian and socio-economic developmental need, support local capacities in their ability to counter the contamination, and provide emergency protection to those at risk — which included the Syrian refugees escaping the Assad regime and the Internally Displaced People (IDP) fleeing the ISIS infiltration.

The neighboring Syrian civil war sparked in early 2011 after peaceful protesters took to the streets to call for their dictatorial president, Bashar al-Assad, to institute democratic principles or to step down. But, instead of addressing their chorus of demands, Bashar responded with a violent crackdown, fragmenting the country into chaos and opening the gates of fire for extremist outfits like ISIS to hijack parts of the opposition.

Disillusioned by who was good and who was evil, scores of civilians scurried over the border to the seeming safety of Iraq, only for Iraq to also descend into its own brand of mayhem with the onslaught of ISIS.

MAG's Integrated Clearance Methodology involved deploying manual teams to remove and destroy landmines, applying machinery to de-mine at a fast rate, but specially-trained mine detection dogs were becoming more and more effective in the clean-up process.

"They are trained on scent recognition, which helps with cost-effectiveness. The dogs can do a lot more squares per day than a de-miner," Neil explained. "We used to use rollers, but they have proven to not be effective. When we arrived in this area, we were finding mines in areas that had been deemed clear by rollers."

However, the issue of landmine clearing was intensely political and problematic. Due to budget conflicts between the Iraqi Central Government in Baghdad and the Kurdish Region Government (KRG), Kurdish officials pronounced that funding for clearance was running low. Iraq signed the 2007 Ottawa Anti-Personnel Mine Ban Treaty, which meant that they had to clear all contaminated land within ten years, automatically making Kurdistan obligated to meet the treaty demands — a feat the experts said was now impossible.

"Donor funding is falling even more. Most [people] see Iraq as a middle-income country, so it should be funding their clearance as well," Neil added. "But as you can see, it's not that simple."

That ten-year agreement would no doubt become a piece of paper — one of many — rendered meaningless. Nothing in Iraq was simple. Its history was not simple. Its wars were not simple.

THE FACES OF EVIL
November, 2014

Some ISIS soldiers will tell you that the reasons they joined were simple, straightforward, woven into the web of basic survival: money, protection, food. Other times, their reasons to pledge allegiance to the terrorist group were complex — deep-seated in sectarian, tribal, and historical grievances dating back centuries.

So, *what is war?* War is a composite of individual stories and reasons, one rarely the same as the other.

Iraqi and Kurdish authorities had already apprehended hundreds of ISIS fighters in those first few months and stuffed their prisons with the terrorist members, including a soldier who told me that he killed as many as seventy people in the service of the radical jihadist army. His reasons weaved a convoluted web of both hatred and self-preservation.

Omar, a twenty-five-year-old ISIS fighter from the Iraqi village of Dor Saladin, admitted that during ISIS's first month in Mosul, he had killed scores of his countrymen and foreign contractors on their behalf.

"They came to our area and forced me to protect their lands," Omar said flatly of his ISIS commanders, his thick monobrow remaining frighteningly still, a physical manifestation of this emotionless figure before me.

"After a while, they told me, 'When are you going to start protecting your own land?'" His eyes burning into mine, he went on to describe the words of his superiors. "They told me to do it or die, and then they killed people in front of me."

Omar was missing four fingers on his left hand from what he claimed was an industrial accident.

A lie? Chopping off hands and fingers was a punishment for stealing.

The disability nearly got him killed by his ISIS handlers, he claimed, until he proved he could shoot right-handed.

Overnight, Omar had burgeoned from a young man, purporting to protect his home turf, to a prolific killer under the ISIS banner; by his count, he had racked up seventy executions in a matter of months. He mandated that he killed his victims with rifle shots and was chillingly candid about why he did it.

"Because they were saying bad words about A'isha (one of Mohammad's wives, known as the 'mother of believers') and burning a mosque," he went on. He insisted that he did not receive any type of reward from ISIS leaders for the large number he killed.

I asked if he had felt any remorse. The clock ticked for a few seconds on the wall, glaringly loud.

"I did not act on my will," Omar responded slowly, flinching as if still embodied by some evil outside influence. We were seated in a tightly-monitored Asayish facility (the Kurdish equivalent of the FBI) in the city of Sulaymaniyah, not far from the Iranian frontier. It had been a long, drizzly day of back-and-forth, navigating the terrain of drawn-out dealings synonymous to the Middle East, before finally it was agreed that ISIS prisoners could be brought in for an interview.

Omar's deflection drew a sharp rebuke from the Kurdish guard inside the room, who barked at him with a scolding I could not understand. Meekly, he corrected himself, apologizing and insisting that he had deflected blame only because he was "uncomfortable around women."

Omar was being held in an undisclosed Asayish prison on the outskirts of Sulaymaniyah, after being convicted weeks earlier in their court-of-law on terrorism charges. He was initially sentenced to death, but I was told a judge commuted the sentence to life in prison.

I was surprised when the security guard offered him tea along with the rest of us, which he nervously but politely accepted. An uncomfortable hush wafted over the room as we all took a few seconds to sip. I took in his impish face, his painfully skinny body, his anxious twitch, and the way his eyes constantly darted and dropped to the cold ground.

Here was a face of evil, a man who had taken lives that were not his lives to take, and yet there remained an odd air of childish innocence about him. Omar was a brutal individual, but he was also a tragic statistic — just one of the tens of thousands of young men to take up arms on behalf of the barbaric group; one of the tens of thousands who could have lived low-profile lives working and tending to a growing family. But instead, he became a statistic in following the path of human destruction and had sabotaged any prospect for a normal future.

As his story unraveled, Omar said he joined ISIS to get away from his new bride. It had been an arranged marriage, and he did not know his wife until the day they were married. After the wedding dancing and chorus of congratulations had ceased, he realized something was wrong with her. He said she had "something in her head — she looked normal on the outside, but she wasn't."

He stuck out the strange nuptials for a few months longer in the hopes of fathering a child, but after multiple doctor visits it was determined that his wife couldn't have babies.

"Something was wrong with her," Omar repeated. He believed that his only option was to leave for work one morning and never come home. He knew that, in fleeing and with no money to his name, as per Islamic law, he left his family responsible for paying his wife's family a fortune in dowry costs. Thus, Omar knew that he could not escape his wife and could not find a safe haven in his family home. And so, he fled into the abyss of Mosul just after its sudden takeover by ISIS.

After weeks of killing, of blood staining his clothes, of living in fear that the terror group's leaders would turn their guns on him for any misstep, Omar decided to run away once again. This time, he deserted during the witching hour and surged into Kurdistan. He hoped that he could blend in with the displaced flow of people and perhaps find a job. But only days later, on October 8, he was captured by police, having been identified by Kurdish intelligence agents.

Omar — along with hundreds of fellow ISIS soldiers and deserters — were being interrogated for intelligence that could help the Kurdish Peshmerga in its fight against the jihadist group.

Evidence against individual former combatants is gathered and presented to a Kurdish judge, who decides whether prisoners are held or released. Omar and many other ex-ISIS fighters convicted of mass murder or terrorism charges would likely spend the rest of their lives behind bars. A small percentage of ex-ISIS members determined not to have participated in the fighting would serve lesser sentences, and someday be released back into the general population.

Omar insisted he was a victim of ISIS — that they had given him no choice but to join and kill for them if he wanted to stay alive. Only he was full of contradictions: the more he talked, the more it was clear that Omar still regarded the so-called "caliphate" with a kind of wistful infatuation, pointing out that living as if they were still in the seventh century was a noble and majestic concept.

I asked him what he would do, hypothetically, if he saw me on the streets under the caliphate's control.

"I would call you to Islam," Omar conjectured, straightening up. "And if you didn't come, I would leave you alone." He recited the sentence as if it were a script, knowing exactly what the guards wanted to hear.

Omar was one of two former Islamic State fighters who spoke to me that day at the Asayish facility. The other, a nineteen-year-old Kurdish teen identified as Dawen, said he was lured to join by the group's Facebook pages, which urged Muslims to join the fight in Syria.

Dawen, a fair-haired and demure youngster, looked like he belonged in a Boy Scout uniform, sleeping in the woods rather than on a bloodied battlefield. He claimed that he had spent just twenty days in the world's most infamous terrorist battery before being arrested two months earlier. He claimed not to have witnessed a single killing, yet he harbored no illusions about ISIS's barbarity.

"I realized that this is not about God, especially after I was captured," he said. "I realized this isn't about God; it is about harming people. Also, the Kurdish people were nice even with my situation."

Again, lines of a script, but somehow delivered a little more earnestly than his cohort.

Dawen explained passionately that he felt regret about joining the group almost immediately. "I called my family and they were not happy; it was shameful... I felt weak because they made me act and think a certain way," he answered, when asked whether joining a terrorist organization made him feel powerful. "I was asking for forgiveness, even while there."

Dawen, who faced terrorism charges and awaited his day in court, also vowed that he was learning more from fellow inmates about other barbarities committed by ISIS. He suggested Kurdish officials "make anti-terror shows and programs" to teach others that "this is not the way to be."

While his words reeked of indoctrinated lines used to please the guards, there were slivers of sincerity in the way he delivered his responses. He was just another tragic statistic.

The facility's director of security noted that most ISIS fighters were uneducated and easily led down the grisly path of violent jihad.

"Some regret their actions, some do not," the guard had said to me earlier, nonchalantly. "Understand that most are young and have no information. They are impressionable. They listen to the second-life paradise story, seventy-two virgins, rivers of wine, and [staying] young forever. That is all they know."

Unlike the prisoners detained by ISIS — many of whom have been marched into the depths of silky desert dunes to have their heads lobbed off with a long sword, or garbed in orange jumpsuits and forced to kneel before being blasted with bullets — these deserters from the terrorist army said they were being treated relatively well by Kurdish authorities. The two men were dressed comfortably and clean-shaven. Kurdish officials insisted that the men were being held under conditions in adherence to international law and monitored by the International Committee of the Red Cross.

Both detainees confirmed they were allowed phone contact with family members and seemed aware of up-to-date news involving ISIS. Both said they feared being captured by ISIS if they were released. Prison was, perhaps, keeping them alive. They articulated that they wanted to join the Peshmerga, to take up arms against the insurgency that had not so long ago enticed them in.

Security officers, however, cautioned against believing the prisoners' expressions of remorse. Neither man could be trusted, multiple authorities underscored, stressing that ISIS was notorious for deploying spies into Kurdistan to gather information about everything from pending military operations to who was hiding in the ever-growing camps.

Kurdish officials privately predicted there was little doubt the two men, and others like them, would be back fighting for ISIS within days if they were ever released.

"We have been dealing with terrorist groups since the beginning, so this is not new for us," said one official, who had experience countering Saddam Hussein's repeated and destructive campaigns against the Kurds. "We specialize in terrorists."

I asked Omar once again what he would do, hypothetically, if he saw me on ISIS-governed streets.

"I would call you to Islam," he conjectured. "And if you did not come, I would kill you."

The script had finally wilted away.

There was some momentary shuffling as the guard cuffed the prisoner and led him toward the exit.

"And," Omar added calmly in his ever-quiet voice, his bowed, pencil-thin legs almost buckling beneath him. "We count Americans like Jews."

The guard, eager to convey a word he knew in English, gave the convicted terrorist a slight slap on the back and bellowed with a wide grin, "Let's go, baby!"

The strange phrase brought with it some comic relief to the sterile room, but deep down I could not help but think Omar was feeble like an infant, hardly a vision of a hardened fighter.

It wasn't until the wet, winding car ride back to Erbil in the dead of that misty night that I remembered it was Thanksgiving in the United States and flags were being burned to ash and buildings set ablaze in the Ferguson, Missouri Black Lives Matter protests.

A STAR-SPANGLED LOVE
December, 2014

The notion of giving thanks to the red, white, and blue was not lost on the people of Kurdistan.

The bald eagle, Old Glory, and the almighty American dollar were king in the Kurdish part of Iraq. Most ethnic Kurds did not hide their affection for the U.S., a concept that had become rare in the predominantly anti-American throngs of the Middle East.

Shops peddled American flags, U.S. military gear was prized, and the locals spoke glowingly of the nation they credited with removing Saddam Hussein — the dictator whose heavy hand so often came down on the minority group clustered into their northern region.

"Imagine if America didn't exist," said accountant Kurdo Amin Agha, whose home was outfitted with Israeli, American, and Kurdistan flags and who wears a U.S. Army shirt and Navy SEAL watch. "Without America, the world would be run by China or Iran."

With dewy eyes, he turned to me in earnest. "America represents freedom," he stressed. "Our dream is to be eternally allied to America."

Throughout the enclave chiseled within Iraq, a U.S. passport gets its bearer waved through security checkpoints, ushered through ministry doors, and served complimentary tea with broad smiles.

The Kurdish region was principally run by the independent Kurdish Regional Government (KRG) and its President, Masoud Barzani, as opposed to being under the thumb of the Iraqi Central Government. It was home to around six million ethnic Kurds and had long been marketed to the world as the "other Iraq" — a relatively safe and economically sound wedge of the country which welcomed westerners with open arms.

Everywhere, hints of red, white, and blue could be bought and sold. One store, tucked away in a local bazaar, owned by a middle-aged man by the name of Zawzad, featured only pro-American merchandise and U.S. military-inspired clothing.

"It's just beautiful," Zawzad said softly as he reverently unfurled a giant flag, holding it up with profound respect and beaming from ear-to-ear after I asked for a photo.

Taxis in Kurdistan often featured seat covers starring the iconic bald eagle pattern, and arrays of household, electronic, and fashion items — from screwdrivers and pots and pans to guitars, phone covers, hats, shirts, shoes, and bags — are adorned in patterns of the stars and stripes.

Local police and military forces proudly sported American-brand 5.11 Tactical Gear and clothing, which could be found mostly in counterfeit varieties in scores of stores. An American flag patch was often sewn on for added oomph.

It was not uncommon to have your drink served with a U.S. flag etched on the side of the glass, or to see American presidential memorabilia behind the workplace desk of locals. A sizable number of official rooms displayed some sort of official certificate proving connection between the Kurdish territory and the United States.

"Students used to have to learn Kurdish and Arabic," an Erbil doctor explained. "Now they just want to learn Kurdish and English."

Bordering Iran, Turkey, Syria, and the Arab-dominated Republic of Iraq, the Kurdish-run region's sense of identity was embodied by its military, the Peshmerga. The roughhewn army, battle-hardened from years of clashing with Saddam's forces, had proven to be an able force in countering ISIS when, just weeks earlier, they had encroached the Kurdish borderline and threatened to swoop in on its terrain.

Kurdish fighters had continued to clash vehemently with ISIS throughout northern Iraq and over the Euphrates into the Kurdish dominion of neighboring Syria, with the fiercest fighting taking place outside the Kurdish-controlled territory. Just sixty miles west of Erbil — an ancient city which was protected by American no-fly zones during Operation Iraqi Freedom — sat Mosul, the country's second-largest city, which was now under ISIS's firm grip.

The roots of the Kurdish affection for America, I learned, were soundly planted during U.S.-led operations Desert Shield and Desert Storm in 1990 in response to Iraq's invasion and the annexation of Kuwait. While the missions commanded by President George H.W. Bush did not topple Saddam, it served notice to the Kurds, who were still reeling from the Halabja and the notion that the dictator would use chemical weapons against his own citizens, that he had fallen into the crosshairs of the United States.

U.S. military forces ousted the Ba'ath party leader in 2003. On the second-to-last day of 2006, an Iraqi tribunal installed by the U.S.-backed interim government brought him to ultimate justice — a grainy video surfaced of the once-feared and hallowed man, standing tall as a noose was wrapped around his neck before dropping to his death with a crack of the neck.

Once Hussein was gone, the oil-rich Kurdish region began to prosper.

Kurds openly expressed their hope that the United States would help them become a completely independent country, although that was never a component of the U.S. policy plan.

When the U.S.-led airstrikes to hamper ISIS were launched in August, entire Kurdish neighborhoods could be seen waving American flags in the streets, with many even marking American Veterans Day this past November.

"We follow American news," Kurdo said. "Like shootings and hurricanes. We care about what happens to the people of the United States."

Most Kurds showed ample respect for President Obama, but it was Bush's name that generated a larger salute. Some were even prepared to get behind potential candidate Jeb Bush in the 2016 presidential elections.

"The first Bush made no secret that he hated Saddam, the second Bush finished him off," Kurdo added. "And the third will be the one to give Kurdistan our independence."

To him, and many like him, there was beauty in hatred. There was a psychological victory in hate, a deep-rooted and powerful emotion that their dictator — their suppressor — would never be able to take away, except in death. And Kurdo was not going to let the dead dictator dissolve their dream of independence.

The very concept of an independent Kurdistan was extremely controversial. With an ethnic population spread across the territory of three nations outside of Iraq — Turkey, Syria, and Iran — the prospect of redrawing the borders of all four countries to create a new state was viewed by critics as a destabilizing idea. Even the notion of independence for the Kurdish-administered area of Northern Iraq was opposed not only by neighboring countries but by the international community, including the Obama administration.

Nonetheless, many Kurds remained steadfastly pro-American. One local even noted Kurdish authorities "get scared" when they see an American passport.

"Nobody wants to upset an American," the local explained. "They worry they might have said or done something wrong."

Kurds, who as a group are overwhelmingly Muslim, also portrayed themselves as more religiously tolerant.

"Right now, I am working with Muslims, Yazidi, Christians — we're all working together," said one high-ranking KRG official. "They celebrate occasions together. It is something very beautiful. I have friends who pray and friends who don't, that is not my problem. That is their choice. That is how Kurdish people think about religion."

On one early December morning, I saw several Kurds busily setting up and decorating Christmas trees. Whether it was done in a secular embrace of a foreign religious rite or simply to make guests more comfortable was not clear.

"We're still new to this," a Kurdish hotel employee said with a smile, bickering with a coworker over how to decorate their tree. "But we love it."

That December, the U.S. announced the Combined Joint Task Force — Operation Inherent Resolve (CJTF-OIR) as the official U.S.-led coalition of countries coming together to defeat the fast-pluming ISIS enemy. The American footprint was once again growing in the country that it had so abruptly left. The internal passion this population held for America in 2014 would only flourish as the Peshmerga continued its battle — often alongside American advisors — in the ensuing years.

But eventually, as I came to compile the memos that make up this book, the U.S. flags would be taken down and Kurdistan would be weighed down by another sense of betrayal. It was hard to imagine that soon a handful of disgruntled Kurds would burn the U.S. flag in the street.

While that physical upset lasted only a few days, a sense of hopeless energy has not since faltered.

SECOND YEAR OF ISIS: 2015

The Ferris Wheels Don't Turn

A TENT TO CALL HOME
June, 2015

Once-barren patches of empty dust across Iraq had been dramatically transformed by countless numbers of sprawling, fast-filling tent camps. Sometimes, those patches of earth contained so many tents that they stretched out into the groove of the horizon beyond what the naked eye could see, and it was impossible to fathom just how many lives had been upended in a single plot.

By the inception of the 2015 Iraqi summer, so many camps had been set up that they all started to look and feel the same. They all carried a kind of energy that was as hopeless as it was desperate. Under the glare of harsh sunshine in the land where life began, the image of a barbed wire displacement camp bobbing with stuffy caravans had become a routine sight for all who traversed the bumpy roads.

Shamefully, I had started to lose track of which camp was which and who was who, and I had grown tired of talking to official after official. I had grown tired of trying to piece together the conflict with the words of suited politicians and executives who only skirted its periphery.

As a journalist, it doesn't take long to recognize that official speak is rarely a true representation of the crumbling reality outside air-conditioned office spaces. It is almost always the testimony of those in the thick of the suffering who paint the most accurate picture.

I wanted to spend more time with those ordinary survivors who languished on those patches of dust; those who could provide hauntingly raw, firsthand accounts of what happened to them to those they loved.

Those were the stories I wanted to tell and the anecdotes I wanted to immortalize with words. It was a Sisyphean, seemingly endless chase to understand how and why such hatred had reared its ugly head. Why had it pounded a country that had already withstood so much butchery?

Every person's sad story is their own story, unique and powerful, but a year into the ISIS invasion it felt as though every sad story had also become one giant sad story. We can hear and see the pain, but we can never really, truly understand it other than comprehending it as universal — nobody was spared. Nobody would ever be able to return to the life they had led before the black flags.

In passing one camp on the periphery of Erbil, I spontaneously motioned for the taxi driver to stop. Even with a press pass, going to an established camp was never a straightforward process. Entrance constituted tea, calls, permission letters, approval, safety checks, more calls, confusion, an ensuing questions.

Those tasked with operating the facility, whose lives now centered out of a portable caravan at the front, typically came across as deeply skeptical of journalists. For them, it was a quagmire of wanting to publicize the agony of the situation — to light up televisions and computer screens across the globe and encourage donors to step up. But at the same time, they also were aware that each camp was a rendition of living purgatory for those stuffed inside. The operators worried that when conditions were exposed, they then had to face a backlash of questions about bloated bureaucracies and how money was being spent.

The operators always ran the risk that a journalist's visit could spawn an outpouring of negative press about the horrid conditions or the lack of resources, amplified by articles peppered with quotes from complaining people. There was also a genuine concern about identifying or photographing people at the camp and how it could endanger other family members, given that almost everyone had loved ones still living under ISIS's control — whether they had not made it out in time or had not wanted to leave.

Would they be retaliated against for their loved ones speaking out against the group? Would they be the next to be executed during Friday prayers, or dumped into a filthy cell to lie for days on end? Would the only reprieve come when they were hung from the ceiling by their ankles and electrocuted during interrogation sessions?

In advance of every visit, I endeavored to set up meetings and ascertain approval for access. But my emails often went unanswered, or I was referred from one person to the next, with little being accomplished, all of which could be chalked up to that bloated bureaucracy catchphrase, inefficiency, chaos, or concern.

Eventually, I configured, my sanity would be best preserved by just showing up with my press badge and politely putting my foot down — this camp was no exception.

Sitting in the little camp office run by a group called the Agency for Technical Cooperation and Development (ACTED), I endured a back-and-forth with the local Kurdish administrator about where I was from and why I was there. Being a journalist wasn't enough — what was my agenda? What was my story angle? What was it I was trying to achieve?

Finally, the administrator gave the green light for me to enter the patchwork of decaying homes, with the strict instruction of only taking photographs after permission was obtained by the head of the family.

I stepped out of the small air-conditioned office into the stifling summer, where the temperature gauge exceeded 120 degrees. Almost immediately, the wind blew a lethal gust in our direction. Smoke rose from a cluster of flimsy, prefabricated homes in the distance and swarms of the camp's residents — children and adults alike — did not retreat, rather rushing toward it, surging into the thickening plumes.

The administrator looked at me with a flickering of agony. His first instinct, I am sure, was to worry about what would be said in the media — a sense of distrust and survival instinct for his own job appeared to permeate every sense of his being. But it quickly dissolved into a shrug of helplessness as I grabbed my notebook and camera and joined those running to the rising flames.

Without missing a beat, the children from all over the flat vicinity gathered whatever they could find to help — blankets, buckets of water, small extinguishers. Some seemed a little fearful, but it was something of a familiar fear. These were the same little humans whose houses had been blown apart; the same little humans who had fled into the unknown as rockets cracked through the air and grenades mushroomed behind them.

They knew what it meant to protect one another, to fight for their right to stay alive.

I quickly learned that the blaze had begun as a cooking fire in a tent at the far end of the camp and was fast prostrating out of control. As the bitter inferno raged, I noticed two weeping children sitting with their threadbare backpacks in the dirt, cradling their clothes and pillows as they looked on.

I assumed that they were clutching all that belonged to them, an instinctual reaction of not wanting to let their few possessions out of sight, prepared to run again.

As if by the grace of God, some higher divine power, or the shadowy conductor of coincidence, a large water tanker rolled down the street outside, and camp workers raced to flag it down. Families stood back and observed as the water designated for their taps and showers and stoves and dehydrated bodies instead flushed through the flames.

Soon, the flare evaporated, leaving in its wake the skeleton remains of a few Band-Aid homes, the unmistakable stench of creosote smoke, and ash sticking to the hot, still air.

Slowly, people started to wander away and resume their monotonous tasks inside the camp confines. A little boy raced into the heap of charred remains and proudly revived the Quran, kissing its singed edges, relieved the holy book had survived. But one person, I was told, had died.

Amid the cluster of kids dispersing as the mayhem simmered, I noticed an especially familiar face. It took me only a moment to place the heart-wrenching, gap-toothed smile. It was Abdullah — the first little boy I had met a year earlier in the first camp I had visited after the ISIS invasion. I hadn't realized we were at the same camp. It looked far different now: much more crowded, drier, and visibly haggard by the summer sun.

Abdullah remembered us and nodded solemnly in recognition. The fresh-faced, happy little boy was nowhere to be found. His once-freckled face had plumped out. It was evident that Abdullah had descended into a new place in his young life, and he would never again feel like a little kid. Children here didn't just lose their homes and baby photographs and toys — they lost their faith, their childhoods.

"Life here is very bad," Abdullah said, defeated. "We don't have money to rent our own place, so we must stay. The organizations come around and ask us what we need, but then they don't ever come back."

From the glistening eyes of a child that once held hope, foreign faces, aid workers, and people dressed in suits had come to symbolize a sequence of disappointments. Abdullah was tired of talking about what he needed most; it had become a fruitless exercise. He and many others had come to believe that the other camps in the area were getting all the money. They felt as though they were the only ones who had been left out and made to suffer.

It was a conspiracy they had configured, that if they spoke of the things they wanted and needed, then the NGOs would go out and purchase the items. But the other camps would be the recipients, so they were better off saying nothing at all.

What is war? It is distrust.

Abdullah no longer rounded up the camp kids and vivaciously led visitors throughout the endless rows of fabricated structures. Instead, he stood by himself with his arms crossed, depleted. He later told me that he had no friends, that he didn't trust the other boys at the camp, and that he was busy taking care of his acutely ill two-year-old sister. There were no glimmers of hope in his scrunched up, exhausted face, but he did express a desire to one day become a journalist because he "wanted the world to know the truth."

He believed the world was being lied to, by everyone and everything.

"I used to every year feel the Eid," Abdullah said, so softly it was almost a whisper, acknowledging that the holy month of Ramadan had just concluded and that Muslims now were supposed to be celebrating with Eid feasts and festivities. "But this year, I do not."

What is war? War is distrust over time. The hope that the mess would be cleaned up quickly or that Superman would swoop in as the savior dissipated as the days melted into months. The other boys that Abdullah had once so blissfully played with had, like him, become introspective loners. Many were angry. Some were scarred, both psychologically and physically.

I recognized another familiar face from that first visit — Mohammed. He had been the joyous creature leading the other boys in song as they sat along the log. Now he slouched around the fire's leftovers, his face slashed. One side of his little body was coated in bloodied bandages.

Mohammed had been hit by a car the previous week while running to the market to collect eggs. I asked him what had happened, how he was feeling, and if he had friends at the growing camp, but he made it clear he didn't want to talk.

"I don't have friends," he murmured bitterly. "And I don't want friends. I want to be alone."

Mohammed was no older than seven or eight. That gash along his face, I thought, was only the tip of the iceberg of the psychological trauma bottled inside.

THE HELP
June, 2015

When the buoyant band of resources is about to snap and survival is paramount, psychological help to ease the pain of war is far down the list of priorities.

Days after the fire incident, I met with a senior representative for ACTED, a New Zealander by the name of Richard Hannah. He struck me as a pragmatic person with a kind of realistic approach to conflict and resolution, who had seen enough hardship to know that there were no good solutions — only ones that were worse than others.

"The biggest issue we have is the sheer number of people," he said. "People are constantly on the move — lots of people at the same time."

They were relying on civilians who had just fled the ISIS strongholds to tell them where the next eruption of displaced people might stem from, so they could prepare in anticipation. ACTED's humanitarian capital was already spread thin over three hundred locations as they attempted to cater to over three million displaced people.

Their mandate, Richard noted, was first and foremost to prioritize food, household protection, and sanitation. The concept of developing a long-term exit strategy was nowhere on the agenda, and establishing a fixed date to hand over responsibilities to the locals seemed the stuff of unicorns. No one seemed to really know if or how ISIS would ever be defeated.

"The situation is still so fluid," Richard went on. "So, until it stabilizes..."

Not so far away, rockets cracked through the air and civilians were hanged in the streets en masse. What was war? What was stability?

Lives pivoted around the immediate needs of the displaced; of keeping them safe and alive. The women feared using public latrines, especially at night, in fear of being raped or assaulted. There were security concerns over who could breach the porous gates and there was persistent worry about what winter would bring.

And many more displaced people would soon be headed in their direction.

"The money is not coming in as fast as displacement is happening," Richard reiterated. "There is simply just not enough."

No amount of money could ever return normalcy to these people's lives. No amount of money could ever return the sanity that was lost. But when aid workers weren't trying to save lives and stop the spiral of madness, they were crying poor and threatening to walk away.

A few days later, on a Saturday morning when most of the workforce was still sleeping, I met with Lisa Grande. She was an eloquent but straight-shooting American diplomat, the Deputy Special Representative of the United Nations Assistance Mission for Iraq.

Lisa was all too aware that the ISIS situation in Iraq far surpassed a humanitarian crisis — it could only be pinpointed as something of a global catastrophe. A year earlier, they had received what she called a "Cinderella donation" from the Kingdom of Saudi Arabia, and it was their way of showing that, while ISIS was predominantly Sunni, "there were good Sunni people too."

But the money had run out, the problem had become too big, and for the sake of "a few million dollars" they had thousands of displaced families from Anbar province returning to the ISIS-held territory they had run from because of the dire humanitarian situation. Perhaps the hell they had left wouldn't be as bad as the hell they had run to. After all, if they laid low and followed orders, maybe they could live in their own homes with dignity. In the Middle East, it was always about dignity.

"What has been frustrating for us is that you can turn on the television in any country in the world and you get a sense of what is going on and yet we still can't scrape together a couple of million dollars to keep these programs running," Lisa lamented. "We are losing the battle."

From her view, if just a small fraction of the military spending — an average of more than six billion dollars per day which was being spent on the U.S. portion of the bombing campaign against ISIS — was rerouted into the humanitarian sector, lives would be saved, and a win would surface on the horizon.

Lisa pointed out that a few weeks earlier, actress and UNHCR special envoy Angelina Jolie had visited some camps in the region to draw some needed attention to the plight — she even penned a front-page op-ed in the New York Times about the crisis. It had barely raised eyebrows in Washington, let alone brought in any extra donation dollars.

"Right now, we are panicked because we don't know what to do, we don't know where this disconnect is coming from," Lisa continued. "There are 154 organizations that are a part of the UN's appeal, and they are all running out of money. We are just hoping someone will say, 'How can we abandon these victims? Let's allow people who are doing God's work to be able to keep doing God's work.'"

What is war? There is never enough money to mend the war wounds.

Lisa believed that those "on the hill" were apprehensive when it came to admitting how wrong the U.S. was when we invaded Iraq twelve years earlier. She conveyed that the moral burden caused lawmakers to shirk away from the issue, rather than come forward to cough up the needed funding.

She insisted that the Iraqi government was doing all it could to tend to the needy, but had become completely "overwhelmed" by the scale of what they were facing and acknowledged that they were having more difficulties with the Kurdish security forces, who refused to let Arabs inside their territory.

"When the retake of Mosul eventually happens, the assumption is that a lot of people will flee," Lisa intoned. "They are going to run for their lives when the heavy fighting starts... will they be able to run to the KRG?"

What is war? War is running; it is not knowing what is on the other side; it is being unwelcome in your own home; it is being unwelcome away from your home. Sometimes war is walking, too — one moment here, and the next in some no-man's-land that could never be home. It is drifting from place to place, both in the mind and the body.

THE BATTLE TO BE BORN
July, 2015

That summer, I drifted between displacement camps. The big ones and the small ones. The ones that were new, only just established to accommodate the constant swell of newcomers. The ones that had been there for years as past wars melted into new wars. Over time, the camps had burgeoned into little towns of their own, complete with banks and bridal stores and markets and places to buy homegoods and sweaters.

On occasion, there were invitations to weddings and engagement parties inside the camp. Life went on and a new normal emerged. People were determined to spend what little money they had on the things that made life worth living. The rituals of life, even in the confines of a camp focused on survival, still mattered.

But the façade was cracking ever so slowly.

Some camps were better equipped to deal with the swell of displaced people than others, but they all shared the common denominator of embodying the notion of entrapment, of a prison, of serving a sentence for no crime and having no idea when you may be able to break free.

What is war? War brings resiliency. It is turning what feels like a prison into something of a home.

But as time dragged on and the weeks turned into months, I tried to go back to many of the displacement camps I had visited in the early days of the ISIS rush. The numbers inside would grow, the resources would diminish, and the ratty tents would turn into permanent structures, the thought of ever returning home no longer a possibility.

What was perhaps worse than not being able to go home was that many did not even want to go home. Their lives had been gutted and hollowed, the shell they projected programmed to keep plugging. All the aspirations that once filled their insides had dissolved with each passing day. Who would want to return to a place strewn with the blood of their people; a place bursting with the memories of the day ISIS came for them? Could that place ever really be home again?

The KRG region alone was brimming with more than two million displaced people. Every day, more people poured in, both because of ISIS swooping up more territory and because other areas were in the process of liberation — the fierce clash between forces had become too much.

In one large facility outside the city of Duhok, Syrians had been squished inside their desolate tents for years before the ISIS invasion, having fled to escape their country's civil war sparked in the Spring of 2011. In the searing summer, the refugees — distinguished from the "displaced" due to having crossed an international border — tried to block out the heat by erecting their own scrap sheet metal walls, failing to understand when we told them that it would only draw more heat into their little spaces.

In and around those stuffy tents, children walked around like ghosts, unable to make eye contact, smile, or show any sign of emotion. It was as if their little bodies were bottled up with trauma so raw and so deep that it possessed them.

Sewage seeped down the dirt paths and into the crevices, where the children continued to play while their parents dug shallow trenches. The adults complained about the lack of water and the aches and pains that could only be tended to when a doctor visited the facility every few months. The generators produced power for just a few hours a day. But many assured me that anything was better than the knowledge that a bomb could detonate in front of them at any given moment.

Some of the scrappy tent homes overflowed with anything that could be hoarded: rusted pots and pans, worn coats and toys. They had wrapped up every part of their lives and accumulated whatever they could along the way to make their existence as comfortable as possible. Other tents were empty — a blunt reminder of those who had fled with nothing, no badges of their old existence.

For many, it wasn't the first time that bombs and bad people had forced them from their homes. That is war and persecution and instability; if it could happen once or twice, surely it could happen again and again. The idea of owning or loving anything material seemed pointless, as it would never really belong to them.

Everyone had a different view of the Syrian war and the ISIS invasion, and they often raised their voices over each other, vying for their opinions to be heard and documented in my fragile notepad. Every person has a unique story — and yet each of those incredible stories of survival blended into one: the story of running from a war for which you bear no responsibility.

I spoke to people who felt as though the world had forgotten them, or as though the world must not know what had happened. I talked to others who bitterly told me that the world knew exactly what had happened and was still happening, but the response was simply to do nothing. Some recalled every excruciating detail of their ordeal with chronological precision, while others could only talk with an amputated recollection.

For everyone swept up, there would always be memories muddied by war — too painful, too extreme to articulate.

The optimism that I had encountered at the same camp just over six months earlier — the belief that somehow the United States would save their country from ruin — had faded fast, replaced with the void of aloneness.

What is war? War is walking for days in the pouring rain with only a paper bag or a dishrag to ward off the elements. War is being stuck in a car, bumper-to-bumper with hundreds of your fleeing neighbors. War is a drive that once took you two hours instead of ten. War is losing the joys, the dancing and the family gatherings. War is losing the basics, a proper stove to cook with and a sturdy wall to sit against while you ate.

War is being a top-notch builder or a devoted farmer and, within a matter of minutes, having your life earnings wiped away by enemy hands. It is living in a place where you cannot find a job and having no alternative but to send your young children off to lay bricks, where you will forever be haunted by the vision of their tiny backs bent over under the burning sun instead of in school.

War is living dependent upon a meal card, enduring constant flashbacks of the days you spent hiding from the persistent rocket and mortar attacks, calming your children as they screamed. War is being jammed into small spaces: cars, trucks, checkpoints, camps, clinics. War is the smell of unwashed flesh and soiled mattresses, a hallmark scent of so many tents.

The refugees, the displaced, the Syrians, the Iraqis, the Muslims, the Christians, the Yazidis, and other ethnicities had developed a language to describe their memories and their lives in grandiose, Hollywood terms, describing the cocktail of militiamen who threatened them as belonging to a range of religions and tribes.

An old man with broken legs, who crawled to make money collecting garbage on the road outside the camp, recalled his run from ISIS as "Armageddon," while another man spoke of his entire family's addiction to sleeping pills and how he sent his son to beg for replenishment. Others detailed that there were "mind-sick" people in the camp who caused trouble late at night by lighting fires at their doorsteps and stealing the wilting sunflowers to instill terror. An old lady insisted that the camp was merely a slow way to kill them.

Then there was the Arab man from outside Mosul, named Musan, who continued to fast for days after the holy month of Ramadan because he believed that it would bring him closer to God. He articulated in vivid, unflinching terms how ISIS operatives had mowed down children with a forklift, leaving nothing but mangled bits of body in their wake.

"Entire families wiped out," he said flatly, like a robotic telemarketer, mentally divorced from the reality of such a horror.

Musan explained that he wanted to stay and protect his home, but he grew scared when ISIS came in. Still, he stayed. When the rattle from the airstrikes started, he told his wife it was time to go as he visualized the terror of aerial bombardment, of being struck from above, of dying slowly — of having holes in his lungs and the air sucked out.

I met a father by the name of Hida, who was no more than thirty years old. He walked around with bags of fluid and tubes attached to his abdomen because he had been diagnosed with colon cancer and it was his only treatment option.

Hida was convinced that the cancer had stemmed from the agony he endured fleeing Mosul with his wife and four babies after the black flags rose outside his home. He told me that he waited as long as he possibly could, barricading their home with tables and chairs until the anxiety grew too much and they held their breath and escaped through the back door.

"I used to have a good life, I went to work in the metal factory," Hida went on, insisting that I take down his mobile number and tent address and photograph his medical documents in the hopes that someone from the outside would help. "Now I am just in pain and dying."

What was perhaps more profound than their words were those that went unspoken. It was in the unspoken language that their agony was most understood, a universal language we could all understand: glazed eyes, slumped shoulders, furrowed brows, crossed arms, the defiance.

Most of the people dressed in the finest attire they could find, trying to scrub themselves clean despite their dank, dirty, makeshift homes. They spent their lives running farms or businesses and are often enterprising people. War may rob them of their personal possessions and their land, but it would not —

it must not — rob them of their pride.

Then there were the wincing stories of the little ones that almost didn't survive.

One old lady, whose crinkled face was dotted with tribal tattoos, told me of her grandson who, in her words, didn't even want to come into this rotten world. She said that her son's wife had been pregnant when they ran barefoot from their Syrian town and her due date came and went — weeks rolled by without the baby being born. She stressed that the "baby was stuck" and they had no money for her to go to the hospital.

Instead, they prayed and prayed for the baby to be born.

What is war? It is turning to the only thing no terrorist can take: faith.

Eventually, the family turned to vending their belongings to make a little money. They all took turns walking along the roadside, begging for spare change, before finally earning enough to present at a local hospital.

Just a week before my visit to the Syrians, that much-anticipated baby boy had finally entered the world. He was healthy for now, but what the world would offer him, she did not know.

Outside that faded blue and white tent with under which the newborn slept, someone had written "smile" in English and Arabic. Somehow, in all the sadness, we still look for silver linings woven within the tragedies and, if we look hard enough, we can always find them.

In a small camp designated especially for displaced Christians, a group of men looked me in the eyes and said sternly that they do not bother trying to read or watch the news anymore because it was all fraudulent — "all lies."

In this camp, everybody knew everybody. They had all lived as neighbors in the village of Alquosh outside of Mosul, and now they lived as neighbors again — this time miles away in a camp, in a way they described as living like their ancestors had lived a hundred years ago.

The men, almost in unison, complained about the lack of resources and

ONLY CRY FOR THE LIVING

how their food portions had gradually decreased with each passing month. They told me that they were hungry, that they drank from the ground, and that they had a number of satellites and televisions that had been donated — only they had no power to make them work. They told me that an Italian NGO came and spent $15,000 to build a soccer field that no one used.

They laughed halfheartedly when they told me this, amused at the farce. They were bouncing back and forth over the undernourished line that distinguished hurt from humor.

I could not help but think of how, in today's modern era of intelligent human rights advocates and NGOs led by folks with PhDs, there were so many blatant failures of our system — something as irritating as building a soccer field while people are drinking polluted water from the ground, or donating televisions when electricity is scarce.

There are many factors of war that we have no control over, but there are also many we do, and too often we get it wrong. The farmers do not hold back in expressing that even they know much of what is given to them is for show. NGOs want to impress their donors with flashy fields and shiny objects to make sure more money keeps flowing in, but it is all at the expense of those suffering.

Then the men were on their way to pray. It was Sunday, and someone had built a small church inside their camp so that they would never have to leave — never have to feel unsafe out in the wild world. One man wanted me to talk to his five-year-old daughter, Sara. "My *bint!*" he said proudly — the Arabic word for "daughter." He wanted me to tell her about life outside the barbed edges of this warring country.

Sara was all smiles. I asked her about the good things in her own life, and what she wanted to do and be when she grew up. Sara shyly explained that she wanted to be a doctor for two reasons: because she was fascinated by metal instruments, and because she wanted to save people.

Sara had just come from Sunday school and she clutched a Bible in the palm of her hand. I felt intimidated by the tenacity of faith that such a young child bestowed.

As I turned to walk away, another man who referred to himself as the wise leader of their Christian community pronounced that he had an important question.

"Why are you wearing black?" he asked me in a bustling staccato.

I glanced down at my black maxi dress that hung shapelessly from my body.

Black had become a color he associated with ISIS and the fateful day the AK-47 men had gutted his village and chewed up everything he owned and loved.

"Next time you come to visit," the wise old man instructed in crisp English. "Please my dear, wear pink for me."

DON'T FORGET US
July 2015

It was the streaks of pink and yellow flushing the early morning skies that could only exist in the Middle East. The region produced the most extraordinary sunrises and sunsets I had ever seen — a beautiful, deceptive umbrella hiding the bloodshed below.

Early one morning, I ventured further north to visit a Yazidi camp stuffed into the wedge where Syria, Iraq, and Turkey converge. As it came into view over the hilltops, awash with a mist of acrid air, I ascertained a sense of something profoundly exhausting.

What struck me most was that — unlike the other camps, where people animatedly voiced their anger and wailed about the lack of water, sharing conspiracy theories about who was really behind ISIS (the CIA, the Iranians, the Damascus regime) and detailing what had happened to them in the flashes after they realized that they could no longer stay — the Yazidis were so grieved that they said very little.

They did not complain. They just looked at me with wide eyes that could brand even the most stoic of souls. They all spoke softly, repeating that all they wanted was for their family members to return and for the chance to go home. Every single person had either lost a family member to death or disappearance or had been maimed when ISIS assaulted their villages less than a year earlier. It did not make sense for them to complain. To complain would be a waste of their precious energy, as they were all as worse off as each other.

An old man, mistaking us for a medical team, asked us to see his wife. Inside her stifling hot tent, the elderly woman lifted her dress to reveal deep red flakes of skin striped across her breasts. It appeared to be a severe bout of heat rash, but I was no medical expert. I felt guilty that I could not prescribe something to ease her discomfort. She frowned, wiping away tears, then pointed out that the pain was the least of her problems.

Her daughters, granddaughters, sisters, and nieces were all on that lengthy list of the missing.

News spread quickly across the camp that there were visitors on the premises and gentle, curious faces emerged around us. There were some giggling girls, some tiny, light-eyed children with shy smiles, but mostly, there were souls so broken that they could barely string together a sentence.

Less than two months after ISIS captured Mosul, the group continued its barrage into the Yazidi villages in and around the ancestral capital of Sinjar, near the Syrian border. ISIS strangled all it could around the mountain until the good people inside were left blue with death, slavery, or forced conversion.

Knowing so many of their people remained unaccounted for was so haunting that it was hard for them to fathom, let alone try to put into words.

Their stories, told like parables without anger, continued until the sun started to dip below the mountain. Many of the Yazidis claimed that the Peshmerga had abandoned them when ISIS came in, leaving them to face the bitter enemy, forcing them to run up the mountain or cross the borders into the Turkish wilderness.

The matter was still under investigation by the KRG, who said they were trying to document what had happened — how the Yazidis were left defenseless at the mercy of terrorists.

I was escorted into a tent where a thin woman had burrowed herself into the corner, weeping silently into her black scarf, shoulders trembling. She was a survivor of sex slavery. She was alive, but she was hardly living. More girls and women tip-toed into the tent behind me. Nobody wanted to speak of this ordeal, the notion of being touched.

The term "sex slave" is a controversial one; many decry that it should not be used; that it is not politically correct, nor accurate — an argument which I hear and understand. But I have chosen to use it because it is a term many of the survivors and their families use, and because it's blunt and embedded in the reality that is... not the reality we want.

Speaking of rape was taboo and terrifying within the closed and staunchly conservative Yazidi community, although the silence was slowly shifting.

But there, inside that suffocating space, the women held each other up, their embraces reassuring each other that they were now safe, if only for that moment in time. And at that moment in time, I understood that the most valuable thing I owned was my 99-cent notebook, with which I could try to capture the plight of these survivors in the hopes that somehow they would not tumble from the world's oblivion.

It was with my notebook that I could recall and write the things these women taught me: what it meant to be extraordinary, what it meant to be brave, what it meant to lose everything and still find the internal spark to go on.

A little girl named Esma wriggled into my lap. She was unable to speak, and nobody seemed able to enunciate why, but she communicated powerfully with her eyes, which vacillated between melancholy, excited, and confused all in a matter of breaths.

I asked if Esma's condition was brought on by the strain of the ISIS invasion. My interpreter, a kind man from Baghdad named Haider, translated her father's words with tears in his eyes.

"This is how she came into the life," he said.

Sometimes, words are lost in translation. Other times, they are even more poignant. She came into the life, I repeated in my mind.

"But the kids here, they all know Da'esh," Haider said. "They know what Da'esh did to their mothers and fathers."

Through the gap in the door flap, I noticed that scores of men and boys had lined up outside, maintaining a respectful distance from the distraught women, but with curiosity etched into their faces. They clearly wanted to be involved somehow, to be part of the healing process, to remind us that men weren't the enemy — bad men were the enemy.

These were the fathers and brothers and sons, the nephews and neighbors. Just as the ladies in their lives were wounded, they too were hurting over what had happened. These were the men and boys who longed to protect their female counterparts, but when ISIS came, their innate duty was torn from them. In those lurid days under attack, they had been rendered helpless. That would be something they would carry for the rest of their lives.

While there had been much focus within the international community on girls' education — given that girls had been subject to deprivation and second-class citizenry in many societies for so long — I also knew that many of these young boys wouldn't receive any more schooling. They would be sent out to the paddies to work until they died.

Yet the education of boys in impoverished, war-torn, and traditionally patriarchal regions is essential in inspiring their desire to shield those they love from harm and in understanding that violence toward girls and women is not a strength, but an abhorrent weakness. To change the course of the next generation of boys is to educate. We need them to lead the charge in shaming the aggressor, not the victim.

I glanced out at the young boys' faces sprinkled in with the adults, and silently hoped the ISIS onslaught would not take that from them, too.

The old man who had approached us when we arrived and asked us to examine his ailing wife was one of the faces waiting patiently outside. He apologized for his tears as we started to walk to the waiting vehicle.

Can you imagine apologizing for having been a victim of such profound horrors?

He told me he had everything he needed at the camp: shelter, food, and some water. He wanted to go home, and he wanted us to not forget the Yazidi people. It reminded me of a book my mother had bought for me one Christmas when I was a university student trying to find my place in the world, A Shadow of the Wind by Spanish author Carlos Ruiz Zafón.

"That as long as we are being remembered, we remain alive."

I knew it was a cliché, but as we drove away that evening, all I could scrawl in my notebook was "misery." I was driving away from a sea of absolute misery. Yet these people understood something that many of us had collectively forgotten: what it means to be grateful.

There seemed to be so much beauty within their little community, but with future visits I would become more aware of the rifts that divided them — rifts on major topics, like whether to align themselves with the central Baghdad government or give their allegiance to the Kurds, or to support neither. Some told me it was only the PKK that they wanted to protect them — the Kurdish separatist group who had long fought the Turkish army in the mountains, a designated terror group.

They had come to save them from the blood bath when everyone else had abandoned them, some Yazidis said. But others doubted that they could be trusted again.

"How do we know who will turn their guns on us?" one young Yazidi father asked me one afternoon as we drank tea in the sunshine.

Many Yazidis did not know if they ever wanted to return to the desecrated villages of Sinjar or continue to scramble and remain dependent on the camp system. Many wanted to go home only if they could protect themselves, but they did not have the means, the money, or the firepower to do so. They had put their lives in the hands of others in the summer of 2014, and they had been burned alive.

It seemed to me that they wanted freedom, but they were also scared of freedom. If they had freedom, that meant others had freedom too — freedom to drive on any road and pass any checkpoint. Those others belonged to the unknown, and could strike them again.

There were Yazidi rifts on minor topics, too, that were equally as self-sabotaging. War rips the fabric discreetly; it expunges families and dismantles deep and loving friendships within once tight-knit communities over things that should never have amounted to more than a silly squabble.

Friends were turning their backs on each other over things as basic as a bag of potatoes — where they came from and who they belonged to. War makes neighbors begrudge their neighbors.

When I was home in the safety of the U.S.A., I often thought of a little girl named Hanin Salo, a Yazidi at a camp outside of Duhok. She was born with a severe case of Ichthyosis, a rare genetic disorder characterized by a thick build-up of dry, scaly skin that painfully cracked across her entire body, from her peeling scalp to her wrinkled toenails.

The rashes, the fevers, and the pain from something as simple as eating — there was no expert care for her condition in the destitute camp. Hanin's body itself burned, and it never stopped. But worse, Hanin also had to endure the scarring stigma of ostracization. She had rosy cheeks and an angelic smile, but had been shunned by the people in her community.

At any other time, her people would have been at the forefront, welcoming and helping her. But that was one of the unspoken side effects of war: a sad but inherent fear brought by the quest to stay alive. No one wanted to go near that mysteriously ill, gentle child. Perhaps they figured it was such a feat to have survived until this point that nothing was going to jeopardize their success to stay alive. They would not risk being around a little girl whose disease they could not understand.

Her father, a handsome Yazidi, had been an Iraqi soldier but ran away when he learned what was happening to his beloved Sinjar amid the ISIS assault. He loved his little girl — a helpless love from a parent whose hands were empty, who every day had to look at his child in deep pain, who could no longer tell her everything was going to be alright.

What is war? War puts people on edge over the simplest of decisions; it sews a subaqueous and often unnecessary suspicion; it brings to the surface a breed of unplacable anger. War makes people feel as though the only one they can rely on — the only person they know will be there when they wake up in the morning — is themself.

One distraught father told me he wasn't even sure of that.

"Not me. Only God I can trust," he said. "One Arab man, he was my neighbor for years, but then even he became ISIS. We cannot trust anyone."

UNDER HEAVY GUARD
August 2015

The shadow of distrust spawned everywhere, and the longer the war went on, the greater it grew. The longer the war seemed to linger, the more those caught up in the chaos felt as though the world had forgotten them. Although ISIS had dominated much of the news cycle, it remained to them a silent war.

Over a year had passed with no progress. The overarching sense was that perhaps people genuinely did not know.

Everywhere I went, victims pleaded with me to sit and listen as they spoke. If only they could tell the world what was happening to them, somehow it would all change — the world would not look away, but would come together to help them.

Just telling their story was, in some way, a means for victims to feel as though they were moving closer to justice. These were people who had been utterly deprived of justice, so to speak out was their way of controlling what had happened to them, of ensuring that the enemy would not go unnoticed in the court of public opinion.

But as the curtain fell on the summer of 2015, a group of soldiers with rifles bulging across their chests took me to a high-security camp near the frontlines. Something had changed. The belief that someone would save them had melted into harsh reality.

"We all have the same story," Abd Al Qader, a Sunni tribal leader from the Mosul area, told me. "The world knows what happened to us."

His voice was calm, monotone. There was neither anger nor desperation in his delivery. He was simple stating the facts.

In many ways, Abd was right. The world did know what had happened to the millions of people propelled from their homes by ISIS.

The terrorist group had dominated global headlines for more than a year and had attracted far more media and political attention than other global tragedies and conflicts. ISIS was a threat to the west, rendering it a high talking-point priority for the United States government and its allies.

But what was perhaps worse was that, despite the attention, the ISIS crisis was only getting worse. The perverse army was only growing. More lives were lost every single day, more land gobbled up by black flags.

This was a small camp, under special control of the Kurdish security branch, the Asayish, because all the people there had lived with ISIS. They required extra eyes for two reasons — not only did they need to be watched with scrutiny in case sleepers had slipped through the cracks, but their lives were also at stake more than most displaced persons. They were prime targets for the militants, and most still had families under the thumb of the terror outfit in and around Mosul. Photographs were strictly forbidden.

What would happen if ISIS recognized a face under the intelligence-gathering Asayish guard, and acted out in retaliation?

Abd explained that ISIS had barged in and took control of half his home in Mosul, and he was forced to live with them for twenty-nine days. The militants told him that they had received direction from their leader, Abu al-Baghdadi, to take over as much property as they could.

One of the headmasters, an Algerian by the name of Abu Alsham, had snuck into the city in a seafood truck prior to the full takedown in order to filter intelligence and get the ball quietly rolling. Then the fighters came, flooding the wide, dusty streets.

For those twenty-nine days, the fighters striding in and out of his home were mostly foreigners — Algerian, Saudi, Syrian, and Palestinian.

"The propaganda ISIS spreads about its cities being all calm and orderly is not true," Abd asserted. "People are dying for food and water. People aren't getting their salaries. And there are only four types of jobs even the smartest people can get: selling oil, ice, in a store or at the market."

Throughout those unnerving twenty-nine days, Abd had overheard ISIS leaders instructing their mignons to torch soldiers and anything that symbolized the Iraqi government or its forces — to set them aflame. He had heard them gloat about the "special offices" they had established to "enjoy the women for an hour or two."

By January of 2015, Abd could not take it anymore — he feared for his life, as ISIS had started to accuse him of spying— so he ran out into the rainy night and never looked back.

Abd told me matter-of-factly that he had three important things he wanted me to write down in my notebook.

"Firstly, the children at the camp need some toys — there aren't any toys here. Second, ISIS is not human, they use Islam as a cover, but they are not true Islam," he paused, his eyes piercing mine — as if to assure me that the Middle East roots of hospitality were not lost in wartime. "And lastly, please drink the 7-Up we gave you, you must, you are our guest."

BULLETS, NOT BOOTS
August 2015

Even in the recesses of fighting in the thick of wartime, the Peshmerga's enthusiasm in attending to their guests was admirable, if not somewhat embarrassing. Days and nights spent in the heart of the battlefield rarely meant deprivation. The soldiers would scrape together whatever food that they could with next to no funds, and there was a continuous supply of freshly brewed black tea.

If anyone needed the extra nourishment, it was the soldiers who spent months fighting, not the foreign visitors.

But, despite their above-and-beyond penchant for accommodating, they weren't afraid to put their guests in confronting positions or let them get away without a barrage of questions about the government's policies toward the ISIS fight. I could never escape a meeting without listening to their leadership recite a laundry list of wants and needs.

For the Peshmerga, the checklist of items they wanted conveyed to the world was long and ceaseless. At the top, it was almost always about expressing desperation for equipment rather than personnel. They didn't want boots-on-the-ground — they felt their decades of fighting rendered them more than capable, but only if they had the necessary weapons.

Second, they wanted to know why the world wasn't doing much — as they viewed it — to help them confront the threat. They felt as if they were stranded on the edge, pushing a global force made up of all corners of the earth.

One especially hot, stuffy day, I visited a joint Iraqi Army and Peshmerga military base in Makhmour for lunch. During the giant feast and grand shisha water pipes, the Special Forces Peshmerga General Helme peppered me with a multitude of questions. He wanted to know why the United States was only giving money to Baghdad, and not to the Kurdish government in Erbil. He wanted to know why we could not arm the Kurds directly. There seemed to be no point explaining that, because Iraq was a unified nation and the Kurdish government only semi-autonomous, the move was against the long-standing U.S. policy of a united Iraq.

The general was not looking for answers, only to dictate that laundry list of questions in his mind. He spoke in lengthy, run-on sentences, one bullet point interrupting the next.

General Helme reminded me that, after the invasion of 2003, no American had been killed on Kurdish soil — a far cry from the blood bath outside their borders.

"We welcomed the U.S. When they crossed into Kurdish terrain, they could put their guns down," he said, almost poetically.

He reminded me that it was the Iraqi Army that had fled their posts in

Mosul just over a year earlier, allowing ISIS to puncture and quickly dominate the city, and yet the U.S. continued arming the same forces who fled and made ISIS all the more lethal by spoon-feeding them a cache of NATO's finest, funded by the American taxpayer.

General Helme's colleague, an Iraqi Army Colonel, looked down sheepishly for a moment and then stood up.

Yes, the colonel said — it was his fellow soldiers that had abandoned their weapons and had run away in the face of the brutal enemy.

Helme instructed me to note that, because of the U.S.'s failure to arm them with more advanced weapons, people were being killed. Children were being killed, old people were being killed, animals were being killed. He also wanted me to note that the Peshmerga was not against the Iraqi Army, but rather worked with them and viewed them as brothers. It was the governments and the politicians who were stirring trouble to further personal agendas.

"We aren't asking for our own country right now, we are only asking for support," the general continued, gaining energy and momentum with every sentence that rolled into a strongman's speech.

The thing they needed, aside from heavy weapons and ammunition, was assistance detecting car bombs. The proud but pleading general lamented that the suicide and car bombs were killing innocent civilians and their brave soldiers. They did not have the means to foil possible plots with sophisticated technology.

"Thousands of Yazidis are in Mosul, and the terrorists are training them and forcing them to become these suicide bombers," he went on.

In an almost foreboding way, he peered through the window at the hot, dusty outside.

"One day we will finish from ISIS, and then what happens after that? What if we are left with a country that is worse?" the general pondered, to nobody in particular.

The conversation soon shifted to the little world erupting just outside.

Makhmour was a burning frontline, considered to be one of the most dangerous hotspots at the time as ISIS launched almost daily attacks. ISIS, Helme assured, was not Islam. He glanced over my shoulder as I scrawled, carefully articulating the familiar tenure that he doesn't even like to refer to them with any kind of Islamic connotation.

"They are just terrorists," he insisted.

That, of course, had been a heated topic: was ISIS a practical manifestation of the religion? Was it just a hardline and twisted interpretation that the vast majority of Muslims had long discarded? Or did it have absolutely nothing to do with the ancient Abrahamic tenants?

Whatever the posturing, for devoted Muslims, who were mostly Sunni Arabs — the same as ISIS — it was disturbing to see their religion being used to justify such bloodletting.

Country before religion, many Kurds would go on to explain to me. *Ethnicity before religion; we are Kurdish before we are Muslim.*

They never wasted an opportunity to explain — to promise — that it wasn't their peaceful religion that encouraged barbarity.

The sun was falling fast outside the joint base that afternoon, and the light breeze kicked up swirls of dust along the plains. ISIS would wait for the first streaks of darkness to appear before they started attacking. We adjusted our Kevlar vests and headed for the frontline. The gyrating road was only a couple of miles long, but it felt much longer.

Starving, skeletal dogs dug for food in the ditches in between homes reduced to piles of rubble.

We stopped to study maps of the area and shared tea and cigarette with the soldiers at the second line of defense. Some of the commanders had earpieces, making them look as though they had stepped off the set of a "Top Gun" movie in their knockoff 5-11 boots, with dozens of patches covering their camouflage uniforms and bazaar-bought berets. I noticed that the earpieces didn't seem to be functioning.

To them, it was perhaps a show of strength, of importance. If they couldn't access the high-tech U.S. equipment that they so desperately wanted, then they could, at the very least, play the part.

We continued down the arid road of destruction through the tainted villages ISIS had controlled until recently, until we reached the final sand-bagged frontline. Twenty soldiers stood in place with their RPGs and rifles, prepared for another night of hostilities. They appeared so small against the vastness of the open plains.

What is war? Most of it is time spent waiting, woven with bursts of intensity. Time seemed to slow and every second labored by, lacquered with anxiousness as the soldiers stood in a formation, surrounding one building that had been spared the chaos.

"We have just fifteen minutes until the sun disappears," the commander in charge explained, handing me his binoculars to observe ISIS's positions in the distance. "It is now at this time that they move in; they creep as close to us as they can, and as soon as the dark hits, they attack. Now is the perfect time to attack!"

The commander spoke in such a way that he could have passed for a football coach, extolling the chess moves of the opposition and how to win. If not for the crushed war zone as far as the eye could see, one might not have known what was at stake.

And then the sun fell, and the sky came to life with fireballs of color.

A couple of weeks later, I learned that the very first assailment of ISIS chemical weapons would hit that Makhmour frontline, escalating the war to an even more critical level of international consternation. Western officials would renew the debate of just how low the terror group would stoop, and reassess the depth of what the world was being forced to confront and defeat.

A POP PRINCESS UNDER FIRE
August 2015

The endeavor to confront and defeat ISIS was being carried out in subtler, soft-power ways, too.

One evening I met emerging pop star Helly Luv for tea and hookah in the lounge of the upscale Rotana Hotel in Erbil. She was dolled up to the nines with long, perfect bleached hair extensions, fake eyelashes, red lips, and strappy stilettos that clashed with her camouflage military pants and loose-fitting white top.

By recording techno-driven, energy-boosting tunes to increase morale and filming music videos in the direct line of fire, Helly was doing what she considered to be her part in the fight: standing vehemently with the soldiers and their will to win.

Much had been said and speculated about Helly's personal life and I wasn't quite sure what to expect, but what I found was a true girl's girl. Underneath the hairspray and larger-than-life persona, Helly was a self-assured young woman who sought only to use her stardom and musical talents for something more than milking the Hollywood machine.

"Some people say I used the Peshmerga to further my own fame, but people will always complain," she said bluntly in her sharply accented English, flicking a perfectly manicured hand. "My country is bleeding, and my weapon is my voice and my music, and for those who have had their voices shot, I felt this was my only way of bringing their story, the story of the Kurdish people, to the world."

Born Helan Abdulla, Helly had been brought tumultuously into the world on November 16, 1988 in Urmia, Iran, as a refugee during the Persian Gulf War. Her parents had narrowly escaped death at the hands of the Saddam regime. That rough start to life, coupled with a passion for fighting back, was firmly imprinted on her DNA.

"I was my parents' first child and I was wrapped in blankets and put on a horse with my mother, and from there we were smuggled all the way to Turkey," she said. "There were hundreds of Kurds running away together, trying to find peace from Saddam. There were so many of us all there that the UN couldn't take us all in. So, my parents were left on the streets begging for money."

Helly reconstructed the story of her life, the epoch she was too young to remember still bringing out a fire from within.

"We were in the same clothes we left in; my father had only brought one bag: milk and diapers for me," she said.

After two weeks of begging, Helly's family was accepted into a refugee camp where they stayed for nine months before being plucked to settle in Finland. As an outlier with unique, dark Middle Eastern looks in the fair-haired Scandinavia and an even more unique language — given that they were among the first wave of Kurdish immigrants — she was spat at and bullied throughout her school years.

"I still have scars on my forehead," Helly continued with a wry smile. "It was difficult. I was the only foreigner, the only one with black hair and black eyes. My teachers suggested to my parents that I find a hobby, something of my own to enjoy life."

That hobby would not only give her an outlet to enjoy at least some parts of life, but would ultimately shape her entire life. Helly's father took her to a musical school, where she spent hours learning to play the piano before discovering a natural talent for singing and musical theater.

"I loved everything about the arts; it was my freedom and my escape. I felt such freedom being on stage," she recalled. "It became a drug and still is a drug. But growing up I had this one problem. There were no Kurdish pop stars I could look up to."

Helly's wall was plastered with posters of Michael Jackson and Whitney Houston, Helly said, but she had nobody from her culture to admire as she fell asleep every night.

"That bothered me a lot," she said. "I wanted that, or at least to become that for that next generation."

When she was eighteen, Helly felt the pull of the American Dream and left her life in Finland for the lure of Hollywood, where a one-way ticket, an under-the-table waitressing job, and a dingy, cockroach-filled apartment served as a lesson in perseverance.

"Very quickly I saw the evil side of the industry, how small it was and how everyone in it was just wolves. I realized what a deep ocean I was in," Helly pressed on. "I met some producers and realized that what they were offering in exchange to promote me was a lie, it was all about sex. It was shocking to me. I almost gave up on everything."

But just before heading back to Finland in defeat, she received a call that felt different from all the porous promises that had preceded it — it was from a producing partner of famed music executive, The Dream, who had heard her tapes.

Within hours, Helly was on a plane to New York, contracts were inked, and the whirlwind began. Her debut single "Risk It All" was released in 2013, inspired by the Kurdish dream of independence. It spread like wild conflagration across her homeland, but her sexy pop princess persona and gyrating dance moves came with some pernicious side effects.

"Straight away, I received death threats from radical Islamic groups and the mullahs at the mosques were insisting I was a bad influence and should be stoned to death," Helly said, her face suddenly clouded by emotion. "My life changed. I was the lion girl. I had all these fans and all this success, but I had this to contend with too."

Helly remained flanked by personal security guards and had to stay holed up in the hotel as threats against her multiplied. What is worse, she said, was that many of the threats came from within her own family, from relatives who abhorred the humiliation they suffered as a result her sinful extravagance and form-fitting clothes.

Nonetheless, Helly had used her spot in the limelight for something she saw as bigger than herself. In the months before ISIS invaded, when the Syrian war was in full force over the border, she started her own charity to help animals and the Kurdish Syrians fleeing from Kobane. Then, after the ISIS onslaught of June 2014, she felt there was more that needed to be done.

"I felt somehow I could bring the Kurdistan voice to the world, I felt like no one really knew what was going on," she explained. "I felt that it was my duty as an artist to do that."

The entertainer then flew back to Los Angeles and, amid a cascade of tears over a piano one balmy night, Helly wrote the hit "Revolution" before returning to Kurdistan.

Stand up, we are united
Together we can survive it
Darkness will never take us
Long live to every nation
Rise up cause we're so much stronger as one

Breaking the silence as loud as a gun
Brothers and sisters, we all come from one
Different religions, we share the same blood...

Over the course of three months, a couple of miles from an ISIS frontline, Helly filmed the "Revolution" music video with real soldiers, real victims, and real blasts of fire in the distance.

"I could have filmed something in the safely of a studio in L.A. but I didn't want that. I wanted something that was the truth," she went on. "I get a lot of criticism that the video is too violent, but it is the truth."

After the plates of hummus and kebabs had been cleared away and the lavish hookah pipes returned to the kitchen, Helly touched my hand and said one last thing, defiance in her eyes:

"It's important to me to keep doing these interviews and to keep getting this message out. Because justice is needed for my people — justice was ripped from them. Only after that, I will go back to Los Angeles and finish my album."

However, I learned a couple of years later that Helly did not go back to her Hollywood world. Instead, she opened a plush, pink-trimmed beauty salon in the heart of Erbil to employ local women and prepare the next generation of women for their weddings and celebrations and for all the good moments that would come into their lives.

I went to see her on a warm April day in 2018. She was exhausted and smiling as Kurdish teens flooded into her salon. She remained flanked by security — her life would likely always be at risk.

But in losing her freedom with the need for constant professional protection, she had perhaps gained it in another, more meaningful way — Helly could be herself. Not a Hollywood girl crafted into the "full package" most male executives looked to groom and sell, but a proud young woman with the skills to help others feel just as special inside and out in an era gripped by terrorism and the great unknown.

THIRD YEAR OF ISIS: 2016
Halo Around the Moon

BOMBS AWAY
January 2016

The blast cut through the air and looks of confusion washed over the faces of those nearby. While everyone expects attacks in a time of insurgency — they are frequent and fill up the twenty-four-hour news cycle — they still come as tremendous shocks. They're things that only happen to everyone else.

What is war? War is something for which no one can prepare. Before you can be scared, you can only be stunned.

This brazen attack struck deep, when no one was ready for it — there had been no intelligence warnings. An ISIS suicide bomber had detonated at a checkpoint outside a small town called Dibis near Kirkuk on November 3, 2015, allowing three fellow fighters to sneak through and temporarily commandeer a local government office.

The men were sentenced to hell and they all died in the attack, but the ISIS bomb expert whose handiwork sent them to their maker did not. Jasim Mohammed Atti'ya was being held in a high-security prison near the oil-rich city. In late January of 2016, guards led Jasim, blindfolded, into the room to meet me.

"What I did were terror acts," Jasim, twenty-two years old, said matter-of-factly, sitting handcuffed in the small office in the Erbil headquarters of the

Asayish. "It was my duty. There are infidels and there is instruction in Quran to stop this and fight all infidels."

The Kurdish security forces had nabbed Jasim weeks after the attack that slaughtered fourteen Kurds and left scores more wounded. Three ISIS fighters had used the checkpoint bombing as a diversion to enter the city, then briefly holed themselves up in the mayor's office.

The standoff ended when they opted to blow their own bodies to bits as police forces closed in.

While that attack served as notice that ISIS was able to strike outside the territory it controlled, the one thwarted by Jasim's capture would have been devastating by comparison.

The Kurdish security officials told me that Jasim had been preparing to rig a powerful truck bomb bound for Erbil when he was arrested by intelligence agents. Jasim had "cried like a big baby" when he was seized, one intelligence official recalled smugly, and had cried that "Allah would be mad at him."

The authorities relished any opportunity to take away the perceived power of ISIS members, to bellow that these fighters were nothing more than pathetic, delusional con artists.

Now, detained along with scores of other ISIS prisoners, Jasim awaited trial on charges of terrorism and plotting suicide bomb attacks. Kurdish officials assured me that the prisoners were held in conditions compliant with international law — another point they took great pains to drive home — and received visits from the International Committee of the Red Cross.

Jasim, wearing casual clothes and orange flip-flops, said he had contact with other prisoners and was not being kept in isolation.

It had been a steep and rapid fall for a youthful killer, who had joined ISIS at the age of twenty and rose through the ranks remarkably fast based on his loyalty and ingenuity. After undergoing extensive training to build explosives, Jasim said he was promoted to the mid-level leadership post of Amir. He then imparted his newfound knowledge of IEDs to recruits and helped plot and execute suicide attacks.

Energy broke through Jasim's dead expression. He grew animated as he reminisced on that slice of time not too long ago. Then, his face fell again.

"When you have all that power you feel like no fears," Jasim said. "I had all this power and then I got arrested."

An Asayish official confirmed that he was "very clever," viewed by ISIS leadership as an up-and-coming top brass. He had more and more power siphoned off to him every day — until Kurdish intelligence officials zeroed in.

Jasim was suspected of leading a sleeper cell in his hometown of Hawija — a large city 170 miles north of Baghdad — before going undercover thirty miles north in the Kurdish-held city of Kirkuk, where he plotted the high-profile November attack.

The exact number of deaths Jasim caused, whether directly or indirectly, remained unclear. He repeatedly gloated about conducting operations that killed and harmed scores of people — including the fighters he outfitted with suicide vests or put behind the wheels of vehicles rigged to explode. He was proud of his monstrous work and craftsmanship, but he was by no means ready to be a martyr himself when I asked if he would have strapped on a vest of his own.

"I never thought of killing myself, I am not convinced to kill myself," he said unapologetically. "Actually, I would leave or escape if they gave me this order. I wouldn't explode myself. That is another level of faith."

He was unconvinced by the Mullah's routine espousing of the paradise replete with seventy-two virgins that don't menstruate or defecate.

Filling in the backstory, Jasim explained that he joined ISIS when it was on the rise in Syria and northern Iraq. A friend had joined first, then introduced him to key members. He gave an oath and was soon learning his lethal trade.

"I spent two weeks in training: one week for IEDs and one week learning how to put explosives in vehicles," he said. "I was introduced to a bunch of other people and after they tested me, I got successful in planting the IEDs and explosives in the cars, they then promoted me to Amir in Kirkuk."

In Kirkuk city, which Kurdish and Iraqi forces had retaken months earlier even as much of the surrounding governate remained under the ISIS fist, Jasim had worked undercover at the direction of an ISIS higher-up who contacted him online.

"He wrote that he was giving me three persons ready to suicide," Jasim said, explaining that he was ordered to send one outfit to be shuffled over to the city courthouse wearing an explosive belt.

At night, he met the person who "wanted to suicide" in a secret hilly area outside the city and took him back into Kirkuk, housing him in his apartment for two days and preparing him for the touted paradise in which Jasmin, deep down, didn't even believe.

Without notice, the ISIS contact called off the operation, saying that Kurdish security had tightened and the risk of failure was too high. Instead, he had a new assignment for Jasim to curate, and it was one which would elevate his stock: an attack on Dibis. It resulted in a high body count — approximately a dozen — and success in bypassing a checkpoint in Kurdish territory.

It was an assorted goody bag that pleased his handlers and led to an even more ambitious mission.

Jasim said he was contacted online and sent the equivalent of $30,500 to buy a car and outfit it with explosives for an attack on Erbil. He didn't question his orders. He went about doing what he did best, only to receive a last-minute call that the plot had been foiled. The planned attack had, at least momentarily, been put on hold.

The wasted money was the least of ISIS's concerns. At that point, the group made an average of two to three million dollars per day on oil operations alone. Then there was all the other black-market trading, taxing, and external donations, all of it bolstering the revenue of the jihadist outfit. Thirty grand was monopoly pennies.

"It is our leaders who make decisions," Jasim said, indicating that freedom of thought definitely wasn't high on his agenda.

He was the type of person looking for absolutes, for the black or white. A group like ISIS — with all its rules and regulations — seemed the bucolic philosophy that brought firm answers to existential questions.

"Our scientists say that there are infidel people in Kirkuk. It is not my decision; we are students and we listen to our teachers," Jasim said. "If somebody pledges allegiance to ISIS, they must take orders and whatever orders they get, they have to do that."

I asked about the scientists and their theoretical determinations of infidel blood, but he didn't seem to know. Jasim had been taught to not question if the scientists were really scientists.

But at the top of the ISIS hierarchy was Abu Bakr al-Baghdadi, who Jasim described as a "good leader" who lived "as a simple soldier" and "was just like everyone else." He had never met nor seen the elusive, self-professed ISIS caliph.

"It's dangerous to meet him. Nobody can see him," Jasim said, his eyes widening in surprise that even suggested such a question. "It is prohibited for anybody to see him."

Alternating between bravado and circumspection brought on by either remorse or the presence of a watchful jailor, Jasim chorused that he would "have to be convinced" not to go back to ISIS if he were released.

"Before I went to prison, I had no problems killing people," he said. "Now I have a bit of regret that maybe some people don't deserve to be killed."

However, in the next breath Jasim called for a worldwide return to the ways of Mohammad. When reminded that life in the seventh century did not include car bombs and suicide belts, Jasim shrugged and said that today's weapons were more effective at accomplishing the prophet's goals.

"During the Prophet's time it is true there was a sword, but now there are AK-47s and that is more effective than a sword," he went on, undisturbed by the glaring contradiction. "But they are all weapons."

Despite the presence of several security officials and likely facing a death sentence if convicted, Jasim called on others to follow his path — he just could not help himself.

"It is better if they join," he said, not talking to me but rather at me. "We want to go to America. We want to spread our ideology all over the world."

Another day, in Kirkuk, I spoke to an overweight and cranky twenty-seven-year-old detainee named Thahir Sahab Jamel. He had held a ringside seat for the entire bloody rise of ISIS and, by his count, killed dozens of uninvolved men, women, and children.

Handcuffed and partially masked, Thahir — who had been in solitary confinement since his arrest two and a half months earlier — said he joined the terror group because, like many other young, Sunni Muslim men, he opposed the Shia-dominant government in Baghdad. To him, and many other ISIS fighters, a savage revolution was better than the status-quo that left them on their knees, suppressed and humiliated.

"A man named Salam talked to me and got me connected to ISIS. He told me I needed to be a jihadist and fight the Shia government. He convinced me to fight the government," Thahir said. "I started getting involved as they were planning operations to begin in Iraq and Syria."

Slapped with a possible death sentence if convicted by the Kurdish courts — or, if he was lucky, life behind bars — Thahir claimed that he had disavowed the black-clad Islamist arm. But his jailers cautioned that they had heard it all before.

On the one hand, it was the authorities' job to try to de-program the savagery with pro-Kurdish indoctrination, even if all it did was make the jails a little safer and squashed some of the terrorist recruitment that festered behind bars. But on the other hand, the guards, the fighters, and I all knew they were mostly empty words.

Thahir detailed how he had joined the Islamic State in 2013. He had served as a foot soldier in the takeover of Mosul a year later and claimed he eventually became disillusioned with the nebulous vision of his fellow fighters.

"At the beginning, ISIS told us we would all go to heaven," Thahir said. "But now that I am in prison, it means I am going to the fire. I am going to hell."

The indoctrination and self-fulfilling fantasy script was evident, but any real sign of remorse was not.

Both Jasim and Thahir had wasted their lives — and the lives of others — on a lie. If they were once men who possessed likable qualities, they were long gone; what was left was the wretched outline of a squandered human.

FAMILY OF VILLANS
February, 2016

The vacuum of war has also contributed to the rise of female jihadists.

I learned in early 2016 that the sister-in-law of self-professed Islamic State "caliph" Abu Bakr al-Baghdadi was being held in a Kurdish prison after attempting a suicide bombing years earlier.

Officials explained that the twenty-four-year-old woman, Duaa Amid Ibrahim, was the sister of one of Al Baghdadi's three wives and had been held by Kurdistan Regional Government (KRG) security forces after she was caught entering Erbil with a suicide vest strapped beneath her burqa.

Authorities told me Al Qaeda had sent her on a mission that long predated her brother-in-law's rise to power. Since Baghdadi had arguably become the most powerful terrorist in the world, Duaa's clout behind bars had also burgeoned. It was a chilling reminder the ideology ingrained among certain patches of the social quilt.

"Her mind might have changed from wanting to be a suicide bomber, but her ideology is still the same. She is very popular, the other women really like her," a KRG intelligence official told me over tea one morning, pointing out that all her years behind bars had done nothing to soften her radical beliefs. "Her mind might have changed from wanting to be a suicide bomber, but her ideology is still the same."

Duaa was the teenage widow of an Al Qaeda fighter when she was arrested in 2011, and she bears a tattoo of his name on her right index finger. She was an attractive young woman, with pale skin and big black eyes. I had wanted to talk to her, but I was told she had vehemently refused.

The high-ranking intelligence and security official explained that Ibrahim's case was still proceeding through the legal system. It was likely she would receive a life sentence, but he didn't know why it was taking so long.

The International Red Cross regularly monitored Duaa along with dozens of other jailed female jihadists, authorities underscored yet again. She had a television in her cell, enabling her and other inmates to follow the bloody exploits of ISIS and the international community's efforts to stamp them out.

Duaa's infamous brother-in-law had risen through the ranks of Al Qaeda's Iraqi arm following his release from the U.S.-run Camp Bucca detention center in southern Iraq in 2004, when he was known as Ibrahim Awad Ibrahim al-Badry. It is not known if he played a role in the suicide bombing plot that would have killed the sister of his wife, Saja al-Dulaimi. Al Dulaimi is the most prominent of the terrorist kingpin's three wives and has been referred to in local reports as "caliphess" or "calipha."

Al Baghdadi announced his split from Al Qaeda and the formation of ISIS in August 2013. Even as the terrorist group seized power, land, and international headlines, the Kurds had no idea — until recently — that the failed suicide bomber they had captured five years earlier was related to Baghdadi.

The connection was made soon after the Lebanese Army detained Al Baghdadi's wife and son as they crossed from Syria in late 2014. While there were conflicting reports at the time about whether Al Dulaimi was still married to the ISIS chief, Duaa was flagged as a vital source of intelligence about the mysterious Al Baghdadi, whose history and movements were so mysterious and guarded that they have taken on a mythical aura.

Duaa's sister, Al Dulaimi, had been released just a couple of months earlier, in late 2015, in a prisoner exchange. The Lebanese government recovered Lebanese soldiers imprisoned by Al Nusra Front, Al Qaeda's Syrian arm. No such exchange had been proposed for Ibrahim.

Authorities would not say what — if any — information Duaa had provided about her brother-in-law. Given the duration of her captivity, whatever information she may have had would likely be of little use. But it cast a spotlight on the deeply-entrenched extremism that ran between bloodlines.

Despite periodic rumors of his death, Kurdish officials believed he was still very much alive and being funneled between Mosul and Ramadi. He had not been seen publicly since the summer of 2014 when a video surfaced of him speaking at the Great Mosque of al-Nuri, declaring himself the caliph and demanding that all Muslims obey him.

"We're getting some more information, but it is not easy to find him," said a Kurdish official, exhausted by the query that no doubt shrouded his waking hours and his dreams.

Baghdadi had become the most wanted man in the world. The U.S. government had horned a $25 million bounty over his head. Someday, someone may pinpoint, capture, or kill him, but his horrid legacy has already burned a painful place in a countless number of souls forever.

HALO AROUND THE MOON
January, 2016

When covering conflicts as a writer, you meet countless special people, but there are always a few that find a special place in your soul where — even if you never see them again — they stay with you.

In January of 2016, I was told about a makeshift camp in the center of Erbil where swaths of Yazidis lived in an abandoned building. It was intended to be a high-rise apartment complex, but when ISIS plundered the country and finances crumbled, construction was stopped and the insides had started to rot.

Scores of severed and hurting Yazidi families had tried to string together new lives for themselves in those grey, gutted foundations. There were sixteen families, a guard outside told me, or maybe seventeen. He had lost track. He couldn't be sure.

My Iraqi friend, Steven Nabil — an Assyrian Christian who had amassed hundreds of thousands of Iraqi fans who followed his Facebook page for updates about the plight of their country — instructed our cab driver to stop at a nearby store. We bought bags of groceries before venturing inside the old building, buying seventeen chickens just in case, as we didn't want anyone to miss out — a roasted chicken for each family.

According to the International Organization for Migration (IOM), around eighty percent of Iraq's displaced persons lived outside the camp system in private settings such as abandoned buildings — schools and pummeled houses — making them more vulnerable to exploitation, violence, disease, and starvation.

As we drove inside the debris of spoiled construction, a group of young children rushed to greet us, wide-eyed and smiling. I felt tender arms slink around my waist and peeked down to see a lovely little girl with blonde-streaked hair, wearing an emerald green sweatshirt to illuminate her deep brown eyes. She the softest of skin and was so graceful and doll-like that she almost seemed ethereal.

There was something extraordinary behind that angelic presence.

I quickly learned that little girl's name was Hala, which meant "halo around the moon" in Arabic, and she was roughly five years old.

Hala was born on a mountain, under a perfect night's moon.

No one seemed to know exact birthdays or ages — there was always a slight guessing game involved. Hala's mother wore dark-colored clothes and sat inside the family's small, hobbled-together room, lighting candles for warmth and perhaps as a symbol of mourning for her eldest daughter.

Her fresh-faced teenage daughter, whose photo hung on the tin wall, had been struck by a grenade in August when ISIS bombarded their Yazidi village. She had been rushed to the nearest medical clinic among the chaos. An hour later, however, the wicked fighters invaded the clinic and snatched away all the doctors.

So there, on that sultry summer day, the teenager could only cry out in confused pain until she could not cry anymore.

Yet time does not stop for the dead.

What is war? War does not rest until the dead are dead and the living are like the dead.

That day in August 2014, as gunshots rang out and panic erupted in the streets, Hala — barely out of toddlerhood — helped her shocked, distraught mother carry her big sister's body all the way up into the mountains of Syria as they fled and then crossing back into Iraq, where she could be buried with dignity.

There was no way they would have left her inside the ruined village.

Just under eighteen months had passed since that terrible day, but the grief was still raw. Hala bravely squeezed her mother's hand as she wept and, with her spare hand, laced her fingers into mine.

We played outside in the muddy plots with the other children until the winter freeze settled for nightfall. Next door, the five-star Divan Hotel loomed in all its golden glory and warmth, laden with expensive rooms and expensive guests. But there was no bitterness among the displaced in having to wake up to that sight every day; exile pained them, but they were grateful to be alive. Yazidis were always grateful — if not confused — to be alive.

We said our goodbyes and climbed back into the taxi. The driver, a middle-aged man from Mosul, had happily helped us load and unload the groceries. He had then waited, happily watching us play with the children and seeing for himself how loving and sweet the families were as they laughed and cried. He had even conversed with the other Yazidi men over a cigarette.

"You shouldn't give them things," the driver suddenly cautioned, his voice deepening as we sped away. "They are worshippers of the devil."

The persecution — the centuries of persecution — was far more submerged than a group of thugs named ISIS.

About six months later, in the summer of 2016, I returned to that little square of abandoned buildings in search of Hala. We delivered some soccer balls and shoes, coloring books and crayons, cooking supplies and clothes. Family numbers had only grown as the displacement deepened and the war went on. Many had come to accept that they may never go home, and that their children would never have a normal childhood. All they could do was rebuild their lives, even if it was in a place that would never really be home.

Upon finding Hala, I knew I was no longer looking into the eyes of the same little being. The twinkle I had fallen in love with the first time was no longer there. Hala had become tinier since the last time I had seen her, the vivacious energy she once held replaced by a heavy shadow.

When I reached for her hand, it fell limply into mine. Smoky bags lined her eyes. She did not say a word, but glanced at her new coloring book without a flicker of emotion. The joy I had hoped for did not come. Hala's life had fallen apart, and while those who saw her every day may not have noticed, to an outsider, it was undeniable.

What is war? All the children looked much younger than they were because they were so small — yet at the same time, they seemed so old. Life experience had matured their facial expressions and sometimes it was like staring into a pained adult soul. These were children who had already been burdened by so much. How would they ever heal?

More than a year later, in late 2017, I again visited that displacement hub. I sifted through the sea of familiar faces, wandering through the abandoned buildings, but I never again did I find little Hala, the special child who had left such a profound impression on me.

Wherever she was in that tick of passing time, I could only hope that she would come to see for herself that the world, though callous, could also be lovely. I could only hope that little Hala, so beautiful in her bravery and so celestial in her demeanor, would one day understand that she was a survivor of the most phenomenal kind — a survivor who had witnessed the annihilation of her family on Mount Sinjar; a survivor who emerged from the storm stronger.

SUN LADIES
January, 2016

The women sitting before me had witnessed the annihilation of their families on the winding arteries of Mount Sinjar. Then, kicking and screaming, they had been forced from their peaceful hamlets into sex slavery. They were the survivors fighting what was left of the storm — fighting for vengeance as well as survival.

They were the "Sun Ladies."

They were a sample of the 2,000 Yazidi women captured in the brutal August 2014 attack on Mount Sinjar, who had managed to escape over the past seventeen months. Driven by the raw memories of captivity and the unspeakable violations that came with it, hundreds of these women had signed up to bear arms and fight the terrorists.

They would not — could not — sit by and just wait to be violated again. The women had all lost something on that fateful day in August, and while they could never get that back, they were not going to rely on others to stop it from reoccurring.

"Whenever a war wages, our women end up as the victims," Captain Khatoon Khider told me from the unit's recourse base — a converted classroom — in Duhok. "Now we are defending ourselves from the evil; we are defending all the minorities in the region."

She paused, appearing divine underneath the streak of daylight pouring into the cold room. "We will do whatever is asked of us," she continued, staring into the cracked ceiling.

Khatoon, at thirty-two years old, was one of 123 Yazidi women who had already undergone training and joined the Peshmerga, skirmishing almost daily with ISIS and preparing for a looming assault on their Iraqi base in Mosul. The women's ages ranged from seventeen to thirty-seven and, Khatoon underscored proudly, there were another 500 women awaiting training.

The full name by which the women referred to themselves was the "Force of the Sun Ladies," shortened to "Sun Ladies," a name that reflected the culture's solar reverence — a monotheistic, ethnoreligious group that embraced elements of the three Abrahamic religions. But for centuries, they were persecuted for their unique faith. ISIS certainly was not the first to harm them, and chillingly, it came with almost certainty that it would not be the last.

While the Sun Ladies needed many things, they most valued foreigners' time and understanding — understanding that their stories were worth something.

Yazidi populations once numbered 650,000 in Iraq, with the majority living near the banks of the Tigris River in northern Nineveh Plain. Their numbers, however, had slowly eroded. ISIS's genocidal campaign to "purify" the land of non-Muslims alone had led to the slaughter of thousands and displaced 200,000 from their homes.

Victims still lay in shallow mass graves; many would never be found.

"Women were throwing their children from the mountains and then jumping themselves because it was a faster way to die," Khatoon said, recalling the days after ISIS surrounded the foot of the mountain. Those who had nowhere to go but to the tops of the mountain slowly died from starvation and heat stroke, deserted by the saviors of the world and all its supposed modern technology.

"Our hands were tied. We couldn't do anything about it," Khatoon continued, repeating a line she would tell me repeatedly in our conversation. "Whenever a war wages, our women end up as the victims."

Some managed to escape when coalition forces pounded ISIS from the air and broke its siege of Mount Sinjar. But in the end, thousands perished. They, too, were ISIS's murder victims.

As for the victims who were captured before they could even run up Sinjar Mountain, gut-wrenching atrocities awaited them.

The terrorists systematically killed men and women deemed too old or too young to be sold into sexual slavery. Boys of age with the potential to be brainwashed and conscripted as child soldiers were kidnapped and carted off in open trucks.

It was not fate, the ladies, the Yazidis, and I refused to call it that.

Women taken as captives were ordered to convert to Islam, subjected to forced marriages, and raped repeatedly. Several escaped after being sold off to low-level fighters, while others were ransomed back to their families. Some were given to high-ranking foreign fighters. Some knew their captors — they had once been their neighbors, Khatoon emphasized.

Sexual activity outside of marriage and outside of the very closed Yazidi community was akin to a death sentence; to indulge was to be cast into a gloom of eternal loneliness, stripped of all honor and dignity. Religious Yazidi leaders sought to reconcile what had happened by insisting that this was not the fault of the women. The leaders urged the community to welcome the returned survivors, and mandated that they were not to be shamed.

The Forces of the Sun Ladies were fighting for their people and for revenge against the terrorists who had enslaved them.

Khatoon had no previous experience with weapons or combat when she approached the Peshmerga senior command a few months earlier, arming herself instead with the idea that they would allow a specialized all-female Yazidi force. She hoped that in forming the force, the women would be able to protect themselves and would inspire other minority groups to follow suit.

"Our elite force is a model for other women in the region," she pressed on. "We want to thank all the other countries who help us in this difficult time. We want everyone to take up weapons and know how to protect themselves from the evil."

The women had willfully stepped into the line of fire as a support force to the Peshmerga on November 13, 2015 — the day the Kurdish Peshmerga forces reclaimed their villages from ISIS occupation. The newly-formed female unit engaged in direct combat, diminishing ISIS forces from the traditionally Yazidi-dominant enclave. The women later helped the Peshmerga soldiers clear the mangled streets and buildings of explosives.

When the jihadists realized they were about to be outrun and outgunned, and that the terrain they were holding was about to fall from their hands, they took great pains to ensure their malevolence lived on by setting copious amounts of booby traps in both conspicuous and inconspicuous places.

And, while Sinjar and some of its skirting villages were freed in the autumn of 2015, the Yazidis — along with everyone else — knew the real test was the impending battle to retake Mosul, which remained the terrorist group's regional base.

Many of the Sun Ladies, at some point, been held captive in Mosul, making them not only extra boots on the battleground, but providers of valuable intelligence on how the gregarious group operated and the methods it deployed to fight and retain control.

I learned that fighting to free the women who had been left behind provided the Sun Ladies their fieriest motivator.

"We have a lot of our women in Mosul being held as slaves," Khatoon said, her voice catching ever so slightly. "Their families are waiting for them. We are waiting for them. The liberation might help bring them home."

I wondered how these people could bear it — the not knowing. How could they move through each passing moment not knowing if those they loved the most were dead or alive, or where the pieces of their flesh were buried?

But what I had also come to learn about the Yazidis was that ISIS had already taken away their hopes and happiness — they would not allow them to take away their sanity, too. The Sun Ladies were strong, always sitting upright. A few tears were shed but hastily wiped away as the morning melted into afternoon.

ISIS had abducted Yazidi girls as young as eight, trading them at the market for a few dollars. I learned of one young mother who was pregnant at the time of capture. She had given birth in a back room of her overlord's home but was not permitted to feed her newborn son.

"The baby cried and cried," Khatoon said flatly. "The Muslim militant beheaded him."

The depth of depravity was hard to swallow, and we all sat in clouded quietude for a small period.

"It's important to us to be able to protect our dignity and honor," a nineteen-year-old Sun Lady named Mesa finally said, softly shattering the wincing silence. "My family is very proud. They encouraged me to join. I'm very proud to protect my people. And after all that has happened to us Yazidis, we are no longer afraid."

As brave and as stoic as the Sun Ladies seemed to me, there was one thing that did frighten them: the notion that Yazidi boys — who had been kidnapped from Mount Sinjar and presumably drugged and brainwashed by ISIS — were now fighting their mothers and sisters under the black flag of ISIS.

"We now have terrorist Yazidis, something that never used to be," Khatoon lamented, more disappointed than angry. "But we have many missions left. We will do whatever is needed."

I revisited the group in a stuffy displacement camp in the summer of 2016, and over that six-month period their numbers had skyrocketed from 123 to more than 400.

"We now have not only Yazidis, but Muslims and Christians too," Khatoon said. "Religion is not important. Anyone who wants to protect our lands can come and join us."

The tragedy had made her fierce, immortal, unstoppable, and comfortable with everything uncomfortable.

In a symbol of Yazidi hospitality, the young children were instructed to wave giant sheets over their guests like human fans. Feeling guilty for their efforts, I pleaded for them to stop. But the elders insisted, and to argue would have been offensive.

Khatoon said that there were still hundreds of girls who wanted to join the special force of women — although many were too young — and that they had become a much greater fighting force since I had met them, not only in numbers but in combat capabilities as well.

"We're better fighters now," she continued. "We watched how the males were fighting, we all wanted to learn."

Before forming the all-female unit, Khatoon was already a known figure in the Yazidi community; an opera singer, who would often perform with her father, Ali, at local gatherings and celebrations. In the aftermath of the defilement, she took to visiting displacement camps — dressed in black — to sing for the mourning families. She had stopped singing after forming the military unit.

That afternoon I asked her to sing for me, and her throat choked a little with tears before her angelic melody rang out. Ali, her father, could not bring himself to join the singing. There was something too melancholic, too reminiscent of their lives before, to evoke those gentle harmonies.

"I am so proud that she protects Kurdistan," her father said from the doorway, his thick grey mustache trembling.

As the final push for Mosul was still in the planning stage and the roles of the different forces undecided, Khatoon busied herself by advocating for her Sun Ladies to undertake direct action in rescue missions to bring back the 3000 Yazidi girls still held captive by the terrorist outfit.

"I told our general we want to rescue girls and he started crying and said he would come with us, but we don't know where they are," Khatoon added. "We don't care how dangerous it is. We don't care about snipers and IEDs. We just want our girls back."

The women fronting the fight had come to define much of this war in different units and forms.

FEMALES AT THE FRONT
June, 2016

In another time and place, I met with a band of women who had been to the front and back of a fight that was far from over.

By the summer of 2016, Mosul remained under ISIS's iron fist. Preparations to liberate the country's second-largest city were finally gaining momentum, with more and more women joining the fighting fray. They did not, however, just want to see the deed done — there was a method to their motivation.

According to the military doctrine espoused by ISIS, there is "no paradise" for Islamic terrorists taken out by a woman. It was deemed haram forbidden to be slain by a lady.

The women claimed that special streak of stimulus with cheeky smiles.

"When they saw women joining the operations against them, ISIS went crazy," a Zeravani soldier named Hurya told me gleefully. "They don't want to be killed by a woman because they won't go to heaven. So, we need even more women to make the Da'esh angry."

Hurya leaned forward and touched my hand, pausing for emphasis.

"When a woman kills Da'esh, it is the best, most satisfying moment," she gushed.

Hurya, at just twenty-six, was credited with creating the all-female Zeravani unit five years earlier in a quest to protect their Kurdish land from outside threats and persecution. It had been a grassroots effort, born when she casually asked her female friends to join. Hurya had then pushed for formal support, successfully forming the all-female fighters into a wing of the Kurdish Peshmerga, with their own name and duties.

"We had been attacked just too many times," Hurya explained. "And it was always my dream to grow up and be a soldier. The enemy gives us courage."

She was slight in stature and wore a goofy smile, but embodied an unmistakably tough disposition, which was enhanced by a tan face and calloused hands from the harsh elements outside.

In addition to acting as security at embassies, government buildings, and along borders and checkpoints, the Zeravani soldiers' duties had further developed: they participated in various anti-ISIS operations, including the freeing of Sinjar Mountain and the ousting of ISIS from their brief takeover of Mosul Dam in early August 2014.

"We came in as support to those on the frontlines, supplying weapons and refreshments, and many of us stayed there for twenty-four hours. We didn't want to leave despite the dangers," Hurya recalled, not boastfully but in a way that oozed determination. "We were in there for the full fight."

The group's commander, Colonel Delshael Maulud, declined to give exact unit numbers. He referred to them as a "huge unit" which only proliferated when ISIS emerged two years earlier, with girls from all over the region signing on.

Most of the girls — between eighteen and twenty-five years old — entered the academy without any prior experience with weapons. Each year they participated in three different types of combat training with both light and heavy weaponry, with each training bloc lasting several weeks under the direction of male soldiers. Some of the women were married with families of their own, while others remained solely devoted to bearing arms.

The women said that, although their force remained a work in progress, they had made much progress in ensuring they received equal training and equipment to that of their greatly-respected male counterparts.

However, being a female fighter still ignited a mixed response within the greater community — their progress was punctured.

"My family really encouraged me to be a Peshmerga," Hurya said. "But some people have told my dad that his daughter should not be in the army, and he just tells them I must do this because I have the courage."

Twenty-four-year-old Zuzan, another member of the Zeravani, noted that they learned to simply brush off the naysayers. "People can say whatever they want but we just ignore it," she said with a shrug. "We make ourselves higher."

The women's ultimate idol was Leyla Qasim, a female Kurdish activist during the Ba'ath regime. She had been captured, tortured, and executed in Baghdad by Saddam Hussein's Iraqi Army in 1974.

"They told her to say she is not a Kurd and they will liberate her. But she had the courage to look at them and say, 'I am a Kurd and I am the daughter of Kurds,' so they hung her," Hurya said. "So when we want to give each other compliments, we say, 'You are smart and brave and you look like Leyla Qasim.'"

When they weren't perfecting their military prowess, the unit dedicated themselves to supplying humanitarian aid in local displacement camps. There were now more than three million displaced people documented to be living on the borders of the Kurdish Regional Government (KRG).

"We know what it is like to be a refugee ourselves; many of us were born in refugee camps in Turkey and Iran," recalled twenty-seven-year-old Kocher of the first eleven years of her life spent as a refugee amid the persecution of the

Kurdish minority under the Saddam Hussein regime. "We want to help them."

LIFE AS A SEX SLAVE
July, 2016

Could they ever really be helped? Was there enough help for every Yazidi woman who had suffered — who had her innocence and life ripped inside out? The mere concept that they were reaching for help, grasping for vessels to share their stories, and holding each other up was a remarkable start.

What is war? War was change; it was detonating customs; it was the forcing in of a new era; it was finding small bouts of control in a situation so out of control.

Yazidi women were breaking the taboos of an otherwise staunchly-conservative culture. Rather than shirking into the shadows in shame, they were coming forward in unprecedented ways to tell the world that they were victims and they were not to be blamed or viewed as tainted for what had happened to them.

They were speaking out not because they wanted sympathy, but because they wanted to help others — to do whatever possible to prevent what had happened to them from happening to another woman.

One blazing summer afternoon I traveled a bumpy couple of hours north to the Office of Kidnapped Affairs in Duhok. It was, perhaps, one of the saddest structures I ever entered — not because of the building itself, painted a bright sunny yellow and standing, indomitable, in the middle of the sprawling city, but rather because of what it represented. The office had been established with support from the KRG Prime Minister after the ISIS eruption of 2014 to find the thousands that had gone missing. I would visit that office many times in the months to come, and every time it would get sadder.

It was the place that the helpless visited day in and day out, tearing their hair out and pacing the garden outside as they waited for news about their missing loved ones with the kind of agony that made me think they would shatter into tears at the slightest touch.

The worst news was no news because the anguish would endure.

But despite the desperation that clung to the walls, the building was a place of profound survival.

One late morning, I sat with Zana, who I had previously Skyped with from the States just weeks after her traumatic rescue from ISIS, where she bravely detailed all she had endured.

An official brought her from her displacement camp to the office to surprise me, and the second I saw her sweet, familiar face in the waiting room — this time in the flesh — everything else on my mind faded away.

Zana and I embraced for a long time, and I did not want to let her go. I wanted her to feel safe and, perhaps more selfishly, I wanted to feel safe in the arms of someone who was living proof of what it meant to overcome the absolute unthinkable.

The first time Zana told me her story over Skype, starting from the day in 2014 that ISIS laid siege to the Yazidi villages on Mount Sinjar, she raised that increasingly familiar scenario.

Zana explained that it was her neighbors — Muslim families they had lived side-by-side with for generations — who ended up turning on them.

"One morning," she said, "our neighbors came for us."

Zana, who was thirty-two years old, had spent more than a year as an ISIS sex slave.

"When ISIS came, they said they didn't want to fight us, they told us to give them our weapons," she said, telling me her story all over again but this time face-to-face, where it felt cruder and more inescapable. "We gave them everything we had — these were our Muslim neighbors. But so many of them had become ISIS and we didn't know."

Zana winced as she recollected the day ISIS assaulted her village at the foot of Mount Sinjar. The elderly, who could not run fast or far enough, were summarily executed. Men and women were separated, with older men dragged off to mosques to be killed. The females — including girls as young as eight — were loaded onto cars and trucks bound for Mosul.

"ISIS took me, my sister, my brother's wife, and my little sister," Zana remembered, her eyes filling with tears. "For thirteen days, we were put in a school — we didn't know what would happen. There were about fifty people — women and children — squashed into a room. There was no water for us to wash ourselves; the children were sick."

Her nightmare was just starting. She spoke in fractured paraphrases, reaching into her memory through troves of ripped lesions. The wounds were still open, still fresh and bleeding, worse than if she had been penetrated by a fatal bullet.

Those invisible wounds could never be stitched back up. They could only be relived over and over. Nobody could ever make them go away. Sometimes she cried, she said, but she knew it wasn't the only thing she could do.

It was clear that Zana did not want to stop even when it hurt; she wanted to tell her story. It was the only mild recourse of justice.

Zana had lied to her captors in telling them that she was married, hoping somehow it might spare her from their evil intentions — that somehow it would save her from being robbed of the one thing she could never get back.

Her captors, however, were undeterred. She and dozens of others were taken to a heavily-guarded building in the ISIS-controlled Iraqi city of Tel Afar. Yazidi girls under the age of fourteen were whisked away and sold at auctions. The remaining women were handed off to ISIS fighters and told they were henceforth their property.

When a fighter grabbed Zana and carted her off into a dust storm, fear paralyzed her from head to toe.

Only it would take weeks of not knowing when the moment would come, every elastic second straining further and further.

In its official propaganda materials, ISIS justified killing, raping, and enslaving Yazidis by calling them "devil worshippers" and linking them to their mandate to reinstitute slavery. Raping them — those unbelievers — had become a core tenant of their theology.

Zana told me that at one point, in the dead of the night, she managed to escape her quarters. She slithered away and knocked on a stranger's door, crying out for help.

"I asked them, 'Please give me a phone to call my relatives, I don't need anything from you. I just want to call my relatives,'" she said.

The family refused to help her, and instead enslaved her for nearly a week. Once her hands had been rubbed raw from the overload of chores, they handed her back to her tormentors.

"They called and said, 'There is a girl who wants to escape, she is with us, come and take her,'" Zana said emphatically. "So, ISIS came... and I cried."

Zana's angry impounders threw her in a prison cell while investigating her escape. Days later, she was transferred to another facility in Tel Afar and forced to convert to Islam under threat of death. Zana had already witnessed a dozen fellow Yazidi captives being executed in cold blood as punishment for their escape attempts. She was not ready to die, but she was not ready to give up on finding her freedom.

Zana and another Yazidi woman were sent to live with a jihadist in the ISIS stronghold of Mosul.

"He took me to his place; they were flats. Small tourist flats. It was a tourist community," Zana said, her eyes cast down.

It was there, Zana noted, that she was violated for the first time.

"Then he raped me," she said forthrightly.

For the next five months, Zana remained inside Mosul and was handed off to another militant, who locked her in a small room. That was how the game was played.

The more she spoke, the more emotions watered her dry façade. She had gone from blunt disconnectedness to melancholy, wistfulness, anger, and revitalization.

"I cooked for him, I washed his clothes, and I cleaned the house. I did everything," Zana said. "But he became very aggressive if I didn't do something just as wanted, and he would attack me."

One night when she couldn't take it anymore, Zana told the ISIS captor that, while they might be killing the Yazidi people now, one day they would take their revenge.

In the ensuing months, Zana was passed along by a string of ISIS fighters from different Arab countries and shuffled from city to city, including the ISIS capital of Raqqa, Syria. When she was sent to Iraq's Anbar Province, west of Baghdad, she managed to lock eyes with a civilian woman.

"I whispered my number to her and said, 'Please call my family,'" Zana recounted. "She told me not to worry. They knew a guy who could help rescue me."

However, rescue missions don't come cheap, as rescuers often have to pay off local tribesmen or hatch elaborate plans to purchase captives from their captors. Scores of Yazidi families had gone into tremendous debt, selling what little they had and taking loans from distant friends and family to liberate their stolen loved ones, even with some assistance from the KRG.

In Zana's case, thousands of dollars had been scraped together, and she was "bought" by a rescuer posing as ISIS in the market. On March 22, 2016, she was freed.

Now living in a straggled camp for the displaced, Zana was clearly and painfully grappling with the scars of her ordeal. Both of her parents had died at the hands of ISIS. Her sisters had been taken, and their fate was unknown.

Rape had always been a weapon of war which thrived on silence — but the Yazidi community was bravely and gradually changing that notion. They were collectively bucking the mortification and the fright and all the repercussions that came with it to speak out and tell the world that they would not be muted.

"It's a tough situation," Zana admitted with a shrug. "But I am still here."

Despite the morbidity of what the Yazidis were enduring, resilience seemed to envelop their whole beings. They may have grown fatigued with the idea of living and dying, yet giving up was not an option. They had started to accept what had happened to their community — the way it had been slashed so savagely — but they were not giving up.

In the face of all the awful, there were many inspiriting moments, too — reminders of the resilience of the human body and mind.

By this time, displaced people of various religions and ethnicities were escaping Mosul in ever-larger droves.

What is war? It was refugees marching on with sweaters and plastic bags over their heads to protect them from the summer sun as they traveled to a safe border.

One morning, I visited a sizable barbed-wire fence stadium that served as a quarantine of sorts. Intelligence officers patrolled the grounds, ensuring none of the inhabitants were ISIS. Children sprawled on the cement floor in trance-like states, tiny faces scrunched with exhaustion and bloated little bellies heaving.

A mother handed me her newborn baby and asked if I would take him; she wanted him to be with someone who could give him a better life — a stunning request, even in such dire circumstances. I pressed the little being against my body for a fleeting moment, feeling the tiny heartbeat pulsating through his ribcage before I smiled and handed him back to his mother, who grimaced with disappointment.

Pink eye had spread like wildfire in the crowded, steamy quarters, but the children did not bemoan the ailment. They wet their tissues in the tank outside and continued to wait. It would take days — maybe weeks — before they would be cleared by security to move on to a proper, more established displacement camp.

Still, the big offensive to liberate their Mosul city had not begun. There were murmurs that it would start any day now, but those murmurs had been dragging on for months. Nobody seemed to know when or if it would ever really commence.

The ISIS tragedy had grown somewhat tiresome to the world's news cycle and had slowly receded from the headlines. The country's economy was crashing, and yet the end was still so far from sight.

FREED FALLUJAH
July, 2016

Finally and suddenly, the July news cycle brought the end into view — even if the road to it was incalculable.

ISIS had transitioned to defensive measures, its offensive days depleted. Reports headlined of the terrorists losing terrain, rather than conquering it. Nonetheless, the fighting was intense, and the death toll was ascending.

And yet we still tried to find the silver linings hidden within the rayless and bloody topography.

While we waited with bated breath for the Mosul mission to ignite, the long-awaited liberation of Fallujah arrived at the end of June.

In January, two years after it had become one of the first prizes claimed by ISIS, residents inside the Pittsburgh-sized community told me that it had become a ghost town — a town where people feared even a peek out the window. At that point, news surfaced of the forthcoming operation to free Fallujah. Residents began turning on one another, and ISIS, desperate, turned against the population, making last-minute slaughter sprees against so-called spies as it prepared for the assault.

ISIS fighters resorted to stealing blood from civilians to heal their wounded, witnesses had lamented. They accosted people on the street and in their homes, forcing them to give blood, leaving some drained and dying in the streets. For a long time, many of the civilians had been lucky to get two meals a day, rendering them already ill and weak. But the terrorist ranks were bloated with large numbers of wounded fighters, and the group was desperate for blood.

Several civilians died in attempts to escape Fallujah leading up to the battle, including some who drowned in makeshift rafts trying to cross the Euphrates.

For weeks, human rights groups had raised grave concern for the absconding residents. Not only were they under the threat of ISIS, but rights defenders worried that the residents would continue to suffer at the hand of Shia militias in revenge attacks.

"We are committed to the human rights treaties and agreements, we conduct our operations as far away as possible from residential areas," said an authorized official of the Saraya Al Ashura PMF faction, which operated alongside the Iraqi Army to reclaim a number of Fallujah-surrounding villages. "We are not interacting with the civilian population and only fighting in close combat against ISIS, so we don't have to use our rockets, which could cause severe damage to them."

An uneasy alliance of government forces, Shia militias, and Sunni tribal units feuded with ISIS on the city's outskirts, signaling the pending — and bloody — campaign. Little information had trickled out from Fallujah since it had been seized by ISIS. The terrorists had informants scattered throughout Fallujah's population, which once stood at 320,000 but had since become a population unknown.

Differing accounts were a testament to the mistrust and fear that pervaded the city. Under ISIS control, Friday morning prayers were followed by mass executions in the public square. Sometimes people were locked in cages with ravenous wild animals; sometimes they were blown up. Sometimes they were set on fire and other times they were driven over by armored vehicles.

"Nobody can stand up to them. If they speak out, they will be killed. All they need is for two witnesses to testify and say that this person has done something wrong and they get killed," an insider of the region said, adding that the accusation of adultery against a woman resulted in beheading. "So, two bad people can make something up and have a person killed."

ISIS members infiltrated local communities to weed out disloyal residents, generating an even more subterranean wariness among members of the community. Scores of residents had been slaughtered trying to leave Fallujah, and those left behind faced constant shortages of water, food, and electricity.

To deter further defection attempts, ISIS stripped locals of identity cards and documentation, making prospects for landing in a safer locale far more challenging. Those who once served in the Iraqi military or police force were hunted down and killed, as were families that had even remote connections to the Iraqi government. A recent and rare case of civilian retaliation had come a few weeks earlier, according to a source in Fallujah — a thirteen-year-old boy killed three ISIS fighters after they tried to stop him from breeding pigeons.

"They slaughtered seventy birds in front of this boy and flogged the father in front of the family. And when the mother tried to step in, ISIS slapped her — causing major anger for the son," claimed a witness.

The boy was said to have seized a fighter's AK-47 and gunned down all three of the afflicters. The boy and his family were then forced into hiding, crawling from basement to basement, unable to stay in one place too long.

Fallujah, like much of Anbar Province, had long been dominated by Sunni Muslims who distrusted the current Shia- led government. When ISIS initially took the city, it had substantial support from local Sunnis, including senior military officers from the reign of Saddam Hussein. The terror group's brutality eventually reduced its popularity among the Sunnis, their hatred for ISIS exceeding even their hatred for the Shia government.

"Now about eighty percent of the people are against ISIS," estimated one inside source in the weeks before the Iraqi government offensive began. "And the other twenty percent either support it or are a part of it themselves. It used to be more."

As in other parts of ISIS's sprawling caliphate, women suspected of adultery were beheaded and men believed to be homosexual were thrown from atop buildings. In the weeks before the final battle, I learned the story of ten young boys who were killed for fleeing ISIS training camps. There was no sense, nor fairness, in any of this nonsense.

During the terrorist's tenure, schools had remained open for a few hours during the day, with boys and girls strictly separated. The only courses taught pertained to weapon use, interpretation of Islamic doctrine, and classical Arabic language classes to replicate the intonation of the Prophet. ISIS requested that families provide at least one or two child fighters — depending on the size of the family — and boys were forced to register for selection when they turned fourteen.

People inside Fallujah recounted ISIS fighters donning Iraqi government uniforms to trick citizens into believing the liberation had begun, only to eradicate them when they ventured from their homes. Others, however, insisted that much of the brutality was carried out by those liberating Shia militias, who were bent on cleansing the city of the Sunni Muslims they despised.

On May 22, 2016, the liberation was given the green light. By June 26, Iraqi forces had claimed victory. Airstrikes homed in on thousands of militants and their vehicles, and explosives-manufacturing hubs were dismantled.

"The city is damaged, but nothing like other cities where ISIS has been dislodged," explained an Iraqi intelligence official who worked closely on the Fallujah campaign. "This was a well-planned operation, led by Iraq's Golden Division."

The Golden Division was Iraq's Special Operations Forces. It had ultimately been created by U.S.-led coalition forces after the 2003 invasion and had received top-notch training.

Some grateful Fallujah residents were eager to move back and rebuild their city, as well as their lives. Most of the city's displaced population were housed in desert camps outside the city while the army cleared the streets and buildings of mines and booby traps — vital work that only began after the last of the ISIS fighters were driven from the city.

"Many sacrifices have been made by the army, police, and the crowd," said Mojtahid Alanbar, a Fallujah resident who survived the two-year ISIS occupation. "If the decision was mine, I would have made a statue for every fighter in the [battle] against terrorism. These heroes are examples of courage when faced with Da'esh."

Fallujah, a predominantly Sunni city, was a place that held a sour taste in most American mouths — they remembered it as a stronghold of insurgents following the U.S.-led incursion thirteen years earlier.

More than one hundred American soldiers had died and hundreds more were wounded in the intense battle. But perhaps most jarringly, it was the memory of four U.S. contractors from the controversial private military firm,

Blackwater, who had been ambushed and savagely burned alive. Their charred corpses had been paraded through the streets before being strung over a bridge on the Euphrates River. Throngs of Iraqis had joined in the celebration, jubilantly posing for pictures with the swinging bodies for all the world to see.

Extremism was so deeply rooted in Fallujah that it had become the first city to fall to ISIS in early 2014, with a sturdy base of support among its local population. Fallujah's infrastructure was drastically damaged in the fight for its freedom, yet it had fared better than Ramadi, thirty miles west.

Ramadi had been brought to its knees; bombs had gouged almost every standing structure. Civilian casualties had amounted to pyrrhic triumph six months earlier.

What is war? War can bring great victory; war can bring great decimation. War can be won — but at what cost?

Ramadi, a city between Baghdad and Syria's Raqqa, had been captured by ISIS in May 2015, sixteen months after Fallujah's fall. Eight months later, Ramadi was freed by Iraqi government troops, but at a high cost. More than 3,000 buildings and nearly four hundred roads and bridges were scorched to the earth. In the once-thriving Hajji Ziad Square, not a single structure was left standing.

Yet by reclaiming Ramadi first, the Iraqi government limited fleeing ISIS fighters' ability to move into the caliphate fortress of Raqqa in neighboring Syria. ISIS members had little choice but to bolt north to Mosul, where they would eventually be boxed in.

Trying to get into Mosul, however, came with severe consequences.

People from Ramadi told me that scores of ISIS fighters were set alight by their own leadership when they arrived at the Mosul gates — punishment for letting Ramadi fall, and failing to fight to the death.

"Cages," one woman said. "I can still remember the screams."

The effort to drive ISIS from Anbar — the Sunni-populated province west of Baghdad containing Fallujah and Ramadi — preluded the looming campaign to retake Mosul. Mosul was deemed the crown jewel by both the invaders and the liberators. Iraqi forces were, at the time, working with Kurdish fighters and coalition airpower to retake surrounding villages, cutting off the jihadist army's supply routes.

On a warm day at the end of June, Iraqi Prime Minister Haider al-Abadi, on a visit to central Fallujah to declare it officially ISIS-free, vowed that the Iraqi flag would next rise above Mosul. The campaign progressed in fits and starts, revealing the deep divisions among the diverse groups that made up the security forces.

What is war? It is many pools of people, all seeking the same outcome but struggling to unite. It is strongmen against strongmen. It is the enemy of your enemy is not always your friend.

The Fallujah operation was effectuated by Iraq's elite counterterrorism troops: the Golden Division, Iraqi federal police, Anbar provincial police, and an umbrella group of government-sanctioned militia fighters — mostly Shiites — known as the Popular Mobilization Forces (PMF) or the Popular Mobilization Units (PMU) or, locally, as the Hashid Shaabi, which directly translates as the Popular Mobilization Committees.

Grievances rose to accuse the Iran-backed mishmash of PMF groups of committing vast human rights abuse against the predominantly Sunni population. The Kurds were not directly involved in the operation as it was out of their territorial reach, but they too were swept up in the quagmire. Kurds are mostly Sunni, but they are always reminding me that they consider themselves Kurdish before they consider themselves Iraqi. Talk circulated of the Turkish Army moving toward Mosul, and nobody was quite sure how the religious and sectarian divisions would play out.

Compounding the complexities of the ISIS war in Iraq — despite all the lost blood and treasure — were the weapons caches and ISIS support cells that would continue to be unearthed for months after liberation. The support for their twisted ideology and the depths of sectarianism remained.

History is a ghost that keeps on haunting; everyone moves in and out, forward and back, ready to reclaim what they believe is rightfully their own.

THE BLACK DEVILS
July, 2016

Almost two years earlier, ISIS had stormed in and taken over lands that had belonged to Christians for centuries, long before Islam had even emerged as a religion. The Christians vowed to retake what was rightfully theirs. The ghost of history had once again reared its head.

On the side of the displaced Christians of Iraq, within the Kurdish people's Peshmerga army, was an especially elite unit tasked with doing just that: it specialized in rooting out ISIS sleeper cells, and responded first when the jihadists struck in northern Iraq's no-man's-land.

They were called the "Black Devils" by the terrorists they hunted, a name they boldly embraced.

Made up of four hundred soldiers, the Black Devils boasted a high enemy body count, a Spartan regimen, and the ability to induce panic in the charcoal hearts of their foes. Their aggressive tactics and effective intelligence-gathering techniques made them as feared by the ISIS enemy as they were despised.

"It is a special kind of hate they have for us," Major Raad, an interpreter for the U.S. Army during the Iraq war, chortled from the nondescript Black Devil headquarters in Teleskof, eight miles outside of Mosul. "They never have mercy on us. They just kill us."

The men were hunkered down in their headquarters inside the key town of Teleskof, which had been seized from ISIS on May 3, 2016 in a ferocious battle gripped by bloodthirstiness, senselessness, and — in many ways — stupidity.

What is war? It was the repetition of fights over land, religion, culture, and control that had been fought many moons ago.

The battle also involved an amalgam of Kurdish, Christian, and American soldiers — in an advisory role — and claimed the life of U.S. Navy SEAL Charles Keating IV on the day of liberation.

Charles, just thirty-one years old, was the son of a U.S. Olympic swimmer and a promising athlete himself — but he had surrendered athletic dreams in order to serve as a Navy SEAL. Posthumously, Charles was awarded the Navy Cross — the USA's third-highest award for valor in combat — for valor in a showdown when he took on an assault by over one hundred ISIS fighters.

Charles's death marked the third loss of U.S. military life in the ongoing ISIS war. He was considered a true hero and leader among the close-knit fighting force of Kurds and Americans. For weeks, those men had prepared and operated shoulder-to-shoulder.

When the Black Devils talked of Charles, they spoke with mournful smiles.

What is war? It is trying to remember those we treasure who were taken, while at the same time trying to let them go.

But with the enemy creeping closer to the town that had not long been liberated, the men had no choice but to cast emotion aside. All they could do was focus; they could not lose any of the gains that had been made, and had to continue making gains.

I sat and watched as the unit surveyed the desert villages on the outskirts of Mosul, collecting information and preparing for the looming battle for Iraq's second-largest city, remaining ready to move at a moment's notice.

"We look for anything that might be strange," Colonel Mahmud Darwesh explained, peering out at the depleted horizon. "When we see extra movements, it is likely an attack might be coming."

Led by Peshmerga General Wahid Majid Mohammed, the Black Devils were formed in May of 2014, just as ISIS was becoming known to locals. General Wahid was something of a luminary to the soldiers, who sketched his image on walls and talked about him with great reverie. At the time of my stay, General Wahid had gone to Lebanon to donate a kidney to a sick little girl.

According to the enthused soldiers, the general was such a good fighter that at the beginning of the insurgency, even ISIS leaders had begged him to join their ranks and had offered him big dollars to do so.

But that was not an option to even be mildly entertained, the men assured me — General Wahid was a freedom fighter, and a fighter only for Kurdistan. His leadership and unrelenting will had rubbed off on his team, who aspired to be as brave and fearless as him. Coincidentally, I had stayed the night at General Wahid's beautiful Duhok home a year earlier. A fixer — a term foreign-focused journalists use to describe well-connected locals who help set up meetings and logistics — had arranged some appointments in the area, and I was informed that a meeting would take place at two o'clock. I later learned that it meant two o'clock in the morning.

That was the Middle East.

We had made our way along some rubble roads through twilight and into darkness. In the distance, snipers shot at the fields and men lay dying with glazed eyes. It was an unsettling time. For the bloodletting to stop, so much bloodletting awaited.

We finally reached the general's lavish mansion, where a superb spread was laid out on the floor. General Wahid had just returned from the heart of the battlefield and held a commanding yet endearing presence, speaking dauntlessly of the ongoing battle skirting Tel Afar.

When the kebabs were eaten and the soup downed, he scuttled back into the hot night to fight until the early hours of the morning when he returned to sleep just a little before waking early to do it all over again.

We spent the morning in General Wahid's sun-drenched living room while he proudly showed off videos of himself leading troops to frontlines, into ISIS towns and dark dungeons filled with enemy munitions and traps. The Kurdish and Iraqi soldiers always loved to show off videos of themselves in the thick of a fight. The way to win their graces was to watch with intense concentration and enthusiasm every single time, even it meant watching the same clash taken from a slightly different angle, from a different phone, of every fighter in a platoon.

General Wahid had not only self-pride, but pride for those around him. He had wanted us to see the courage of his men, and how well they fought. He also wanted us to watch as they stomped on the heads of the dead ISIS operatives who dared try to blow them back.

These were his Devils.

The unit — whose youngest member was twenty and oldest was fifty-five — included fathers and sons, uncles and brothers, cousins and childhood friends.

At that point, the Black Devils had seen seven members killed and fifty-seven wounded fighting ISIS. Every day, their errant frontline was hit with everything from Soviet-style heavy weapons, such as Doshkas, to 120mm mortars and artillery launched from Katysha tanks. ISIS snipers often took advantage of darkness, dust, and fog to creep close to their sandbagged line and hide in ditches before striking.

"If anyone has a problem and gets attacked," said Raad, snapping me from my internal dance down memory lane, "That is where we go, to save them."

Much of the Black Devils' work was focused inside cities recaptured from ISIS such as Kirkuk, Makhmour, and Sinjar Mountain. Liberated but damaged, the cities were nonetheless still plagued by sleeper cells and boogey persons.

The unit routinely foiled suicide bombers, including one whose story made international news as an emblem of the hapless desperation of ISIS's deadly dupes. The would-be bomber was captured before he could detonate his vest, then begged the Black Devil captors to kill him because the "Prophet was waiting" and he was due in heaven by sun- down.

The retelling of the tale incited a chorus of laughs. The futility, the ridiculousness.

The Black Devils had listened in on the ISIS fighter's cell phone call, where he told his handlers with distress that his mission was halted and he had been captured. They instructed him to kill himself immediately so he would not miss his divine appointment. Instead, the fighter was arrested, medically treated for his injuries, interrogated, and handed over to the authorities.

The prominent intelligence forces in the area relied heavily on the information that emerged from the work of the Black Devils. The Devils insisted that ISIS was deteriorating, as their ranks were becoming increasingly younger and less experienced, and often fueled by amphetamines.

After the Teleskof liberation in May, members of the unit had walked out to the ditches a few hundred meters away and proudly hoisted their red and green striped Kurdish flag, with its yellow sun emblazoned in the middle. When eight ISIS fighters snuck forth and took the flag down — just two weeks before my arrival — each paid with their lives, Raad said with a smile.

In their callow and roughened barracks in a house that had once belonged to a Christian family, the Devils trained with weapons and loaded magazines. They listened to a mixture of classical and Kurdish music. They sipped tea and smoked wispy cigarettes.

They also dedicated countless hours to cracking codes used by ISIS in radio transmissions. ISIS communicated via a strange brew of military terms and odd phrases.

I learned that "visiting the farmer" meant that the terrorists believed an airstrike was imminent, and "taxi" referred to the preparation to launch heavy fire. When ISIS fighters sought to announce a mortar directed toward the Black Devils, they called it "sending a bird."

Although they slept in a different abandoned home, there were several exclusively Christian forces who occasionally joined the Devils on missions and received U.S. training. It was important to include them not only on a practical level to bolster numbers, but on a symbolic level as well — this was their history and they could not let others be responsible for its erasure.

Teleskof served as a crucial gateway to liberating Mosul due to its proximity to the city and symbolic importance as the largest of all Christian ancestral homes. Two years earlier, Christians had fled in the face of a fierce ISIS advance. Too dangerous and too decimated, the town that was once home to 11,000 people remained largely uninhabited other than for military use.

Christians wanted, more than anything, to go home.

"This village is for all Christian people and we do want to protect them," said Colonel Ziravan Bavoshky, the manager of security in Teleskof, who operated in conjunction with the Black Devils. "Sometimes the people who lived here come just to collect things they need from their houses. We want to make it our duty to protect it for when they are able to come back when the Da'esh is gone."

This week was Ramadan, and even though the soldiers were told they need not fast due to the heavy demands of war, they chose to anyway. Their wives took turns bringing them bountiful trays of home-cooked delights to break the fast after the sun had fallen.

The Black Devils, like all soldiers, waited. They waited for smaller things, like the next rocket cracking through the air. They waited for bigger things too, like Mosul. When would the liberation of Mosul begin? There was so much anticipation, yet still no one knew how or where or when it would officially commence. The Black Devils hoped it would be soon — they had families at home who needed their love and attention. There was frustration over the waiting game. They wanted to be at the forefront, but they wanted it to be done with, and quickly. They were convinced they could run the enemy out of the stronghold within a few weeks.

I smiled politely. The confidence was only to be admired.

We ate in pitch darkness to the musical score of rifles firing in the distance and the roar of starving dogs pattering through the broken village. Each soldier, in his own way, made sure to tell me that he would fight until the end — until the very last ISIS fighter's blood was spattered on the ground.

What is war? It is waiting to kill; it is waiting to be killed; it is waiting.

There was little sleep for the Black Devils. When there was, I was certain they only dreamt of danger or anticipation of danger. And when they woke, normal living would be at a faraway orbit.

They slept on the frontlines, sometimes manning positions for twenty-four hours straight if someone else was sick or injured. They typically rotated on either a day or night shift.

When they went home, their time and minds were occupied by the wait to return to battle. If they died, it would be with bravado on their lips.

What is war? It is shaping every decision around the notion of death.

Raad said he only had one child, a son, and he didn't want more — a strange statement in that part of the world, where family sizes usually swelled, sometimes into the double digits. But he did not want to leave a burden if he died and, more poignantly, he felt that there was no future for the young in a country in a perpetual state of battle.

In the first sprinkles of sunlight, I sat with the Black Devils on the blanket among the spread of yogurt and pita bread, waiting. They took their fighting positions. The incoming rounds started and they went to work, faces contorted into concentration.

Some months later, General Wahid — who had survived battle after battle — died suddenly of what the Kurds described to me as a "brain attack," meaning a stroke.

It happened quickly, I was informed. Perhaps he had come to do what he needed to do and exited with grace, but the Black Devils were still heartbroken. General Wahid never got to see the lands for which he fought so hard, for so long; he never got to bask, finally, in the smell of freedom.

PRISON BREAK
July, 2016

The smell of freedom, a distorted brand of it, drifted on the other side of the iron bars. For days that had stretched into months — and sometimes years — the detainees had faced torture and the constant threat of execution at the hands of their ISIS incarcerators.

Through the cracks, they longed for the freedom they never realized they once had.

And then one night in early 2016, a few of the detainees used a discarded piece of serrated metal to scrape through the crumbling wall of their prison, fashioning a hole just big enough for a human body — a body reduced to skin and bone — to squeeze through.

Asir was one of about twenty men who fled the jail in the small Syrian city of al-Thawrah, a name which translates to "The Revolution." The prisoners held their breath as they poured out of the hand-hewn tunnel and scattered in all directions into the night. Nobody had thought of where they would go or what they would do upon their successful escape.

A booming siren and the guttering wails of escapees as they were recaptured spurred the then thirty-year-old Asir to focus. Do not look back, he told himself. Run. Run. Faster. Harder. Run.

Exhausted, he had eventually scrambled into a stranger's home and begged for protection. The brave family hid him in a swath of blankets in the basement as he called a friend and waited anxiously for a familiar face.

Out in the sooty streets, ISIS members with AK-47s strapped over their shoulders had been sent door-to-door to locate the wanted detainees.

"Every day for three months they tortured me," Asir recalled from where he sat, stranded on the Syrian side of the shuttered Turkish border. "But after a while, the torture just became routine."

He was one of the thousands of prisoners arrested by ISIS for so-called "crimes" like wearing "western jeans" or smoking a cigarette. But he was also one of a select few who had managed to claw their way out of the terrorist group's dungeons with all his limbs intact. Short of a jail liberated by opposing forces, such escapes were considered rare.

Occasionally prisoners were released after finishing their "sentences."

Few like Asir made successful prison breaks without being hunted down.

"One cannot get out, the roads around are usually under control of the Da'esh," he said. "In Raqqa seven months ago, some escaped in an airstrike. After that, almost no one."

Nasrah, another former captive who had just been freed from an ISIS prison in Mosul, explained that ISIS operated three types of lockups. One type was for government workers, police, and military. Another was for public offenders, and the third was for high-value persons or ISIS enemies captured amid the theater of war.

The dank, lightless basements of seized churches, hospitals, stadiums, schools, and office buildings served as prisons. Within the blood-spattered walls, the prisoners were almost universally tortured to varying degrees, interrogated, and often killed.

"ISIS told us, 'We will give you safety if you give up your weapons,'" Nasrah recounted, remembering the way the terrorists had offered the police and military free passage if they surrendered their arms in an ambush. "But they lied to us — they took our weapons and then they arrested us."

Many of Nasrah's fellow soldiers had since been executed, but many remained incarcerated. There were no rights to attorneys, due process, trials, or even a phone call home. He estimated that as many as 2,000 Iraqi Army soldiers had been slain since succumbing to ISIS over the past two years. He also estimated that 5,000, at that time, remained in prison bowels across the country.

But the jihadist outfit went above and beyond to prove that they were anything but a rag-tag JV militia without governing skills. ISIS took mug shots of prisoners and meticulously recorded details of their lives and, in due course, their deaths. Prison records were vast and kept in tightly-bound office cabinets.

The cages were so small, Nasrah said, that their torsos were marked by the folds of skin and their limbs tinged blue from the hours of crouching, curled like a fetus in the womb.

Inside those cold confines into which Nasrah was wedged, food had been scarce — two meals on a good day. Breakfast was typically curdled yogurt with tea and days-old bread, and lunch or dinner consisted of a little bit of potato, tomato, and eggplant swimming in rancid cooking oil.

Sometimes, the food was tossed on the filthy floor, depriving the prisoners of dignity, forcing them to scavenge like dogs on their knees.

The rancid oil that dripped down their dirty hands as they stuffed the slivers of scrappy food into their mouths is what Nasrah believed kept him alive. Their lives were reduced to squalid dumpsters, to the stench of overflowing toilets, to the snapping of whips by masked men.

Then one strange day, after months of misery, they let Nasrah go, barking that he had done enough time in the overstuffed cell.

The second type of prison operated by the jihadists was referred to as a "public prison," run by ISIS's Department of Enforcements. Those types held civilians who were deemed to be working against the occupying force.

"The number of people in these public prisons goes up and down depending on the situation inside the city. There are many hundreds still in there," Nasrah continued.

Offensive crimes warranting captivity in one of these prisons included communicating with the Iraqi government, insulting an ISIS member, or trying to escape the caliphate.

Almost anything could have you thrown behind bars — and much of it was based on rumor. Maybe it was a rumor that you were smoking, or that you had arrived late for prayers, or that you didn't shut your store during prayer time. Or maybe you were tossed behind bars and had a hand amputated because of gossip suggesting that you ate your neighbor's goat without permission.

What is war? War is a war inside the war which the world cannot see. But sometimes, if you get close enough, you can hear it: it is inmates being endlessly beaten, lashed, maimed with sadistic tools, and kept in small cages.

All the prisons were varying shades of fire and brimstone, but the worst ISIS prisons were reserved for prisoners of war — the third type of lockup.

Iraqi Army and Kurdish soldiers captured in the heat of battle were kept alive just long enough to hover on the delicate threshold between life and death. Prisoners were kept alive only so they could suffer, and only so they could be used for prisoner exchanges.

"But when there is a big battle and ISIS is attacked, they kill some of the prisoners in retaliation," Nasrah said. "Or sometimes they just kill so they can use it to boost the morale of their fighters."

Women arrested by ISIS typically disappeared behind the prison's exterior, held separately from the men, and often were never seen again.

One document I obtained from an ISIS jail in Iraq's Saladin Province detailed the arrest of a woman in her mid-20s who was charged with "prostitution." It listed her full name and her mother's name, in addition to details such as her date and place of birth, her occupation, her place of residence, her marital status, and the location of her arrest.

I mentioned her case to some Iraqi officials in the hopes that she had been accounted for and was home in the protection of her parents, but they all shrugged and presumed she was long dead by now.

Although nobody wanted to talk about it, the reality was that no one knew what happened to those women. They were swallowed up by a building where even their cries could not be heard. In many ways, nobody wanted to know. Only the worst could be assumed — and that worst meant ultimate dishonor for her and her family. Such a life would not be worth living for a young woman, even if she were to make it through the storm.

Children are not exempt from the torment, either.

"A large number of children have been arrested by ISIS," my friend, Hussam — a member of the Syrian activist group, Raqqa is Being Slaughtered Silently — explained over Facebook messenger one night. "The most common charges are insulting Allah and cooperating with apostates. They are being tortured just like men, and some of them have died under torture."

Refusing to take part in the obligatory five-a-day prayers, listening to pop music, or disrespecting ISIS elders can all result in torture for children, Hussam wrote, essentially repeating the notion of a benign crime smorgasbord that had become all too familiar.

"They torture the children too — mostly flogging, beating on the hands and feet," he continued. "And psychological torture."

According to the Office of the United Nations Human Rights Office of the High Commissioner (OHCHR), "ISIS continues to treat its detainees with brutality, subjecting some to torture and other ill-treatment, as well as to summary executions after unfair trials."

The commission had published several reports documenting the extreme "violations of international human rights law" such as punishments involving amputation, overcrowded and insect-infested cells, and public displays of crucified captives.

It was unknown exactly how many people were held in ISIS jails across Iraq and Syria at that time, or even how many jails the terrorist group operated.

"I was administered with electric shocks; my bones were broken. I was hung by my feet from the ceiling and beaten with my hands tied behind my back," said Ali, a professional in his mid-forties who had been arrested in the early days of the terrorist onslaught on suspicion of being an atheist. "They swore on a Quran that I would be cut into pieces."

In addition to the daily indoctrination of ISIS's interpretation of the Quran and torture at the hands of their detainers, the inmates lived in constant fear of air attacks from coalition forces.

"They put us in a room where we could hear the planes echoing, the planes that fly over Mosul," Nasrah explained. "This scares the prisoners; we feel like we could be attacked at any minute."

To live in such anticipation was exhausting, and shaved years off their lives, stabbing wrinkles of stress into their skin and peppering their dark beards with white.

Several ISIS prison survivors emphasized that it was the psychological torture — being rousted from their quarters for mock executions, hearing the piercing cries of fellow inmates, and the constant reminders that each day could be their last — that was undoubtedly the worst part of captivity inside the caliphate.

Ali told me that he spent only a few days in the ISIS lockup — he was released after connections affiliated with ISIS negotiated an exchange. But those few days were enough to sentence him to a lifetime of hell.

After he was freed, Ali walked away from that haunted place with his head high, but everything about those days and nights lived on inside him. It was in the hazy moments between consciousness and sleep when it ravaged him the most.

"I still feel like I am in jail," Ali concluded. "But my mind is strong. I will keep fighting it."

The common thread among the torture victims I met was that their need to flee would never leave them. Their minds and bodies would never again belong to them. They would forever feel the burning urgency to escape from their own skin — only there would be nowhere from them to go.

The broken bones might heal and the open wounds might close, but victims of such merciless torture would never again have a safe place in the world to call home. Their flesh would be the prison walls against which their mind would thrash, but they would be unable to run.

Over time, I lost contact with Asir, Nasrah, and Ali. I have tried several times since 2016 to find out if they managed to flee the fighting, to find out where they were living and what they were doing with their lives, to see if they had been reunited with their families — but their names disappeared into the fog of war.

You can take a life without killing. That's what torture does.

What is war? A human shell might have made it through the storm in one piece, but what is inside will forever be filled with the dull pain of waiting... waiting for evil to enter, to violate the person they once were one more time.

DRUGGED-UP CHILDREN
August, 2016

Suddenly, it seemed the waiting game was almost over. The battle for the Iraqi bulwark of Mosul loomed. Many military officials in Baghdad said any day now the offensive would begin.

The macabre flipside, however, was that an increasingly desperate ISIS had set about replacing its depleted senior ranks with foreign fighters and child soldiers, who they drugged into fake macho oblivion.

Ever since ISIS had captured Mosul — the country's second-largest city — over two years earlier, the daily quarrels with the Kurds and Iraqi government forces, as well as the coalition air attacks, had taken a heavy toll. In the early days, ISIS's strength thrived from its swell of experienced and battle-hardened soldiers. Many of them had once been part of Saddam Hussein's extensively-trained cadre of Ba'ath loyalists and had endured decades in the trenches. After the U.S. invasion in 2003 and the subsequent dismantling of Saddam's poisoned political party, they were left marginalized by the new Shia-centric leadership — and hungry for revenge.

But years into the ISIS reign, with thousands of its top brass dead or heavily wounded, the attacks against them had also left their weaponry destroyed or degraded.

"In the beginning, they had powerful weapons they stole from the Iraqi Army, but over time the coalition strikes have destroyed such weapons," Jaffar Ibrahim Eminki, deputy speaker of the Kurdistan Parliament, told me from his office one morning. "And ISIS is being defeated at many strategic points."

Earlier in 2016, Baghdad officials had projected the fight to retake Mosul would be done and dusted before the year was out. However, U.S. Marine Lieutenant General Vincent Stewart, director of the Defense Intelligence Agency, had tempered those expectations. He instead told the Senate Armed Services Committee that the city would not be recaptured inside the 2016 calendar year, and remarked on just how extensive the forthcoming operation would be.

The General also underscored that the greatest challenge would be reconciling the differences between the Sunnis and the Shia, between the Iraqi forces and the Kurdish ones. Then there was the ever-daunting issue of the Popular Mobilization Forces. The U.S.-led coalition vowed that it would not work with them, given their adherence to Iran.

One chilly afternoon, I visited Kamal Kirkuki — the spokesman for the Kurdistan Democratic Party — and his team on the frontlines of Kirkuk. We weaved through the familiar tracks of dun-colored roads lined with sandbags, where fighters waited. War was always about waiting and smoking and waiting and attacking and being attacked.

Kirkuk, Iraq's "cultural capital," had for centuries been a multilingual and diverse place. It was poised above the antediluvian ruins of the Kirkuk Citadel, dating back to the middle of the third millennium B.C. Much of the extended province was under ISIS control, and the city itself was ripe for assaults and sleeper cells.

"In the beginning, the Da'esh was all former Iraqi military and Ba'ath party leaders. They had experience, top bomb tech specialists and most were very skilled," Kirkuki explained later that week, reinforcing the emerging theory that many of those original professionals have since gone down in the long hostilities. "The new ones who have contacted them online and come to join have much less experience."

In Iraq, ISIS was bolstering its fighting ranks by bringing in more "reserve fighters," many of whom were as young as twelve or thirteen and with little or no combat experience, according to Kurdish military leaders who frequently clashed with the terrorist wing.

ISIS demonstrated their lack of battlefield know-how in a recent skirmish in northwest Kirkuk. ISIS had planted scores of IEDs between the two opposing frontlines, prompting the Peshmerga soldiers to circle around and attack from behind.

"They were waiting for us face-to-face and they didn't think of that option, something so simple," Kirkuki mused. "ISIS is really stupid. If they weren't stupid, they wouldn't join ISIS."

The costly mistake evidenced the few seasoned military experts left to advise ISIS forces. While the terror outfit remained in control of significant dollops of Iraq and Syria, the U.S.-led coalition airstrikes and local ground forces had killed several senior leaders in recent months.

There were no official figures on the number of ISIS fighters annihilated, but the Pentagon reported more than twenty thousand fighters killed as of October the previous year — some 5,000 of them killed over a single three-month period.

The Iraqi Interior Ministry had also sporadically — and proudly — announced that numerous key members had been killed.

Among the deceased was Abu Ahmad al-Alwani, a former officer in Saddam's Republican Guard, and high-ranking commander Abu Saad al-

Anbari, who had headed the Islamic police in Iraq's Anbar province and was an assumed Second-in-Command to Baghdadi. Then there was the security and intelligence honcho Abu Arkan al-Ameri, and the Georgian Chechen missile-making expert they called Abu Omar al-Shishani. All dead.

What is war? The good guys don't always win. But sometimes, the bad guys do go down.

U.S. Special Operations forces in 2015 had also killed prominent ISIS commander Abu Sayyaf, who was believed to have supervised the terror group's black market oil and gas trade. A year prior it had been reported that half of ISIS's top commanders serving on the ruling council — including former Iraqi Army lieutenant colonel Abu Muslim al-Turkmani and a key aide to ISIS head Abu Bakr al-Baghdadi, named Abu Abdulrahman al-Bilawi — had also died in battle.

Between the summers of 2015 and 2016, ISIS had been on an especially vicious rampage to compensate for the loss of seasoned soldiers and had taken to drugging those it radicalized or forced into its lair.

"ISIS is using special tablets; the fighters take the drug and they don't know where they are or what they are doing. They are just shooting and fighting," one Kurdish intelligence official explained. "They lose their minds. Some can be shot twenty times before they go down."

That ominous drug was known as Captagon, a methamphetamine-like variant of the banned pharmaceutical Fenethylline. It was manufactured in copious quantities, primarily in Lebanon and neighboring Syria, where it was sold to ISIS through middlemen.

Cali Estes, founder of The Addictions Coach, explained to me over email that the drug was commonly referred to as the "Super Soldier Pill" because its effects could last up to forty-eight hours. It gave users bursts of energy — and rendered them impervious to pain.

"In a sense, it removes any barriers they would have to fighting and getting killed," Cali wrote. "There is no second-guessing; they just go in and kill."

ISIS's increasing brutality to its own fighters had not gone unnoticed by supporters, who at an earlier point in time had believed that the extremist army could insulate them from the Baghdad Shia-dominant government and wage a war of revenge.

The two sects of Islam have been at odds since the faith's earliest days in the seventh century.

"The Sunni people have been pushed by the Shiite Iraqi government a lot. They were looking for a window to help, so at the beginning when ISIS came in, they thought it would help them against the sectarian government, so they joined them," the Kurdish official said in an effort to articulate how ISIS was able to gain so much ground so rapidly.

It was that civilian support.

"There were entire villages of them, entire villages that were rooting for the Da'esh," the official continued. "They thought at the beginning that ISIS was very good, but then started to realize they were not human."

THE BOY WHO GOT AWAY
August, 2016

There was nothing human about stealing little boys from their homes and indoctrinating their fragile minds at gunpoint.

Among the ranks of the captured, brainwashed, and drugged were scores of Yazidi boys whose minds had been twisted to turn against their own people. They had been propelled into training regimes that included Islamist indoctrination and weapons instruction. They had been forced into learning the finer points of beheading; forced into becoming suicide bombers and into serving as human shields.

The handfuls fortunate enough to have escaped were housed in ordinary displacement camps. There was no home to return to — most dwellings in the Sinjar villages had been ransacked and blown to bits. The traditionally peaceful ethnic community was trying to heal with little professional help. It was painful to observe.

"Psychologically, they are hurting. They have been influenced a lot, especially the young boys aged four to five," said Hussein Al-Qaidi, director of the Office of Kidnapped Affairs. "They forget how to speak Kurdish. Some still insist on praying five times a day. Many no longer have fathers and mothers."

Hussein, a Yazidi himself, looked over at a photograph of his smiling children. "This is a difficult thing."

In the earlier days of ISIS, his office had established a few basic agreements with non-governmental European organizations who helped with de-radicalization programs. But funding had since dried up, Hussein lamented, and this devastated populace was left mostly to fend on its own.

As it stood then, there were just over 700 children who had fled or been rescued from ISIS camps, with thousands still missing. ISIS operatives shuffled many of them to Raqqa as talk of the Mosul operation gained momentum. But many of these boys, according to Hussein, were being executed or used as cannon fodder.

Time was a ticking bomb, and with every passing second it was too late for a Yazidi to return to the light. Mosul was not far from where we sat, and yet it was so far away — a whole other, ruptured universe.

I felt the chill of Hussein's office, a room as somber as it was necessary. People floated through the tiny waiting room looking for news of their loved ones, their eyes haunting and desperate.

One aging man, dressed in his most elegant suit, pulled out his phone and started showing me photographs of smiling children. All eight of them had been missing since the morning ISIS marauded through their village two summers ago. The goats on his farm had mostly died, he said. Maybe of heartache. Maybe of dehydration.

Another, younger man in farmer's trousers stared out into the sunshine, nervously yanking at strands of hair until small chunks fell upon his plaid suit coat as he slowly went mad with infirmity.

In a quiet room across the hall, a Yazidi boy named Ahmed — who was sixteen but looked no older than twelve — lifted his shirt. It had been more than eighteen months since he and his little brother broke free from the jihadist bivouac and walked for days in the sweltering Iraq heat before finally reaching safety. His ribs were still raw and purple from the daily lashings.

The scabs became his stories.

The timid teen — with skin peeling from his freckled nose and light eyes that never stopped wandering — wanted to draw a picture for me. From the jar of writing utensils, he selected the black ink and scrawled an ISIS member holding up the jihadist flag. Switching to a red pen, Ahmed then inscribed a large "X" across the drawing to prove that ISIS was wrong.

This boy was a rare exception — a teenager who had made it through ISIS captivity with his Yazidi identity intact. For nine hellish months, Ahmed had been kept under the terrorists' brutal grip, a student of their incessant indoctrination bent on shaping the vulnerable.

Ahmed was just thirteen when ISIS laid siege to Mount Sinjar in August of 2014. For days, Yazidis — the ancient religious minority insultingly regarded by ISIS as "devil worshippers" — remained trapped in the towns dotting the mountainside as the world watched uselessly.

In those uncertain first hours under the panicked siege, Yazidis formed convoys to flee down the only road leading off the mountain. Ahmed's father had desperately hoisted him and his little brother into a relative's vehicle and stayed behind to assist others. But within minutes, ISIS fighters manning a checkpoint on the road stopped the car.

"At first they told us, 'We have no problem with you, you are all our brothers and our sisters,'" the soft-spoken Ahmed remembered. "At first they told us they wouldn't hurt us."

What is war? It is ugly. It is lies. It is ugly lies.

An ISIS fighter took the wheel, whisking Ahmed and the other children fifty miles east to the ISIS-controlled town of Tel Afar while the Islamist army moved up the mountain with savage precision, destroying villages and burying countless men and women alive in a horrific scene that eventually galvanized international disgust.

Witnesses would later provide similar grim accounts of military-age men summarily executed. People of other faiths were at least given the option to convert to Islam or die. Of the half a million Yazidis in Iraq, more than two hundred thousand had been displaced or killed since the rise of ISIS, according to a United Nations report at the time.

Ahmed and his brother ended up in what ISIS called an "education camp," where as many as fifteen hundred other Yazidi children were beaten, starved, forced to memorize the Quran, and taught to kill.

"It wasn't a school, it was like a prison," Ahmed said. "We were forced to prayer; we were told we were jihadists and we were not Yazidi anymore."

The children were awakened before sunrise for morning prayers and given scraps and contaminated water that left them buckled with dysentery, he remembered. Yazidi girls with frightened eyes — more each day — were taken away to be sold to ISIS fighters. Ahmed recalled one mother's desperate plea for mercy on her young daughter.

"The mom cried that her little girl was too young, and she didn't know anything about marriage or sex," Ahmed continued. "But they didn't care and took her anyway."

Young women told their captors that their little brothers were their sons, in the hope that it would make them less desirable. If a virginity test conducted by an ISIS doctor proved them wrong, however, they were whipped for lying.

"The girls were covering their faces with dirt, trying to make themselves less beautiful," Ahmed pressed on. "But if they were caught doing that, they were beaten. They were all beaten and taken away. ISIS beat us too."

After one month, Ahmed and his brother were moved to a jihadist military training camp closer to Mosul, where they were forced to memorize the Quran. A single mistake resulted in severe punishment, usually lashings that would make the children cry a lifetime's worth of tears in less than a day. Boys were trained day and night on the use of different guns, in hand-to-hand combat, and on fighting in close quarters.

ISIS's instructors used real prisoners as their guinea pigs. The boys had to watch as crying men took their last breaths. Wasted lives.

The trainees were told that they were being groomed for the frontline to fight the Kurdish and Yazidi people. Eight months into their ordeal and a matter of days before they would be sent to sacrifice, Ahmed knew that he and his brother had to escape.

The brothers were shuffled off to Tel Afar again, but soon after they arrived in the ISIS-controlled city, the group's enforcers mounted a crackdown. In fits of gunshots and grenades, ISIS rounded up men and boys in a monstrous repeat of the scene on Mount Sinjar. They needed more folks to fight their dirty fight. Quick-thinking Ahmed took advantage of the frenzied confusion as ISIS violently swept students from the streets and plucked military-aged men from the markets — he and his brother hid under the rubble of a damaged mosque until night fell and the danger of being taken back to the ISIS haunt passed with the fading of the ISIS footsteps and flashlights.

In the morning, the brothers began their arduous quest across the desert to return to their mountain home. Ahmed recounted how he and his brother waited for hours outside an ISIS base until its occupants went inside a mosque for prayers, then darted into a building to fill their water bottles.

"We knew we would die without water," he said. "We were so thirsty we drank it all and walked again until we found a small stream to fill them up again."

The shadow of danger followed them for fifty miles, setting off close calls and games of cat-and-mouse with ISIS men who had no doubt been instructed to nab the defectors.

As he recalled his experience, we sat in a big, empty restaurant eating lunch. Ahmed could have ordered anything he wanted, but ordered only a large bowl overflowing with buttery rice. He ate every kernel slowly, savoring it like it might be his last.

They never made it to Mount Sinjar, but they did stumble with blistered feet into a Kurdish-controlled village, where locals were all-too familiar with the Yazidi plight and gave them shelter and a phone to call loved ones.

"We stayed quiet and still until it was dark — we couldn't walk anymore. We were starving," Ahmed said, his voice dropping to a whisper. "Relatives came in the car to get us. Nobody knew before that we had been trying to escape."

The brothers had leaped without looking, and it had saved them. What had also saved Ahmed was the knowledge that those who loved him most were missing him, mourning for him.

He soon realized that there was no Sinjar home left to go to, and that many of those people who loved him were gone. Ahmed and his brother were, however, reunited with their mother and sister in a displacement camp. There was no time to recover, as war has no patience. The boys quickly set about getting jobs to support their broken family. They attended school in a makeshift classroom inside the camp. Everything they had gone through was wrapped up in the void of memory.

Of an estimated 5,000 Yazidis captured in the ISIS assault on Mount Sinjar, about a third had escaped, been ransomed, or smuggled to sovereignty. But most troubling to the fractured community — as Khatoon from the Sun Ladies had emphasized months earlier — was the prospect that the Yazidi sons and brothers had been brainwashed and turned against their own people.

In Ahmed's case, eight months of intense indoctrination had not shaken his sense of right and wrong. Instead of fury, he expressed only a glum resignation and a wistful longing for his old life.

"For a moment, if I feel happy, my neighbors are not. We cannot be happy. We think of others who are with ISIS. It is a difficult life," he said, staring out the closed window. "I want to see my dad again... I want to go back to Sinjar, and I want to live peacefully with all my community — all of us — safe and together again."

I touched his forehead, wiping back the wisps of his hair that kept falling, and lied that such a day would come.

Ahmed insisted that his father "was missing." Yazidis would never use the word dead. Until their bodies were unearthed, those unaccounted for would always be referred to as missing. No one could bear the thought of their loved ones dying alone or in fear.

Yazidi leaders firmly ensured victims like Ahmed were welcomed back into their communities. The leaders hoped that more boys would return after the liberation of Mosul. They believed time, coupled with the warm embrace of their people, would heal the boys.

"These children are victims," Hussein, from the Office of Kidnapped Affairs, stressed. "What happened to them was not their fault."

A SPECIAL REGISTRY
August, 2016

It was, of course, not their fault. But there was some poetic justice in that many Yazidi women would not allow themselves to be blamed for what had happened to them. They would not let themselves fall as too many victims of wartime rape fell over the decades.

For the thousands of Yazidi girls and women kidnapped by ISIS and forced into sex slavery, their honor had been stolen from them. But the survivors, as well as members of the broader community, were taking extra steps to ensure that those rescued were not plagued by shame; to ensure that they could pick up the pieces of their lives by continuing to marry and raise families of their own if they desired. It would take time, but there were footprints embossed into something of a recovery road.

I learned that, as part of one community initiative, a special registry had been established. Yazidi men could sign up specifically to be matched for marriage with a female survivor, who may have otherwise been ostracized for no longer being a virgin.

"We want to make sure they felt accepted again as Yazidis and accepted just as they were before this tragedy happened," said Hussein al-Qaidi, director of the Ministry of Kidnapped Affairs when I revisited the desolate building. "At first when the girls were taken, there was a lot of worry that they would not be accepted and not treated well, but that is not true. There are many Yazidi men who want to marry the returning girls."

The new list had apparently attracted eight names in just a few days, but the word was spreading.

The first Yazidi couple to be matched was Adab, a Pershmerga soldier. He told me that he was twenty-nine, but he seemed at least ten years older in his demeanor and manner of speaking. Calculating ages was not easy within the Yazidi community, and many often turned to significant events to calculate their age. Beside Adab on a leather couch sat his new wife, Dunya, a painfully thin twenty-year-old swathed in a long black dress and hijab to mirror the dark mourning flooding from inside her. They had been married for a month.

Adab and Dunya had lived in adjacent villages skirting Sinjar Mountain when the Islamic militants invaded in August 2014. Dunya was captured and held as a slave by the brutal jihadists for nine months until her escape in April 2015. Adab had known of Dunya through relatives before ISIS upended their lives, admiring her from afar. He had refused to allow her treacherous ordeal to stand in the way of marriage.

"The first reason I wanted to marry her was to protect her and her family honor," Adab told me. "And the second reason is because she is very beautiful."

He also acknowledged that, while it was a very tough situation, he was trying to help his new wife "forget what happened to her." Only, Dunya's emotional scars were so deep, he was at a loss over what he could do to scrape away the invisible trauma.

"We are just hoping one day for healthy children who can live a healthy life," Adab said, glancing at his wife, whose sorrow-filled eyes burned into the cracked tile floor. Her arms folded tightly across her chest — she did not want to be hugged, nor even lightly touched.

In the first few months following the ISIS invasion, some Yazidi girls were said to have refused to return even when the opportunity for freedom arose. The anxiety and shame of how they would be perceived — even by those who loved them — dangled on the gates of their minds. Many admitted that they could not tell even their closest loved one about the abuses they suffered. Many, dreading the stigma that would make it impossible to find suitable husbands, were adamant that they had not been violated; that somehow, they had been spared.

However, the group's spiritual leader, Baba Sheikh, made a prompt public appeal to the community to accept the women returning from ISIS territory and to help them move forward. He said that they had been "subjected to a matter outside their control."

His words had significant effect in mobilizing the community to support rather than shun.

Historically, Yazidis could only marry and procreate within their religion to keep their bloodlines pure, and converts into the religion were not permitted. For centuries, that was the Yazidi code, and their lives were quiet among the olive groves and green pastures. Until ISIS came and took their history away.

Adab and Dunya lived together at a camp for displaced Yazidis in Duhok, but they had no money for a proper wedding ceremony. Dunya, with her overcast eyes still fixated on the floor, noted that a ceremony of celebration did not yet feel appropriate as most of her family had either been killed or kidnapped. She wanted closure on the fate of her missing loved ones before she took to a cheery night of food and dancing.

"I can't forget what happened to me and my relatives. I lost eighteen members of my family and I want to know their fate. We want confirmation if they are alive or dead," she announced bitterly. "And we want to know that we will be protected, and this won't happen again."

Dunya spoke softly, without conviction. Perhaps she knew — perhaps all of us in that room knew — that such a demand would never be met. Maybe the ceremony would never come.

However, Hussein pointed out that, once they added another fifteen to twenty names to the registry and made successful matches, they hoped to fund a combined wedding party — including Adab and Dunya — attended by the KRG Prime Minister, Nechirvan Barzani. Hussein wished to commemorate not just the marriages but all that the people had endured and survived.

"We are injured in our heart," he added. "But we want to provide Yazidis with all their needs."

How, though, could they begin to think of moving on when more than 3,000

Yazidi women and children were still knotted inside ISIS's web of captivity and suffering?

As we sat there on that hot afternoon, in the office with its buzzing air-conditioner, the unspoken reality was that this shattered community was expected to both let go and move forward, as well as hold on and find hope at the same time. Although an estimated 2,000 Yazidis had been rescued at that point, the number of those making it out alive had slowed as the militants tightened their grip on the terrain they still held. With the battle of Mosul imminent, the prices to buy back the girls had increased in recent months.

Before meeting the couple that day and knowing little about the registry, I had idealistically envisioned writing a Yazidi story of love, light, and silver linings rising from the dark clouds to overcome the tribulations of the past.

But as I gazed at the newlyweds on the couch in front of me, I realized that was not possible.

Adab came across as a pleasant man, if not somewhat lost in the world. Dunya was clearly still trapped in a cycle of pain that no man could pull her out of, no matter how much he loved her and no matter how many times he told her she was beautiful. She did not look at her new husband, let alone lift her eyes. Some memories had to be bound tightly for self-preservation.

ISIS still clung to the walls of her fragile body and there was no telling when — or if — she would ever smile or move forward again.

THE DAY THEY CAME
August, 2016

The bars that had imprisoned the soldier for months still caged him within the walls of his memory, suffocating him, nauseating him, crowding him. Would they ever really go away?

"I don't think that they will," Issa (the Arabic name for Jesus) said.

He went through the motions of life as if he was still stuck inside those bloody prison walls. His was a life now riddled with guilt, confusion, uncertainty, fear, and hopelessness.

Just a few days after ISIS overran Mosul, Issa Saido had been standing at his post on the Iraqi-Syrian border. And like that, the world he knew slipped away and there was a war.

Word had filtered to Issa and his fellow Iraqi Army soldiers through their radios of a pending army of angry terrorists were heading straight for them.

But the warning had come too late. Before they had time to figure out where to go or how to fight back, a truck sped along the chalky road and slammed on the brakes. Muzzles flashed and a brutal firefight ensued, the twenty-six-year-old recalled. Outnumbered and outgunned, Issa and a handful of fellow soldiers ran across the border into Syria in a last-ditch bid for their lives.

To stay and fight would have been the noble thing to do, Issa knew, but defeat was so clear. Only a few of the Iraqi soldiers survived the sudden assault. Not long after the survivors stumbled into Syria, all of them — including Issa — were taken prisoner by the insurgents who trailed in their shadows.

"There were fifteen prisoners, three were Sunnis and they let them go once they repented and promised not to return to active duty with the government," Issa remembered. "ISIS gave me the option to either die or convert... I converted out of fear."

But Issa, a Yazidi native to Sinjar Mountain, said that in this situation, there was one subsect given no options.

"Four were Shia and they didn't get a choice," he remembered. "Just executed."

Earlier that year, the U.S. State Department officially declared the Yazidis — along with the Christians and Shia —victims of genocide. Under international law, that carried a great deal of weight: it meant the onus was on the international community to act fast. But from the outside, it felt as though little had changed.

Issa and his fellow detainees were transferred into an old prison in Al-

Shaddadah, a small town in northeastern Syria close to the Iraqi border. On the way, four Iraqi soldiers begged for water, clearly suffering severe dehydration as they threw up and their flesh turned a pasty white. In an act borne of pure humiliation and evil, their jailers pulled out bottles of coveted water only to pour it over their open wounds, watch them squirm, and then proceed with the final slaughter — the price for having dared complain.

Shortly after arriving at the prison, the captives were joined by approximately forty more frightened individuals. Issa had observed the numbers fluctuate over a matter of minutes, thinning and thickening as dozens were taken outside and killed en masse before being replaced by new groups.

Issa watched helplessly, preparing for what he thought would be his last moments on earth. At ten o'clock that night, he was taken to ISIS's newly-proclaimed headquarters in the region. It was there that he came face-to-face with Abu Omar al-Shishani, the ginger-bearded Chechen ISIS leader who would soon be regarded as one of the world's most wanted men.

"They requested our rank, name, religion, and the places where we served," Issa stated. "Then one of Shishani's guards cut the ropes that had been used to tie me up. Shishani took our military belt and said it was so that we can't try to commit suicide."

After intense interrogation, each hostage was placed in a separate room and the torture commenced.

"They tortured me a lot more than the others that night, beat me up a lot because I was wearing a replica of a U.S. Marine uniform which got the bad attention of Omar Shishani," Issa said. "I still had two cigarettes in my pocket. They used them to burn my hands."

Days labored on and simple survival became the young soldier's sole focus. As a feigned Islamic convert, Issa prayed and prayed. He spent hours absorbing the heavy-handed interpretation of Islamic doctrine, endured painful interrogation sessions, and watched, frozen, as men around him were executed mercilessly. Issa had taught himself to think and move with a hardened heart; to offer no physical response when fellow prisoners bellowed in agony or took their last breaths. In some ways, it was a moral achievement — a refusal to let his jailers see the impact of the wretched hole on his mind.

Issa remembered seeing "two pretty girls" somewhere between eighteen and twenty-four years old brought to the old prison and then whipped away. They spoke French, and he believed that they were foreign workers. They were the only females he saw for the duration of his imprisonment. Every morning and night since that day, Issa thought of their eyes wide in horror and wondered what became of them.

Once his captors were satisfied with his Islamic conversion, Issa was granted a little more freedom to make occasional telephone calls. He used this time artfully, quietly collecting "ransom" funds. He organized the sale of everything he owned — his rusty old car and his cattle — and borrowed money from his family and friends until he had scrounged together thousands of dollars.

Some four months into captivity, Issa paid his way out of the inferno and his cuffs were removed. He was reunited with his family, who had lost everything in the barrage on Sinjar Mountain two months earlier that had taken place while he sat in a dirty cell.

Issa did not return to the crushed Iraqi Army, but instead rounded up his destitute remaining family members and fled the country he once-proudly served. When we spoke in 2016, he was living as a refugee in a neighboring country.

Karma would come. In July 2016, it was announced that the high-ranking leader Shishani — often referred to as the "Minister of War" or "Omar the Chechen" — had been killed in combat south of Mosul. The tides had turned.

On another afternoon in Baghdad, I visited the home of an airport Homeland Security official in the Shakook area. He never told me his name. He was sharply dressed, wearing stylish leather shoes and a striped black polo shirt with square-framed glasses and a thin, perfectly-shaped mustache.

His son prepared a palisade of fresh Middle Eastern delicacies on a colorful mat before us.

We spoke casually about the ISIS threat, and the official acknowledged that the group was indeed losing its power — and fast.

"They have started giving up," he said. In the earlier days, many ISIS fighters funneled in and out of Baghdad International Airport, their true intentions and pasts disguised with the use of fake ID cards and passports. Earlier in the year it was revealed that the terror group had developed an entire industry in making fake passports, getting its hands on the legitimate printing machines and paper supplies used by Iraq's authorized passport offices. The capability sent a shiver through the spine of the global intelligence community.

The number of suspected ISIS operatives arriving and departing from the airport had waned significantly in recent days.

After our meal, the official and the other men who had joined us went outside to smoke cigarettes and watch the sunset while I stayed in the big room to catch up on some work. I noticed a couple pairs of eyes peeking out at me through the vinyl accordion door. It was the ladies of the house — the young girls and the middle-aged mothers, aunts, and elderly.

I motioned for them to come into the room, and after cautiously ensuring no male presence, they tip-toed over for hugs and the standard three cheek kisses. The women were the sort who latched on, holding my hand and interlocked their knees with mine as we sat cross-legged on the ground. They wanted to know who I was, where I was from, and what I did. They giggled every time I did or said anything, as if I was the funniest person in the world. They wanted to take selfies with me and run their hands through my long, untamed hair and poke at the holes in my jeans.

Each of the women had lofty black eyes, pale skin, and wore brightly colored dresses. They giggled more when I asked for my tea without sugar. Sometimes, lovely moments arise in the bedim of wartime. Language and cultural barriers don't exist, and just through tea and touch, the basic, common experience of being human can be shared.

The sound of male voices approaching, however, sent the females into a mild panic. Since they weren't wearing hijabs, they hurried back behind the folding doors before I had a proper chance to say my goodbyes — my ma'salma (which translates to "peace be with you").

As I turned to leave, I felt inquisitive eyes on my back once again and heard the hush of excited whispers. I looked back just once to see the gap slowly close, the female forms disappearing behind it along with the dropping daylight.

DEMOCRACY HAS FAILED
October, 2016

The harsh October sun had long dropped, the crescent moon shrouded by smoke and smog in the blackness of night. The dense Baghdad heat slapped me squarely as I stepped off the largely empty, almost all-male flight from the Gulf, embarking on another visit to blood-stained Iraq.

My arrival felt different from arrivals past. The U.S. Department of Defense was steadily deploying more and more troops to the region in a push to rid the country of ISIS's scourge once and for all. There was a sense of something big to come. But then again, we had been believing that for so long.

I had returned to Iraq with my good Iraqi Christian friend, Steven Nabil, on a last-minute venture to the scorched capital. I could no longer sit still. It felt like all we did was ask questions, but getting answers was arbitrary, especially when it came to the many victims of genocide. I wanted to understand what was being done to end the ISIS war so that those caught in the crossfire would no longer need to flee the soil that belonged to them.

But, more importantly, I wanted to understand Iraq's vision of and commitment to justice, so that those responsible for the atrocities would not walk the streets with impunity when all was said and done. I did not want to admit it to myself then, but my passion for justice would always be something of a pipe dream. I am not sure if justice was ever really a viable goal, but I knew that we could not stop fighting for it.

Some of the evil would die on the battlefield while some would surrender or be captured and tossed behind bars, left to either face the gallows or rot there for the rest of their lives. Others still would escape, slipping through the smoke and ashes to roam among the very people whose lives they had gutted.

Over-caffeinated and slumped in the backseat of a private car, we sped down the infamous — and recently remodeled— Airport Road, towards a dark city reminiscent of an unraveled conflict. The seven-and-a-half mile highway, which eventually ended in the heavily-fortified Green Zone — once the palace of Saddam Hussein — had been a popular locale for kidnappings, roadside bombs, and drive-by shootings since the U.S. invasion of 2003.

For now, the relative utopia of the Green Zone was not the destination. We abruptly pulled off the highway into the jungle of residential homes and the Baghdad grit.

Since the U.S. pulled its troops in 2011, Baghdad was technically no longer at war, nor was it under external occupation. Yet it so clearly remained a land torn apart by sectarian divisions, insurgency, and unpredictability. In the weeks following the Mosul capture in 2014, ISIS breached the strategic southwest outskirts of the city in large numbers, spreading genuine fear across the world that the capital would be eroded, endangering global security. But the Iraqi Army, aided — or, more likely, led — by PMF Shiite militias, blew them back.

There were no frontlines here, just that chimerical instinct of persistent jeopardy. The presence of the terrorist outfit prowled, spreading its blood across markets, malls, mosques, and checkpoints day in and day out, killing those who wanted nothing to do with the conflict of caliphate and anger. The war was one that seemed like it would never really end. Outside the confines of the car was a city of 7.2 million, still exploding with bombs. Earlier that year, I had read in an Arabic newspaper that the average death count was up to one every twelve minutes. Baghdad held the unappealing accolade of terrorism cardinal of the world.

The Institute for Economics and Peace's 2015 Global Terrorism Index pointed out that seventy-eight percent of the world's terrorism-related deaths in 2014 — the latest year for which such data was available — took place in just five countries: Iraq, Nigeria, Afghanistan, Pakistan, and Syria. Of those, Iraq and Nigeria had accounted for more than half of all terrorism deaths that year, and Baghdad had officially become the deadliest city on the planet in terms of terrorism.

However, I quickly learned that the state of such dire affairs was not at the forefront of topics that locals sought to discuss over tea. The people of Baghdad were by no means in denial, and whenever I raised the issue of city-saturated acts of terrorism, animated conversation ensued. They always had thoughts and anecdotes and opinions — yet such topics had become a monotonous fact of their lives. Of course, the avoidance of terror talk also stemmed from an unmistakable Baghdad pride and a desire to show foreigners the upside — the gloss, the gaudy opulence, the bright lights.

But at the same time, it spoke to the instability of a city enduring an identity crisis, still unsure what to say and what not to say. Baghdad was a microcosm of an uncertain country not quite sure who it was in the decade since its long-running dictator was captured subsequently executed years later. Now, de-Baathed and pulled apart at the seams, Iraq teemed with the Shi'a Iranian influence, still purporting to restore the nationalism and military prowess it had once embodied. Iraq, it appeared, wanted to be Iraq, but had become an extension of Iran, too. The consequential upset and alienated Sunni presence will forever maintain a powerful mark. Countries everywhere have a stake in its future.

In the final quarter of 2016, Iraq was still in a delicate post-dictatorship — but not exactly democratic — holding period.

We stopped at a high-gated home. The air glowed orange from the faint light of the streetlamps. A car of young men that had been waiting for us at the airport and traveled behind us said their goodbyes. I was told that they belonged to the controversial Popular Mobilization Force that Shi'a militia hailed for fierce fighting against ISIS but condemned for human rights atrocities. With hipster jeans and slicked-back hair, they were far from a vision of fear.

Apparently, the PMFs wanted to escort us safely out of the airport and through the web of uncertainty. Or maybe they wanted to make certain they knew where we were. I did not know the reason, but I remembered what a close Iraqi friend had told me before I left — "Eyes," he had cautioned, "are everywhere. The good ones and the bad. Trust no one."

We arrived at the dwellings of Mamoul Al-Samraaii, the Baghdad-based head of the Al Itfaq political party, a non-sectarian, economy-focused bloc. I couldn't quite tell if it was a home or an office; the sitting room was painted an almost unbearably bright white and lined with gold ornaments and trimmings, and the dining room provided a similarly grandiose design with throne-like chairs.

Mamoul represented the "new Iraq" as a businessman who had taken on a political posture in the hopes of ushering the country into a new era of prosperity. He was the kind of leader who was not afraid to point out corruption and nepotism in the leadership or the idiocy of appointing illiterate tribal leaders into high-ranking military and political posts rather than seeking out the best fit for the job.

"I believe in capitalism. Right now, we have a singular economy that relies on oil money to eat and that is it," he said. "We need to compete with China. We need to export more than just oil."

Over a lavish dinner of lamb and dolma with warm bread and grilled eggplant, Mamoul continued with his idealism in what resembled a perfectly-manicured campaign speech. He was an economy person, he told me.

"Governments do not build countries. People build countries, we must start with the children — we are not raising our children the right way," he went on. "School is like punishment. Children walk around with twenty pounds of books and are given too much homework. This will not help them succeed."

Rather, he said, the answer to a thriving education system and a subsequently thriving Iraq would come from practical excursions — taking children to airports and teaching them what it would take to become a pilot, then to factories to show the technology of how things are made, and finally to jails, where they would have to confront "criminals in cages" and learn firsthand why and how they had ended up there.

"We want to be teaching technology, not just handing out books," Mamoul elaborated. "We don't want to be teaching history. Those things don't matter anymore."

To that, I said nothing.

Earlier, Mamoul had instructed his elegant, sharply dressed wife to venture across town to meet me. We shook hands, and I had assumed she would be joining us for the meal — after all, she had come all that way so late at night. But she — a modernly assembled lady — disappeared into oblivion when the food came. Iraq remained, for all the talk of progress, a fiercely patriarchal world of rigidly-defined places. While I was warmly welcomed at the suits-only table, it was on that familiar, yet unspoken premise of the third gender.

In most places I have traveled, the female western journalist is slotted into a unique category, not beholden to the "rules" of their women, but not to those of their men, either. It came with the advantage of drifting between the two distinct groups, providing access to almost the entire population.

"Democracy has failed," Mamoul declared on a parting note, tugging at the red-tinged tie that matched the hue of his large, gold watch. "But democracy can work if we have a better electoral process, debates like America, and if the educated class lead — and we don't leave the decisions to the religious societies."

A few days later, I visited his party's headquarters nearby. One of his advisors had learned that I was — in what now felt like my former life — a ballet dancer. He insisted that I see the old theater they had transformed into a Parliament-like hearing room with an extensive sound system and towering podium poised in the center of the stage.

The blend of old Iraqi fixtures was contrasted by a western boy band soundtrack blaring through the speakers: "What Makes a Man" by Irish pop group Westlife. The commixture of bodies in front of me — suits, skinny jeans, traditional attire — created a clashing combination of the past and the present.

THROUGH THE TRIANGLE OF DEATH
October, 2016

In the morning light, when the sky was still gentle and pink and the Tigris River shone in front of me, the dualities between Baghdad's past and present were most pronounced. For a place thrashed by decades of war, it still possessed such voluptuous beauty.

I sat alone on the balcony of the Al-Mansoor hotel in the city's center. The hotel itself was a plain, dull brown tower with various layers of security arranged outside. Like most major hotels in Baghdad, it had been a target of insurgent attacks throughout the U.S. occupation. In June 2007, twelve had died in a suicide detonation, including a Shiite lawmaker and some Sunni tribal sheikhs. Yet its view remained peaceful and unparalleled.

As the sun crept higher against the humming of the day's first call to prayer, I admired the reflection of the palm trees, the light flapping of the row of flags, the quiet. Baghdad held a raw, unexpected beauty.

Across the street stood mortar-fissured apartments that once housed Saddam's elite guards. Adjacent to those, there was the General Arts and Theater, once a beloved place of the dead dictator. I was told that the theater had been assaulted repeatedly "by the Americans" with bombs lined with uranium. That was how they justified why it had not been repaired or rebuilt — to get close would be too dangerous.

A study by Dutch peace group Pax released that week, found that U.S. forces fired depleted uranium (DU) into civilian areas soon after the 2003 invasion, although the issue has been one of contentious debate. DU is deemed to be less radioactive than the original, but is still considered a toxic chemical. When it comes to the use of mines and cluster munitions, biological and chemical weapons — even blinding lasers — there are international treaties devoted to regulating their production and deployment. But little was made clear about the creation and dissemination of DU weapons.

Nonetheless, some defense experts I spoke to said no such weapons were ever used in Baghdad.

Our driver, Hassan, wove through the maze of streets, narrating as if he were a war tour guide. He pointed out Saddam's shattered old Prime Ministry, the bomb-blistered structures, and the shells that remained, routinely citing the presence of uranium. Little kids played happily in the trash, roving for treasures.

The city was lined with religious flags — some of which commemorated the Shia Imam Hussain's fight for justice almost 1,400 years ago and some of which were Iraqi flags — in a display of nationalism and religious adherence to the Ashura, which was just seven days away.

Every time I attempted to scrawl in my fast-filling notebook, Hassan instructed me to look up and out at their beloved country. He was a doctor, he said, but had given up the medical profession to venture into politics; he wanted to do something more for his country. Everyone everywhere, it seemed, wanted to exercise their political prowess.

We reached the highway to make the seventy-mile journey to Kabala, the holiest of holy sites in the Shi'a religion, home to the Shrine of Imam Hussein. Outside of Mecca and Medina, his tomb was one of the most important places for Shi'ites. Millions of pilgrims visited the city annually to observe Ashura, which marked the anniversary of Imam Hussein's death.

Hussein, the grandson of the Prophet Muhammad, was slain in battle at Karbala in the seventh century. His martyrdom, celebrated on the day they now call Ashura, was considered a pivotal occurrence in the Sunni-Shia discord that would rock the Islamic world and energize ISIS and its predecessors.

The Sunni militants of ISIS regarded Shia as apostates who must be wiped out so that one purified form of Islam could be established. The Shiites believed that Islam was imparted through the household of the Prophet Muhammad, while the Sunnis believed that it ascended through followers of the Prophet Muhammad — his chosen people. The sects were ultimately divided over who was the true inheritor of the mantle of the Prophet.

We continued down Karbala Road, a passage that contained a wealth of memory — from the spiritual to the malefic. I could not help but envision the lives lost in roadside attacks, from all sides of the spectrum. The region was renowned for heavy fighting ten years ago. If I closed my eyes for long enough, I could see it: my own countrymen and women sacrificing their lives for a cause none of us were entirely sure of all these years later. I could see them taking their final breaths along the desert road, graphed by withered palm trees, blood crusted into the tar and greenery, and into energy that could never die.

We soon arrived at what was known as the "triangle of death." During the U.S. occupation — or invasion, depending on who you talk to — the rural area was the ultimate Al-Qaeda playground. It was a site of high unemployment for locals, frequent American kidnappings, and savage attacks on the Musayyib Power Plant, a crucial supplier of Iraq's electricity.

"Nobody could pass through here," Hassan said, glancing out at the remnants of war — skeletons and fragments of fighter tanks and missile launchers. He again reminded me that the waste couldn't be removed because of the uranium.

Checkpoints were dotted with posters of wanted terrorists, designed like old-fashioned posters from the Wild West of the American frontier. At every checkpoint, kids would come to the car window flashing peace signs and smiles, trying to make a buck or two to get by. The soldiers were sweet with them, patting them softly on the back.

We stopped for a cigarette by the blue-green Euphrates River, its edges brushed by overgrown greens and palm trees. Along with the Tigris, the Euphrates is one of the two decisive rivers of Mesopotamia, the cradle of civilization. Originating in Turkey, it streams through Iraq and Syria and empties into the Persian Gulf. Religious scholars often cite the Euphrates as the location of the Garden of Eden, referencing the Book of Genesis.

According to Biblical prophecy, just before Jesus returns to earth, God will compel the river to dry up. Then all the armies of the world can assemble to battle Jesus on his return to earth. That battle will mark the last of the world wars humankind will ever have to fight. It will mark the end of the world.

We finally arrived at Karbala. As the lone female in the group, I was cautioned against shaking anyone's hand and told not to get out of the car until I was fully covered in a black abaya. After the hasty wardrobe change, I watched the faces of the Iraqi men change. Before, I was a western woman defined by my own dress and rules. And suddenly, now — looking the same as every other black-cloaked female in the street and barely visible — I was deemed "more beautiful."

Was beauty not to be seen — or to be seen only as pure and pious?

The streets were busy but calm, full of people going about their daily lives, bustling in and out of markets, to and from the stalls that had been set up to offer free food near the shrine's entrance. But there was always a precipice of uncertainty to Iraq.

Just a couple of weeks earlier, eighteen people had been killed in a vicious bomb attack just west of the holy city. And, two days earlier, another round of ISIS attacks had been thwarted. Suicide bombers had been busted at the city's conduits, allegedly with the intention to detonate during the changing of the flags. Intelligence officials tracked every single person entering Karbala. They surveilled cars from the moment they left their homes until they reached the city, employing thousands of "secret volunteers" to help arrest suspects. The direct connection across the Western Desert from the Sunni-majority Anbar province to Karbala was an especially monitored location.

At the Holy Provincial Council, officials touted the shrine like executives in a board room. One told me that the greatest challenge — greater even than keeping terrorists out — was ensuring that diseases didn't spread. Some twenty-five million people each year lay their naked hands on the Imam Hussein Shrine throughout the forty-day Ashura period alone. They had hired experts to test for germs that may be thriving on the shrine, but everything had "come out clean," the official assured me.

Nseeif Al-Khattabi, a Shia Muslim and governor of the Holy Province Council, invited us for tea. He wanted us to listen to him preach of peace and espouse the lessons we could all learn from the great Iman of the Shi'a sect.

"He led a revolution to fix corruption," Nseeif boasted. "And he paid with his life. Without him, humanity would be in a dark sleep right now."

He assured me that Iraqis were the ones "fighting ISIS on behalf of the world." It was a phrase I had heard numerous times from the Kurdish side. What was the cause of the ISIS existence? How much were Iraqis to blame for their own dark reality? Was it the western invasion on their land? Who was really to blame and at what proportions?

After an almost poetic soliloquy about Iraq's future — a future that will be unified, tolerant, and accepting of all religions and sects — Nseeif noted that such peace would only come if the U.S.A. — the world's commander — supported the Shi'a over the Sunni.

We flounced from meeting to meeting, office to office. In almost every room, there were "No Smoking" signs, but every room stank of cigarette smoke. Rules were voluntary. Various men entered and exited. I was often addressed last.

Ironically, inside the great shrine, the element of male and female seemed to dissipate. There was a feeling of equality that came from people from all walks of life worshipping one leader. In the end, they were all children under God. While the genders had separate areas, there were sections on the floor where everyone sat together reading, praying, discovering, and dreaming, all deeply devoted to something much bigger than themselves. There were also those taking selfies and giggling, absorbing the moment in a far less orthodox way.

One young woman excitedly approached Steven — ever the Facebook superstar, with an extensive following of his journalism — for a photograph. All these miles away from home, and somehow she knew about our lives and embraced us like long-lost friends. As it turned out, the young woman — via my friendship with Steven — also followed me on Instagram.

It was dark when we left to head back to Baghdad, unveiling the darker side of Ashura. We passed men self-flagellating in the streets, their eyes damp and their clothes daubed with their blood of self-sacrifice. Self-flagellation was the religious ritual adopted by Shiites leading up to the Day of Ashura in remembrance of the Battle of Karbala and the martyrdom of Imam Hussein.

Five weeks later, another truck stuffed with ammonia nitrate and other explosive material would explode at a gas station and restaurant in the nearby town of Hilla, slaughtering some seventy-seven pilgrims who had journeyed from Iran and Afghanistan.

What is war? Everyone is ensnared in the violence; the violence does not discriminate. The pilgrims had merely stopped to rest and eat after commemorating in the holy city of Karbala. I never knew their names, but their rest was to be eternal.

THESE WERE THE ORDINARY
October, 2016

Families of Baghdad had come to accept that an eternal military structure would define their lives. Just as religion would forever play a profound role, perhaps so too would the armed forces rolling through the flat, wide streets.

Past midnight, past streets lined with armored trucks and tanks and the echoing of gunshots, we met with a military family and weaved through the traffic into their humble home in the al-Benok region of Baghdad. I was not sure who they were — Steven had orchestrated the visit. I had momentarily resigned myself to stop asking questions. Sometimes not knowing the plan is knowing the plan. That was the way people here existed; one second to the next.

Steven knew the young father of the house, Omar, an Iraqi Special Forces soldier, who lived with his wife, Noor, and their two little boys.

Steven and Omar played with the guns in the living room for a while, then wanted to play with more and ventured out to a cafe in Adhamiya in the early hours, where other soldiers would meet them with their firearms to compare and contrast. After the death of Iraq's widely revered Sunni imam, Abu Hanifa An-Nu'man in 772, Adhamiya — one of Baghdad's oldest districts — became a fierce Sunni resistance. Sunnis congregated there to protect the imam's resting place from Persian invaders. Adhamiya became known as the intellectual enclave for artists and wise thinkers, as well as a neighborhood storied for its bursts of sectarian violence during the war with the U.S.

I desperately wanted to see it, but I was not invited. I was, without anyone needing to express it, supposed to stay with the young mother and children. I felt that pang — my place as a woman. I was jealous, but didn't say so; this was the boys' club, to which I didn't belong. Perhaps I had become used to being the accepted "third gender," and it didn't always work.

In this case, the female regulations remained, and it was unthinkable for me to join the army men inspecting their latest arsenal.

With the men gone, I sat with Noor drinking coffee and playing with her young boys. She slowly unraveled her red hijab and her beautiful, waist-length black hair fell to the floor. She lit a thin menthol cigarette for me and insisted I bite the end before smoking it.

Girl time. There were no Green Zones, no warm water, no electricity. We fell asleep watching dramatic soap operas from India until the generator died.

Despite the unease that accompanied visiting strange places, I slept better than I had in a long time. I was exhausted, but felt very comfortable with the ordinary — the people who had lost their sons and husbands and fathers in the wars that had stained their country for years. There was an honesty to their lives that calmed me much more than the heavily-secured hotels surrounded by guards.

The ordinary — the ones that raised their babies in times of steep uncertainty — were of great intrigue to me. Life for this young family had indeed been hard, but it seemed not to occur to Noor that it could have been any different or easier.

In the early morning, she watched in astonishment as I attempted a kind of pathetic workout running in place in the back room. Later, she asked, perplexity etched on her face, how old I was turning (wahid wathalathin!). How was it possible that I would be thirty-one that day and yet not married? The notion of me, "ghyr mutazawij," not married, seemed to be a source of bewilderment in a culture that generally weds — mostly through arrangement — in early adulthood.

Still, she said she would pray for me, and in return I promised to pray for her. In the ordinary, we find the extraordinary. I had tried to document their lives and stories, even if just in a flimsy notebook for nobody else to see. Because that way, they would always remain present in my mind.

Outside, gunshots became louder, but nobody inside flinched — not even the young boys, who had grown so used to that tenure of life. I ventured to open the window, but Noor grabbed my arm and shook her head, a flash of distress in her eyes.

"Very dangerous," she cautioned in Arabic.

The men, barely having returned from the overnight adventures, were still asleep in another room. It was my turn to watch silently as Noor played with her boys.

She popped Maltesers in my mouth for breakfast. Then, suddenly, as I was dressing in her room for the day, she began pulling random items from her closet to gift me: sunglasses, a leather purse, a bracelet, lipstick, strappy platform shoes. Middle Eastern hospitality goes unparalleled.

"Hello," Noor repeated over and over in a beautiful singsong voice each time I said shukran, meaning "thank you" in Arabic. It was the only English word she knew, and she recited it proudly.

Baghdad was an extraordinary city checkered with both beauty and brutality. Its past and present were blemished by invasions, occupations, oppressions, and persecutions, but was also awash with a remarkable defiance and a willingness to keep moving on even though the burn could come at any time. And it did.

After the men woke up, Noor and I took photographs together. I vowed they were only for my private collection and they wouldn't be posted anywhere. Even so, she hid her face with her thick handfuls of hair. It would have been shameful for a married woman to be exposed to strangers without her proper hijab.

The boys and Omar had identical haircuts — short, sharp, staple military undercuts with straight-cut bangs. The boys observed their father with awe and pride as he adjusted his fatigues and laced his combat boots. They wanted to be just like him, Noor informed me. I couldn't help but wonder what — not if — war would still be waging when they reached military age.

Noor and I kissed goodbye, both a little wet-eyed. She said she hoped I would get married and that I would come back to visit. I said I hoped to return, but I was careful not to promise. A promise was as good as a dotted contract in Arab culture; it was not to be case. I left with a wave of the hand and an inshallah — God Willing — into the cutthroat heat.

Even in the fall morning, Baghdad burned — in more ways than one.

MOSUL OPERATION READY
October, 2016

Smoke clouds rose from the gritty road ahead. A bomb? An accident? A fire? No one knew yet. More tellingly, no one batted an eye in the bitter endeavor to make it to work and bring something home to feed the family.

In bumper-to-bumper traffic, with the soundtrack of screeching horns amplified by suffocating heat, I studied faces — the cigarettes dangling from lips, the eyes glued to phone screens.

I rolled down my window just a few inches and quickly got schooled — again. That was a safety no-no. I returned to examining the dust swirls and exhaust pipes, scribbling in my little black book. Omar nonchalantly pointed out the charred remains of a suicide vehicle on the side of the bridge.

No one in the car seemed to know how long it had been there or how many had died, but it remained under the blistering sun as something of a haunting reminder of the fight the Iraqi people routinely faced just to get from point A to point B.

"Happy Birthday," Steven suddenly chimed.

We picked up bags of fresh dates from the roadside for breakfast, selecting ripe bunches from the humidity of tent shelters inside a little tropical spot known as the Bahamas. It resembled the tropical paradise, with palm trees and dew on one side — but chaos and soldiers lined the other. Omar showed me a video on his phone of a young Iraqi boy in a classroom, crying as he was slapped repeatedly by a teacher. I wasn't entirely sure why he was showing it to me, but when I looked up — part perplexed, part horrified — he nodded pensively. It was as if to make sure I knew the difficulties here that everyone faced.

Finally, after what felt like an eternity in the terrible Baghdad traffic, we arrived at Omar's Iraqi military base near the airport.

As far as military bases go, this one — home to the elite Special Forces Unit Emergency Response Division (ERD) — was as upper crust as they come. Gated by large, white cement blocks, the inside rooms were spacious, air-conditioned, and filled with more Ashura flags, golden warrior statues, and royal blue velvet thrones.

The soldiers, most of them in their twenties, had grouped around a bullet-seared Humvee.

"The vehicle was injured," I said to no one in particular, suddenly realizing that I was applying human terms to non-human objects.

What is war? It makes you think of everything as either a causality or a survivor — babies, buildings, bad guys.

"From Fallujah," explained one soldier, donning a blue Navy SEAL shirt and motioning to the Humvee.

He glanced over at another Humvee, blemish-free, almost idyllic as it shimmered and shined in the sunshine. "For Mosul," he said.

Iraqi forces were trying to retake the prized city without destroying it or worsening the already burgeoning humanitarian crisis. They knew their vision — to free the city house by house — would be slowed by the terrorist army.

"ISIS is using a lot of snipers and plenty of IEDs," Omar — who had now adopted his captain persona as head of the elite unit in the Iraqi Emergency Response Division — pointed out, pulling out maps and photographs to illustrate their victory. "They have booby-trapped a lot of homes and they are moving civilians around to use them as human shields."

The battle for Fallujah had been strategic as well as symbolic. Fallujah was ISIS's second-in-line entrenchment in Iraq. Mosul was the first.

In past liberation efforts, entire villages and large dollops of cities — from Sinjar to Ramadi — had been razed to the ground; it was the price of victory against ISIS. But who was going to rebuild the cities? Who was going to rebuild Mosul if ziggurat butchery was the only way out?

Sitting with the soldiers in Baghdad, the consequences of that liberation became apparent on a far more human level. Some nursed broken bones; some had holes dotting their flesh and shrapnel littering their bodies. But they were back at it in an instance, ready for the next deluge.

Soldiers and officials came in and out, stamping their feet in the standard sign of respect for superiors. Some put their hands across their chest and nodded toward me, signaling a hello, while others didn't even acknowledge me or make eye contact.

The highly-anticipated Mosul liberation was in the final phase of preparation, poised to begin as early as the following week. The darkest days of the ISIS fight were yet to come. It was going to be long, and it was going to be fierce.

I was informed that forces had been amassing along Mosul's outskirts for months, with periodic skirmishes in the towns and villages circling the city. The jihadist organization still had a granite grip inside city limits, and they were busily planting roots, fortifying positions, placing booby traps, and preparing for the showdown.

"The coalition has trained us very well in joint operations, medical training, our snipers, advanced bomb units and street guerrilla tactics," said Colonel Thamar Mohamed Ismael, commander of the Iraqi Army Emergency Response Division (ERD).

He had a hardened look; every facial muscle was chiseled and steeled. The colonel was the sort of person with an undoubtedly complex history, who had done more than they were willing to let on.

Thamar said that Iraqi and coalition forces had, in recent days, bombarded Mosul with radio broadcasts and leaflets instructing civilians of the coming offensive and notifying them of their exit routes, ginning up speculation of imminent action.

Aerial attacks were expected to soften known ISIS targets first, and then Iraqi special operations battalions would spearhead the ground assault. Iraqi troops would then move in, with the grim possibility of fighting block-to-block and door-to-door. The Kurdish Peshmerga would be tasked with keeping the frontlines to the north secure, while Sunni militias would guard the outside of the city. It remained unclear what role the Shia militias would play.

United Nations officials and non-governmental organization leaders had converged in Erbil that week in preparation for the displacement flow that the offensive would undoubtedly produce. However, the deteriorating security situation and increasing frequency of suicide bombings surrounding Mosul had made it extremely difficult to set up aid bases and camps.

The fight for Mosul mattered in many more ways than one. The Iraqi army was humiliated when the city was overrun more than two years ago. Soldiers had fled their posts, leaving behind weapons, munitions, and even uniforms in a display that demonstrated the military's shocking inability to protect the nation from the growing threat of ISIS. Over the next two years, the terrorist regiment overran much of northwestern Iraq, claiming a caliphate the size of the United Kingdom.

Iraqi soldiers were now eager to reclaim both the city and their army's reputation. It was in the next room, in his formal work setting, that I got to sit with our gracious night host, Omar Nazar, and learn his story.

He was a twenty-eight-year-old ERD Captain. He had grown up wanting to be a "military man," as it was his father's profession, and he viewed it as something noble. In the Saddam era, everyone was conscripted to join the armed forces in accordance with article 31 of the 1968 Constitution, which described military service as a "sacred duty and an honor for citizens." After the Iran-Iraq war began in 1980, almost everyone was called to the helm.

But Omar wasn't made to join — he chose to.

"The best part is the training to really prepare for each battle, I get to train to lead my troops into battle," he said proudly. "We are an ancient civilization, and we will rise again. We will defend everything we stand for as Iraqis."

Omar wanted Americans to know that their training and their "modern weapons" cache was much appreciated. He was confident that Mosul civilians had turned on ISIS and their cooperation was going to be key to the operation's success.

"We expect many civilians to stay there," Omar explained, gaining momentum. "ISIS isn't the same ISIS as before, we have conquered them emotionally. Their morale is gone."

Another Omar, First Soldier Omar Salah al Wad, sat down. He was a twenty-nine-year-old father of four from Ramadi. He had joined the military the moment the Saddam regime fell in 2003 and had already been wounded seven times in battles against ISIS. Two of his toes had been cut off and a grenade had shattered his shoulder. During the fight earlier that year to free his home city, a piece of debris had entered his eye, leaving Omar partially blind; it was still swollen and oozing fluid. He shrugged it off.

"It's very exciting to liberate towns from these criminals," he continued. "It is my honor; it is my desire to protect my country. I want my country to be as good as it can for my kids."

The second Omar assured me that, despite some advocacy to split Iraq into three — the north for the Kurds, the middle for the Sunnis, and the south for the Shia — there were no "sectarian issues" in the towns after liberation. He said that in his dream, his country would remain united.

Over lunch — soup, lamb, and limitless mounds of fresh bread — Ismael talked about how he liked to empower his soldiers. He joked darkly that he threatened to beat them up if they did something stupid — like getting killed or injured. We were joined for the meal by an imam who told me he was studying law.

"He is our religious leader," Thamar enthused. "He could do more to help."

It, too, was a joke... I think.

The imam said he joined the army in 2003 — the "new army," so to speak — but his demeanor suggested a man who had been militarily wizened years before that. His voice dropped to an almost Saddam-era whisper as I prodded on. I quickly got the signal that some secrets were better left buried in the trenches of the past.

What is war? With the Iraqis, there was never a discussion of medals and honors; only endless videos and photos of soldiers killing ISIS and dragging the dead bodies into the backs of pickup trucks, or capturing them alive and letting them sob like helpless children begging to be spared. That was their Medal of Honor.

We talked a little about the dramatic presence of foreign ISIS fighters. Many of the soldiers, officials, and displaced people I had talked to over the past couple of years placed great emphasis on foreign fighters from Afghanistan, Tunisia, China, Europe and America. It was all these other countries wreaking havoc.

Analysts had started to use the term "Iraq's Civil War," but whenever I raised that assessment, it was almost immediately rejected.

Some saw it as Iraq and Kurdistan doing the world a favor by ridding them of the terrorists that had left their countries. Iraqis and Kurds alike saw the war as being advantageous to all the other countries but their own; they saw it as the terrorists fleeing home turf to kill their people and destroy their country.

For others, there was a deeper denial that Iraq was to blame. It was hard to accept that Iraqis could be doing these grotesque things to their own people.

Out back, beyond a jagged cobblestone path reminiscent of a children's book illustration, was the unit's own little farm full of turkeys and chickens and birds of all kinds. One soldier explained in hushed tones that he made sure every day that no one killed his bird. He liked her a lot but hadn't thought to give her a name.

We parted ways and headed over to the other side of the base to meet with Haitham al-Malaki, the head of military intelligence for the ERD. One of the soldiers nervously scurried inside the trailer to wake him up. When he emerged, he was bleary-eyed and exhausted. I could see that he had been sleeping over a ton of ISIS-related documents.

Iraqi military officials had keen intelligence from inside Mosul, much of which had been gleaned from spies within ISIS, Haitham said. Working closely with the U.S.-led coalition, he had obtained troves of critical documents and sources that paved the path for the Mosul offensive.

"We've identified most of their communications and financial supplies," he told me with confidence.

A significant part of the plan included safeguarding the thousands of Yazidi women believed to be held hostage as sex slaves in the city.

"The minute we are on the verge of the city, we will notify those assets to go in and collect as many girls as possible before going in," Haitham went on. "We will also open a rescue path to ensure safe passage for the ones we can't get beforehand."

Perhaps the biggest question looming ahead of the operation was the whereabouts of shadowy ISIS leader Abu Bakr al-Baghdadi. Occasionally, reports claimed that he had been injured — or even killed — but intelligence sources believed he was alive and hiding somewhere around Mosul.

Several military officials postured that the offensive to take control of Mosul could happen as fast as four days, but Malaki anticipated that it would likely take two months to regain full power, clear the city of threats, and root out hiding fighters.

"It will take longer than the others due to the vast majority of people there and the size of the land," he noted.

I poured my favorite kind of milky Arabic coffee into an elegant little cup from a courtly dallah coffee pot — a vessel with a bulbous, gold-tinted body, elongated spout, and crescent-like beak that had been used for centuries throughout the Arabian Peninsula.

I gestured politely for more. The server, a sweet-faced elderly soldier, instructed that I must always hold my little cup out with my right hand. If I put it out and held it still, it meant I wanted a refill. If I put it out and shook it, that signified I was finished, and the cup would then be collected.

Conditions inside Mosul had deteriorated significantly in the recent months. Families were starving due to inflated food costs and limited supplies. Medicine was also scarce, and ISIS was said to have stopped supplying civilians with the services they once offered, their desire to govern shredded as they focused on pure survival.

In the months and years since that meeting, I have often thought about those men. The Iraqi Army had been dealt a lot of flak since the ISIS invasion, and not just for their disastrous error that allowed ISIS into Mosul, but repeatedly after that for running from their positions. The media, and many U.S. veterans of the Iraq war, perpetually blasted them in regards to the billions of dollars that had been poured into their training and development during the U.S. occupation. Iraqis themselves, many in the diaspora, simply hung their heads in embarrassment when the topic came up.

I pictured the brave soldiers I met that day, envisioning their young faces and their families at home. I could not help but think — as wrong as it was to run when one had willfully committed to the noble duty of protecting and serving — how difficult it must have been to react rationally to such an irrational situation. No amount of training or drilling could ever prepare one for death dressed as a jihadist attacker.

I understood the human instinct to turn and flee; to slip instantly into that primordial space of fight-or-flight; to think only of your own family rather than the thousands of strange families you had sworn to defend. Self-preservation trumped. While many may have pledged their willingness to die for Iraq, when the reality dawned, nobody was going to go willfully. If there was a way to run and stay alive, they would find it.

LADIES FIRST
October, 2016

Nobody wanted to die. But the fear of death and the threats that prowled did not stop the regular people of Baghdad from living their lives. They lived with a kind of fullness — food, family, friends, fun, resilience.

That evening, we took a cab through the thick traffic that clogged Karrada, which was considered an especially dangerous area of Baghdad. Bombs continually dropped on the Shia-dominant area. I glanced out at the blistered remains of the mall that had been blown to bits a few months earlier. On July 3, as families set out to celebrate the end of Ramadan, more than 323 of them had been murdered, with hundreds more injured. It was a suicide truck-bomb attack on the mall, sending the building up in flames with scores of victims trapped inside.

Karrada was haunted. We all felt it and we did not like to linger in the densely-populated main street. But if it weren't for the deep burns and guttered bits of buildings that had not yet been swept up and glossed over, one would think that there was no history to be feared. Of course, terrorists thrived on the protocol of fear — it was as useful an armament as a shrapnel-lined explosive vest. Regular Iraqis were not going to give in to that fear, though.

What is war? Not caving to fear or becoming so accustomed to it that it went away.

Unlike other countries I had visited during tumultuous times of attack, Iraqis never seemed in a hurry to clean and dismiss the evidence. They moved on, but in a way that didn't discard the past. Life here was smeared with the tacit knowledge that anything could and would happen; but they also seemed to understand that the only thing in their control was to pick up the pieces and put them back together.

People — mostly men — ventured out every night to smoke hookah and cigarettes. They read newspapers and played chess with their friends in restaurants and tea houses. They played in the streets with the food vendors, hedging bets while sitting in gutters beside the burning piles of trash. There were mosques tucked in between shops and strip-light cafes, and tables spilled from the sidewalks and out into the road. Soldiers and police were everywhere, also smoking cigarettes and standing in line for kafta with their rifles strung across their chests like baby carriers. The air was still and soothing, scented with smoky food and illuminated by lights from store fronts. Karrada ballooned with life.

As we drove, Steven's friend Saif — a perpetually smiling, twenty-something charity worker — pointed out little local hotspots like a gleeful tour guide. There was FAGMA, the "very famous" ice-cream place, and Abu Afiff, the "very famous" sweets store. He loved chocolate, he said. It was the best thing in the world.

We rounded the road's fork and entered a much darker street brightened only by a few weak streetlights and the new crescent moon. We had arrived at the Mary Yousif Church. I had wanted to acknowledge my birthday — my new year of life — somewhere sacred, and a Baghdad church symbolized the epicenter of human consciousness's beginning.

Months earlier, on July 26, ISIS assailants had attacked churchgoers in the sleepy town of Normandy in the north of France. They stormed the sixteenth century church of Saint-Étienne-du-Rouvray and slit the throat of eighty-five-year-old priest Jacques Hamel in broad morning light.

I found myself deeply impacted by the priest's death. It kept me awake for nights on end as I envisioned his pain, his fear, his bravery. It had triggered something in me — a staunch defensiveness to protect my Christian roots, even though I had not considered myself religious or practicing in a theological sense. But it had made me want to stand up for something that had been a small part of my childhood, something that was now not only under attack, but under the umbrella of a genocide.

After that murder, home in Los Angeles, I drove for hours across the Californian desert to the Nevada border with my Egyptian friend, Georges, to attend mass at the Coptic monastery. My head wrapped in a white lace mantilla tied tightly under my chin like the drawings of Mary, I lit candles with the monks. Tears rolled down my cheeks and I didn't bother to wipe them away.

The Baghdad church was closed when we arrived. A kind worker opened one of the heavy wooden doors and I wandered inside the cool, unlit space and took my place in the wooden pew. Despite the destruction that surrounded the simple building, the church felt like an odd little refuge from the misery.

For a couple of the Muslim men with us, it was their first time visiting a church. They followed me — past the colossal sculpture of Mary standing under the gleam of a dull green spotlight and past the children playing soccer on the patch of courtyard grass — with open eyes and a twinge of gracious excitement.

Afterwards, Steven and I sat with some church workers in the management office next door. It smelled musty from age, like the pages of an eighteenth-century book, and was peppered with trinkets and crosses. There was something very comforting about that distinct scent and the old, rustic furniture and wooden floors. It reminded me of being a little girl in the 1980s, spinning through our little home in rural Australia.

And, for the first time since I was a little girl, I wanted my mother. I wanted to be taken care of, to be folded into her soft arms. To feel safe. That was the beginning of a strange omen — the need for my mother — that would carry me through the months to come.

Steven and the church official engaged animatedly, but soon the tone grew more hostile. I shifted uncomfortably and Steven said abruptly and with sternness that we were leaving. He distrusted motives of some of the workers who weren't Christians. He said it wasn't clear where their fundraising monies were going or if they were really helping Christians displaced by ISIS's persecution.

That was the thing — nothing was ever straightforward, especially not in times involving extra monies. There were good people everywhere doing the righteous thing. But would the unleashed corruption ever be put back in its box? That's what drives a war and flourishes during it; that is what war does to people. Money triumphed. Among the poor and the rich, money was almost always the thing.

What is war? War was always about money. Many benefited, while many paid with their lives and limbs.

We traversed through the traffic in another cab. I couldn't help but raise the topic of Iraq's former Prime Minister, Noori al-Malaki, whose popularity was again rising. Steven had been trying to coordinate an interview with him that day, and had come very close, but was told at the last minute he had decided to wait until after the U.S. presidential elections — which were just over a month away — as he didn't want to be asked the inevitable question of who he hoped would win.

Nouri Kamil Mohammed Hasan al-Maliki was a decisive figure. He had been demoted from the prime minister position formally by resignation two months after the ISIS invasion. He was then sworn into the mostly-symbolic role as one of three vice presidents to the country. Malaki, as Iraqis called him, was installed initially with the blessing of the American government in 2006. He represented hope — hope that he would take on the duty of peace and inclusion following the de-Baathifcation of Iraq. Those hopes, however, quickly crumbled as corruption ran rampant, and Sunnis felt painstakingly oppressed by his Shia rule.

Still, Malaki possessed both lovers and haters.

"He is a loser," the cab driver said in crisp, British-clipped English. I had not realized that he spoke English as he hadn't said a word until then, but clearly couldn't resist on such an inflammatory topic.

Saif disagreed. He argued that Malaki was a "strong man," but that people had unfairly targeted him. Without him, ISIS had only become stronger, Saif concluded. The group went back and forth with their thoughts and analysis, respectfully dissecting each other's arguments.

"You have started a debate," Steven told me with a wink.

To engage in such a debate before Saddam's takedown was not only unthinkable but explicitly dangerous. His dictatorship thrived on the suppression of discerning views. Citizens were forced to cheer for the authoritarian strongman or face steep consequences.

We passed the Tigris, reflecting columns of color from the city lights, and sealed off my birthday night with a stroll through the Al-Mansoor mall. Mansoor was once an affluent neighborhood of diplomats and professionals, but during the U.S.-led war it descended into a killing field. The neighborhood had since regained some of its former prestige and safety, but who knew if it would ever be the same again. How could it be?

More of Steven's friends joined us and we walked through the crowded mall spruced with a big-lettered, colorful "I love Iraq" statue outside. People in this part of the world liked to walk through malls, not necessarily shopping or eating, but just hanging out. It was a recreational pleasure to see who you might run into, to see families out to play, and life in its full force.

"Ladies first," Saif gestured as I stepped onto the escalator. Later, he explained to me that this was an "Iraqi joke" that stemmed from an old fable like Romeo & Juliet, in which a couple in love was forbidden to marry by their families. They agreed to jump off a bridge together so they could be with one another in the afterworld.

"We say ladies first, because the lady jumped first and then the man chickened out," Saif continued. "Because we men, we always chicken out. Ladies are the brave ones here."

Saif, my new friend, had surprised me with a rich, dripping chocolate cake — his favorite, he reminded me. We sat upstairs by the air-conditioner to eat and were joined by an assortment of young Iraqi men. They were poets and bankers and teachers and politicians. Most wore skinny jeans and tight, trendy tops. These men, the Iraqi military- aged men, struck me as hopeless romantics. They spoke in hushed tones, glanced at their reflections in the shop mirrors, and held hands with one another the way teen girls did — a sign of platonic love. They wished me a happy birthday with songs and ululations — that high-pitched trill emulated from the tongue moving back and forth, a token of good times.

Saif pronounced my name as Holy instead of Hollie. Embarrassed, I tried to correct him, but he assured me that Holy was my name, a special name, and I shouldn't try to change it. I just smiled. These were some of the loveliest people one could ever meet.

I learned other morsels about daily life in Iraq as the days went on. For all that week, between the hours of eight and ten in the morning, internets everywhere went dark — the government's doing. High schoolers were in exam week and were notoriously known for cheating, selling answers to one another through earpieces and internet apps. Cutting the net during exam time was the solution.

"Iraqi kids cheat," Steven said simply. "So, they're just trying to be fair."

Later that week, I relocated from random floors of small hotels and people's private homes to the Babylon Warwick Hotel. The hotel had become a guilty favorite, with its sprawling outdoor terrace, the little artist alcove with dazzling paintings, the big swimming pools, and the pyramidal structure. Famed Slovenian architect Edvard Ravnikar designed it with the intention for it to be a beach resort at Budva in Montenegro, in Yugoslavia. But the project had fallen through and it was reimagined for Baghdad in the early 1980s.

To stay there was a treat. I would sometimes spend hours on the balcony answering emails and staring out at the Tigris before the fierce heat came in and made sitting in the sunshine unbearable. As with most hotels in Iraq, unless they were married, women and men were not permitted to share rooms. I had heard horror stories about being invaded in the night by the religious police — the mutawa — who demanded to see the passports or marriage certificates of the sleeping guests, having heard rumors that an unmarried couple was there together.

But I very much relished this alone time.

The previous year, the hotel had been the site of a deadly car bomb attack that killed fifteen people. Five years earlier, more than thirty-six people lost their lives in a similar blast. Despite its gashed past, the Babylon remained a place frequented by dignitaries, foreign businessmen, and high-ranking diplomats.

The lesson I learned from Baghdadis was that there was no point living life defensively. My nana in Australia always told me as a small girl that, in the moment you are born, your name is entered in a large book in the skies with your date to die, and nothing can change that date. This world here, in the heart of humanity's beginning, embodied that sensibility.

Over breakfast, as I sipped coffee and nibbled on pecans and fresh yogurt, a dear friend in Aleppo, Syria sent me images of the aftermath of yet another attack on his already decimated village. He wasn't sure who was killing who — the Assad regime, ISIS, or another rebel faction. Children's eyes had been gouged in the blast, their blood-soaked limbs contorted, grey bodies lined up for collection. People he knew and loved were there one day and gone the next. Life was cheap, it seemed.

"I am very sad," was all he wrote. There wasn't much left to write.

What is war? It is lives that should be valued, lost instead like commodities.

I needed to venture back up to the northern part of the country. Mosul was tipping. It was in the curious, dull days before the big bang and all we could do was wait. Baghdad lived on a precipice of constant conflict, but the north was where the brunt of death and decay idled. I booked an Iraqi Airways flight bound for Erbil.

As I left the illustrious dining room, I turned to a torn page from an English-translated collection by famed Persian poet, Hafez, that I had stuffed into my oversized duffel bag. There was something so profound about the Persian poets from centuries ago — the way that they could capture a situation and make you feel things you didn't know you were already feeling.

I wish I could show you, when you are lonely or in darkness, the astonishing light of your own being.

AND THEN THEY BURNED THE BABIES
October, 2016

As the sun sank into desert darkness, I made my way down the cleft road, swerving around potholes until I reached Lalish, the holiest site in the Yazidi religion.

The last time I had come here, it had been in the January crux of winter. Our socks had been wetted by the melting snow as we leaped over doorsteps into the frigid temples. Yazidis never touch foot on doorsteps; they are thick stone sills to be kissed, blessed, and revered.

We had worn black as we mourned.

But by the time I reached Lalish this time, accompanied by my Kurdish friend

Yakhi — a young entrepreneur who had started his own medical NGO, the 1st NAEF, with a deep passion for assisting their beleaguered community — the night was sprinkled with color and life. I made my way up the steep cobblestone hill where the single streetlight shone a gentle gold. To enter Lalish was to glide into another world belonging to a treasured, bygone era.

Yazidis say that Lalish was brought into being at the fall of Tawsi Melek — the Peacock Angel — who tumbled to the earth when the planet was still empty and beset by earthquakes and volcanoes. Tawsi Melek was sent as a beautiful peacock to remedy the tumultuous terror and fleece the sterile landscape with luminosity.

On this night, the street was lined with little fires to warm the families who had traveled far from the Yazidi diaspora for the annual pilgrimage known as Jamayi. For seven days each October, Yazidis from all over the world converged on Lalish to complete their odyssey. It was a time to be showered with blessings and to share their blessings.

There was an air of celebration, of laughter, of togetherness. I took a moment to hold onto it, intuiting that what was to come that night would be anything but celebratory.

We were received at the temple gates by His Holiness, Baba Chawish, the spiritual guardian of the precious temple, who looked regal in his traditional, flowing white dress. Yazidis often wore white as a representation of purity. He led me up the stone steps to his office, a warm, square room with exposed brick wall on one side and stones holding together the other side. The space was embellished with bronzed pillows, antiques, and clocks frozen in time, which felt symbolic of something deeper. For Yazidis, time had stopped on August 3, two summers earlier, when ISIS had invaded. There was only life before that date and the lesser life that came after.

Beside the large photograph of Baba Chawish taped on the wall — which accentuated his long beard and gentle, inky eyes — sat figurines of the Peacock Angel, the Eiffel Tower, and the Statue of Liberty. Baba Chawish had recently gone to New York to visit the United Nations with Nadia Murad, who had become a goodwill ambassador and candidate for the Nobel Peace Prize speaking out about the Yazidi plight. He still seemed fascinated by the endless cabs and chaos of Manhattan, and he kept asking if the Nobel Prize winner had been announced.

I sat beside Baba Chawish on his small brown couch, rolling unfiltered cigarettes with fresh tobacco from the fields outside. The other Yazidi men in the room taught me a few phrases in Kurmanji, their native Kurdish dialect, as we chatted.

I asked about Yazidi traditions, like why they didn't wear blue or eat lettuce. I was trying to gather a richer understanding of the religion. But Baba Chawish grew visibly uncomfortable — it wasn't that he didn't want to share his ancient theology with an outsider, but more as a sign of how gravely they had been persecuted over the centuries for their beliefs and how so much had been misconstrued to hurt them. There was a palpable apprehension to share their religion with the yonder world for fear it could again be used against them. For now, he wanted to hold the spiritual side close.

Who could blame him? War is distrust.

Baba Chawish politely requested that we talk only about what had happened to them. Subsequently, our talks ventured into a more ominous place: the ongoing genocide that no one, not even the U.S.-led joint taskforce, had the power to stop.

Three men sat on the floor beneath the large open window. One of them — Umer, who would go on to become a dear friend — had arrived from Arizona where he had relocated four years earlier. He, too, had just returned to Lalish.

"This happened to us all because of religion," he lamented. "We are all harmed because of this one religion."

Umer was bitter and had every right to be. He had returned to Iraq to piece together the whereabouts of eighteen missing members of his family. He wanted answers. His elderly mother had just been rescued and he intended to drive to Sinjar in the early morning to surprise her. I hoped it would be a sliver of light amid the eclipse that had struck their tight-knit community.

To illustrate their loss, Baba pulled out photographs of the dead. Some were children. Some had been deceased for days — their grey, distended bodies decaying, their faces buried in the dust, insects nibbling their rotting flesh.

Others had succumbed to heat exhaustion, the life sucked from their limp little structures.

"Look," Baba Chawish said to me, monotonously, as if he were merely pointing out paintings in a gallery. "They cooked the children."

The rage he may have once felt bubbling in his gut was now stillborn. The incense had burned out. Baba Chawish seemed to understand there was no point in outwardly showing his anger; it wouldn't bring back the burned babies. Maybe someday he would forgive — but he would never forget.

I counted seven shriveled babies curled into fetal positions in the photographs, tiny bodies still roasting beyond recognition on what appeared to have been a slate of tin shed. The silent tears wetting my cheeks had turned into guttural sobs I was powerless to control.

I stared at the floor and sobbed. No one knew what to say. Those hushed seconds seemed to last forever. Perhaps it was unprofessional to cry so voraciously, but it was a flow I could not stop. I often scold myself for not having thicker skin. Of course, it is naive to think the world and all its children can be kept harbored from evil. But these babies, their broken bodies captured in full gorge of the sun, could have been saved — I am certain of that. And I was almost certain these graceful people would never see even a little justice for what was done to them. They knew it, too.

Finally, someone passed a tissue to wipe my eyes. I glanced up through the glaze and saw the faces around me bereft of emotion.

"This is nothing. We don't react anymore," Umer said nonchalantly, by way of explanation. "There are far worse things that have happened."

I realized then that the Yazidis were beyond the point of pain. Their grief had entered a place few in this world could ever comprehend. Their torment and desperation had dried up and dissolved. They had no emotion left to give.

For them, there was no fog of war. Everything was reconstructed with precise attention to detail: the numbers of the missing and enslaved, and where they were exactly when their world stopped turning. Every abuse could be recited like a nebulous monologue, but without the theatrical cues and vocals. There was no need to dramatize what had happened to them.

At that point, in early October 2016, they had more than 400,000 displaced persons from their community, Baba Chawish told me. 1,293 men had been executed, 1,103 children had been orphaned, 5,878 hostages had gone missing, 238 female and 2,650 male, and forty-two Yazidi shrines and holy sites had been blown up. Only 2,364 had been rescued — 876 women, 318 men, 572 girls, and 598 boys.

Men drifted in and out of the room. Some expressed a resigned frustration with the U.S. State Department. Earlier in the year, Secretary of State John Kerry had officially designated the Yazidi community as victims of genocide. But the men said the announcement had brought about no change, no extra help. They felt as though the world, in all its bloated bureaucracy, had discarded them.

Baba Chawish stressed that the most important thing America could do was help with bring their hostages home.

"We can't do anything for the dead," he said. "But nobody is doing anything in the world, it's all just talk."

Another Yazidi man chimed in that there were too many thoughts and prayers, but not enough action. "Thinking about it doesn't do anything," he said.

We talked some more about the covert, complex rescue missions to secure the captured Yazidis from the clutches of ISIS, and about the brave prisoners who concocted their own plans to break free. One young boy, a brother to one of the men on the floor, had been forced into a training camp in Syria. He killed a leader by stealing the keys to his car and running him over.

"ISIS beheads women, too, the ones who refuse to convert," Baba Chawish said, pulling out collaged pictures of both male and female Yazidis, mostly elderly. The pictures showed side-by-side images of them smiling in the before, and then the after — their heads severed off. Sometimes, the photos featured just the head, cut cleanly with a blade and left on a dirty concrete floor.

One old man had enormous blue eyes in his before photo. In his after one, his eyes were even larger, crippled in shock, in agony — mouth wide open in a final gasp, as if in a final, silent plea to be saved. Only no one had come for him.

He died a slow and horrific death — a righteous old man in the sundown of his hard-working life — alone. And for what?

We smoked more fresh tobacco in the dining room. Large ceramic bowls filled with rice, chicken, soup, olives, and figs — straight from the magical trees of Lalish — were placed in front of us. We all picked idly at the food. It seemed nobody felt much like eating.

Before he went to sleep that night, Baba Chawish wanted to share a story with me. Days earlier, an old woman had been rescued from ISIS and was transported to Lalish. He led the old lady into the temple and it was there, in their most sacred space, that she drew her last breath. They didn't know why she had died so suddenly, but I could only imagine the trauma that had clung to her woman's heart.

I cried some more, thinking about how that lady had lived through so much. I thought of the years of brutal torture and enslavement capped by a terrifying rescue mission — only to die within minutes of making it back, before she could really reclaim her right to life.

But to Baba Chawish, the moment was a magical one. She had held on just for that moment, and when she passed, she passed on her terms — inside the love and protection of her hallowed home.

"She died in the temple," he whispered. "In Yazidi religion, it is very special to die inside the temple."

The old woman had departed inside the cradle of life. Death was not her end — it was her dawn to a new beginning. Yazidis believed that death was only the end of time in that body.

Later that night, I was tended to by two lovely teenage sisters — Hami and Layla. Both were petite, no taller than five feet, with magnificent black eyebrows and multiple ear piercings. They moved with a soft femininity and had a kind of insatiable desire to be held — and there is nothing comparable to a Yazidi hug; they envelope your whole being, long and tight, complete with kisses on the cheeks and lips.

Hami assured me that we were family even though we had just met, and she wanted me to know that they were here to help me with whatever I needed. When people with very little want to give their all to you, a trait so innate to the Yazidi community, one cannot help but be profoundly moved. For such a historically closed community, they are incredibly accepting of outsiders.

The girls held my hands and furled their dainty bodies into my shoulders. We wandered barefoot, ducking beneath the arched doorways and across the concrete maze of the temple roof to the old-fashioned bathrooms across the way. Every moment we were together, their skin touched mine.

While the men slept scattered across the roof and beneath the stars, the dozen-odd women had a designated room with lime green cement walls and a bevy of mattresses and pillows. Hami and Layla, on either side, wrapped me in the stiff sheets. We rested our heads on the same pillow until morning came — until the roosters crowed and the sun dusted our little sleeping nest.

When I woke, the street was already teeming and Jamayi had very much begun. From the rooftop, I could see freckles of color from the vibrant dresses and white hijabs, growing even more plentiful as more people climbed down from the rooftops and mountainside to collect water and make breakfast. The sharp, triangular tops of the temple were graced with rays of misty light through the masses of surrounding green trees.

I showered in rubber flip-flops with a bar of soap and a bucket of cool water tossed over my body. The heat outside rose fast and sharp. Hami brushed my matted hair with her fingers, twisting my unruly mane into a ballet bun just like hers.

I was greeted by a young man named Baxtiar, who I had met at dinner the night before. He spoke in endearing, truncated English. I loved listening to him talk; his voice was like a musical instrument, smooth and melodic. He volunteered to walk me through the festival and offered to go and find me my shoes, seeming pleased when I told him no.

"It is good for the feet," Baxtiar chimed. "To be barefoot on the earth."

Baxtiar was a Lalish local. He used to catch a bus every day to go to school, but after "what happened to them," he quit to be a man of the land. He had a well-heeled vernacular and a lovely way of translating; he seemed to love sharing his religion and its long history. His young life had already been filled with heartache and loss, but there was no acerbity in the way he spoke.

The morning sky was already bursting, blue and spotless with a dash of pink from fires burning in the distance.

Downstairs, women sat, knitting on piles of pillows. Men shaved slabs of raw meat and peeled vegetables. Aromas of cardamom and coffee wafted through the various food stands. Baxtiar brought me some "special spices" unique to their mountains. Svok and Samak, little girls with plastic flower headbands, played with other young girls in the sunshine.

A large portrait of Noah and his ark was painted one side of the building. In the Yazidi religion, Lalish is where Noah's ark first encountered dry land after the flood and is therefore considered the origin of new civilization.

Out in the courtyard, a blown-up picture of Nadia Murad speaking at the United Nations was taped to the stairwell. Yazidis lined up to take pictures beside it. She had already become a superstar — someone who could reach the world on their behalf.

That day, the Nobel Peace Prize winner was announced, and Nadia did not win. Rather, the Norwegian committee gave the prize to Colombian President Juan Manuel Santos for his efforts to bring the country's fifty-year-long civil war to a formal close. But the mood was not dimmed by that disappointment.

"The festival used to be much bigger," Baxtiar said. "Now, just small."

The previous two years, Jamayi Festival had been canceled altogether due to the instability of the security situation, but this year the Yazidis had resumed their pilgrimage and brought back what was rightfully theirs to own and enjoy. The festival would perhaps never be what it once was — long days of laughter and celebration. Too much had changed for that, but the Yazidis were not to be stripped of what mattered most, and that was their faith.

After walking up into the mountains to take in a birds-eye view, Baxtiar guided me toward their precious place: the White Spring. It was the place where Yazidis, young and old, went to be baptized. It was a small, grey concrete room with a single light beaming down from the back.

"They put water on their heads. We have some words, and we must say those words," Baxtiar explained. "It is holy water on their face and head."

To be baptized from the water of their sacred springs, tucked away and protected by the undulating hills, was something which Yazidis were to do at least once in their lifetime. It had also become a method of reintegrating their stolen women back into the tight community.

As I am not Yazidi, I could not venture inside the White Spring, but I watched from the arched doorway. For many — even the elderly — it was the first time they ever made the three-hour journey from Sinjar to Lalish, Baxtiar explained. It was the first time they had been baptized in their holiest of waters.

"Many people from Sinjar are very poor and homeless and lived their lives poor," he noted as a middle-aged man stepped inside for his baptism. "He became a big man not yet baptized — but today that changes, and there is hope."

An older lady, colorfully dressed, performed the ceremony, which lasted just seconds. Baxtiar told me the lady was his aunty.

"She is very nice," he said, waving to her. "We are like friends."

The festival was a mix of old and new. Women wore the traditional, flowing white dresses of purity and the men in the khirque — which denotes the cloak of the Sufis — wore t-shirts and jeans. Some ate traditional foods and listened to traditional music, while others opted for burgers and Kurdish pop music. A little girl dressed like a princess sat in the middle of the street, sobbing wildly. A Yazidi soldier approached to lift her up, hold her hand, and wipe her tears. Minutes later an announcement over the loudspeaker claimed a girl fitting her description had been separated from her parents.

On my way out of Lalish that afternoon, Baba Chawish led me by car to see a little sliver of history in their land: the ancient caves that Baba dated to be 800 years old.

However, Yakhi pointed to the Romanesque carvings and observed that it was likely they were older — so old that it is believed Alexander the Great rode through them around 331 B.C.

The tiny, ornately-carved rectangular windows let in streaks of blinding sunshine, casting long and lithe shadows on the stony grey floors. Baba Chawish, his ever-noble presence standing defiant in that mist of light, waved goodbye.

GOD SEES EVERYONE
October, 2016

I waved at the young children scattered along the roadside selling water bottles and vegetables, fluttering their little fingers to draw our attention as we drove by. We churned through the serpentine streets past the sunburned shepherds herding their flocks and the cement dwellings with mats hanging from the rooftops until we came to an abandoned, decaying structure where torn sheets served as walls and clothes hung to dry from a strip of thin wire tied to a flimsy pole.

In these ravaged villages, it was far too common to see Yazidis seeking shelter wherever possible. These were the ones who could not even make it to the relative safety of a displacement camp.

Behind those ripped sheets, salvaged from a UNHCR set-up somewhere, were extraordinary survivors.

A crippled man with a cane, dressed all in white with a traditional red-and-white scarf tied around his head — called the shma'ag — hobbled barefoot across the dirt floor to welcome us. His name was Murad, and he seemed far older than his seventy years. Deep wrinkles lined his forehead; his thick grey moustache curved into a permanent frown. But, most jarring of all, Murad heaved with exhaustion, tired with what the world had handed him.

He sat on his iron bed frame and I sat beside him on the floor, folding myself in between the cardboard boxes stuffed with canned tomatoes and paper towels and blocks of bread rolls so stale that they looked as hard as rocks. The room was dank, fuming with unwashed flesh and despair.

Slowly but willingly, Murad started to patch together what had happened to him on August 3, 2014 — the morning that ISIS changed the Yazidis forever. It had started like any other searing summer day in their town of Telekasa, just outside of Sinjar. He was heading down the road around 8:00 A.M., pushing his disabled, wheelchair-bound wife, Guly, to gather food when the jihadists blocked their way.

"They were yelling, yelling that we must convert then and there or be killed. People were getting killed," Murad said, his eyes closed as if to carefully collect his thoughts and reflect on his intense pain. "There were women and children all around me. For the sake of the women and children, I converted. I didn't want them to see another person slaughtered."

Many of the disabled hadn't made it. Many tried to flee, he stressed. But they didn't make it.

Trucks rolled up. A sinking feeling hit Murad and he wept inside, not knowing where he would be taken but recognizing that it could be his last ride in this life. His chilling description of that moment later reminded me of a letter acquired by the U.S. Holocaust Memorial Museum, written by Wilma Grunwald hours before she was sent to her death in the gas chambers.

The famous trucks are here now, and we are waiting for it to begin.
Take care of my golden boy and don't spoil him too much with your love.
Have a great life; we must board the trucks now.
Into eternity.
Yours, Wilma.

Murad, his wife, and other Yazidis, too, had been thrown into trucks and taken to a village for forty days of starvation, torture, and fear. Then they were moved to Tel Afar where thousands more prisoners were being held in squalor. After three months, the couple was hauled to Mosul and held in what Murad called a factory of sorts. There, alongside one another, they prepared — readying themselves to die.

"We didn't know when they were going to take us out and end us. One day they just pulled six people out and executed them in front of us," Murad went on, mimicking pulling a trigger. "Pistol to the back of the head. They said it was because these people had planned to run away."

It was in the gun gesture that I noticed Murad was partially missing two fingers from his right hand.

"It was all terrible conditions. They didn't feed us. My friends died around me," he continued, clutching his right leg. "I lost my leg. I cannot feel my leg."

When the first winter in captivity came and ISIS did not give them blankets or clothes, Yazidis dropped dead from the cold and the hunger that sent them into fits of anguish, their muscles eating away at themselves. The whole time, Murad said, babies were being separated from their mothers and murdered in front of them.

"They are savages; they have no faith. Anyone with faith would not take a small baby and kill [it]," he cried. "They were killing babies like they were killing sheep."

Murad told me that all he could think about — all that got him through the darkest of days — were thoughts of his family. He had four sons and six daughters, all between fourteen and thirty-five years old. Three of them were actually his grandchildren, but he called them his own. Some are still missing. He thought of them playing in the sunshine and sleeping under stars, and he remembered what it felt like to hold their milky little hands and how he wanted to hold them just once more.

A young woman, perilously thin and bedecked in a light purple scarf, entered the room and sat beside me, drawing her legs to her chest and rolling onto the floor like a baby in the womb. She seemed flighty, terrified, and curious all at once. After a few minutes of listening, her face fell, and she flounced out again.

"I am sorry for her," Murad said. "Her mind has gone somewhere else."

I learned that she was his eldest daughter. She had been held as a sex slave and was been rescued just weeks before. The young woman felt ashamed for what she had gone through, Murad said — ashamed even though she was the victim.

Those who made it through that first frigid winter were separated into two groups. The disabled were tossed into trucks and the rest dredged back to confinement in Tel Afar. Murad considered himself lucky to have been dumped at the Kurdish border. Being disabled rendered him and others useless to ISIS. I concluded that most likely, there was money involved in their return by smugglers somewhere along the line.

Murad never referred to his captors by any of their self-styled names —
ISIS, IS, Islamic State, or Da'esh. He only ever referenced them as "they." Murad
stopped suddenly and lit a cigarette, glancing at me with a cheeky smile.

"I like to smoke," he explained. "They didn't let me smoke for all those
months."

I laughed and told him that sometimes I liked to smoke too, so we shared
a cigarette and a few moments of silence. Murad's smoke rings hung in the
warm, static air; perfect, circular puffs that persisted for longer than normal
before gracefully fading away.

Murad said that one day, he hoped he could return to his village to live
out his final days — but only if they were guaranteed protection and if the
persecution wouldn't return. He missed everything about the life he referred
to as simple but nice — a happy life of peace and quiet.

Life now, in the deserted construction, was a far cry from his pre-ISIS past.
They had little money, little medicine, little food.

"Look, we live under a tent," he exclaimed. "I need surgery for my leg.
We have no money. Nobody gives us anything. If we do get a little money,
we spend it on medicine." Murad pointed this out without fret, only with
frankness. "The children cannot go to school. There are no jobs. We are stuck
here in this unfinished building."

I plucked up the courage to ask about his half-sliced fingers. Sometime in
the seventies, during the ongoing Kurdish- Iraqi conflict in which the Kurds
sought independence, Murad was captured and tossed into an Iraqi jail,
labeled a Kurdish dissident, and execution orders hung over his head. His
fingers were chopped off during a routine torture session. Murad was granted
amnesty after the Iraq and Kurdish leaders reached some sort of political
prisoner agreement.

He later worked as a food distribution agent for the government's long-
running socialist program that issued monthly food staples to Iraqis, but his
disabilities forced him into early retirement, where he and his family went
about their days in peace and quiet.

Yet Murad was itching to get back on track and returned to detailing what happened to him under the terrorist regime.

"They were taking out girls and raping them in front of us. There are still hundreds of girls gone and we don't know about their destiny," Murad noted, grief snagging in his throat. "I think of them always."

He turned to me. His enameled eyes stared straight into mine.

"How can I forget?" he asked.

I shook my head. I had nothing appropriate to say. He would not forget — he did not want to forget. This was what had been done to his people. Those heinous recollections would go with him to the grave.

"What is worse," Murad said, blanching, heartsick voice dropping. "When you know them, the ones who are hurting you."

He said that the people torturing them, threatening them every single day in captivity, were faces all too familiar.

"It is very difficult when someone takes your religion away from you. We were told we could not be Yazidi. It is more difficult when it is someone you know and once loved," Murad went on, a slight tremor again cracking his speech. "How can we trust the Arabs again? We can't ever trust them again. They looted us. They hurt us."

Murad gestured for me to move into the adjoining room to see his wife, Guly. Freckles of light poked through the frayed curtain walls. On one side, an assortment of brightly-colored clothes hung neatly beside a little cupboard piled with boxes of soap and cigarettes.

In any other circumstance, it could have been abstract art. But in this circumstance, it was a painful admission of all they had left to call home.

Guly sat on a gaunt mattress in a white head scarf and clashing red-and-pink dress. Her glassy eyes lit up as I approached, and she smiled, her ailing body slumped forward. She motioned for me to sit in the plastic purple chair, but I chose to sit beside her on the ground. Her daughter floated beside me.

We wrapped Guly in blankets to cover her legs so her exposed skin would not be seen; so she could preserve her dignity in what felt like her dwindling days.

Guly was disabled from what she referred to as a "brain attack" — a stroke — and ISIS had thrown away her wheelchair when they kidnapped her. They had no money for a new one. Her life was now relegated to sitting helplessly in that one spot on the arid earth, waiting for someone, anyone, to come.

For months, ISIS had dragged this old woman around by her neck from torture place to torture place. She recalled how the cold came and, just as Murad had said, there were no blankets or warm clothes. The frost had eaten away the feeling in one of Guly's hands, which she now clutched and shook in despair. She cried for something she could no longer feel. It was painful to watch.

I reached for her good hand and entwined my fingers in hers. It was all I could do. I did not want to ask her questions of her ordeal. I could not ask her to relive the tribulation. I wanted only to be there. Somehow.

Where was the world? The aid agencies? The do-gooders? The angels and the God? These people couldn't even make it to an established camp. In my time abroad, stories like Murad's and Guly's fell into infinite binders that would be tossed away to collect dust. There was no justice. This was genocide.

"We don't have anything," Guly sobbed. "But we are thankful."

As I eventually motioned to leave, she kissed my hand and wouldn't let it go.

"I will pray for you in my religion. The Yazidi," she whispered. "God sees you. God sees everybody."

Guly's power had been ripped from her, but never her pride. Her faith was tenacious.

As I stepped outside into the heat, Murad shuffled to the door to say goodbye. "The people that took us — threatened us — were our neighbors. They were the people who, for years, would come to our house and eat with us. We considered them brothers," he asserted, defiant. "Our neighbors. And then... they became ISIS. They turned their guns on us."

Murad's words echoed through me. I turned for one last time and glanced through the gaping hole in the ripped sheet where Guly sat, staring into nothingness. There she would wait for help that, deep down, both she and I knew would never come.

But a person who believed — really believed, without the faintest shadow of doubt — would never be lonely. I believed she would never give in.

JEWS COME OUT OF HIDING
October, 2016

It was a Friday when I attended my first Shabbat dinner. These were people who refused to give in to the dominant religion around them, even in the face of immense persecution. It was ironic to attend that first Shabbat in Iraq, in a land that the Jews had been almost entirely run out of years ago. Roughly twenty people attended the dinner in a private home.

I enjoyed the eager conversations, the prayers, and the pride among the Jewish people. To express their faith with such ease — only a year or two ago — would have been unthinkable. But the Kurdish Regional Government had been active in trying to bring back a sense of religious freedom, which felt ever more pertinent amid the fragile backdrop of ISIS's movements.

But could the Jews ever be truly safe and welcome in the ancient Babylonian land, where many of their ancestors once peacefully coexisted? Could the thousands of Kurdish Jews in Israel build lives in a place that had not always been so hospitable to them?

"Jews would be surprised to find that they are freer and safer here than in certain European capitals," insisted Sherzad Omer Mamsani, a Jewish government representative.

For the first time that year, the KRG officially marked Holocaust Remembrance Day with the first-ever ceremony in Erbil. The occasion came amid the somber atmosphere of suffering as well as the current genocide of Christians, Yazidis, and Shia taking place just fifty miles away in Mosul.

Under heavy guard, participants held a moment of silence and watched as six candles were lit, each symbolizing a million Jews killed in the Holocaust. For many in attendance, it was the first time they had ever worn the traditional brimless cap — known as the kippah — in public.

For 2,600 years, the Jewish community prospered in what was once called Mesopotamia and was now known as Iraq. In the early 20th century, they were considered an affluent and politically important part of the country and made up one-third of Baghdad's population. The Jewish community was most esteemed in the years after the first World War, but as the Second World War dawned, scores were forced to flee.

After Israel was etched into the neighborhood in 1948, their net of safety fell to tatters. Iraq subsequently fought the new nation in what became the Arab-Israeli war, the remaining Jews in the Mesopotamian land branded as Zionist traitors. Their numbers dwindled to around 6,000 in the 1960s after being forced to carry yellow identity cards. They were banned from selling property, and the population continued to descend as the persecution mounted. Today, only a handful of Jews pepper Iraq, living secret lives and praying secret prayers.

The Kurdish enclave was, at least, purporting to change that, leaders said.

Sherzad had long advocated for Jewish rights, and it had cost him the use of his right hand. In 1997, he published a book on Jewish affairs. Soon after that, he was targeted in a bomb attack.

There are an estimated 300,000 Kurdish Jews in the world, mostly in Israel. There are several hundred in the Kurdish part of Iraq. Yet there was some debate as to whether they were newcomers — people suddenly embracing the faith of their earlier lineage — or simply misclassified people. For generations, the small number of Jews in Iraq hid their faith, even registering as Muslim on the mandatory identification cards required by Baghdad. In the Shia-dominated southern part of the country, several Jewish families, formally registered as Muslim for their safety, were believed to practice Judaism in the cloaked seclusion of their homes.

"Since we're still part of Iraq, all IDs must indicate the religion of the holder," Sherzad explained. "Judaism is not an option, and most individuals concerned with their safety and their family, would not attempt to register as such with the central government."

Sherzad insisted that the ranks of Kurdish Jews in the region were in fact slowly growing, as some from the UK, Germany, and even Israel returned to their ancestral homeland.

"The number of known Jews or families with Jewish heritage grows as we discover individuals who have been quiet for decades, or as some Kurdish and Iraqi Jews return from the diaspora for long-term business," he told me.

Practicing the faith of their families without threat of persecution is new for many. One high-level official revealed that he never left home without the Star of David secured in his pocket, while another proudly flew an Israeli flag alongside the Kurdish flag inside his home.

Jaffar Ibrahim Eminki, the deputy speaker of the Kurdistan Parliament, assured me that lawmakers valued strong social relations with the Jewish populace.

"We believe they can live here," he said sternly.

However, the present and future of Jews in Iraq remained a subject of contention. Mordechai Zaken, an Israel-based expert on Kurdish and Middle Eastern affairs and a former Arab affairs advisor to the Israeli prime minister's office, denied that such relocations were happening or that there was much of a Jewish community in Kurdistan.

"There were several dozen families that had some distant family connection to Judaism," he told the Jerusalem Post. "Most of these people are Muslim Kurds who perhaps have a grandmother or great-grandmother of Jewish origin who converted to Islam two or three generations ago."

Edwin Shuker — a Baghdad-born Iraqi-Jewish businessman, activist who worked to preserve Jewish shrines in the Middle East, and former vice president of the European Jewish Congress — echoed that, while progress had been made in helping Jewish people to find comfort in the Kurdish areas, they were not returning to live there permanently.

"They are not moving back from anywhere; they are simply more comfortable to reveal a Jewish connection," he noted. "This is the oldest Jewish community in the world that has managed to keep its identity in exile. People who are of Jewish descent have now been more willing to associate themselves with the Jewish heritage."

There were still no synagogues or public places for Jewish prayer and gathering. Some KRG officials said that they were trying to open temples in the region, but others claimed that such efforts were hindered by sour relations with Baghdad, along with concerns over Iranian-funded militias and the ongoing jihadist threat.

For now, Sherzad was taking things one step at a time — gathering to mark the Holocaust was one of the biggest strides to date, and a tradition he was intent on upkeeping.

"We don't want to put our lives and hundreds of Jewish families in trouble," he said. "We're starting with teaching and learning about the Jewish religion. It is one step at a time."

THIEVES OF FORTUNE
October, 2016

War — and repairing what it ruined — could only be done one step at a time, in micro portions. Needs were too vast; if you thought about it on a macro level, it became the stuff of nightmares.

Late at night, Yakhi and I would often sit in a little Greek restaurant in a housing complex called the American Village, where workers played cheesy pop ballads and we would talk about what victims of the genocide needed — medical supplies, mostly. Gunshots would sometimes scream out and entropy would ensue as local guards scrambled to protect high-ranking government officials, yet nobody looked twice. Nobody stopped their conversation. Nobody bothered to peep outside and see what was going on.

Life chugged on. That is what war after war after war does to people. Weapons become the harmony, the earworm that slithers inside of everyone. The more you will it away, the longer it lasts. So, you just get on with things.

What is war? War is a way of life.

One morning, we ventured out to the Baharka IDP camp, a place I had visited several times. Before ISIS invaded Mosul, the block of dead land had been a cement factory, but as displaced persons flooded north, officials had to turn industrial areas into makeshift shelters. Over time, those temporary shelters became painfully permanent.

Baharka was a lifeless place, permeated by the grief of the people who had no choice but to be there. Rows of cracked cement shell trailers swelled as far as the eye could see. Kids played on the hardened earth and chickens pecked at the dust. A few fruit stands were strewn across the entrance, apples and plastic water bottles melting in the heat, emitting the ripe smell of overflowing trash and leaking sewage.

I met a young father named Wasim, who was of the Shabak minority and had once lived in a village called Hamodarnya in Alquosh, outside of Mosul. He was gap-toothed, had light hazel eyes — the whites of which were stained yellow — and was withered to the bone. His abnormally sunken face and the way he quailed when he moved indicated something was wrong.

"The Peshmerga warned us to leave because ISIS was on its way," Wasim told me, cross-legged on the cement floor. "Everybody left; my whole village left. We didn't leave anyone behind, and ISIS got it all. All we ever knew."

Wasim said that his entire village now resided in the crusty factory grounds except for the neighbors who had joined ISIS. His little home was nearly empty, but had a thin mattress in one corner and a blinking, 80s-style television sitting on a milk crate in the other.

Wasim wanted to go home, he said; to his real home . . . if it was still there.

"Sometimes we get donations from people in the town," Wasim went on, pointing to the refrigerator by the entrance. "A nice person came one day and gave us the fridge, but we don't have much electricity."

Moreover, the family didn't have much food. They were hungry, he admitted. Wasim's three small sons sat beside him, quiet and with gentle demeanors but each with the air of old men, weathered by hardship.

Wasim had four children in total, between seven and fourteen years old — three boys and one girl. Every day was the same, he murmured. His daughter, Duha, the second eldest at thirteen, had left school in the fourth grade to help her mother run the household.

The eldest, fourteen-year-old Saif, held the pertinent job of selling pickles in the nearby streets for four hours every day. He tried to go to school when he could, but it was evident that the burden of being the family's breadwinner rested heavy on his shoulders.

"I walk around," Saif explained, dense in his concentration as he demonstrated his job. "I see who needs pickles. Some days, the people need pickles. Some days they don't."

On the former days, the family could afford to buy food from the open-air market close by — on the latter, they subsisted on old food or scraps from neighbors.

Saif watched his childhood wither away. He had been forced to grow into the man of the house all too fast; he did not want to let down those he loved, who needed him most.

I had expected there to be a hint of pride in Saif's tone at being the family's money-maker, but I did not detect any. He was just doing what needed to be done to get by. His younger brothers sometimes joined him on the streets at the crack of dawn, before school, with jars of pickles. But Saif said one day he would like to become a doctor: "To help people."

"That would be a dream," he whispered, almost wary of speaking too loudly, as if afraid someone might laugh in his face or jinx his hopes. "But maybe I will have to keep selling pickles instead."

I wanted to tell these boys that their dreams would be fulfilled and that their childhoods were not wasted — only it would have been a lie. I didn't know if they would grow up only to keep selling pickles; I didn't know if they would ever leave this camp.

Confirming my initial reflection, Wasim was unable to work. He was ill. A couple of years before ISIS came, he was working as a police officer in Baghdad when an insurgent-driven explosion injured him, costing him a kidney, some nerve endings, and much of his dignity as the family leader.

Wasim lamented about being weak and, in his words, useless. But at least he had become a little more accustomed to the pain, and it bothered him less now. When the family had fled their home, he had to leave his medicines behind. They left everything behind, taking only their ID cards, with no time to gather anything else. They were too poor to have a car of their own, so a neighbor jammed them and many others into his, tearing out along the rubble road before their village was captured.

I often wonder, in situations like that, when the children are so young, how parents explain — amid all the mayhem — that they must leave behind life as they know it for no fault of their own. In Wasim's case, he told his children that they were going on an impromptu picnic.

"And now we are here. Now they understand what is going on and I don't have to explain," he said, nervously twisting the prayer beads in his hand faster and faster.

Still, I thought. How do you explain that you were targeted because of your religion — something that serves as the backbone to your existence; something so near and dear to your heart?

"No matter who said my religion was wrong and no matter who said it was right," Wasim continued, as if reading my mind, "I would never convert. I am Shabak."

Wasim was upset by the fact that missionaries from all over the world were coming into the camps and bribing Shabak families to convert to Christianity. He said he knew of three families that had converted in the last week just as a means of survival.

"They come in a car, they knock on the doors, and they give the families who convert money," he explained. "About every five days, I see them around here."

I had heard from various sources that such bribed conversions were becoming commonplace in numerous camps and areas rife with refugees and IDPs — different religious groups capitalizing on the dire situation to build their numbers and exert their power. It wasn't just Christians, however. Shia and Sunni offshoot groups were also said to be luring in hapless prey. Camp supervisors had much bigger fish to fry than keeping tabs on missionary and NGO behaviors.

Wasim pulled out a cigarette and the youngest boy, Husam, so angelic in the way he flicked his hair and smiled, jumped up to light it. The little one brought me a cigarette and struck another match, but I quickly refused. The notion of a seven-year-old lighting a smoke in the dank room certainly did not feel appropriate.

I asked Wasim what it was that they needed most there, at the camp — a question that had outworn its welcome.

"Thousands of NGOs come and ask us what we want, and we tell them, but it doesn't change," Wasim said. "Our problems are obvious."

He was right. Their problems were obvious. I glanced through the single window at the all-too-familiar sight of children, their backs bent over under the fierce sunshine, laboring to make ends meet. I surveyed the squalor and the flapping signs featuring dozens of branded NGO logos, as if advertising for a community concert series and seeking back pats.

Wasim's most significant criticism was of the United States.

"America came in and removed a dictator, which was good, but then you don't protect us," Wasim said, turning his hazel eyes on me. "Why? Then ISIS came. Why?"

Embarrassed, I simply nodded in acknowledgment. Tension cut the air as Wasim's passion gained momentum. It was the first time I had seen vitality seep into his drained disposition. So I let him roll, uninterrupted.

"I am not talking about politics. Political people cannot even bother themselves to come and sit with us. But someone let ISIS come in. The question is why?" he continued. "We are nobody. We are just poor people. I don't know anything about American politicians. But what I do know is that the Iraqi politicians are all thieves. They call themselves religious people, people of God, but they are thieves."

Wasim pulled out a few crumpled Iraqi dinar notes and loose coins from his pocket and tossed them on the floor.

"That is my fortune. That's what I have to raise my family. I have worked every single day of my life since I was seven years old," he said. "Politicians live in the high life. They steal. And yet they expect people to be united for Iraq? To want to fight for the country? To be proud of Iraq?"

Wasim retained every ounce of honor that he could — every ounce of being an honest and simple man. He may not have been the most educated or the most articulate, but he wanted to be heard. He knew it was his right to express that opinion, and it was his right to be angry. I could not blame him. Conflict and persecution had ripped away his health, his home, his family, his future. The only life he knew was one of work, wounds, and war.

Wasim looked down at his prayer beads, worn from his continuous touch. Faith was the only thing that conflict could not take from him. Time slowed for a little while, and I wondered what he prayed for.

Suddenly, Yakhi's phone rang. He jumped up and said we needed to leave — it was the call we had been awaiting. The family waved us goodbye.

We were headed for the frontlines; for Mosul in the twilight before the big battle — before the big liberation began.

FAMILIES OF THE FRONTLINES
October, 2016

The chatter centered on the impending battle as we approached the final Peshmerga checkpoint during those strange few days before the official push into Mosul, the pocket of placidity before the storm. A sense of confidence alit — that the effort to dismantle ISIS in Iraq was commencing — coupled with a fear that the worst in this war was yet to come.

The worst was yet to come.

Florence Welch's "Ship to Wreck" whistled through the broken car radio.

"And oh, my love remind me, what was it that I said?
I can't help but pull the earth around me, to make my bed And oh my love
remind me, what was it that I did?
Did I drink too much? Am I losing touch?
Did I build this ship to wreck?"

That final checkpoint stood just eighteen miles from the center of Mosul along the Mosul Main Road, the only route between Erbil and the ISIS-inhabited city. When would I be able to ride this road into the city center and how much blood would freely be spilled along the way?

I stopped taking notes and appreciated that serene afternoon with its spotless sky. A young soldier at the checkpoint highlighted that with spotless days came a bombardment of bombs. It wasn't clear if it was a joke.

I hadn't obtained the necessary permissions to cross beyond the last checkpoint into the military-only zone. But I had figured that, when there is a will, there was always a way. We were told that because the Mosul offensive was slated to start at any moment, the U.S.-led coalition had asked the KRG's President's office not to allow journalists past this point out of concern that secret military positions would be compromised.

But we made some calls, worked some connections and, finally, we were waved through. I was politely instructed not to ask questions, but to be something of a silent observer and a ghost on the wall. We climbed into the armored vehicle driven by a Peshmerga Commander, snapped our armor into place, and continued forth.

Sometimes a conflict can't always be seen, but can be heard and smelled — the waft of metallic blood, gunpowder, exhaust fumes, and burning trash — miles before its trail of madness even begins, perpetuating the thousands of years of unrest stagnant in the warm air.

That concluding track between the last checkpoint and the frontline was an eerily quiet one. There was the occasional sight of a handful of soldiers or an ambulance casually coming and going. The silence was striking.

Yet, in that silence, the tension rumbled below the ruined road, like the proverbial childhood monster beneath the bed that could burst through the brittle mattress at any moment.

Along the roadside were remnants of the horrors that not too long ago had plagued this very parcel of the Mosul outskirts, still a disputed land area between the Bagdad Central Government and the Kurdish Regional one, where entire villages had been swallowed by airstrikes and heavy fighting.

Decapitated power lines swooped down across the terrain. Cement roofs sat on the road and cracks riddled the few buildings still standing — so discolored that they blended with the dirt. Exposed, masticated furniture and what was once someone's sanctuary silently exhibited agony. Charred carcasses of cars and a burned school bus sat stranded in the road. A mere barbed wire fence barricaded vast expanses of land, not yet cleared of the mines planted over the last two-and-a-half years of chaos.

Miles of trenches had recently been dug to stop car bombers from breaching the Peshmerga-controlled area, but everyone remained on high alert regardless. ISIS sent their paradise-seekers sneaking through the deadened plains, strapped with explosives, almost every day.

"At one point," the Kurdish official accompanying us said spiritedly. "ISIS even had armored lifts it was using to put bombs inside the ditch."

Another few miles down the highly-restricted stretch of road — past the occasional armored vehicle strapped with supplies — led to an array of Peshmerga frontline positions. A scattering of soldiers spread along the trail of sandbags and flimsy huts, armed and waiting. Of course, they were always waiting.

What is war? Waiting and boredom and then action and exhaustion.

Less than half a mile ahead of the men was the enemy frontline and their central base — a tower of sorts — inside what was once a brick factory.

After a few more twists and turns, we traversed into the frontline village of Mufti, a minority Shabak and Kakayi village, which had only been freed from ISIS four months before. All that remained were clumps of brick and guts of homes.

Still intact, however, were the intricate, expertly-constructed underground tunnels the terrorists had built. The tunnels originated from what was once their firing line and cleverly led to every house they occupied, concealing the jihadists from the intensity of the routine airstrikes.

I got out and peered into the raven void. With a deep breath, I followed the soldier's lead and lowered myself down carefully, feeling less like Spiderman and more like Alice in Wonderland toppling into the rabbit hole. The tunnel opening was just under three feet wide, requiring a drop-down roughly 5'10" height.

With a less than stellar flashlight, I wandered through, examining the crafty construction of the little hallway and rooms built off to the side.

I was cautioned to put one foot in front of the other and not stray into the rooms.

"Bombs," the soldier quipped breezily. "Everywhere."

Lived in just weeks ago, the tunnel was strewn with odds and ends — soiled prayer mats, pillows and blankets, slippers, severed electrical cords, a phone charger, a broken fan, bottles of engine oil and antiseptics, cans of food and yogurt tubs, water bottles, and empty cigarette packets.

"ISIS might tell everyone else smoking is haram [forbidden]," observed the guiding soldier. "But their fighters did what they wanted."

We reached a room with a high ceiling, outfitted with an old but unscathed ceiling fan and ringed by cracks of filtered sunlight and mortar holes carved into the stone like a rock-climbing wall. The tunnel had an empty energy about it, as if everything that the walls once harbored had been wiped from the face of the earth.

Barricades blocked the rest of the long tunnel, and the soldier clarified that the rest had "not yet been cleaned" of explosives — a job that would take "many, many months."

I finished taking my notes and maneuvered back up into the light of day, and we drove onward to meet the special battalion of Kakayi fighters that had assembled to protect their lands and had reclaimed some control over what was so swiftly stolen from them soon after Mosul fell in June of 2014.

"After that happened to us, the Peshmerga called on our military-aged men to take up arms, so we could have the chance to protect ourselves and our people and a special battalion just for us," explained one of the senior ranking soldiers from their central base in Tulaband. "And we've participated in every offense to retake the village."

Tulaband was the Kakayi's ancestral home which ISIS had controlled for years, and while the locals had taken it back, it was merely a ghost village, smashed beyond comprehension — uninhabitable.

Under the guise of the Ministry of Peshmerga, around six hundred Kakayi men had banded together to fight back. The dozen I met stationed at their little base of operations, complete with a few roaming chickens and a small green garden, ranged from about eighteen to forty years old. They all had fabulously bushy, almost identical mustaches contouring their top lips and protracting down to their chins — a signature of the Kakayi, I was informed.

"It is important we have the resources to protect ourselves, our people," one soldier said. "For two years ISIS was here, and all we could do was run away and watch from afar."

The Kakayi are part of the ancient Yarsan, or Ahl el-Haqq, which means "people of truth" in Persian. Their faith is a syncretistic, mystical one with elements of Islam and various Mesopotamian religions, believed to have started in Kurdish-dominated parts of Iran in the 14th century. They speak in a Kurdish dialect known as Gorani, believed in reincarnation, and for much of Iraq's modern history suffered intense persecution and marginalization.

Much like the Yazidis, the minority Kakayi were threatened with annihilation after ISIS branded them "infidels." Exact numbers of the remaining endangered religion's population are unknown, but their community leaders estimate around 75,000 followers.

It took two full days of ardent fighting in Tulaband to finally push ISIS out in late May of that year. They lost nine of their men in that battle alone, but more than sixty had already paid the ultimate price since the battalion had been formed.

We climbed back into our vehicle and drove deeper into the destruction, stopping outside a home to sit with some civilians who had assembled on plastic chairs in the afternoon sultriness.

These were a few of the thirty-odd Kakayi families who had returned to their homes upon their recent liberated from ISIS. Their homes were now poised on the firing frontline — but they preferred to live on luck, or perhaps on faith. They preferred to take back what had been ripped from them than to languish any longer in overcrowded displacement camps or try to pay rent they could not afford.

"This is where I was born and raised. This village belongs to us, to our grandfathers," said Falah, who had returned three weeks ago with his wife and two young daughters. "That is why I came back. It's a strange feeling, an exciting feeling."

But since returning, his youngest daughter, Raifa, had stopped speaking. Falah said that she refused to walk or stand. He said she always "stuck to someone" — most often her mother — with trembling lips.

Raifa — a name meaning tenderhearted — was a beautiful, delicate little girl with enormous brown eyes and light olive skin. She sat on her mother's lap in the shade, playing with an empty soda bottle, staring into nothingness. When I tried to speak to her, her long black lashes fluttered closed, as if she were retreating into another world far from this one; as if to protect herself from the horror of reality.

"We think she has a sickness, maybe," Falah whispered to me. "She has shock from coming back. She is hurting."

Most of the women, all in-laws, wore black abayas woven with tiny sparkles. They spent their days together making tea, talking, and praying in that shady spot underneath the house awning. Two women lay on the floor, moaning — it was hard to know if they were awake or dreaming. Falah told me no one there was ever really sleeping.

Falah's other brother, Dyab, noted that he could not yet return to his home in the neighboring village of Wardak, but he was helping his brother rebuild. Their other brother Ahmed, however, had moved back to his nearby home eighteen days earlier with his four children, even though only part of his house was still standing — the rest of it ensanguined by multiple rocket attacks.

"We couldn't keep paying rent anymore," Ahmed explained helplessly.

At one point, the brothers had good jobs as soldiers-turned-truck drivers and construction contractors. Dyab proudly showed me a Certificate of Appreciation he had received for his service to American troops during the U.S.-led occupation.

"Your hard work and dedication with the 950th Maintenance and Coalition forces has been a great asset not only to the Pedestrian Gate but to the success of Operation Iraqi Freedom," read the creased piece of paper, impressed with both the U.S. and Iraqi flags.

The certificate, he said, was all he took when the approaching black flags forced them to flee.

The brothers had all been rendered jobless by the ISIS onrush and now had nothing but distant memories to their name.

"ISIS looted everything, everything," one of Ahmed's son said in fluent English as he guided us through his home, which still featured the graffitied name of the fighter — Abu Janat — who had seized it. "Even the doors and windows. Everything. They took everything."

Dyab had the opposite problem; he said when he returned to his house, it was bursting to the brim with beat-up furniture and random objects.

"My house was the ISIS headquarters," he explained. "So they threw everything in there. I had everyone come in. Some of our neighbors were able to recognize their things and take them back."

Given the families' premature return, there was no running water or electricity. They shared a well for water and a small generator that gave them two hours of electricity a day to cook some food and charge their phones.

Falah's spacious home was nearly empty, but so spotless you could see your reflection twinkling in the marble tiles. The furniture consisted of a few mattresses, mops, and buckets. The cleanliness was how they retained their self-respect, their ownership. The view from the large window was one of burned belongings, window palings, and dead plants.

The men took turns guarding the roof overnight to watch for ISIS infiltrators. The parents were on constant high alert to ensure that the children did not cross the road into the fields littered with landmines. And how easy it was to forget they were children as they carried such heaviness on their shoulders. They often slept with their eyes open, one mother told me. Terrorists had pounded the place, and they worried it would happen all over again.

"They know what is going on. They are careful that they don't get too far away from the house," Falah said. "They are good kids."

They needed a school for the children, he continued. Some days, he drove them down a treacherous road twenty miles to the nearest school in Kalak.... but that was just some days.

I sat on the steps and watched the families mingle until the sun started to turn pink.

A few of the children squealed in delight, chasing each other in tiny circles. One of them, no older than six and mentally disabled, showed me the scar bored into the back of his head from a traumatic head surgery. No one could — or wanted to — detail what had happened to him. The child smiled and high-fived me, his eyeballs rolling, before returning to run in circles within the safety of the perimeter.

I noticed that most of the young always needed to be close to their fathers, either holding their hands or clinging to their sides, desiring to touch all they had left to protect them.

From the surface, it appeared as though these families' lives were broken. Everything they had was broken; but they were not. Living together in their butchered village was not only survival, but part of a broader, collective healing. They had each other.

Five of their Kakayi shrines had been bombed into oblivion.

"Look." Falah beckoned me over to see a devoid hilltop across the way where one of the shrines perched. "This was the second time our village was destroyed. Yesterday it was Saddam. Today it is ISIS. Tomorrow will be something else. We are always under threat."

Only one business had reopened. It used to be a medical clinic and was now a window repair shop to help the returnees with reconstruction. Graffiti smeared its lavender sidewalls. The black words "Medical Clinic" had been written over in grey with the words "Islamic State Remains," over which, even more recently, "Viva Peshmerga" had been scrawled.

I finished my tea and we parted ways with smiles and waves. In a few days' time, mayhem would again reign around them. Would they stay, or would they run for their lives once again?

Echoing that the ISIS war in Iraq was in its twilight, I stopped on the returning ride and watched a handful of laborers. They had already taken to repairing the road adjoining Al-Khazer Bridge over the murky green Tigris. At one point, that bridge had served as a critical supply route for ISIS between towns. At another point, it was a casualty of an airstrike intended to cut ISIS's ease of access. Now, it was on the mend for the Iraqi people.

A couple of weeks later, those tents would fill with homeless families trying to make sense of the past several years of ISIS's domination and wondering what would come next.

DO NOT PITY THEM
October, 2016

Despite the reality slap accompanying all the horror, carnage, and devastation, there was something that still felt unreal about war and terrorism — something an outsider could never really make sense of; that made it hard to imagine stability. As outsiders, we have the luxury to walk away, record the suffering of another, analyze it, share it, and then escape it.

There is something about time spent in a war hospital — time spent holding the hand of a once strong and noble young man who wanted nothing more than to protect — that robs one of that escapism. The vision of soldiers whose lives had not been lost, with the life once inside fizzled to nothing, cements itself into one's soul. It becomes something that will sit inside one's mind forever.

Doctors are never given enough credit for saving lives, not in the immediate moment nor in the weeks and months following that moment — they keep hearts beating and encourage their patients to stay strong.

It was a suffocating morning when I visited the Emergency Medical Center (EMC) in the Erbil city center, a crumpled collection of chipped white walls and rectangular rooms. There was a small courtyard with dying geraniums and a towering minaret in the background. Hospital officials led me past faded doors labeled "Spinal Injury Unit" and into a conference room lit by bright fluorescent lights, furnished with an old-fashioned projector and a table cluttered with translucent plastic tubes. It smelled faintly of disinfectant. But mostly, it smelled somber — or what I imagined somber would smell like if it could be a fragrance.

The moments spent in war hospitals are rubberlike moments, stretched out and on the verge of snapping. They are either riddled in chaos or filled with an almost terrible silence. What was worse? Sometimes chaos is a dreadful thing and silence is good. No casualties in this hour. But sometimes, the chaos means the fallen have at least survived; sometimes, the silence means that no one made it through.

What does war look like? It isn't just blistered buildings and empty brass casings and displacement camps. War looks like wounds, and soldiers who don't resemble fierce fighters but are mere men in unfathomable pain. Soldiers belong to someone; they are a mother's child. Someone created them and brought them into the world, only for the world to rip them apart. And for what? Was it worth it? It was always the question on my mind, but ever the hardest to ask.

Some of the injured men were already seated at the conference table when I entered. Others slowly wafted in. Shadows idled beside them; I felt as though I could see who they used to be. There was always the before. And then the after. Life for people living under the constant threat of war is organized into intervals. The beginning of one war, the end of one war, and then the start of the next — the beginning of one power struggle and the end of the next. They could be an individual one day, and the next, someone they no longer recognized.

The hospital suits sat down and we started the conversation on something of a positive note — ISIS was losing. The Peshmerga had clocked up several battlefield victories, liberating villages and expanding their border. But nothing in this war had come easy. According to medical personnel, the soldier death toll stood at 1,600 since the ISIS war began, but would have been far higher had they not had training from the U.S.-led coalition.

"In the early days, we would have seventy wounded soldiers coming in all at once from one battle, only a few nurses and doctors who would work three shifts without a break," Pshtiwan Aziz, Manager of the Emergency Management Center (EMC), told me. "But now they have had American training; many less are coming in with wounds. Just a few from even big battles."

For many, even basic training was brand new — learning how to use tourniquets and appropriately bandage bodily bullet holes, understanding the correct side position to place the injured during transport, and memorizing resuscitation techniques. Training for thousands — mostly conducted in large units — lasted several weeks, and each training block was tailored toward the needs of that unit. According to the Department of Defense (DOD), Improvised Explosive Devices (IEDs) had caused the majority of casualties — eighty to eighty-five percent, urging coalition personnel to teach techniques and strategies to remedy that threat.

The training was said to have been particularly crucial leading up to the highly-anticipated Mosul offensive, especially given that the Kurds did not have the medical-evacuation helicopters and extensive dispatch of well-equipped mobile hospitals that many wealthier armies maintained. Relying on their brothers-in-arms was the best chance they had.

But now, soldiers and medical staff faced a fight of a different kind — no money and no medicine to treat the almost 9,500 that had been seriously wounded. The tiny hospital — if one could even call it that — had no MRI equipment or CT scanners. It reminded me of poor clinics of a Soviet time and place.

Despite sitting atop some of the planet's most prominent oil refineries, the brutal war had ravished the economy. Some referred to the piling debt as a "worse threat than ISIS."

A combination of substantial military costs associated with the ongoing operation, the deluge of refugees and displaced persons from Iraq, and continued federal budget bickering with Baghdad had cast a dire financial gloom that was likely to linger long after the brutal jihadist group had gone. And soldiers would bear the brunt of the increasing economic woes.

Thousands of battered soldiers were taken to public hospitals across the region, many miles from the frontlines, where they had to compete with other casualties in an overburdened healthcare system. A handful of what doctors described as "fortunate" soldiers — severely injured ones requiring complex surgeries — had been sent to places like India, Turkey, Jordan, and Germany. But absorbing those costs also meant more mass debt for the government.

Inside the EMC, the frustration was barefaced. There were thousands of open, unresolved case files. Several soldiers — young faces, old faces, and with body parts gone — came forward to outline their predicaments and pain, to reconstruct the blows to their bodies. I feverishly jotted down all I could in my fraying notebook. They had each brought with them a plastic case that contained their diagnosis, clinical evidence of their condition confined to a simple folder.

Phwan Ishmael, thirty-one years old, was an engineering student who wore a white shirt that said "LOVE" in silver block letters. He had been diffusing a roadside bomb for the Peshmerga on Christmas Eve in 2014 when it exploded. His two comrades died, much of his body was burned, and his thigh skin had been reduced to ash. Phwan passed out immediately and woke to feel warm blood gushing from his eyes. He stared at his white-gold wedding band as he said the worst part was losing his hearing, and the constant humming noise in his head. He knew the noises didn't exist, at least not to anyone but himself.

Karwan Saeed, thirty-seven years old, attended the hospital meeting proudly dressed in his soldier's uniform. He was one of the first victims of an ISIS chemical attack. Just outside of Mosul a year earlier, Saeed had gone to inspect a Katyusha rocket that hit a few meters in front — not knowing of its "chemical element," or that ISIS even had chemical capabilities at that stage. Ever since, his body and eyes welled up incessantly and his skin erupted into excruciating rashes. He pulled out a bar of oatmeal soap and bottles of medicines with dramatic names.

"I use all the pills and the soap," Saeed told me earnestly, like a child assuring his teacher that he had been following all the playground rules. "But I feel it is not working."

Karwan was still fighting on the frontline. But he constantly itched, he could not sleep, and he felt as though he was "always agitated." You could see it — the way his eyes crawled.

Meanwhile, Khider Merkir, a forty-two-year-old and a twenty-five-year Peshmerga serviceman, had been ambushed by an ISIS vehicle on December 18, 2015 while patrolling in the Makhmour area. A round from a BKC — also known as a PKM machine gun — cleaved below his left ear and lodged a few millimeters from the top disc in his back. The round remained in there, infected and inflamed. His hands were numb, and his head persistently ached.

"I want to remove the bullet," Khider said. "But it is a sensitive operation, and they can't do it here."

Khider did not remember being scared when the bullet penetrated his body. He remembered being frustrated, not fearful. He remembered refusing to go to the hospital until two of his fellow soldiers — lying face down on the soggy terrain, dead — had been removed from the hot zone. He stayed just two nights in the hospital before his wife and seven children took over his care at home.

Then there was Bazhar Hussein, a thirty-two-year-old who had been working on the frontlines for the region's leading security and intelligence branch, the Asayish, when the crucial first and second discs in his back were struck by a sniper's bullet in broad daylight. Reduced from a strong, able-bodied man into an almost infantile physical and mental state, Hussein could no longer control his legs, nor could he control his head and eye movements. Occasionally, he could speak slowly. But other times, his eyes just swelled with confused tears as the words would not come out.

"He wasn't like this before; he used to be able to talk. But now it is getting worse and worse," one nurse explained softly, helping him reach for the walker. "But that's what this war has done to people."

Pummeled by four bullets in Kirkuk on June 29, 2015, twenty-nine-year-old Mohammad Othman needed a new elbow, as did Shakhawan Mohammad, thirty-four, who had been gorged by a rocket blast on January 27, 2016.

Akmad Ailli, thirty-three, soon stumbled in on crutches. He had been hurt inside the Syrian border town of Rabia on June 23, 2014. He had gotten word through his radio that a roadside bomb had just struck some members of his unit. On his way up the mountain to help, he too was injured by a hidden explosive device. Akmad woke up seven meters away from where his vehicle burned, his weapon in hand. He had wanted to fire back.

"I tried to stand up and couldn't," he said slowly. "I looked down and I saw then that my leg was backward."

Bundles of nerves and muscles and bone had since been extracted. Akmad said that he missed the small things — being able to use the standard hole in the ground toilet; to sit without squirming in discomfort; to get in and out of vehicles on his own; to feel his leg —and above all, being able to fight.

Sometimes, soldiers can't claim direct combat for their injury. It was in the more mundane moments of their war-devoted lives that tragedy befell them.

Khnabi Othman, sixty-five years old, had been hurrying to the frontline on August 5, 2015 when his car and legs were mangled in a collision. Mihedini Miho, who appeared far older than his forty-five years, had been shot on five separate occasions throughout the conflict in the 90s. These old war wounds were still haunting.

"Problems with my bladder," he said sheepishly when I asked about his biggest medical challenge.

But the person who had waited the longest for treatment was thirty-six-year-old Nabil Majeed. He had become the first Peshmerga casualty of the war in July 2014. He had been inside a Christian village near Mosul when he sniped an ISIS operative putting up propaganda posters in the street. In return, a rash of bullets battered Majeed's body — then another rash. He recalled vividly how the shots kept coming. Even when he thought he could take no more, they kept coming. He drew a breath and took them all in — and he survived.

Since that day, Nabil had part of his tongue and nine teeth removed. He could no longer close his left eye or chew. Because his nerves were riddled with damage, two of his ribs were removed in a complicated bone graft operation and inserted into his face where his jaw had once existed. Life for him was full of was hospital visits and useless surgeries.

I held his x-rays and photographs up to the light, examining how the flesh had been ripped from his cheeks and the pockets of blood had turned black and bubbly, the holes in his insides glowing an uncooked pink.

Only he showed no anger. His eyes were loving and calm.

"I miss going outside in the sun. Now the sun makes my eye swell, and I always feel like something is in front of my eye," he explained, nostalgia in his voice. "Something is always in front of me. And I don't know what it is."

In the coming weeks, the sight of infected mortar rounds and lodged bullets too risky to remove became commonplace. I would meet more and more soldiers with crippled bodies and anguished faces, but rarely would I meet one who complained. There were no regrets. Hospitals had become their prison, a place they could never be free from — but if asked to answer that most difficult question, they said price they paid was worth it.

"I would do it all over again," Hassan Kheder, fifty-two, assured me without a moment's hesitation.

Hassan had run out of ammunition in a firefight on the chilly autumn night of November 16, 2015. ISIS attacked them at their post, having snuck through the bushes under the starless evening sky. In a split second, as Hassan was changing magazines, a round from an AK-47 at close range clipped his shoulder bone. For forty-five minutes, Hassan fought back until four of his enemies were killed and the rest had retreated. Hassan had been preparing to retire from the military that very day — before he lost the ability to raise his arm and before his clavicle bone was removed in emergency surgery.

The doctors told him there was nothing more they could do to help.

These men had been robbed of bones and body parts that could not grow back. Some had lost their minds. But none had lost their self-respect; they were heroes who did not look like conventional heroes, but constituted what the Hollywood depiction of heroes should have been.

For the Peshmerga, there was no questions as to why they were fighting. They knew exactly what they were fighting for and for whom they were fighting — they were fighting an enemy called ISIS, and they were fighting for

Kurdistan.

Late that night, I made the quick flight to Beirut, Lebanon for some meetings. I wandered through the bustling, French-colonized city with its cultural cafes, artist enclaves, trendy hookah bars, and light ocean breezes. I visited the quiet Lady of Lebanon and took photographs from the spiral staircase that looked out upon the dainty country, still scarred from its own fifteen-year war. From 1975 to 1990, a quarter of a million Lebanese people died in the multi-sectarian conflict for power and control. The destruction was still raw, the pain still apparent.

I lit candles and sent silent thoughts for Iraq; for Syria; for the civilians caught in the crossfire; for the brave men and women; for the many friends I had met along the way.

I had received official word that the Mosul offensive would begin within hours. Striking another match, I prayed for the ones who would survive — and the ones who would not. As I walked past a shop front before heading back to the airport, I stopped to read a small wooden plaque taped in a glass window. It was the poem "Pity the Nation," published in 1934 by acclaimed Lebanese American writer and artist, Kahlil Gibran.

"Pity the nation that is full of beliefs and empty of religion.
Pity the nation that wears a cloth it does not weave
and eats a bread it does not harvest.

Pity the nation that acclaims the bully as hero,
and that deems the glittering conqueror bountiful.

Pity a nation that despises a passion in its dream,
yet submits in its awakening.

Pity the nation that raises not its voice
save when it walks in a funeral,
boasts not except among its ruins,
and will rebel not save when its neck is laid
between the sword and the block.

Pity the nation whose statesman is a fox,

whose philosopher is a juggler,
and whose art is the art of patching and mimicking

Pity the nation that welcomes its new ruler with trumpeting,
and farewells him with hooting,
only to welcome another with trumpeting again.

Pity the nation whose sages are dumb with years
and whose strongmen are yet in the cradle.

Pity the nation divided into fragments,
each fragment deeming itself a nation."

SLEEPERS IGNITE IN KIRKUK
October, 2016

ISIS was desperate to cling to its fragmenting territory. And to do that, it was growing ever more rash and violent.

It was days into the official start on the Mosul onslaught. The noose around the big city was tightening. The Iraqi forces were moving in from the west and the Kurdish fighters from the east. Both armies were smashing through villages and cleansing them of the terrorists. Coalition airplanes were dropping bombs from high in the sky with the flashes of fire leaving large plumes in their wake.

Mini victories were being called, and officials were quick to praise the progress on social media. But behind the curtain of applause, IEDs exploded; civilians ran from their homes, and soldiers dropped. It was a chaos that military planners knew would come when the highly-anticipated operation went underway, but it came with a prohibitive cost, in a currency that could not be repaid: the currency of good peoples' blood.

That was war.

Local Kurdish friends spent one especially harrowing night in October scooping up dozens of dead bodies from the battlefields of nearby Christian villages — beloved members of their tribes. As I flew in the predawn hours from Istanbul, they went door-to-door delivering the news to families and the lifeless frames to the morgue. Most of the fallen soldiers were in their twenties and thirties, married, with young families. Most came from poor, working-class families. Without the man of the house, those families now faced a future of abysmal financial hardship. But before their surviving loved ones could even think of how they would possibly make ends meet, they would mourn.

After just a couple hours of sleep — the kind of troubled, dreamless sleep — I woke on Friday to the Call to Prayer and the news that Kirkuk was ablaze with battles. It was characterized as a "sneak attack" intended to distract from the Mosul operation and launched by an ISIS sleeper cell, stoking fears that more jihadists were submerged in the vast sea of displaced people.

I chugged down some bitter Arabic coffee and grabbed my vest — I was going to Kirkuk. Located about one hundred miles southeast of Mosul, Kirkuk was a source of tension between Iraqi and Kurdish forces. Technically, it belonged to the territory of the Central Government, but the Kurds had stepped in and taken over in 2014 after Iraqi army units reportedly fled upon ISIS's approach. It was a quick bid to stop the terrorists from dominating the oil-rich domain, and a strategic win for the savvy Kurdish government.

The closer we came to the Kirkuk entry checkpoint, the murkier the sky became, obscured by strips of smoke from the burning oil rigs. Everything was tainted by exhaust flames and the smell of cordite. We slowed a couple of miles from the checkpoint, examining the protracted line of halted incoming oil trucks. No one was going in, and no was going out. A stymied scrum of news crews set up live positions as close as they could get. Scores of families sat in the dirt staring at the sun, parents chain-smoking cigarettes as kids kicked at stones, unable to reach their home.

"Cluster fuck," were the precise words I scribbled into my notebook. There was no other appropriate description.

Checkpoint closed? No problem. It paid to have friends of friends who specialized in smuggling. After making some phone calls, we disappeared into the lush corn fields and narrow backroads strewn with empty farmhouses, trailing an old beat-up car that knew the "smugglers route." For thirty years under Saddam's reign, the green patches set against the dun plains were a military-only zone. Guarded by uniformed men, Arab nomads were forced to do the laborious work.

After 2003, the Kurdish villagers slowly started to return and reclaim their pastures and sun-beaten slate roofs.

We sped through twists and turns until we entered Kirkuk city — until I saw the red "WELCOME" block letters I had seen several times before.

Today, not even the ghosts were even out to play. The city was without signs of life. Imams had shut down all mosques in Kirkuk, canceling Friday prayers as the place had been turned into an urban battle zone. Overnight, the government had instituted a curfew, and nobody dared step out. The shops had been barred and locked, and the curtains of houses drawn. Families stayed inside and cowered as the city around them was strangled.

Just hours earlier, multiple suicide bombers had detonated on police posts inside the city. Shooters took up positions in a mosque, a school, a hotel, and on top of other buildings, shooting like rabid dogs from the roof.

We made our way through the wide, empty roads towards fierce clouds of smoke where the brunt of the battle raged.

I spotted a patrolling Iraqi Federal policeman, his rifle slung tight across his chest, and I rolled down the window. He told me that the terrorists had spread into three locations and questioned how I got inside, glaring like I was crazy. Maybe I was. Suicide bombers were sparking. Gun powder stuck to the air.

Although sensing uncertainty, we continued to the gates of the Peshmerga base that teemed with guards. After flashing my press pass, my driver and I were granted access to the fortified building. Dozens of soldiers and intelligence personnel skirted around bucolically, bracing for possible attacks, scanning the streets below. Others sat around the television watching the mayhem unfold, sipping tea and cracking jokes. It was like 2003 all over again, one of them exclaimed with a cheeky smile. Soon after the fall of Saddam Hussein, Kirkuk transformed into a hotbed of looting and jihadism. The city settled throughout the U.S. occupation but was still subject to random outbursts of flying shrapnel and bullets. In August 2011, five churches were targeted by insurgent bombs. Eleven months later, thirty-eight people went out to a local café for food and never came home — blown to bits.

"We have been facing this kind of disease for years now. We know how to respond," said Adnan Kocher, senior adviser to Lahur Talabani, the head of intelligence and counterterrorism for Kurdistan. Adnan had smoky, sleepless rings around his eyes and a composed, stoic demeanor.

The enemy had pushed his buttons, and now he was pushing back — this time on his terms.

Adnan explained that around 3:00 A.M., jihadists who had been living among the 70,000 refugees in surrounding camps had packed their children into six cars and drove through a checkpoint into Kirkuk. Once inside, they rallied an estimated one hundred confederates inside the city for the pre-planned attack. The mob then opened fire on citizens, security forces, and Iranians working at a power plant. At least thirty people were already dead, including ten suspected ISIS fighters who had detonated suicide belts as the security forces closed in.

In between cigarettes and phone calls, Adnan narrated that officials had received intelligence five days earlier from their sources within ISIS about a sleeper cell that was preparing to wake up. They did not know exactly where or how the cell would act out, but it had afforded them some time to brace.

However, he cautioned that the problem extended beyond the threat that lay among the displacement camps. Arab villages inside Kirkuk included ISIS supporters who helped — and then harbored — the killers. Adnan believed that dozens of members of the cell that struck that day melted into a population of thousands of citizens who quietly backed the ISIS ideology.

Frantic authorities had spent the morning calling for troops to return from the Mosul area. The distraction had worked.

Adnan lamented that the left-driven media and human rights groups had made their task next to impossible. He said that they were "part of the problem," and for weeks had accused the security forces of human rights abuse for detaining families with known jihadist ties. He insisted that their intense public criticism had made it difficult for law enforcement to carry out stringent security checks.

"But we have a good plan," Adnan assured me, adding that the cell would be hunted down and eliminated over the next few days. And he had more fingers to point.

"Turkey is trying to bring problems to Kirkuk," he went on.

Weeks earlier, Turkish President Recep Tayyip Erdogan vowed that his troops would play a role in the battle for Mosul. He made it clear that he intended to ramp up the Turkish involvement in Iraq. The bold proclamations had alarmed the Iraqi government and threatened a sideshow war outside of ISIS's mission. Erdogan postured that the Sunni-majority Mosul was part of his historical responsibility, while the Shia-dominant Baghdad government cautioned the Turks to stay out.

Kirkuk was a garrison of support for the Patriotic Union of Kurdistan (PUK) stronghold, a predominant political party opposing the KRG. The PUK had tighter relations with Tehran, who considered Ankara its archenemy. Complicating matters further, the KRG boasted strong diplomatic relations with the Turkish leadership given oil trade relations. Tensions from all sides were boiling over.

Outside, the sun was falling. I mingled in with the soldiers in the compound until the sky faded from blue and pink to navy and black. I felt as though I was in a gilded ivory palace with its high wrought iron gates and swaths of armed guards. But there was no Rapunzel on the roof — just half a dozen uniformed men with binoculars and sniper rifles who eyed me suspiciously until I gave them a wave, to which they smiled and enthusiastically waved back.

That night, more Kurdish and Iraqi police swarmed the city to squash the threat. More ISIS snipers circled, more lives were lost, and more anxiety trickled in. Over the next few days, the fighting raged on. Several jihadists attempted to open fire but were met with bullets to the backs of their heads. Others blew up their own bodies when cornered by authorities.

The 2016 Raid of Kirkuk, as it became known, finally ended after Iraqi forces killed the local ISIS commander, Abu Qudama. Several more ISIS members were detained, including Saddam's cousin, Mahmud Abdul Ghani. By the time the militants had been mopped up, ninety-nine civilians and members of the security forces were dead and one hundred and fifty were wounded, while sixty-three of ISIS's own were slain.

JUST ASH AND BONES
October, 2016

The vapor of the slain ambled even miles away. People will always tell you in times of war they can smell the slain from far, far away. Maybe it's just instinct — but it becomes a smell, real or otherwise.

I hadn't been to Sinjar since the summer of 2015. At that time, fifteen months earlier, the city below the curling mountain was still occupied by ISIS. We had taken a different route as we made our way up the rugged incline to the Peshmerga base on top, a base where you could gaze down on the Yazidi-majority city under the wrath of airstrikes and the iron fists of terrorists. I remember marveling at that mountain, built like a spiral staircase, a classic, breached anticline structure. Rumors persisted that Saddam's notoriously barbarian and bluntly evil son, Uday Hussein, used those twists and turns to race his many decked-out sports cars.

With each twist and turn of that summer journey, we ascended further into a world belonging to the beginning of time. Our driver that day had been fast and reckless, and there were so many of us squished into the vehicle that we needed to take turns lying down in the trunk. Each of us had our turn of being thrown against the roof, heads cracking on the hardtop. Begging to "slow down" became meaningless, and I gave way to putting my fate in the driver's hands as the car lurched up and down the braided edges of the mountain.

Finally, the villages bloomed into view and we weaved through the devastating remnants of those who had tried to flee. Overturned picnic tables and clothes were strewn across the road along with vehicles burned to the frame and trucks on their sides, withering under the strain of the summer sunshine.

Among it all, people walked barefoot on the earth and coasted on the backs of donkeys. Instinctively, I took off my sunglasses as I wanted to make eye contact when I waved. Every person I encountered waved back.

In many ways, I remember thinking that mountain protected them. They roamed freely through their forsaken streets, even if a little lost. In contrast, below them, you could see the towns still oppressed by the ISIS rule. At night, as we waited at that frontline Peshmerga base on the mountaintop drinking tea, the counter-intelligence officers would explain how ISIS operations were changing.

"They used to be out in the open, but now there are more airstrikes, so it has driven them underground," one official told me.

The operatives would call in coordinates for the airstrikes with a simple telephone call to the coalition, and they would share information at checkpoints through the open radio.

It was all they had, the Peshmerga official explained helplessly. They did not possess advanced, covert communication contraptions. But the simplicity worked both ways. One afternoon, we climbed on a roof at the base to take photos of the city below. A sweet soldier quickly cautioned us to come down because "we hear on the radio that the ISIS snipers can see you too."

On this visit, in the late fall of 2016, it was a straight shot to Sinjar along what they called the Syria Road, an artery that bordered the neighboring country — a country also spilling its blood in more ways than one.

The hours spent bumping alongside the colossal plains gives one plenty of time to think — sometimes about existential things like human life and its value, sometimes about more trivial things like the fabrics I wanted to buy at the bazaar, and what I could make out of them when I returned home. I didn't like thinking about going home; there was a part of me that wanted to stay in the war bubble forever with these people.

To deeply understand the situation — the genocide — I felt very strongly that I had to be there to experience it. But even so, I could not comprehend how humans could go on doing this to other humans. One cannot make sense of things that truly don't make any sense. And yet, still we try. Why? Because even if there is no sense to it, we have to try make sense of what remains when the war does not want war anymore.

On the way to Sinjar with Yakhi that day, we stopped by the ancient Christian village of Alquosh to collect a bottle of aged red wine from the cellar of the Monastery of the Virgin Mary. The village was poised atop a featherbed hill, the grounds silent and serene and filled with secrets. The sky's light streamed into the open courtyard and candles burned below the mural of the Virgin Mary and the Christ Child above the main altar — both figures of God pictured standing in a wheat field, a symbol of heaven's blessing for bountiful harvests.

It was easy to forget that just miles away through the flat plains of no-man's-land was ISIS-held territory. And the vicious fighting between factions was etching closer and closer to that large city.

I was told the monastery was mostly a "Monk School," as most of the Christian community went to prayer services closer to the towns instead. There was also a monk cemetery below the floor. I peered down into the pitch-black wedge. The young church caretaker explained that three monks were resting, locked in a cupboard below my feet. By tradition, they didn't bury them. Their bodies were preserved, and five years after they died, the cupboards would be opened.

"Just ash and bones are left," the caretaker quipped.

There was an orphanage as well. The children moved through the gardens and schisms of daylight — the children of God.

We ventured into the tiny old village — a place I had come to love over the years. So rich in religion and history, with its primitive stone huts and shy residents peeping from the hand-crafted archways, it was the kind of place you wanted to cocoon you because it felt like you would never grow old. There, it was as if time had frozen... as if everything was at peace and nothing more could be taken from you — even though almost everything had, indeed, been taken from the dwindling Christian community in Iraq.

But we had to drive on.

Occasionally, I saw a man by the roadside roaming aimlessly with a rifle in hand. Sometimes I saw congregations of men by the fruit stands playing cards. Young children — children who should have been in school — sold water bottles and cigarettes on the road with towels wrapped around their heads to protect them from the heat. Women walked together, sheathed in black burkas, covering the fronts of their strollers with sheets to protect their infants from the spring wrath.

The lone tin sheds and infinite fields reminded me of my childhood in North Queensland, spent on my grandfather's sugarcane fields, dotted by rusted tractors plowing in the distance.

There always seemed to be someone there to help the broken-down cars at the side of the road. There was a sense of togetherness despite the fractured continuance of history wracking the region.

What is war? The best of humanity shoved in with the worst of it.

We passed Ferris wheels, erected to climb into the sky, that never moved. There were water slides too, but they often stopped several feet from the concrete ground below.

Our driver was a gentleman named Fareed. He had big, hazel eyes and a childlike softness in the way he spoke. He was a Kurdish Jew and a Star of David swung from the review mirror. He told me "bad petrol" had ruined the engine of his armored vehicle — an irony given we were in the land of oil. So instead, we took a standard four-wheel drive despite heading into the hot zone. I was cautioned multiple times by worried officials that they were expecting ISIS to launch attacks around Sinjar that night as another diversion from the Mosul operation.

We reached the final security checkpoint for civilians. From this point, there were to be no journalists, Kurdish civilians, or any other type of foreigner moving through. Only approved military personnel and Yazidis were granted access.

Two men had just been found dead near Sinjar Mountain after joining the Peshmerga forces, with Kurdish officials pointing their fingers at both the Kurdistan Workers Party (PKK), a Kurdish militia, which the U.S. State Department officially designated as a terrorist group. Although the leaders of both groups denied responsibility, it was a sign of things getting nasty with factions — all of whom were on the side of fighting ISIS. Reports of engineers abducted in the region also filtered in and raised alarm. No one knew what this footnote could evolve into.

I waited in the hot sun for hours as Yakhi navigated the approval process, passing the time by sketching the faded army-green crevices of the mountains. Fareed whispered that I should put my notebook away; it was making the security guards nervous.

I watched the weathered supply trucks come in, loaded with diapers, chip packets, fizzy orange drinks, and sunflower oil. The workers unloaded everything, box by box, for inspection, as buckets of sweat poured from their pores. Once they approved the load, they spent hours repacking everything, strapping the boxes down with frayed ropes. The process could have easily been avoided with technology, but there were no high-tech scanners here. Fareed told me this was why everyone wanted to leave the region — it's the trivial things, he said, like making the poor food traders burn their bodies up with all the unnecessary loading and reloading. He was excited to have started learning English and said that he wanted to live in Washington, D.C. someday.

"It's a disaster for all humanity in the Middle East," Fareed went on, busting open a potato chip packet given to us by one of the food traders, telling me that he thought the security was worried every time they saw us smiling and laughing. "Maybe they are used to seeing people laugh and then blow themselves up."

Even laughter had become a dangerous concept to those consumed by this war.

Finally, we were issued the clearance to pass through. I gave Fareed a tight hug goodbye and hopped into the vehicle of a Yazidi Peshmerga soldier named Amer. A Kurdish flag hung proudly from his mirror and now and then I would catch him glancing at it with affection. Hours passed as we drove on. The old-fashioned power lines looked like aisles of divine crosses trimming the barren road. The round sun was the boldest I had ever seen it, but the way it glimmered down on the destruction below was almost insulting. Syria stood on one side of the road, Iraq on the other.

There was no border sign, wall, or fence to tell you where one country ended and the other began — just landmines.

A VICTORY FOR GENOCIDE
October, 2016

We made it to the Yazidi village of Sinonwy where families had recently started to return. It had taken months to cleanse the village of landmines, and still nobody could be sure it was totally safe.

Amer owned a bakery on the ground floor within the town and, above it, a clothing store that featured tons headless mannequins modeling cheap western-style clothes in the window. He said he had something he needed to collect on our way. I waited in the car outside his little set-up — adorned with a "Shangal Mall" sign — while they retrieved a 50-caliber machine gun, which they harnessed to the back of the truck as if it were the most normal thing in the world. Then we drove onward to the frontlines of Sino.

Yazidi soldiers sat in tiny huts at sunset, making tea and smoking cigarettes, the light flurries of their smoke disappearing into the sky's strips of pink.

Of course, the incoming attacks could begin at any moment, but it clearly did not frighten them. They were as ready as they ever could be. They were always ready. The post had been viciously attacked the night before by bombs from the air and bombs tied to bodies. ISIS infiltrators had snuck to their position, but not close enough to kill their enemy. They sent themselves to hell with a push of a button. They had torn the limbs from their sockets and heads from their shoulders. I studied the photographs. Some had died with their eyes wide open in shock and others had bled out — their hair falling over their faceless heads.

One thing was for sure: none of them looked as though they were anywhere near the coveted "paradise." What was left of them was packed into trucks and sent away to a final resting place. No one seemed to know where or how, nor did they seem to care.

According to high-ranking soldiers and later affirmed by local officials, the brutal jihadist group had reached a new level of brutality since the start of the Mosul operation. They were digging deeper into the bowels of brutality, taking civilians off the streets and forcing them to the frontlines in the nearby city of Tel Afar.

The terrorists had misleadingly told residents a couple of days earlier that the sleeper cells in Kirkuk were unleashed. They lied that they had successfully "liberated" Kirkuk and regained full control of the oil-swathed city as news of heavy fighting in the region wafted out.

Tel Afar had long been marked as having one of the strongest support bases for the terrorist outfit and was considered one of the preeminent places for ISIS recruits. Much of the ISIS training happened in the mixed Shia and Sunni city, as well as weapons and bomb construction.

"When people from the town heard that Kirkuk had been taken over by ISIS, many came out to the streets to celebrate," said a prominent intel source from the Yazidi-controlled frontline of Sino, the closest frontline to Tel Afar. "With all the families out on the street, ISIS members then executed their scheme and had trucks ready, they filled them with young boys and imported them to the frontline Friday night."

ISIS was said to have used two tanker trucks, two pick-up trucks, and two armored vehicles to scoop up the minors, aged between eight and sixteen years old.

"ISIS has used all sorts of tactics and human shields many times before," Amer, who I learned was forty-three and a Lieutenant Colonel in the Yazidi Forces noted. "But this way we just saw last night, this is new."

ISIS was using the young boys for three main functions on the fateful frontline: as direct fighters, as human shields, and as suicide bombers. At around 5:30 A.M., the morning after the sleepers were ignited, just as the first rays of light rose over the Iraqi desert, a suicide vehicle came toward the Sino front from the Tel Afar line. One soldier showed me a video of the remnants of the cauterized truck and told me the three inside were just kids taken from the Tel Afar streets just a day earlier.

Two Yazidi soldiers were hurt in the suicide detonation, and they were bracing for similar attacks in coming days. The two opposing frontlines were 1.6 miles apart. By using children as shields, ISIS fighters were able to push forward with greater ease as it put their opposition on the defense rather the offense.

"The Yazidi Peshmerga tries to snipe behind the shields, but that's very hard," the official continued. "But if the shields open fire first, we have no choice but to shoot back. Otherwise, more and more of our soldiers will get killed."

Colonel Marwan Sabri, a thirty-five-year-old who oversaw the Yazidi brigade, told me later that the sick development came as no surprise.

"ISIS does not follow any international laws, they used banned weapons and children shields," he said sternly. "This is a group without any morals."

However, the notion of using young boys — who may or may not have been radicalized — in the frontline fight was one that hit hard for the Yazidi community. According to Marwan, based on their intelligence, Yazidis were fed and groomed for the very strategic purpose of fighting their own.

Thousands of Yazidis were captured on that apocalyptic day in August 2014 when the jihadists invaded in a litany of murder and evil smoke. Scores of girls and women were kidnapped and sold into sex slavery, the boys forced into jihadist training camps and radicalized to kill those who loved them most.

"The use of the children is making things very difficult for us; we don't know who those children are or if they are one of ours," Amer said, glancing wistfully over at his uniformed eighteen-year-old son, Rayan, who was also a Yazidi soldier.

Nobody flinched at the soundtrack of outgoing rockets and mortar rounds blasting from a nearby defense post.

Amer and his family lived in Germany, known to have a prominent Yazidi diaspora when their homeland was attacked. Almost immediately, he and his wife, along with their six children aged between six and twenty-two years old, returned to help protect the embattled region that they had left in 2008. Amer had been learning English before the ISIS maraud, but the war had stolen that passion from him. There was no time for such a learning luxury.

What is war? They lived their lives only to defend. That was war.

Amer and his two eldest sons joined the Yazidi brigade, made up of around 8,800 male soldiers from the heavily persecuted minority. The battalion was formed the previous year after their native region in Iraq — centered on and around Sinjar Mountain — had been overrun.

His eldest son, Aqeed, barely twenty years old, was severely injured when an ISIS mortar round slid through his back three months earlier.

"This is genocide," Amer stated flatly, now living in the devoured city of Sinjar. "We have no water, no electricity. But this is our home. We will never leave it again."

In the darkness, we made our way to the abandoned schoolhouse inside the eaten-up city of Sinjar. It was one of the few buildings that had survived, only out of luck. I was instructed to run from the vehicle and into the house as quickly as possible. If ISIS knew a foreign journalist was there, they would waste no time in striking. I was led upstairs to what would be my room — an old couch pushed against the window. The view outside was one of crushed satellite dishes, debris, books, and broomsticks. At night, the room shook with the mayhem of mortar and rockets surrounding the city. I quickly became accustomed to the noise and falling asleep with my mud-caked boots in sight by the door — ready to run if I needed to.

But, once asleep, my dreams were plagued by a nightmare — an odd nightmare, a different variation of losing my mother.

I went to bed each night with a candle still flickering, casting silhouettes against the punctured wall. I did not want to blow it out because, like a child, I found comfort in the light. Yet night after night, I would dream of losing my mother in unusual ways and forms. It had felt so real.

The dream that felt the most real of all — and the one that never left me — was hearing the news that my mother had died. Overwhelmed by shock and sadness, I stumbled outside to an old-fashioned letterbox that I remembered from my childhood: a silver box on a pole at the end of the driveway, with a door that flips up just enough for you to stick your hand inside and pull out the letters. In my haze of despair, I put my hand into the box only to be fiercely electrocuted.

I thought back to my thirty-first birthday in a Baghdad church, when all I wanted was my mother. In all the madness, I had wanted someone to take care of me.

Several of the Yazidi soldiers who stayed with me in the abandoned house — and on its bomb-wracked roof — did not know where their mothers were as they had been taken years ago by ISIS. But from a son's pained eyes, they believed that someday their mothers would come home.

The meals with the men were always the same; eggs, yogurt, and bread for breakfast, then salad with pomegranate seeds and chicken for lunch and dinner. I felt very guilty, although fortunate, to fill my stomach so well when those scattered in the ruined streets were starving.

There was no electricity outside, no running water, no sign of real life under the night sky beyond a few soldiers coming and going. The civilians who had returned to the destroyed city hid inside ravished abodes.

But in the light of day, one could see the degree to which Sinjar was a triumph for genocide. There was nothing left of their past. It was hard to imagine the lives that had lived here. The trash was heaped in piles; books, toys, and food packets burning in little fires along the streets. ISIS and airstrikes had chewed up the city so badly a year earlier that officials told me they were not even bothering to rebuild it. The first anniversary was far from celebratory. Sinjar has been buried alive by this war. The once-bustling municipal could never be again.

"We will build an entirely new city next to this town," the Sinjar Mayor, Mahma Khalil, told me one night from his makeshift headquarters — a relinquished home that had since been acquired by officials inside the extirpated city. "Economically, it is easier than to reconstruct. The infrastructure is destroyed. And there are too many bad memories here. Who wants to come back to these memories?"

The city of Sinjar once stood proud on the foot of the famous mountain with the same name.

It had been a picture of happy inhabitants, ancient traditions, farmer's markets, festive freedom, and ancient Yazidi temples for the persecuted Iraqi minority who made up eighty-three percent of the township. Now, almost every building had been butchered and burned to bits by bullets and bombs. Frames of furniture hung from mortar-fissured homes, and smoke still rose from the ashes in the streets, which had been reduced to something comparable to the end of the world.

Sinjar reeked of burned rubber. ISIS was burning tires and lighting up factories a few miles away. The houses, hospitals, schools, and cafes were all cracked or flattened to the ground.

Mahma also pointed to the practical impossibility of ensuring it could ever be safe enough for civilian populations.

"ISIS had chemical bombs here, and light uranium has been found in neighborhoods," he explained. "We don't want to infect the people."

There were the masses of hollowed buildings rife with hidden IEDs and booby traps. Before being killed or driven out, the terrorist operatives laid waste to whatever they could find. A week earlier, two soldiers entered a building, and one stepped on what appeared to be a strip of metal on the floor. In an instant, the whole remaining construct came crashing down — the result of a meticulously embedded tripwire.

Flyers that were dropped from the skies by Iraqi Forces before the offensive, informing those inside — the good folk and the bad — that "ISIS is over and there is no return" still freckled the gutted rooftops. Written in Arabic, the flyers warned them that only the Iraqi government was their rightful protector and that ISIS fighters must surrender themselves immediately or face the ultimate consequence.

Before the ISIS invasion of early August 2014, the city boasted a population of around 152,000 with a total area population of 450,000, according to the mayor. Many Sinjar villages were still in ISIS hands. Although no one could quite agree on precise figures, around 35,000 were thought to be living in desolate conditions across the countryside. That included 170 families that had filtered back into the bullet-battered, broken city because they had nowhere else to go.

Sometimes, I saw timid women step outside to find fragments of food, or children peering through gaps in the gouged fences. But mostly, they remained inside their skeleton homes, living out their traumatized lives in helplessness and fear of another assault. One morning, I saw a little girl playing in a bombed-out garden with a plastic flower. A headless doll in a blue dress lay submerged in the dirt beside her. She picked it up, stared into the void where the head should have been, and gently buried it back into the earth.

The doll felt like a cruel symbol of what this entire war had become: literal decapitation, faceless victims, lost childhoods, and shattered girls who may never be put back together again. If a little girl lost in the ruined city had wanted a hundred dolls before ISIS came, she would probably only want one now. And if she had a hundred dreams before ISIS came, she would probably be left with just one arbitrary goal going forward.

Distant rounds of incoming and outgoing mortar and rockets, followed by periods of perilous silence, was the chorus to which they had become accustomed.

Except for a few generators and wells, there was no electricity, running water, heating, telephones, schools, or services. Sinjar was an eerie Peshmerga military town made up a few officials and soldiers who slept on the roof of their command post — once a children's school — to keep guard.

There was also a sizable — albeit controversial — presence of hardened female fighters belonging to the Kurdistan Workers Party, known as the PKK, manning checkpoints and areas. While designated a terrorist organization in the U.S. due to their decades-long war with NATO-partner Turkey over Kurdish independence, the group was also attributed to saving many Yazidi lives in the ISIS incursion. Thus, they felt a sense of ownership of the land and had set up a permanent base.

The mayor told me that local administrators had already started putting together a "master plan" for the new city, and he anticipated that they would need at least $600 million to begin the process. Officials were said to have spoken to an array of government and non-government organizations in the U.S., but no practical steps forward had been reached.

"Morale to build this is very high, to give the local community jobs," Mahma assured me. "I believe, together, we can do this in two years."

But it had not yet been agreed where the "New Sinjar" would be built.

"Some want it on the left of the city, some say right," said Luqman Ibrahim, Battalion Head of the Yazidi fighters. "And then some say the city should be built upon the mountain."

Furthermore, Sinjar remained contested land between the Baghdad Central Government and the Kurdish Regional Government (KRG). That meant that the decision over which region to belong would likely need to be put to the people.

Some locals advocated for completely erasing the ruins and the horrors it held, while others had different ideas.

One Kurdish official said that they might leave the location in its state of medieval devastation, but they would turn safe areas into a monument to remember the genocide against the Yazidi people. Other town leaders said it would retain its name — one of ancestral and historical importance to their origins.

The once largest hospital in Sinjar was now a teeming mess of panels, bricks, and shell casings. Blood smeared the walls. A few rooms were still erect, spared by sheer fluke. The building that remained still served in what locals continued to call a "hospital." A doctor came from a neighboring town just once a week. Other days, a handful of brave physician's assistants tried to help those in need with a tiny cabinet holding a few outdated basics: tranquilizers, oral rehydration salts, and clofen for spinal cord injuries.

There was a little garden outside that had also been spared from heavy destruction, with lush, overgrown trees, and rusted but upright chairs. It looked as though it had been a very long time since anyone had sat inside.

Nearby, a general health clinic — a cement three-story dwelling — had also survived the bombardment. After ISIS took over the city, the clinic functioned as a hospital for its aggrieved and injured members. It was a cursed place; civilian medical files trashed the filthy floor along with Iraq-imported medications such as water purification tablets, penicillin, and syringes.

The oddly ominous words, "Don't Steal God's Property," were graffitied on a wall. Nearby was the ceremony hall. Everything around it had been gobbled up and spat out. I imagined all the weddings and birthdays and parties that had happened inside the large marble building, now coated in broken glass. I was told that the owner, a Sunni Arab, had "become ISIS" and allowed his fellow terrorists to use the room as an operations base.

However, the military approach to liberating the area — which relied heavily on aerial bombardment by the U.S.-led coalition and which was largely responsible for the complete ruination — had since been met with mixed views.

"We could have preserved Sinjar," one leading security officer for the Kurdish Asayish in the area lamented. "There are other ways we could have done this, but this method was chosen. I still don't know why."

But Mahma disagreed.

"The military and coalition did a good job. If ISIS is in a building, they need to strike and kill them," he said. "They needed to do whatever it took, even if it meant I was in that building when it was struck."

A SPECIAL CLINIC
November, 2016

For many who had been struck in the war and survived, life was reduced to waiting on other people — waiting for the magical thing that could give you back what you lost.

So much time in Iraq was spent in hospitals or thrown-together medical facilities. Hospitals had become the centerpiece for not only the living and the dead, but also for those caught on the cusp between life and death.

There was one clinic atop Sinjar, erected at the place where thousands had died of starvation and dehydration in the thick of the ISIS barrage below. The farming community, left languishing on the mountain, had since survived scorching summers and snowy, bitter winters with next to no outside assistance. That single medical facility near the winding mountain peak had saved them.

The clinic was an ad-hoc room with six patient beds and a handful of medications, run by a thirty-six-year-old woman the locals lovingly called "Hero Doctor Khansa." She was, in fact, not a doctor, but a nurse from Rojava and a refugee herself, having fled Syria after ISIS attacked in 2014. Late one night, Khansa Ali told me that she had simply started visiting displacement tents of those in need. In early 2015, demand for her aid had grown so big that she decided to set up a small clinic near the peak.

"I stay here, and I work twenty-four hours if I have to, whenever someone walks in," Khansa passionately explained from the clinic. "People have many problems — skin diseases, pregnancy complications. The hardest part to help is with the psychological illnesses. The children suffer the worst."

Khansa and her small team lived and breathed what was left of life at that clinic. Every day, dozens of the desperate came in — sometimes with mumps or measles, sometimes with their skin raw and bloody from skin infections.

Sometimes they came in with nausea, and sometimes they came in simply because they just needed to know that somebody was there. Their lives had been inscribed into stories, written with tears and blood and sickness, but their stories would not be erased.

The notion that someone like Khansa Ali cared and might help them was a powerful one.

"The Yazidi people are very kind people," Khansa said. "They will give you everything they have. That pushes me to want to help them. It is an obligation for me."

Since she was a small child, Khansa had a zest for healing. She loved books and movies about doctors; she was fascinated by medical objects and operation rooms.

Several months later, I was on a flight to Afghanistan when I learned from Yakhi that the Yazidis' only medical clinic on Mount Sinjar — Khansa's pride — had been damaged by Turkish airstrikes. Many of the genocide survivors living in squalid, ripped tents with little aid, electricity, or medical care had again fled for their lives. This time, they were running down the mountain as Turkish warplanes struck in and around the mountaintop for almost an hour.

Khansa had survived the sudden Turkish bombing by luck. She woke up to loud noises of hovering aircraft nearby, quickly rousing her patients. And they all ran... just as shells suddenly began to fall.

Several of the doubly-displaced Yazidis were rendered terrified again, huddling in tents at the mountain bed, including those just rescued from the clutches of ISIS in Mosul.

The strikes were reported to have killed at least twenty in the Iraq/Syria border area. A missile also struck a communications tower in the area, destroying a vital lifeline to the outside world for the deeply impoverished and traumatized Yazidi community.

For days afterward, the stretch of road connecting the Yazidis to the world outside remained closed.

Turkish officials justified the attack as necessary for decimating the "terror hubs" of the PKK militants and stopping them from transporting terrorists and arms into Turkey, and thus committing acts of violence against the Turkish people.

But the U.S. State Department expressed "deep concern" over the strikes. Then-spokesperson Mark Toner inferred that Turkey could not pursue its grievances against the Kurdish PKK at the expense of the fight against ISIS. The U.S.-led coalition is said to have received a one-hour warning before the attack and requested that it not be conducted due to concerns over coordination. However, Turkey — a nefarious NATO ally — went forth, targeting positions in Syria and Sinjar Mountain. To Ankara and most Kurdish people, the YPG and PKK were one in the same.

The predominantly Kurdish YPG was the primary ground force supported by the U.S. in the fight against ISIS in Syria. The closely affiliated PKK had for decades fought for Kurdish independence inside Turkey, leading to unrest and violent flare-ups. While it was not unusual for Turkish planes to bomb the mountainous region between Iraq and Turkey — some seventy miles from Sinjar and where the PKK was mostly situated — the air assault on Iraq and Syria was met with surprise and anger. Tensions between the NATO alliance were simmering.

Erdogan had vowed not to let Sinjar become a PKK base and cautioned that the strikes would continue.

"Everyone is scared. But they knew straight away that this was Turkey, the threats had been coming," one Yazidi affirmed to me over messenger. "If someone doesn't do something, it will happen again. Yazidis don't want this war."

Clusters of PKK remained scattered around Sinjar and its surrounding villages. Some Yazidis viewed them as crucial protectors given that the Peshmerga and Iraqi Army withdrew from their positions the morning ISIS marched in, allowing their slaughter. Many Yazidis have since persisted that the PKK militia came to their defense — fighting fearlessly against ISIS and rescuing vulnerable women and children. Others didn't like them, perceiving them as just another external force that sought to take territory that did not belong to them. Some worried their presence would only further endanger the fragile community.

Meanwhile, a YPG soldier in the Syrian Rojava side told me that their media center had been flattened. Evacuations from their area continued in the aftermath of the Turkish bomb blasts, and much of their medical personnel treating the wounded were in hiding.

The soldier accentuated that they were still determining the dead.

What is war? War is the reason you wake up.

There is no life outside of the conflict you eat and breathe. When you're in it, it is impossible to have a life outside of it even if you attempt the ritualistic movements of daily life. The soldiers I met may have had their families, but war always came first. It was not a choice; they had no option but to live it and breathe it. They had all abandoned their studies or deserted their livestock or quit their jobs to defend their people for a paltry paycheck — a paycheck that often did not come on time, if at all. There was no time for anything but war.

One morning in early November 2016, as sun streaks brushed the sky, ISIS launched a massive attack on Sinjar city. Shells snapping around the paper-thin wall woke me. It was the largest attack my accompanying soldiers had seen since the liberation effort. I jumped to my feet, still wearing the hoodie and running pants I had slept in. I hoisted myself up an outside wall and onto the hacked roof, where the soldiers had already set up a few plastic chairs. They were gathered like teenagers at an open-air cinema, ready to watch a war movie — only this was real.

There were family members and dear friends out on the firing line. The whistles and crackles of missiles grew louder and more frequent. Smoke plumes rose and mushroomed on for miles. They surrounded the whole east side of the city, curving around to the west as ISIS burned tires to conceal their positions. The coalition airplanes came in, and the aerial bombardment began.

Even with the strength of the air backing, the fighting did not ease. It lasted for hours. I paced, wrote, watched. It was an odd sensation, observing lives lighting up and out in front of you.

Across from my position was the Yazidi military headquarters, which had become a flurry of activity.

What is war? It is rushing in to reload ammo at the HQ and rushing back out to face the enemy; it is rushing in those mangled, and rushing back out to face the enemy, knowing you could be next on the stretcher.

I laced my boots to head to the headquarters. I had to be driven in an armored vehicle simply to cross the street; it seemed the security situation was only worsening as the Mosul offensive heated. Colonel Marwan's office reminded me of an early twentieth-century English office. An old-fashioned handgun, dagger, and cigar pipe were framed on the wall. I collapsed in a chair so soft that I slept deeply until the strong Arabic coffee came. Other Yazidi soldiers wandered in and out, each with a mustache thicker and more fabulous than the next.

According to Colonel Marwan, the Yazidi mustache originated 300 or 400 years ago when they were attacked and had to pretend to be Muslim to avoid persecution.

"But in order to tell each other who was Yazidi, the Yazidis grew their mustaches slightly longer than the Muslims," Marwan said with a smile. "It was like a little code."

Their fighting strained on into the day and the late afternoon, until I convinced them to let me come along.

THE CHEMICAL CAPITAL
November, 2016

I clicked my vest and helmet into place. A skinny soldier strapped my suitcase to the back of the truck, and with the Doshka nestled beside it, we journeyed to the frontline that they called the "chemical capital."

A slender mountain of dirt was all that separated hundreds of Yazidi soldiers from an ISIS bombardment of bombs — bombs possibly filled with chemical compounds. The frontline post, called Domiz, was poised on disputed land three miles from the city center. Ever since the area had been liberated by the Peshmerga a year earlier, after more than fourteen months of ISIS occupation, their post had become a "chemical capital." ISIS had hit them with the toxic agents thirty-one times on February 11, 2016 alone.

Luqman Ibrahim, the Battalion Leader of the Yazidi Forces, explained that the terrorist group had used three main types of chloride bombs: "sophisticated Russian-made ones, ones manufactured by the former Ba'ath Party Iraqi Army, and then they had two types of homemade chloride bombs." The first type was a rocket that disseminated the agent, and the second type was a double whammy for damage — it had a chloride-filled rocket with an attached propane gas can.

A series of U.S. airstrikes over the past five weeks was reported to have destroyed major chemical weapons factories used by ISIS in Iraq. But despite those hits, local leaders braced for ISIS to unleash its remaining chemical arsenal across its shrinking battleground. Domiz was a hot target, but the jihadists had fired their crude chemical stashes on several different frontlines in the past, even aiming at U.S. troops.

"They are still in the process of making these bombs," Colonel Marwan said. "They will use everything they can on us."

A senior official with the Asayish affirmed that "there are still many factories and places that ISIS is using to make these weapons" and they were "absolutely" sure there were many more yet to discharge.

What was most concerning to the local Sinjar leadership was not that the chemical weapons could reach their frontlines, but that they could make it inside their embattled city. That was what had happened in February of that year. Even though the once-bustling urban center was host to some 151,500 people pre-ISIS invasion, it now resembled a rubbished apocalyptic wasteland. About 170 families had trickled back into their bombed-out husks. Those lives mattered.

While no civilians were injured by the chemical warfare that had made it to the city, the fact that ISIS could reach that far was of particular concern.

Overall, thirteen of their soldiers suffered severe injuries in the chemical onslaught. A few had been able to receive treatment at a hospital in the Duhok, while some were sent to Germany for more advanced care. But more than fifty soldiers within their team had been affected to different degrees, enduring a catalog of complications from vomiting and skin rashes to swelling eyes and difficulties in breathing.

After Sinjar was taken back the previous year, liberating Yazidi forces discovered scores of ready-to-go chloride bombs and supplies hidden in warehouses, indicating that the city was likely a hub for developing and storing the deadly toxins.

The ensuing attacks prompted the forces to go through the chain of command and request some form of protective gear. However, the Ministry of Peshmerga was, according to Marwan, only able to send 100 gas masks even though their special minority force was made up of 8,000 fighters. The Kurdish government appealed to Washington and other western capitals for help in supplying masks to protect their warriors, and U.S. officials recently stated that 9,000 masks had since been issued.

Despite the lingering possibility of another chemical attack at any moment, there were no masks or protective suits in sight as the sun made its way over the Domiz front that autumn Sunday. Instead, the very young group of Yazidi soldiers — fresh-faced recruits — hoisted their rifles with strings of affixed ammunition, tightened the straps to their Kevlar helmets, and gathered up little mounds of blankets and bread.

I followed them past the Kurdish flags and stalks of fake flowers into their half-concealed positions behind the sandbags. Through the binoculars, I watched as ISIS vehicles flurried and dirt shot up at their head-quartered factory. Just as the sun fell and the cold crept in, someone wrapped a thin blanket around my shoulders.

The men stepped into their designated positions for what was to be another long night of unknowns, facing an enemy stationed less than half a mile away.

Their Domiz post, which snaked around the parched desert plain, had endured a particularly hefty attack two days earlier that wounded three. Although no chemical weapons had been used, it was suspected to be part of a technique by ISIS leadership to yet again distract from the Mosul operation by striking elsewhere.

Even amid the uptick of ISIS violence — the almost daily bombardment and sneaky incursions — Luqman, the battalion leader, was confident that the jihadist outfit was dimming.

As the warfare raged on, I sipped tea with him under the weak protection of his office roof, a house that ISIS had not so long ago inhabited.

"They used to come at us in bigger groups — now much smaller. It means they are lacking in fighter numbers," he noted. "Their morale is broken; they are still dangerous, but definitely not like before."

Russian graffiti from what was believed to be a Chechnyan fighter still stood stark across the wall. The men had better things to do than bother themselves trying to remove it. To them, it was a daily reminder that they were not just fighting a terror group, but that they were fighting the world's terror group; they were fighting the spread of Islamic extremism from every direction.

Days later, when back in Erbil with a phone signal, I messaged a Russian friend to find out what the words meant.

"The first word means clean as in well kept. The second word is *abdurachman*. The third word is *firgani*," he wrote back. "That is the literal translation. Figuratively, it could mean 'Get rid of this guy, *Abdurachman!*'"

I still didn't know what it meant, but I figured it meant to exterminate someone — something ISIS had been adept at for too long. They had operated with a scorched earth policy, intent on erasing people, places, and centuries of memories.

ISIS TOOK THEM FROM THE CURVES
November, 2016

If the sight of a township almost erased from the map was not morbid enough, the grim journey up the corked mountain where most aid agencies refused to venture could only be articulated as depressing.

The most confronting miscarriages of justice had happened on that mountain. Burned cars and clothes littered the dirt-peppered tracks; a few trees sprouted on the otherwise dead mountainside, cinders of the earth swirling the languid hills, which carried with them so many ciphers that would be buried forever.

It was just as I had remembered from the summer of 2015, only the clothes were a little more sun-faded.

When ISIS invaded, they surrounded the hoof of the mountain, opening fire and grabbing weeping victims. Thousands of Yazidis had nowhere to flee but up.

"ISIS took them from the curves," Amer told me, gesturing to the spiral of the ascending road.

There's one point in the mountain where it becomes "anti-gravity," where you can spill water and it trickles up instead of down — where you can stop the car and put it in neutral, and it rolls upwards. It's one of the planet's rare magnetic pulls, and we played there for a few minutes. To the Yazidis, that little place still had the power to bring a small smile to their faces.

But the smiles fast faded as we ventured deeper into the mountain, into a space so forgotten it felt like the edge of the earth. There, in the infinite plains that seemed to sweep on forever, was a spattering of lacerated sheets — not even dignified enough to be called tents. They were shacks where the lost and the brave lived, where women wept for what they could not get back, and where children headed out to the farms to work. School was both a distant memory and an unnecessary luxury in an era of such hardship. What they needed most, many Yazidis stressed, was medical care.

"The elderly are dying. People have no money. When somebody gives birth, there are no doctors. They are alone in a dirty tent," grieved Baker, a thirty-year-old farmer living on the mountain with his young family. "Babies are dying after just a couple of days, and our women are dying too."

Baker stumped into our vehicle with deep wrinkles chiseled into his skin. He carried a unique heaviness as he moved — bowed and slow. It was as if life had been sucked out of him, and he was barely holding on to its curtain call.

With winter on the horizon and a light frosting the mountain tops, Baker was bracing for the worst.

"There are a lot of diseases now among the children, measles and skin infections," he noted, his face falling. "Everyone gets too sick in the winter. And it will rain. When it rains it gets muddy and the children, the children get sicker."

We passed an imposing Doshka poised on the roadside. Amer told me that the sophisticated heavy weapons system had saved them. A man not famous in the world, but famous in their community, Qasim Shesho, had protected them all and fired back as the ISIS army invaded. He was a rock star in their eyes.

The Doshka he took control of had been a lifeline for the lucky that safeguarded many from death, Baker explained. And God had preserved them, too. Even with all the carnage and loss, this young man praised God for his life.

Without hesitation, he believed in divine intervention.

Baker had been living in a village south of Sinjar on August 3, 2014 when the world he knew was hacked into a million pieces. He ran up the mountain and past his childhood home. Bullets kicked up dust in his wake as he carted his six-month-old son, Habib, in his weary arms.

But the enemy bullets bit closer like sharks at Baker's feet, and his exhausted legs slowed. He felt he could no longer run fast enough to survive, given the burden of cradling a baby, while at the same time propelling his aging parents.

The young father made a difficult decision.

"I had to leave Habib behind a rock as we were all under attack," Baker said matter-of-factly. "He was heavy, and we were running."

I thought how strange it was that someone would choose to save the life of an elderly person over an infant. It was totally against the grain of what I had always been taught was the right thing to do. The unlived life of a child always took precedence over that of an adult.

"I wanted to save my mother and the elderly," Baker went on. "I thought if they find a child, they would not kill him. I thought nobody kills kids."

How wrong Baker was. As the weeks and months unfolded, burned and battered bodies of babies inflamed social media and anecdotes emerged of horrific child beheadings and murder. Distraught mothers told me of their child's death and village elders would show pictures of the young that had been taken too soon. There was no mercy for the tiny.

Baker said he hid far enough away from ISIS to stay alive, but close enough where he could just make out the blur of the rock that bulwarked his son. As his people were killed and kidnapped in the war theater, all he could do was hold his breath. Hours later, when the ISIS ammunition had run out, and there was nothing left around him but the vision of death, Baker raced back down and found Habib, still wrapped in cloth and fast asleep. The war could not break him from his dreams, but his father could.

"There is no life for us here on the mountain, but we are alive," Baker said. "God saved us."

A week later, I met little Habib. He lived on the mountain in a blue tent with his family. He wore bright green trousers and a grey sweatshirt, his bare and calloused feet moved sleepily along the chilled earth. He had a chubby, heart-shaped face with rosy cheeks flushed even more by the impression of a pillow. We played together with his deflated soccer ball in the frigid autumn afternoon. His nose dripped unremittingly, and his little lungs wheezed and wheezed.

Never-ending nose drips and wheezing. Smog. Smoke. Cold. Coughs and rasps.

Deadened flakes caked everyone's scalp, and their faces were mottled with raw blotches. Strange brownish bubbles burst from the pores.

What is war? That is war.

Habib clutched a little packet of biscuits for dear life, nervously offering me one after his mother gestured him to do so. I could not and would not take his treat. Habib burrowed beside me with a warmth that could only come from a small child. I paused for a moment as I examined his angelic face, wondering if he would ever come to know what he had already survived as a tiny baby hidden behind a rock. One of the saddest perils of being a child caught up in the craziness was that one does not have to comprehend what has happened to still feel it deep down. The children there knew something was wrong, even if they did not understand or remember.

Baker was convinced that it was the Arab neighbors in his village who had turned their weapons on them. He believed that they had been in communication with ISIS elites days before the meticulously planned assault.

"It was planned. When our neighbors heard ISIS was advancing, getting close, they told us not to leave and promised they would protect us," he said. "But they deceived us. Hours later, they put their black flags on their houses and took up arms. They used weapons against us."

Habib was just a child, but he had the carriage of an old man. He led me down the dirt road to where the roosters crowed, to a lady who wanted to talk to me. She stared at the cloudless sky and told me her name was Gooley, and that she was living on that mountain in a tent given to her by the PKK. She was a mother to eleven children — four girls and seven boys — but ISIS had killed her oldest son just south of Sinjar on the day they attacked.

Citing financial reasons, she only had the means to send four of her children to school. She kept touching her blotchy face, which appeared as though it had been bitten by frost and then by sun time and time again. Gooley said she had undergone surgery recently and now she struggled to walk, but in her pained emotional state, she could not remember what kind of surgery she had endured or why. It didn't seem to matter. It was as if she was living outside her body in a faraway world, telling me her story in broken fables.

Habib led me onwards to another tent where an old man with a long silver beard, dressed regally in white, sat in the shadows — seemingly unaffected by the frozen air. It was already so cold, and winter had not even begun.

The old man, whose name I never learned, said that although they lived like dead people, the mercy of God and their Angel Tawis Malak kept them alive so they could tell their tales to the world.

He had the animation of a trained actor, and he rolled cigarettes with tobacco from the fields nearby. The man said they called him the "grandfather" because he knew all the prophecies. But the one he most wanted to share was about the Temple of Sharfuddin.

The Arabs would rise against everyone, the old man cautioned. He said that the Jews and the Yazidis would unite against them and that the Persians would be divided into two groups. Some Persians would fight with them, and some would fight alongside the Arabs. And the last battle would take place at the Gates of Sharfuddin.

"That is how the world ends," the man vowed.

He said he felt the prophecy was coming soon. And so, one morning, we went to the Gates of Sharfuddin.

TO THE GATES OF SHARAFUDDIN
November, 2016

As we approached the Gates of Sharfuddin, that local legend Qasim Shesho was already waiting. I had no idea what he looked like, but I had assumed it was him by the way he stood up straight, the younger soldiers at a respectful distance behind. When they passed, they kissed his hand.

Qasim had the signature thick mustache and smoked cigarette after cigarette on the dim green couch that matched his khaki fatigues.

He and his soldiers had been sleeping on the floors of an old hall, cradling their weapons the way some people would hold their newborn baby. They slept across from the Temple of Sharfuddin, more than eight hundred years old and one of the most sacred places for followers of the Yazidi religion.

The soldiers had prepared an elegant spread for us; brass plates overflowed with rice and goat meat fresh from slaughter. Meals in the Middle East were almost always elaborate affairs, with each dish offering a bite of history — the wins, the losses, the pains, and the glories.

One soldier reminded me that the battle for Sharfuddin would be the last battle on earth.

In August of 2014, hundreds of ISIS fighters had stormed the gates of the temple. Qasim — a storied fighter since the 1970s — and just eighteen of his men spotted the black dots in the distance, surging forward at a pace faster than they could holler for help. The men were prepared to die to ensure that that their temple did not fall. Too much history — too much of divination — was at stake.

Vastly outnumbered and outgunned, the men — with what little ammunition and weapons they had — propelled the ISIS fighters back bullet by bullet in a siege that lasted for months. Over time, reinforcements trickled in to help. But it was not until December, after more than four months of fighting for Sharfuddin, that U.S.-led airstrikes finally helped propel ISIS back into the horizon.

Qasim and his men had wept.

After lunch, I walked aimlessly around the hall, garnished with loose AK-47s and rockets, staring out at what was once a village. There was little left; rubble, a wild dog, a cemetery on the nearby hill. But that pale-colored temple stood, a testament to their faith and the power of the brave. On paper, the story seemed unfathomable, but I believed them — I believed in their conviction.

As if the daily assaults were not enough, I found a group of soldiers huddled in the backroom playing Call of Duty. They emulated war by day and ventured off to the real war by night. They took selfies, smoked cigarettes, listened to music, and bided time telling dark jokes before the next swath of bombs rained.

Maybe that was how most Americans viewed war, too — a video game in a faraway alternate universe. Real, but not real enough to care.

Qasim wanted to take me inside Sharfuddin. I ran out in front of the group so I could capture the unflappable men as they marched together in full armor through those gates.

In keeping with the protocol of the Yazidi religion in which one's feet should never touch the doorway, as doorways were often kissed and blessed by pilgrims, I skipped over in my bare feet. It was Wednesday, which meant it was the Yazidi Holy Day. We sat on thin mattresses with our backs against the pale yellow brick.

In the corner, there was a small skeleton of a tree decorated with rainbow-colored eggs. Yazidis celebrated their new year in April, and one of the key features of Yazidi New Year festivities was the coloring of eggs, a tradition that could be traced back to ancient Sumerian and Babylonian times. The eggs were principally colored red, blue, green, and yellow. They illustrated the arrival of spring and the arrival of the new year under the guise of God's creation.

April was long past, but the eggs stayed.

Qasim told me more about the day that ISIS had come so close. They had made it all the way to the front of the gate and had even sent in a tanker. How close they had come, he kept saying, to the world falling apart.

What is war? It was full of small victories... of accepting all that was at risk.

He led me into a room with radiantly colored fabrics. We each tied a knot, silently saying our prayers. The Yazidi ritual of tying the soft silks stemmed from the belief that prayers made while doing it would be granted when another pilgrim untied them.

Only most of these silks were tied, and it was hard finding one not already knotted; silent testament that so much of their ravished community was over the hills, their status unknown.

THE PRICE YOU CAN'T PAY
November, 2016

The ravished community still longed for their beloved to return. Often, when I stayed with Yazidi families, soft moans emanated from the rooms. They possessed a pining that no words could describe. I felt that way every time I wrote about the Yazidis. But I had come to realize that you could print and reprint their stories and woes many times over, but there is always the one that — for no particular reason — breaks you; the one story that makes you really and truly understand what it means to be poor and powerless against the forces of evil.

In a street still littered with landmines, I found a forty-five-year-old Yazidi father named Mirza, chewed up and burned alive. He had just returned to the ruins of his home with his children. ISIS had taken his wife as a sex slave. Three months earlier, the Raqqa-based enslaver contacted him and said he would sell her back for $30,000. Mirza told me he had scrounged and saved and begged and borrowed to get that money.

But by the time he had it, he called the seller — who told him the price had doubled.

"I couldn't afford it," he said with a look so lost and sad that it ripped through me. "I couldn't afford to save her."

I wanted to help Mirza, but I could not. To have given money or tried to fundraise for him would have been illegal in the United States, as it would have been considered giving money to a foreign terrorist organization. Mirza had since lost contact with the ISIS enslaver.

He didn't know whether the children would ever see their mother again, he said.

A gentle afternoon rain sifted through the splinters in the canopy caused by mortars and madmen. Mirza held himself together through the helplessness, and I was the one falling apart.

These were the small voices. They represented every part of you that identifies with their pain but doesn't know what to do. They were sick of being scared, sick of being sick, and sick of being cold and impoverished; they were sick of weeping inside their wasteland and nobody hearing them; they were sick of living as though there was no longer any sense of time.

When I first met the Yazidis, they never complained. But as the war dragged on and their situation puckered, they found their voice. Then again when it peaked, they stopped complaining. It made no sense to complain. Everyone was in agony, and there was no superhero striding in to hold their hand.

But perhaps as upset with the world as they were, nothing could take away their innate giving nature. Some afternoons we would drive through Sinonwy and stop by Umer's bakery, which not long ago ISIS had stormed and closed down. I would watch the women — young and old — fire up the old, traditional stove and flip and fold the dough as traditional music hummed behind them and the naan rose to life. They smiled shyly and always wanted me to try more. They simply soldiered on.

What is war? That was war, too — soldiering on.

One day, Amer took me into his little clothes shop and insisted I pick out something new. I was notorious for only wearing black, but that day I picked out a plum-colored blouse. We then went to his home in the township, and he rushed out to collect fresh figs from the garden. Amer wasn't sure who had lived there before, but when he arrived with his family, someone had told him it was abandoned. He needed somewhere to stay when he wasn't on military duty and a place for his family to live and wait for the war to pass. And so they had moved into the random abode.

There was no electricity and no running water. At night, I would wrap myself in layers of blankets and yet still feel my bones freeze. I tried drinking whiskey to stave off the cold that only the desert approaching winter could bring. Still, my bones felt like ice. I dared not whine. It was my choice to be there, and it would have been silly to whine about something so trivial.

When I needed to burn off the anger and the sadness, I would climb to the open rooftop and run on the spot, overlooking the cows and llamas and ground powdered in frost. The old Yazidi women would boil water and, when it cooled to lukewarm, would toss it over me in the bathroom and lather my hair and body with soap before I ventured back into the frigid air.

As much as I longed for a proper shower with a spout of flowing water, there was a magical simplicity to this life I had grown to love. I knew I would miss it whenever I returned to the States.

I often think of the quiet breakfasts seated in plastic chairs on the driveway as music played, with fresh coffee, eggs, and yogurt. Amer's son, Aqeed — the one who had been wounded — often served us. He was always well-dressed with a crisp, green shirt tucked neatly into his black dress pants. He looked younger than his twenty years, his weight wasted. I felt terrible, watching him struggle as he bent down to bring me food and tea, envisioning the mortar still lodged in his spine.

I wanted to do it myself, but he politely gestured that it was okay. I realized that even though he could no longer fight in uniform, he felt it his duty to serve and work in any way he could. Even if it meant contorting his face with every hobbled step and gritting his teeth in agony with each incline forward, he had his dignity. This war could not rob him of his dignity.

THE WAITING LIST
November, 2016

In the Middle East translation of dignity, asking for help is often left out of the definition. But desperate measures called a broadening of the meaning.

One night, heading back from Sinjar, we stopped in the Khanke camp in Duhok which had become the prefabricated home to many Yazidis. A woman named Basima had called Yakhi earlier asking for someone — anyone — to listen to her story and perhaps help her husband. We wandered through the maze of tents in the nightfall and Basima emerged with a lantern to guide us. Still swathed in a dignity she would not relinquish, Basima refused to let the war take the man she loved without a fight.

Months earlier, her husband Zedan — a construction worker who had quit his job to become a Peshmerga soldier after the ISIS emergence — had been hit by an ISIS sniper bullet in the left side of his head on the Sinjar frontlines. She pulled out the paperwork, which showed he was born in 1981.

Although Zedan had undergone surgery, Basima said it had not worked and there was no doctor supervision for them. She detailed the way their lives had been dismantled with a mix of both pragmatism and pain.

"He is paralyzed on his left side," she said. "He always feels cold. He cannot hold conversations anymore."

Basima wore a floor-length, shapeless, faded bronze dress and electric blue earrings. A tribal tattoo dotted her face. There was something very buoyant and bold about her, in the way she held her chin up and in her robust features. Since her husband's injury, she had become the man of the house — or the displaced tent — taking care of matters and their seven young children. In turn, Basima had developed an unrelenting vigor to advocate for her husband's survival. She was not going to let his life go to waste. She had developed a veneer exterior to fight hard for him.

Zedan, once a broad-shouldered and tough young father, lay inert on the floor, asleep against the wall, swaddled in a flowery blanket. He appeared as dead as a living person could be. He did not — could not — move except for the occasional shudder or agonious cry like a wolf's howl in the wild.

"We have no income. I must watch him twenty-four-seven," Basima explained. "Still, I have tried to get a job in construction inside the camp, but the staff refuses to hire me."

I stopped writing and studied Zedan's curled body. The slowing of his breaths, each with which he seemed to deflate and let go a little more. I thought about what a priest had once told me during a sermon when I was a little girl. He had said that nobody teaches us how to be born, but along the journey, we learn how to live; people teach us how to live. But nobody can ever teach us how to die. Death is a path we walk without the knowledge of the living. Zedan looked lonely on that path, gasping for air. His time was coming too soon.

"The Ministry of Peshmerga has a list and a small budget for surgeries for the wounded," Basima said. "But I worry he will die before his turn comes."

She looked at Zedan with such a depth of love, like there would be no world if the world were to go on without him. She outstretched her five fingers, but she stroked the air instead of her withering husband. Perhaps it would be too

249

real at that moment, if she were to meet his limp flesh with her own.

I needed air — I needed to temporarily remove myself from the heaviness. I had that ability — an ability that felt like a luxury because those around me could not do that. They endured the gut-punching all day, every day. Even if they wanted to leave, there was nowhere for them to go.

Selfishly, I went outside and closed my eyes as the cool air washed over my face. Then I went to play with the camp's children before they were called to sleep. A handicapped boy pedaled an old, rusted bicycle and girls in princess dresses milled around with an old car tire. These were not children who were afraid of the dark. They marched into the camp's rims, far from the generator's lights, where it was so black you could not see your hand before your eyes. They played in the ditches they had dug for themselves under the starless sky.

On my way toward the exit gate, a man with a thin, silvering mustache called me over to his little camp shop, where he was selling canned goods. He insisted I take a fizzy orange drink. I looked down and saw a contorted, decaying leg and a foot that faced backwards entirely, black with dirt and infection burbling through the slashed flesh.

I sat on the ground beside his wheelchair and we talked for a few minutes in broken Arabic. Waves of civilians had walked toward his home, he remembered, "pretending to be refugees fleeing ISIS." He said that they told him ISIS was in the town, only they were ISIS. The village was ambushed, and his family was killed in front of him.

Perhaps, he pondered, he survived because he had somehow stayed one step in front of death. He was crippled, of no use to ISIS — not worth wasting a bullet.

How easy it was for me to wander into their lives and then, with a honk of a horn from the awaiting car, wander out.

RESCUED FROM HELL
November, 2016

One autumn afternoon, a mud-spattered Land Cruiser sped down a lane at the back of a remote displacement camp close to Duhok, Iraq. It came to a halt where a growing circle of mostly women and children had gathered. A fragile young woman with a toddler in her arms leaped out and into the arms of the small cluster.

The commotion was bittersweet: weeping, hugs, cries from young children.

The new arrival was Gazal, a twenty-two-year-old Yazidi who had spent the last two years and two-and-a-half months of her life as an ISIS sex slave. She had just travelled from the depths of hell in Syria and, in the final phase of a complex rescue operation, was delivered back to what was left of her community.

"Thanks to God," was all Gazal could utter, cowering in the corner of a flimsy cabin. She was joined by her two sister-in-laws: Nadifa, twenty-two, and Basima, seventeen, who had also been captured by ISIS but were rescued a year ago.

"Our father and brother — Gazal's husband — were taken by ISIS at the same time we all were," Basima told me. "Since then, we haven't seen or heard from them. They are still missing."

In any other western or wealthy place on the planet, Gazal could have been mistaken for a supermodel or Hollywood prodigy. She had exotic facial features and a tall, statuesque presence. But in the cruel world in which she existed, her natural beauty had only worked against her. As we talked that afternoon, I understood that Gazal's mind was a file stuffed with stories, memories, and a type of sadness I could not begin to comprehend.

It was August 3, 2014, when the terrorist legion assaulted the Sinjar in Iraq's Nineveh Plains, calling them "devil worshippers" due to their ancient religion so unlike their strict version of Islam. While Christians believed that Lucifer fell from the heavens to hell, Yazidi doctrine asserted that he was forgiven and reappointed as God's closest angel.

In the gnarled ISIS mind, it made them devotees of Satan.

Thousands had nowhere to run but up the mountain and into the deadly summer heat with no reprieve. These girls would sneak back down each day to collect water for their family's survival. They got away with it for the first few days, tiptoeing around the ISIS nests in the villages below. Then, on August 8, the jihadists caught them — and their lives would never be the same again.

"First they put us in a school in Tel Afar and held us for twenty days. They didn't let us eat or drink, only the children were given a little bread; but we had to go to bathrooms to share it. If they caught us sharing we were tortured," Basima said, speaking as if she were a historian, restoring someone else's story. "The children were dying, starving. They wouldn't drink the little amount of dirty water. So, we found some toothpaste and put it in the water to pretend it was milk, so they would drink and not die from dehydration."

Dulled of emotion, Basima recalled everything down to the most minor detail: how they were transferred to Mosul in cattle trucks and stashed in a traditional ceremony hall; how the elderly had to give the children their urine to drink "to keep them alive" after ISIS cut their only water pipe; how everyone became so sick and malnourished that clumps of their hair would fall to the floor.

But the worst was yet to come.

"In the middle of the night, the ISIS men were coming in and yelling to know who was still a virgin," Basima whispered. "And from the age of eight, they were taking girls to the market to sell for a cigarette."

However, Basima and several of her siblings "thought up a plan" to avoid being violated. They "tried to look like ugly boys" by using a piece of broken plate to shave their heads and dressed in the men's clothes they found hidden away.

"We thought that if they mistook us for boys, we would be taken out and killed rather than raped," she explained. "But instead, when they knew our trick, the men came in and stripped us in front of everybody. In front of everybody, hundreds, they touched us everywhere, sexually abused us. My father and brother had to watch. And that was the last I saw of them."

Basima did not shudder when she talked about the abuse. She was telling her story, but she was also telling somebody else's story. She was telling the story of so many other women. Perhaps that is how she was able to get through it with strength — by separating herself from the narrative.

When initially snatched, Gazal was with her six-month-old son, Bakhtyar, and five-year-old daughter, Darin. While Gazal clutched her screaming son, Basima claimed to be the mother of Darin in the hope that the ISIS operatives wouldn't sell her if it was clear she was no longer a virgin. Darin stayed with Basima through the months of terror and together they were rescued twelve months earlier.

It had been years since the little girl had laid eyes on Gazal, her real mother.

Now, Darin was brought in through the tent flap to reunite with her real mom in a reunion that was as deeply sorrowful as it was delightful. Their bond was broken, but they had a mother-daughter love that could not be killed. I had seen Darin waiting in the pool of people outside but had not known her connection as she twirled in the mud and clapped her hands in giddy anticipation. I had not known she was waiting to see her mother after all this time.

The story went on.

Basima, Nadifa, Gazal, and their other close relatives were soon transferred to a prison in the so-called caliphate capital of Raqqa, Syria. They were shoved in a line. They were again made to remove their clothes, and — in Basima's words — "it was ordered everyone had to be looked at by the Wali." The Wali was referred to as Abu Habis, and she described him as nothing short of "scary" — a fat Iraqi, blinded in one eye, disabled, and "like a devil."

"But he chose her, and he said she is the most beautiful," Basima said, motioning to Gazal, whose large eyes, so fair they appeared almost colorless, were cast down. "He said he likes her eyes."

Gazal spoke of her ordeal in a tempered rhythm, relentlessly tugging at her dress and glaring at her raw, cracked hands. At first, she said, she refused to go with the Wali. But he dragged her by her hair and took her and Bakhtyar to the Syrian city of Minbij near the Turkish border. They were yanked into a house "like the headquarters" where there were already two other Yazidi slaves and a constant ebb of foreign fighters.

"The Wali said I must marry him, but I refused, so he took my son and I didn't see him for two days. After that, I begged and cried. He started torturing me and said I had no option but to marry him," Gazal said. "Only it wasn't a real marriage. There was no contract, no real ceremony. It was just rape. I was forced to be a Muslim, to pray five times a day."

The coalition bombs soon started falling on ISIS installations, bases, and homes. But they also fell on people who were already scared and suffering; who had no arms and no choice but to be there.

After Gazal was gone, Basima said that she and scores of others — including young Darin — were wounded in an airstrike on the prison. Shrapnel pierced her head. Basima's only "treatment" was her long ebony locks getting shaved off — she received no medicine. The slaves were propelled down twenty-two skewed steps into an underground weapons storage "filled with guns and bombs," which would become their living quarters for more than a year.

"We were tortured. There were no toilets. We had to eat, sleep, and 'do the necessary' all in the same place. All kinds of insects and flies were in there," Basima continued. "They forced us to convert to Islam. We were made look at beheaded bodies through the little window. We didn't know when our time was up. All we could think about was whether it was better to live or to die."

Finally, on October 13, 2015, several of the girls were piled into an old van and told they were being traded at a market. But instead, they were left on the Kurdish border in something of an intricately executed rescue operation.

Meanwhile, Gazal's tale of torment persisted.

"The Wali gave me so many birth control pills my kidney hurt. After five months, when I got so hopeless, I wouldn't let him have sex with me anymore, so he sold me cheap to another fighter, and I was taken to Mosul," she continued.

That fighter was a twenty-eight-year-old Jordanian named Batar, who was married to a local Sunni woman named Sadr. Together, they beat her — she was his "sex tool" and her full time "maid."

"They threatened to hurt my son if I didn't obey. But still," Gazal paused, pulling her screaming son closer, "they hit him and tortured him. Now he is always hungry and aggressive and can't understand my language Kurdish, only Arabic. When he sees a bunch of men together, he gets angry and cries."

After about a year, Batar gave her his phone and told her to find someone to buy her for $25,000. She remembered her brother's number, and for weeks he scrounged the money together from others and gleaned strategic support from the KRG Prime Minister's Office of Kidnapped Affairs. Then, finally, she was taken to a family's home in Raqqa. They were paid to harbor her there for ten days.

"They weren't nice people," Gazal remembered. "But at least they did not rape me."

At long last a vehicle came. She was brought to the Yazidi displacement camp — now her home.

"Location is not important to us anymore. We survived," Basima added with a shrug. "Our only hope is that we get back our father and brother.... and that maybe someone will help us here. We haven't been helped yet. We don't know what to do."

Basima was open and loving, her hand gripping my knee as she spoke. I could tell she didn't want to just survive — she wanted to live. But Gazal's anguish was too fresh, her eyes piercing the walls of that prefabricated existence, a place she knew none of them belonged.

Months later, I heard that the women were still waiting for help and waiting for their loved ones. The triumph of having survived felt like a pale triumph. How would they ever put the pieces of living back together again? I also learned in the dwindling days of the ISIS territorial war that secret proposals were being drawn up to establish a communal home for some Yazidi women who had given birth to ISIS babies.

Although the narrative for almost all of the survivors was that their enslavers had given them birth control pills and did not force pregnancy on them, it wasn't always a successful plan.

"The women who have been violated are being welcomed back to the community, but the babies who have ISIS fathers are not," one government official, not authorized to speak on-record, told me. Her voice dropped to a whisper as if afraid somebody would hear. "So, we are developing a plan for them if we can get the money. These mothers will probably never be able to marry, so we want them to be able to live together and raise their children together."

The Yazidi religion did not accept converts, and to stay Yazidi, one had to marry and procreate only within their community. The women were wounded by their memories and the taboos they had to slash through. But the boys suffered, too. Scars ran through their blood.

A CALIPHATE CUB
November, 2016

The scarred little boy was of an age where he should have been playing outside in the puddles with his friends. But Zed seemed to have no friends, nor did he seem to want them.

A ferocious winter storm had just swept through the small Iraqi-Kurdistan border town of Zakho, and while the other displaced children his age squealed as they played in the oily puddles outside, eight-year-old Zed sat with his back against the flimsy tent wall, arms folded. He was just a child who did not yet have the words to yell, so he sat silently instead, glaring with eyes of blind rage.

"We are trying to convert him back to Yazidi," his mother, Seve, told me. "But sometimes he does not agree. When he gets angry, he recites verses from the Quran. And he yells we should never have escaped; we should never have come back here."

Zed's entire family, including his mother, father, and three sisters, had been ambushed and captured by ISIS as it overran their village. They were forced to convert to Islam, traded at the market for the equivalent of $50, and moved from Mosul to Raqqa. Seve was held as a sex slave as her young girls — now between five and ten years old, including one with special needs — looked on, their tiny bodies starved and beaten in captivity.

Seve's husband had not been heard from since. He was among "the missing."

Zed had been forced into a "caliphate cubs" jihadist training camp.

"They were breaking his teeth every day — his teeth are all broken. They took him to training and were making him use a large weapon for three to four hours a day," Seve said dryly. "Only, he was too small. He couldn't hold the weapon, let alone shoot it. Eventually, they brought him back to me."

She took a moment as if to count her blessings.

"But normally," she whispered, "those children are never coming back."

Seve didn't know how long her family was in the grip of ISIS, her recollection mellowed by the fear and hopelessness of the entire ordeal. The days dragged into months and time folded unto itself in a giant blur.

Zed was not the only one whose brainwashing disfigured his daily life. Many of the Yazidi returnees still adhered to the Call to Prayer when it chimed from a nearby mosque. Many had forgotten what it meant to be Yazidi, and many were extremely violent toward their loved ones.

"He beats his siblings," Seve continued as her silent son fidgeted and slumped in the corner.

But she could not bring herself to punish him. Abuse contorts and deprives a child's innate instinct to love and be loved.

With the assistance of smugglers and a network of rescuers, the family finally made it out of Syria and to the relative safety of the camp on June 2, just over four months before I met them. They were physically safe, but would likely never be whole again.

For every Yazidi in Iraq, life was made up of two parts. There was the quiet, peaceful farming life in mountain villages before August 3, 2014, and then there was the lesser life from that day forward — the day the genocide of their ancient religion at the fist of ISIS systematically started.

Their men were missing and, in most cases, presumed dead. Their women had endured the unspeakable degradation of sexual slavery. Their homes had been destroyed. Many children of the ancient faith which predated Islam and Christianity had become terrorists, weaponized against the people they once loved — and who still loved them.

Baba Chawish, a leading Yazidi spiritual authority and the guardian of their holiest site, Lalish, repeatedly called for the community not to shun the returnees, but rather to make sure they were embraced.

However, the sense of helplessness was, at times, overwhelming.

"As a community, we don't have a problem accepting them back," Colonel Marwan Sabri, who headed the Peshmerga brigade in Northern Iraq, had explained to me. "But we have no experience in this and no resources to help. We don't know how to help them."

A senior Kurdish intelligence official also assured me that returning Yazidi boys would not face repercussions despite what they may have been forced to do in the service of ISIS. He also expressed that de-radicalization and psychological help was pivotal — but it was not there.

I thought back to my time atop the parched Sinjar Mountain — where thousands of Yazidis fled amid the ISIS assault and subsequently died of dehydration in the scorch of summer — as I sat with Syrian Kurdish nurse, Khansa Ali. A refugee herself from Rojava, Khansa had been doing her best to save children, working out of that shoebox clinic with a few medicine bottles and beds.

"Psychological problems are the number one thing. They come here broken and in shock," Khansa explained to me. "But all we can do is try to sit with them. Talk to them."

Down in the masticated streets of the mountain foot village of Sinonwy, once occupied by ISIS, local schoolteachers encountered similar frustrations. Sixth-grade teacher Hadi Murad said depression, isolation, and fear were just a few of the symptoms plaguing the survivors.

Professional and long-term psychological and de-radicalization programs, experts agreed, were desperately needed.

"Many have been forced to kill, and they are now desensitized to killing," said Dr. Anne Speckhard, adjunct associate professor of psychiatry at Georgetown University School of Medicine and director of the International Center for Violent Extremism. "They will need programs similar to other forcibly conscripted child soldiers. PTSD and deprogramming-type therapy will be needed intensively at the beginning. They will need to be restored to safety and security to be able to participate in therapy in a meaningful way."

That, she noted in an email, was particularly challenging, given that many had lost their family to the genocide.

"But this can be treated," Speckhard said.

While Seve was trying to heal her lost child, she too was trying to heal herself. The mother, born in 1975, recalled how she and her family were fleeing their village towards the mountain when she spotted a well. Glancing over at her babies howling with thirst and hunger, she walked towards the well. As they desperately flushed water into their mouths with their bare hands, gunshots rang out. ISIS fighters marched methodically, painstakingly toward them, surrounding them.

Seve, eager to tell her story, remembered each of the days that followed distinctly. Those days turned into weeks and months and then into over a year. The whole family was forced to convert to Islam and forced to make the pledge of faith, the Shahada. The men and women were separated, moved from place to place, herded like cattle in trucks. They were transferred from a cement building in Tel Afar to two different schools, and then to a prison glutted with manic people — from babies to the old and crippled.

"There was not even room to sit," Seve said. "Then they took out all the people who were seventy years or older, they took them somewhere, but we never knew where."

If they were lucky, they were given some rice to eat once a day. Some of them died from starvation, some from the heat, some from the cold, and some from the bullets and blasts and beatings. Seve held cornbread in her hand the whole time she spoke, but she dared not touch it. Maybe she was not — or could not — be hungry. Or maybe she was afraid that if she started eating, she would realize the depths of her hunger and her trauma.

She never smiled. Anything they owned and had tried to hide, like baby photographs or jewelry, had been stripped from them — the last links to their old life, gone.

"And then someone came in with a notebook in his hands, and they said he was the Wali from Saudi. He said he would reunite all the broken families, so we started to write all our names. But it was a trick," Seve continued. "They separated all the girls who were seven or older from their mothers."

A hint of hatred broke through Seve's robotic voice. In her view, a liar was worse than a thief.

Seve said she could still hear those mothers screaming as their little ones disappeared into the gloomy night in trucks. Those screams still curdled through her head whenever it got too quiet.

Then, a plane flew overhead, and a blast hit the side of the Tel Afar prison just inches from where she was sitting. The scared ISIS men ran away from the strike. Some of the children, capitalizing on the chaos, were able to jump out of the truck and run back to their families. After midnight, they were all bundled up and relocated to a school that had not yet been compromised by outside intelligence.

Later, they were moved again, this time to an empty house under ISIS guard. Seve was squished into the house with other families and her four tiny children — one was Imaan, the special needs child with a big, beautiful smile and a playful spirit. In the mornings, the guards would throw them a piece of hardened naan. For three months, they lived on that small piece of morning naan. Along with some salvaged scraps, it was just enough to stay alive.

As the gentle mother unfurled her harrows in words, the children danced. The rain outside got heavier, crashing on the muddied tent as lightning struck, sending chaotic flashes of light across us. The children didn't stop their dance. The distant chant of the Call to Prayer rang, and immediate recognition flashed in Imaan's eyes, indicative of the indoctrination that may never go away.

Another of Seve's young daughters, Kinder, had her name changed to an Arabic name while they were under the ISIS fist. Sometimes when Kinder got angry, Seve said, she yelled that her Arabic name was better, and she was no longer Yazidi.

"The ISIS tricked us again. They told us they would take us to find our men, and after midnight one day a truck came, and we went to Raqqa," Seve went on, chronologically replaying their plight. "But when [we] got there, our men weren't there, and they took the girls seven and over, they said they were being taken to serve the Wali. They were again moved from the village and left for ten days without food."

When the growling inside their empty stomachs became too much and the ISIS operatives were not looking, they would sneak to the dumpster to wrangle food, which they would shove down their throats without chewing. They were pedaled from apartment to apartment. At one point, an ISIS-appointed judge moved into the village, and Seve and several other Yazidi women were "given as a present to that judge."

One day, Seve claimed, American soldiers came to a house next door. It was sometime in May 2015, around the time that the Army's elite counterterrorism unit, Delta Force — under the Joint Special Operations Command — raided deep into that ISIS territory. They killed the high-value Tunisian operative known as Abu Sayyaf, the ISIS oil and gas "minister." Seve had hoped that the Americans might rescue them from that underworld, so she tried to make eye contact with them through the open window, but they were there and then, in a flash, they were gone.

For the next year, Seve was raped and beaten daily, her entire family sold at markets for $50. The small children were bashed until blue — the captives cautioned that if they cried, they would be killed. The children were hung from the ceiling fan and whirled around until the fear — until the ability to feel — had been guttered from them. When her babies screamed, Seve was hit harder in retaliation.

Imaan, who had a bladder control problem, was punished in a way her mother could not bring herself to say aloud. She whispered it instead, privately — and it chilled me.

In any and every war since the beginning of time, children are always hit the hardest. They are victims mangled into the folds of collateral damage. But there is something especially evil about one who would target a small, disabled child. How could such a mindset ever be rehabilitated?

Seve slaved for those fighters. She had no choice. She cooked for those evil men and their families; she cleaned from dusk until dawn. Secretly, she would line her pockets with bread bits to feed her children when her slave master turned his head. The children had their teeth broken with bats. They were not permitted to take showers. Then they were sold again — this time, Seve worked on a farm outside of Raqqa, taking care of the sheep and cows and cleaning the house.

Until one day, Seve snapped like a wild animal who could no longer be caged. By falling into the ocean of the insane, she was restoring sanity to her situation. She knew this could not go on.

"I just couldn't stop screaming. I begged the fighter to let me call my brother. He said no, but I insisted. The oldest wife at the house finally, finally said I could. I asked him to find money to pay for me," she recalled. "And then one night we were all bundled up and taken to Mosul. I cooked and cleaned for the family like normal. I gave them their pills like normal. They went to sleep. And I grabbed my children and told them we were leaving."

They tip-toed through the night for over an hour, hailing car rides from strangers and walking some more, switching cars and holding their breath all the way to the YPG-controlled border of Syria.

Seve said that a French person had visited their displacement hub a few weeks ago to give them some counseling, but they had not come back. No one else had come to help them through the psychological injuries.

As I rose to leave the humble canvas home, Zed, who had just started first grade at the camp, suddenly — as if slowly warming back to life — had something to say.

He told me that earlier that day, he had been taught the English alphabet and he wanted to practice it. Perhaps it was his way of saying he wanted to be part of the world once again.

EXECUTING 'SPIES'
November, 2016

The world Zed was edging back into was a world transfixed on the operation to liberate Mosul. ISIS was being cracked both from the outside and the inside. Disenfranchised fighters from within the insurgent outfit played key intelligence roles, feeding information to the opposing forces outside.

"I will give you more money for information," one senior intelligence and security leader in the Kurdish region stated firmly over a cell phone from the safe house in Kirkuk as the city outside exploded with sniper fire and suicide bombers. "But remember that if you lie, if you give me wrong information, we will find you wherever you are, and we will get you."

The official was talking to one of his sources within the ranks of ISIS, piecing together information on where the cell may strike next. As it turned out, he was not the only one who made effective use of the enemy to glean necessary information.

Many high-ranking soldiers scattered across various units of the Iraqi Security Forces, and Kurdish Peshmerga had also developed key contacts from deep inside enemy lines. It was a strategy they employed from the start, which mushroomed as ISIS started to lose its grip, its disillusioned members looking for a buck and a way out.

"We have a mixture of some working for ISIS intelligence and others who are in a fighting role — or both. Civilians too. They give us all kinds of information," Amer explained over dinner, glancing out into the wrecked streets of a liberated Northern Iraq village.

I started peppering him with questions about attacks brewing in the nearby ISIS fortress, the city of Tel Afar.

"I am not sure of all the details for your questions, but want me to call them now to find out?"

Without pause, the intel-focused soldier phoned his ISIS "insider" and had a brief but civil exchange in Iraqi-dialect Arabic before hanging up abruptly. Later, he explained the finer points of the well-etched internal network. He said that generally, only male sources were used, and with a few rare exceptions, he typically wasn't the one to initiate the phone calls.

"They call me," Amer insisted. "From a secret phone, a secret phone they can only use to call me and vice versa."

Phones and "other equipment" were sometimes provided or "smuggled" in by the liberating forces, and other times the assets — or informants —

provided their own means of communication.

Given the success so far of the ongoing Mosul offensive, they were calling more and more.

I was told that there were two main reasons the ISIS associates agreed to dish dirt to their enemy. There were those working for money, who were recruited and vetted through the highest level of intelligence and security agencies and delineated as trustworthy enough to give accurate information.

Then there were those who "volunteered" because they wanted to negotiate a life-sparing alternative to their atrocities, which amounted to not being purposely targeted and killed — or they volunteered because they sought safe passage for their families to escape ISIS territory.

I was sternly informed by multiple security top-brass, however, that it was made very clear to the fighters that they were not to attempt to seek asylum no matter how useful their intelligence. On that note, relying on a brutal or delusional jihadist to tell the truth was hardly a clean-cut victory for information gatherers.

"Sometimes they lie," Amer acknowledged. "So, we have to have many sources. If they tell us something, we must check it and check it with others."

Another high-level counter-terrorism military official concurred that the "insiders" were known to give some correct information and some incorrect information at the same time, creating a guessing game for the recipients. But more than two years into the fight, the officials insisted that they had acquired the necessary experience to analyze and determine fact from fiction.

For the gossips, the stakes were high.

The top echelons of ISIS were street smart; their leaders knew that critical information was being leaked by many of their own. This instilled a rabid paranoia within the leadership. ISIS operatives consistently rounded up soldiers and civilians, slaughtering them in the most primitive ways for their alleged "spy" activities.

However, external authorities doubted that the group was particularly apt at tracking down the real leakers.

"The way ISIS determines who is a 'spy' isn't by any high-level hunt, they will often arrest anyone found to have a phone," explained one official. "They will take the phone and 'investigate' and brand them a spy."

Another top official with the Asayish — the leading Kurdish security and intelligence branch — assured me that none of his informants had been caught or killed. He said that, from the beginning, ISIS was obsessed with "sim chips" for phones, believing that switching sims was a tactic only used by spies. Thus, early on, possessing multiple sim cards was prohibited. Subsequently, ISIS had gone about butchering anyone found with one.

Moreover, the spy system worked both ways. One Kurdish official said that he understood they likely had a few moles mottled among their own ranks, dishing the dirt to the ISIS side, mainly because the group had arrested and threatened to kill their families inside ISIS terrain if they failed to partake.

Iraqi Forces had also spent more than two years tightening their terrorist spy network inside Mosul in preparation for the offensive. Haitham al-Malaki, head of military intelligence for the Iraqi Army's Emergency Response Division (ERD), noted that these internal agents had provided information and documents that helped identify "most of the ISIS communication and financial routes." Haitham also pointed out that these same sources were critical in helping establish safe routes for civilians when forces finally reached the city perimeter.

According to another well-placed Iraqi military insider, the secret networks were comprised mostly of locals, both within ISIS and civilians, as "outsiders are generally more hesitant to do it."

And those with some form of connection to ISIS also played a pivotal role in the complex process to rescue Yazidi sex slaves and forced jihadists.

According to Hussein Al-Qaidi, Director of the Office of Kidnapped Affairs in Duhok, all parties involved were playing with fire.

"Dealing in any fashion with a terrorist organization is always difficult," said Hussein, highlighting problem points such as middlemen running away with the money, inability to do their job, or worse.

"If they get caught by ISIS — someone facilitating these missions," he added. "They automatically get beheaded."

Only, the distrust that permeated life in a war zone was hardly limited to the bad guys.

What is war? War is distrust, dishonesty, skepticism.

War is living in your village for years, sharing food with your neighbors and minding their children. It is feeling as though praying in a church, bowing in a mosque, and kneeling in a temple is one in the same. And then it is suddenly waking up one morning to learn your front door has become a frontline; to feel the barrel of your neighbor's gun staring down at you against the soundtrack of rockets cracking the air.

It is running for your life, not knowing who is your friend and who is your foe. It is falling down a sinkhole in a road you used to travel day in and day out and realizing that you will never return to that state of being alive — a sinkhole from which you can never really climb out.

What is war? War is bleeding on the outside, but even more on the inside. It is not knowing who will compress your wound and who will slash it open again. Just when you think it has healed and the skin has melded together again, a knife stabs into the same exact spot.

WHICH CIVILIANS TO TRUST?
November, 2016

There is an old Iraqi proverb: "When a camel falls to the ground; the knives are many." The saying can symbolize sympathy for the victim or the rush for something edible. Where the knives will come from, who will use you for their nourishment, and who wants to minimize your suffering are persistent rhetorical questions in times of war.

It was the early days of the 2016 winter, and Iraqi forces etched closer to the city of Mosul. Cooperation and support from civilians inside the ISIS stronghold were considered crucial components to the operation's success. But trust remained a problem.

Despite the atrocities committed by the Islamic terrorist organization, it was far from a given that a prominent portion of insiders would side with the liberators and rise against them.

A Kurdish military leader maintained that when the Iraq Forces began to encircle Tel Kaif — also known as Tel Keppe— days earlier, "waves of civilians" rushed toward them. He said that they were poised as disgruntled and grateful civilians running from the caliphate. They had been praising the incoming offensive, declaring that "ISIS is out of the town."

Tel Kaif was a historically Christian farming town located just northeast of Mosul. As of 2004, its population was half Christian and half Muslim, but the former gradually declined in the ensuing years. In early August 2014, ISIS overran the region, prompting the remaining Christians to flee or face slaughter.

However, when the forces moved closer to the civilians, they were ambushed by the awaiting jihadists — resulting in a bloody showdown.

"It was a giant human shield in some ways," one official observed. "But it also shows the depths of the ideology. ISIS will go, but the ideology is a much harder war to win."

Many Iraqi officials were quick to point fingers at Sunni-dominant areas. They vowed that such pockets still saw ISIS as a better alternative to the Shia-led government.

I thought of the earlier incident with the activated sleeper cell in Kirkuk and the litany of snipers and suicide bombers storming the streets. It had been quickly revealed that almost all the participants in the cell were from neighboring Arab villages. They had come to the now Kurdish-controlled city of Kirkuk seeking sanctuary from the ISIS conflict. Much of the surrounding province was still tight under ISIS's grip, replenished by swaths of civilian supporters in the region.

"This is a big problem for us; even we were surprised by the support," said Adnan Kocher, senior advisor to Lahur Talabani, head of intelligence and counterterrorism for Kurdistan. "This kind of ideology is a disease. We have been dealing with it for years now."

However, Baghdad worked overtime to convince residents in and around Mosul — areas still monopolized by the jihadists — that they would be the righteous and only protectors of the innocent. The government asserted that the ISIS members would not walk away from the war with impunity.

"Warning: for all Iraqis who are involved with ISIS, ISIS is over, and there is no return," read a leaflet I found coated in debris. It had been dropped from the sky by Iraqi Forces and featured their national flag on one side, the harsh words of caution on the other.

"For those who are seeking mercy and amnesty, they have to capture an ISIS, either Arab or foreigner, and turn him into the hands of security forces or else you will be killed," the flyer continued, reminding the Mosul inhabitants of who was in charge. *"ISIS brought destruction to your sweet cities. Your government is more merciful, and Iraq is the one who takes care of you."*

The distrust was palpable, if not unbearable for those inside. Trusting governments, security forces, and even neighbors had burned them before — why wouldn't they burn them again? That's how ISIS catches you. They find the crevices in the corruption, the persecution, the misgivings. They tell the people that no one can be trusted and that the only thing that will save them is God — their version of God.

Those stuck inside were divided over whether to believe that the government, which they blamed for not doing enough to stop ISIS from forming in the first place, could ever be a savior for good.

EVERYONE WANTS A PIECE OF MOSUL
November, 2016

The role of the international community, of the footprint of foreigners, was something that had divided the Iraqi people. Since the U.S.-led invasion of 2003, the country had been swept over by Iran — for better or for worse, depending on who you talked to.

The coordination between various countries and interests in the operation to liberate Mosul was being heralded as a success. Officials spoke from the same script. But as the different teams got closer to breaching the city, the bigger concern was that cracks in coordination would hurt the well-heeled plan.

"It is complete madness. I haven't seen anything like it. It is Iraq we are supposed to be helping in this, but essentially we are helping Iran," one U.S. military source, connected to Operation Inherent Resolve, told me. "The Iraq government is of course influenced by Iran, and we are telling Iraq what to do, so what does that say? All parties here have an agenda here, and it seems the U.S. is the only ones whose only priority is getting rid of ISIS."

Iraqi national forces claimed that they oversaw the Mosul effort, which U.S. officials echoed. But given the enmity between the various groups — Kurds, Iraqis, U.S. forces, Iranians, Sunnis, and Shia — questions remained as to who really ran the show, or rather the showdown. There was also the issue of to what degree the United States was working with Iran, either directly or indirectly, given the undeniable influence Tehran had over Baghdad and the number of boots it had on the ground.

"The Mosul offensive is being led by the government of Iraq and we, the coalition, are providing support by training police and military. We are supporting them in terms of providing logistics, targeting, and providing advising to the unit commanders involved in that operation," said Adrian Rankine-Galloway, a U.S. Marine Corps Major and spokesperson for the Department of Defense (DOD). "We have specific rules that govern who it is that we can provide support to specifically, we only provide support to those forces that are under operational control of the Government of Iraq."

Controversy continued to crawl around the Iranian-backed Shiite militias, the Population Mobilization Forces (PMF), and what they stood to glean from the U.S. weapons arsenal. But Adrian assured me that the U.S. "does not work with units that have histories of human rights abuses or officials with the government of Iran."

However, he declined to comment on the strength of Iranian influence because "that would entail revealing classified information."

"U.S. troops answer to the commanding general Lieutenant General Steve Townsend, commanding general of the combined joint task force international task force primarily manned by American forces," he affirmed. "But other nations as well."

With the recent deployment of more than six hundred troops, the U.S. had almost five thousand of its forces on Iraqi soil and some two hundred "advisors" nestled alongside Iraqi and Kurdish soldiers on the Mosul outskirts.

"Americans are in harm's way as part of this fight," Pentagon Press Secretary Peter Cook stated. "They are playing a support role... but they are behind the forward line of troops."

Yet Iran-linked militias and the Popular Mobilization Forces continued to play vital roles in operations — particularly in clearing areas around Mosul ahead of the final swell.

"There is a reason we haven't been targeted by the Shia militias — yet," noted another U.S. military source, who was not authorized to speak on-record and thus requested anonymity. "We are helping them get rid of their enemy, which is ISIS but helping them gain a lot of power in the process."

During the U.S. occupation of Iraq, Shia militias, openly supplied with advanced bombs and weapons by Iran, were said to be responsible for more than 500 American service member deaths.

Over coffee on a Friday afternoon, Shwan Mohammad Tihi, a former Iraqi Parliament member and Head of the Security and Defense Committee in Baghdad between 2010 and 2014, called the mishmash of alliances "complicated." He had little doubt that each country endeavored to gain strength in Iraq.

"Iraq is Shi'a dominated, so naturally Iran is going to have a lot of influence and Iran is not afraid to play here," Shwan said over his cup of black coffee, indicating that a "bipolar" policy and weakening American military presence had prompted Iran "not to be afraid" to take charge.

"Iran is gaining land," he continued, looking me squarely in the eye. "And popularity because of this war in Iraq, and the success of its proxies."

It seemed like an omen of sorts, and it was words he wanted Washington — pre-occupied with the presidential election a day or two away — to hear.

Earlier in 2016, Moen Al Kadmi, deputy of the state-sponsored Popular

Mobilization Forces (PMF) half-laughed when I questioned their working relationship with the Iraqi troops. Indeed, they were a crucial part of the Iraqi Forces; he had scoffed, stressing that the two "can't work without the other."

"We need their equipment," he had said, referring to the mostly U.S.-supplied weapons and armament given to the Iraqi forces. "Cooperation between us is what has led to our success in liberating towns and cities."

But Moen had also noted that they "don't want to work with U.S. troops" and insisted that U.S. forces had "fired on them."

"We won't kill them, but we can't guarantee that other militias won't kill them," he continued, adding that their long- term goal was to have an official, withstanding role in Iraq's government to protect the country.

The looming question was — despite the U.S. policy that forbade the Iraqis from handing off issued weapons to the Iranian proxy force — how much control did they have in stopping it? And when it came to fighting ISIS, could the enemy of the enemy be a friend?

The PMF was formed in 2014 following a fatwa from Iraq's Grand Ayatollah, Ali Sistani, requesting able-bodied Iraqi men to help expel ISIS from Iraq. While it had proven to be a strong fighting force, it was thought to be permeated with Iranian-controlled militias, all beholden to the Iranian Revolutionary Guards Corps (ICRG) elite Quds Force's commander, Qasim Soleimani.

Wedged deep within the IRGC was arguably its most potent branch — the elite intelligence wing called Quds Force — which itself had been a designated terror group since 2007 and was estimated to be 20,000 men strong.

Its long-running leader, routinely referred to as the "shadow commander" or "spymaster," was considered one of the most powerful persons in Iran. General Qasim was the man who had long been responsible for "recruiting Shia Iraqis into militias, training them in Iran, and returning them to Iraq equipped with increasingly sophisticated weaponry." Much of that weaponry, the Pentagon underscored, was used to kill more than 600 U.S. service members between 2003 and 2004 in the Iraq war.

However, the prominent Qasim's foothold extended beyond just Baghdad. While he was said to be a regular inside the Iraqi capital, given Tehran's tight reign over its neighboring government, he had sent tongues wagging a couple of weeks earlier after he was spotted inside the Kurdish areas. However, multiple Kurdish officials dismissed this as nothing out of the ordinary — he went to the Kurdish city of Sulaymaniyah frequently, they told me, as he had good relations with their dominant party, the PUK. They mostly discussed "the lengthy border they share and all issues that stem from that."

But in the ever-complicated ISIS web of war, mutual enemies doesn't automatically mean the fire will be friendly. In the minds of various high-ranking Kurdish Peshmerga stationed in the North near the Syrian border, close to that seemingly coveted land pocket leading to the Mediterranean, there was "no difference between Shia militias and ISIS."

"If we see militias here in our area," cautioned one Lieutenant General, "we will kill them."

One senior official with the Asayish told me that the Shia militias not only "carry out mass atrocities," but had another "dangerous agenda" that entailed extending their influence across Iraq and Syria. The murmur was that they were exploiting the ISIS offensive to place their forces in a land strip west of Mosul and extend their hold through to the Mediterranean Sea. This would enable a safe and secure route through historically Sunni Arab terrain — much to the embitterment of Turkey.

Adding to the convolution of the situation was the presence of Turkish troops outside of Mosul. Turkey was not technically part of the Mosul mission and was not wanted by the Iraqi Government. Subsequently, the PMF had threatened to attack Ankara's contingent, illuminating the degree to which other escalating conflicts could hamper the Mosul operation.

"Everyone wants a part of Mosul," said one Kurdish official. "Including Turkey."

But as tensions rose between Ankara and Baghdad, the U.S. was again propelled to play middleman given its NATO alliance with Turkey. Captain Jeff Davis told Pentagon reporters that the Turkish were considered "friendly forces" despite their aircraft not being part of the coalition's air tasking order

(ATO). He urged both sides to "talk."

What is war? A lot of talk about talk. What about listening?

While everyone wanted a slice of the Mosul mayhem in favor of their agendas, there was a lot more walk than talk needed before any of the fragmented forces could claim their riches. It was then anticipated that over six thousand ISIS fighters were still inside Iraq's second-largest city, and they were expected to wage bloody warfare on soldiers and civilians until their dying day.

Yet, given Mosul's majority Sunni population, Baghdad officials had assured the public that Shia militias would not enter the city. It was their way of avoiding sectarian flares. But could a government's word be trusted? Could the militias be trusted to adhere to the government's word?

Tehran certainly wasn't shying away from making its support for the Mosul operation known. Iran's Foreign Ministry spokesperson, Bahram Qassemi, declared that the Iranian government would stand alongside Iraq in the Mosul Operation. He urged the international community to support the Iraqi government "more effectively" in its ISIS- obliterating efforts.

I was told that militias within the PMF had used a well-oiled tactic during the freeing of Fallujah earlier in the year; "Staying on outskirts for a while then building trust with tribe leaders, after that, getting permission to enter the town."

Everyone knew that they weren't going to stay out of the biggest fight of all.

"But in Mosul, this is not going to work. They don't want to give Turkey a reason to interfere. So, there is an agreement with (Prime Minister Haider) Al-Abadi to stay out of the city and take a role in a Shi'a town (Tel-Afar) and support the Army with logistics," the Iraqi intelligence insider quipped. "But the Shi'a militias are there. Who knows what they will do? Everything changes on a daily basis."

SMUGGLING INTO IRAN
November, 2016

The smugglers' trek from Iraq to Iran was one of the few things that did not change on a daily basis. The demand was high, and it would be idyllic if it weren't so dangerous.

An opaque fog swirled over the snow-capped mountain range as the sunlight faded. The cold settled around us. But even during the summer months, it was an isolated, whimsically frozen place — too cold even for wild animals— reached only by a single, writhing road hours from any central city, peppered with nomads and quaint village huts protected by grand canyons and velvety sierras.

At its end was an Iraqi-Kurdistan borderline without displacement camps or battle bases. There were no traditional sand-bagged frontlines, tanks, or camera crews. But there was something of a small war there.

We drove for hours along a narrow road trimmed by vast rock walls streaked black, silken hills, and farming villages. It was a road known to be infected by landmines from the war between Iran and Iraq that claimed the occasional life, most often a child playing in the fields, born years after the conflict had ended.

We passed tiny children operating creaky bicycles and nomadic donkeys stacked with blankets and guided by farm dogs. We stopped at a small gas station where the attendant listened to opera and stared into the gray skylight. We stopped for tea in tiny towns with clay huts that blended into the colors of the white-dipped mountainside. We made our way up a jagged street to pray with a heartbroken family who had lost a brother in the ISIS fight ten days earlier.

It was a Friday. Young women came from the mosques and the markets, laughing, wrapped in black and gold abayas. It was hard to imagine how these beautiful places had once been so soaked in blood. Cemeteries dotted the distance, erected under the long-frozen contours of the mountainside.

Along that mountainside was the countryside that belonged to Iran — and it was smuggling central.

In the far scope of the eye was a cluster of a dozen hunched men trekking through the frost and up the steep mountain path. They were on a smuggling mission from Iraq to Iran, their rucksacks loaded with a commixture of basic goods like food and electronics. The most coveted of their carries, however, was the one which was outright prohibited at their destination: alcohol.

Brooding on the mountain above the men was a medieval Iranian border patrol tower. As smuggling insiders elucidated in hushed tones, the patrollers were known to shoot any infiltrators they spotted outright. Other smugglers were brought down by bullets from hidden border patrol points. The odd man would step on a landmine — again, a bitter reminder of the blood spilled during their 1980–1988 war.

Some succumbed to the harsh elements, and many were captured by Iranian authorities every year, tortured in obscurity with nobody to fight for them before they were eventually sent to the gallows.

At just this point of entry alone, one longtime smuggling operative told me, an average of fifteen men died every month. Some went in armed, but most accepted that whatever happens — happens. It was an illicit endeavor that happened multiple times a day, 365 days a year, irrespective of the gushing snow and rain and sub-zero temperatures and deaths.

Not far below the weighed-down human dots disappearing into the darkness, a little ways to the east, the Iranian flag shimmered beside the large stock picture of the Supreme Leader Ayatollah Ali Khamenei signaling the official border into Iran. There was a strange emptiness. A few cargo trucks waited at a no-man's-land customs checkpoint between Iraqi Kurdistan and Iran. Roosters crowed. I turned around just in time to see each of the faraway bootleggers fade from purview, concealed only by the congestion of forest greens.

There were said to be more than twenty of these "open secret" contraband routes into Iran, but only a few — like this one in the very north of Iraq's Kurdish turf, an area known as Hajji Omaran — were fit for transporting the banned beverages.

"Other things are okay to smuggle during the day," one suited and shoe-shined local co-coordinator explained. "But alcohol only in the dead of night between the hours of eleven and two."

Special vehicle paths were used to transfer bigger items like oil, but moving alcohol was a process as old-fashioned as it comes. If it was not on foot, it was by burdened horseback — hundreds of hooves hauling daily.

A string of four-wheel drives arrived, filled with the night's liquor goods. The men got out and began preparing the boxes hours before the night's operation was scheduled to start.

Typically, smugglers — usually poor Kurdish farmers, young and old, from both sides of the border — made around $60 per tortuous trip, each of which took about six hours from pick-up to drop-off, while the brains behind the business stood to make thousands a month.

And there was no slowing in this game.

Smuggling was a lethal but booming trade. The demand for alcohol inside Iran had been steadily rising ever since it was outlawed following the 1979 revolution. Consuming it was deemed a "Crime Against God" and remained punishable with lashes, or even execution for multiple offenses.

Most of the alcohol was purchased in bulk and on the cheap from Armenia — Absolut vodka, Johnnie Walker scotch, counterfeit Grey Goose, and Ozo being the most requested. The alcohol was sent into Kurdistan, then snuck into Iran. By the time it got there, the consumer paid triple the market value — and even more in the winter as the transporters received a little extra for their life-endangering wades through fifteen-foot snow mounds.

What's more, illicit breweries and home concoctions bubbled behind closed doors in many Iranian homes. Prohibition had generated an epidemic of alcoholics, and it had become the nation's second-largest addiction issue after opiates. In recent years, Iranian authorities had begrudgingly acknowledged the growing problem and in 2013 opened Iran's first and only detox center in Tehran.

Now, the Iraq-based bigwigs behind the black-market trade were hastily aligning for an even bigger smuggling trade into their own perimeter. It seemed Iran's war on alcohol had infiltrated its neighbor.

Late last month, as Iraq's attention was almost solely devoted to the heralded inauguration of the Mosul operation, Iraqi Parliament "slipped" in and approved a bill to ban alcohol. Violators were to face fines of up to $21,000.

It was not yet clear when it would come into effect or if it would just get tossed by the Supreme Court, but the controversy continued. Supporters of the new law insisted that it was justified as Iraq was an "Islamic democracy," and the constitution forbade the passage of anything contradicting Islam. However, many critics saw it as an ominous reflection of Iran's influence; they saw it as something that would lead to black market mayhem and something that sought to endanger further Iraq's already dwindling minorities — like Yazidis and Christians — who enjoyed drinking as a rite of passage.

"For decades, Iran has wanted to control Iraq, and this is their opportunity to bring more conservative Islamic values into Iraq and shape it into its own second Shiite Iran," lamented Juliana Tamoorazi, founder of U.S.-based Iraqi Christian Relief Council, an Assyrian who fled Iran as a refugee after the revolution. "A bi-product of this legislation is the further marginalization of persecuted minorities; it appears laws like this want to push minorities out of the country."

Khalid Rumi, a Member of Iraqi Parliament and a third-term member of the Council of Representatives — the sole representative for his near-extinct Christian-related ethnoreligious group called the Mandaean — acknowledged that while such decrees as the alcohol prohibition "choke minorities and force them to leave," the booze ban was a symbol of something far more sinister.

"This isn't just about suppressing minorities; it is about targeting personal freedoms for everybody. The danger isn't only banning alcohol, there is a bigger goal to target more personal freedoms," Khalid vowed from the tiny, newly-constructed Mandaean temple nestled in Erbil's Christian enclave of Ankawa, a temple more symbolic than used due to their dwindling populous stemming from relentless years of persecution.

He insisted that there was an ever-growing faction within Iraqi Parliament and government that "supports the Islamization of society."

"It starts with alcohol," Khalid paused. "But later they will talk about dresses and head covers."

There was, however, a willingness from a prominent portion of the Iraqi people to not simply accept this fate. Many Iraqis — young and old, religious and secular — spoke out against the law. They sensed where it was headed.

"To pass this law is one of the most stupid decisions ever made," sighed twenty-nine-year-old Baghdad-based financial expert and author, Rusly Almaleky. "There is no doubt Iran is controlling many things in Iraq. This may be their idea to distract public opinion."

The war against ISIS had, many experts and officials concurred, been a major booster for Iran to insert its dominance militarily, economically, socially, and religiously.

From Khalid Rumi's viewpoint, the threat of Islamization — or Iranianzation — was one that ought to be given close international monitoring and nipped before it became too late.

"Those who brought the rule, take them away from the rule," Khalid added. "The U.S. was the ones who removed the regime and brought the Islamists to rule.... then they walked away from it."

THE LOST BOYS OF ISIS
November, 2016

Even if they had wanted to walk away, loathed by the savagery they saw, the boys who willingly joined ISIS likely would have been killed or their families would have paid the ultimate price for such a defection.

These were part of Iraq's modern-day lost boys.

I woke up one morning and drove to Kirkuk, into a fortress that, just a little while ago, had been spattered with ISIS snipers on the roof in a sleeper cell attack on the city. It was the police headquarters, where I had organized to meet with some child ISIS members recently captured by authorities whose futures were yet to be determined.

I was not sure quite what to expect — I had interviewed many ISIS jihadists before, but child recruits were a different game. Children were always victims by standards of international law, but how destructive would these victims be?

A meek, bone-thin boy sat inside a darkened office. Shreds of light from a film camera cast gnarled shapes around his young face, mottled by hints of adolescent acne. His deep brown eyes darted relentlessly from side to side — part confusion, part fear, part cowardice.

This was fourteen-year-old Awad Arkan Helal Mohammed. Although an arrested ISIS operative, he did not resemble anything remotely akin to a hardened fighter. Awad was just one of the thousands of child soldiers to have been voluntarily enlisted by the Islamist command.

"The Caliphate Abu Bakr Al-Baghdadi, to listen and obey in times of hardship and ease, in difficulty and prosperity," he shouted pitifully to the camera.

Awad's interrogation by Iraqi Kurdish authorities was carefully filmed to present as evidence to the judge at his forthcoming trial on terrorism charges.

"I am not to dispute his orders, only when I see evident infidelity regarding which there is a proof from Allah," the juvenile squawked. "Allah is my witness."

Awad explained how he had joined the brutal organization with this simple pledge of allegiance recited on April 16, 2015, after being recruited by his friend, Mahmood Ibrahim Shukoor, in the local Kirkuk village of Smata Olya.

"My dad was also ISIS," Awad admitted, before insisting that he didn't tell his parents he was joining the group because they may have stopped him. "So, I just ran away."

His father, Awad noted with a pause, was killed by an airstrike in September of 2015. But that did not deter him from escaping the group — instead, it fueled his motivation for martyrdom. Awad didn't join ISIS for sectarian and ethnic thrill kills, nor for the money, nor because he was forced to do so.

His reasoning was clear.

"The leaders told me I would go the paradise," Awad said bluntly. "Where there would be many angel women waiting."

I sat through the interrogation session and then subsequently interviewed the child recruits myself.

Encircled by a thick cement wall and layers of security, the Kirkuk Police Department was a nondescript, signless building in the city center. Snipers guarded the roofs above the peeling walls, and uniformed men meandered, smoking cigarettes with their rifles slung tight, sitting on the patch of courtyard grass — the only badge of brightness in the colorless collection of buildings.

After his initial pledge to the self-styled ISIS "caliph," the then thirteen-year-old Awad was taken to the nearby village of Albo Najim for thirty-seven days of intense weapons training. The training focused on the use of AK-47s, M16 rifles, and the Soviet-style machine gun BKC — known as the PKM outside Iraq. There were two ISIS trainers, and thirty trainees — half of them minors, he recalled.

Awad said he spent four months working for ISIS in the Kirkuk village of Al Bonajim, earning a salary of $50 per month. He was then relocated to the terrorist bulwark of Tel Afar, where he underwent forty-five days of more intense training alongside a bevy of other Iraqi and foreign fighter kids. This was intended to give the children an augmented proficiency in the same three weapons with the added extra of what Awad called "body fitness" training.

The leaders, according to Awad, would yell at them during the boot camp to "kill Peshmerga" as well as the Shia militia, PMF, or Hashd Al Shahbi in the local dialect.

Awad's next ISIS duty was commanding a guard post in Kirkuk's Sehel village with eight others — all from neighboring Qahara Village in Daqoq. With an AK-47 in his hand at all times, his task was to inform the ISIS intelligence agents if anyone "came close" to their post. But around nine months in, on August 23, 2016, the Kurdish Peshmerga assailed the guards. Before he could sound the alert, Awad and his kid cohorts were carted away in handcuffs.

"I wasn't scared," he said emphatically. "They treated me well."

Awad slouched hopelessly and gazed into the cement floor. The police interrogator, who embodied something of an old-school military drill sergeant, barked at him to look back up and into the lens. Awad heeded the command sharply — a trained fighter to the core.

"I don't think," he told me slowly, "that I will go to the Paradise anymore."

Kirkuk Police Brigadier General Sarhad K. Muhammad — known in the local community as "Rambo" for his no- nonsense persona and for having survived countless bullet batterings and assassination attempts — burst into the stuffy room. He ordered Awad to stand in the corner, and the next ISIS teen took a seat on the blue plastic interrogation chair.

General Sarhad towered over the impish teenagers, ordering them around, lightly slapping them across the ears, blazing into their eyes with a belittling twinge. It was a small victory to have caught these naughty boys before they had the chance to inflict severe damage on human life.

"ISIS told us this is the Islamic State that the Prophet commanded. If you get killed, you will enter the Paradise, and there are women for you," said fifteen-year-old Mostafa Qais Ahmed Dawood, explaining why he joined before demonstrating that he knew the ill pledge of allegiance to Baghdadi by heart, just like his fellow detainee.

There was something much more militant about Mostafa. He had a strong jawline that he constantly clenched as if to stop himself from breaking into a smile during questioning. His eyes flashed wild defiance. When Mostafa's hands weren't fidgeting in his lap, they were reaching to tug at a beard that was no longer there.

Recruited by a local Sharia Law Judge named Abu Rashid, Mostafa had sworn his way into ISIS in July that year. He and seven other newcomers — all minors — were given "brutal" training by three ISIS leaders. He learned the ins and outs of "the AK-47 weapon, BKC weapon, and the 12.5mm machine gun weapon and body fitness."

Mostafa's first ISIS "job" was with ten other adolescents in Abbasi Village in Kirkuk province guarding ISIS vehicles. By September, local authorities had caught on and moved swiftly to shut the shop down. He was caught and cuffed. As Mostafa detailed his short jihadist journey, I glanced over at Awad. He stood timidly in the dark, transfixed by the multitude of framed photographs and certificates of Kirkuk Police Department accolades on the walls.

I wondered what he was thinking. I wondered if he missed his dead father and how hard it was to mourn him from behind bars. I wondered what he had been taught as a small child that would prompt him to want to live like a seventh-century swashbuckler.

The interrogator later confirmed to me that neither one of the boys had participated in combat operations against security forces, nor were they known to have made any kills — but both recognized that they had ruined their adolescence by aligning themselves with an organization that slaughtered, enslaved, and waged savage warfare on millions worldwide.

"I do regret it. If I saw my young friends, I would tell them to leave ISIS because it is outlawed," Mostafa lamented. "I would tell them to surrender to Iraq."

It was almost too systematic to be convincing.

Later, over tea, General Sarmad affirmed that the oft-heard "regret" spiels are usually just fibs of ear.

"They are obliged to say that, but we don't believe them," he observed. "So, we investigate."

Kirkuk authorities alone had, by then, apprehended "tens of children" belonging to ISIS — just less than one hundred, according to the General. They were held in an undisclosed children's correctional facility which was set up like "a hall," in which fifty people were detained together rather than in single cells as they awaited trial. Their time in court typically came between two and six months after their arrest, Sarmad said.

The General underscored that the juveniles in the system — there for an array of offenses — tended to radicalize one another. He pointed out that sentences handed out by a judge varied, but that minors usually get "half" of what an adult would for the same crime. Another police official in the room predicted that these child soldiers would probably spend six or seven years behind bars.

There was no mention of the amnesty or rehabilitation programs that routinely drove the discourse of western media and human rights groups when it came to such an issue.

Of course, the use of child soldiers in conflict was not a new concept, but ISIS had taken its enrollment of the young to an unprecedented level. ISIS schooled them to be everything from spies and swordsmen to human shields and suicide bombers, which posed a particular challenge for opposing forces on the battlefield.

"ISIS uses every technique, every way, to get everyone," Sarmad said. "They take women, train children; they find every possible way to infect the community."

For a few minutes, the two accused jihadists — flanked by security — were permitted to stand in the bright mid-morning sunshine as officials talked amongst themselves on the other side of the garden. The boys stood together with their backs against the wall, both staring out with deadened expressions. I locked eyes with Mostafa — his gaze stoic for a split second before it dropped in apparent shame.

Sharing a single handcuff, the boys were led back down the hallway to their holding hall.

"It is not easy for these children to forget their ideology, forget something that they wanted to die for," General Sarmad added passionately. "But this ISIS ideology is like a cancer. It spreads if you don't treat it accordingly."

Later that night, I pulled out my notes, hoping to find some a common thread between all the jihadist fighters I had encountered over the years. What I had come to understand about many of these ISIS fighters, even the ones who were technically adults, was that they were looking for absolutes and acknowledgment — like children who would never grow up.

FEMALES OF THE CALIPHATE
November, 2016

Even the ISIS women I had met were like children in every sense of the word — rebellious and sheepish.

In the epicenter of a bustling commercial road in the Kurdish capital of Erbil stood a bleak brown building constrained by a high barbed wire fence. A few armed men sat in the decrepit watchtower above.

Behind the graffiti-riddled walls, an array of female ISIS jihadists languished with scores of other criminals. It was the only Women and Children's Correctional Facility in the province.

"Some have been trialed, some are still waiting for their sentences," the facility's female manager, Diman Bayeez, told me from her office. "They are here for various offenses — honor crimes like cheating on their husbands, theft, murder, and now because of ISIS, we have more and more terrorists too."

Down a flight of stairs and across a concrete courtyard, I entered a small room at the back of the prison caged by thick metal bars over the high windows, reeking of fried food and heavy cleaning products. Disheveled ISIS women waited, fidgeting, in the hallway.

"I got fifteen years," one plump fifty-four-year-old woman said, flopping onto the office couch. "For being an ISIS terrorist. I wanted to be a suicide bomber."

It was on March 9, eight months earlier, that a Judge had handed her that final fate. As directed by prison officials, she could only be referred to in print by her initials, "KS".

KS wore a long, purple velvet dress, flip flops, a tethered black hijab, and an exhausted face of ever-changing expressions. She had been at the prison for one year and four months.

KS wanted to tell her story in a jagged timeline, a biography bound by battles. She was the daughter of an Arab father and Kurdish mother. She grew up speaking her grandfather's language of Turkmen. She ended up in ISIS after her marriage fell apart.

"I wanted a divorce. I was very poor; I have schizophrenia and was just diagnosed with blood cancer, and my only daughter wasn't treating me well. I was borrowing money from people for the treatment," KS lamented, eyes welling. "But then I grew desperate."

In the obscure days after Mosul was snatched by ISIS in June 2014, when the terrorist group was quickly capturing territory across Iraq, she had detailed her situation to a cab driver named Mahmoud in her home city of Kirkuk. He offered her a solution.

"He was ISIS and said if I join, they would treat me well and pay me," KS continued. "I said I would join on one condition. That they make me a suicide bomber and got me out of my misery. The only thing I was seeking was to be bombed and die."

KS explained that she tried to contact that driver for weeks afterwards, even going to his house, but never received a response — learning later from his wife that he had been killed fighting in Hawija. Soon after that, two other ISIS members found her number in the dead man's phone. She and her husband — who she later divorced — were quickly recruited. ISIS paid her then-husband their combined salary.

"But she never saw a dime of it," she exclaimed.

He was now in a Kurdish prison somewhere, too, but they had no contact.

In her old pre-ISIS life, KS was a primary school teacher. But after twenty-three years in education — five years ago — she was forced to resign due to her "mental condition." Fluctuating between heavy weeps and girlish laughter, KS pointed out that she was a longtime member of the Iraqi Ba'ath party, but in 1992 was incarcerated and accused of selling secrets to the Kurdish Peshmerga. A neighbor came to her defense at the gallows as she awaited execution, and she was spared at the eleventh hour. It was after that trauma, the woman moaned, that a doctor diagnosed her with schizophrenia.

KS vowed that she never received any formal training and that she never pledged allegiance to the Caliph, but she admitted that she allowed two ISIS soldiers to stay at her home.

"I was too scared to refuse," she said, her eyes widening. KS scratched her temple for a moment as if trying to organize her catatonic thoughts.

It was on the Islamic holy day of Eid — the day which breaks the month-long Muslim fast of Ramadan — of last year that KS was scheduled to don a suicide vest. The day came in a burst of celebration in the streets, and she claimed she got cold feet. She swore that her "sane" personality returned and suddenly, she realized she would be killing civilians if she went through with the mission. So she planned a different mission: to run away.

KS said she sold some property and found an apartment in Turkey where she intended to stay for nine months. Then she purchased a plane ticket. When those nine months were up, KS said she was going to make her way to Europe and seek asylum. Her whipped up itinerary, however, was squashed when the Asayish arrived at her door just as she was about to depart.

She thought, looking back, that one of the men in her home — named Abu Haki — was actually a Kurdish spy all along.

"When they arrested me, I told them I did all these bad things I didn't do because I wanted to be executed. I still wanted to die," KS continued, her leathery face crinkling, before recalling an early suicide attempt with a kitchen knife in jail.

"But now, I am thankful to God. I know I have committed no crime," she wailed, her eyes darting up to the heavens of the dirty ceiling. "I don't care about human judgment. God knows I did no wrong."

But authorities differed. According to the Deputy Manager of the Correctional Center, Zhino Azad, KS was entrenched in the ISIS corrugation. She co-coordinated for them and guarded their female prisons — potentially filled with captured Yazidi sex slaves. Furthermore, she received substantial amounts of money from the terrorists for her work.

"Her daughter, a lawyer, is even terrified of her," Zhino noted later over lunch. "She is a dangerous woman. A little psychotic, that's the type of people ISIS takes advantage of."

Yet in KS's own words, "it is like heaven in this jail." She was safeguarded from ISIS, given the standard three-square meals a day, a television, and because she only ever had "one bad daughter" she had been rewarded with hundreds of women under her wing to call her own. Guards took her to a local cancer hospital for treatment once a month — paid for by prison funds and NGO's — and she loved her social worker so much she referred to her as being like "half my body."

"I get to read the Quran all day and sleep," KS said with a bright smile. "And I interpret dreams for the other women, my daughters."

When I asked if she ever believed that she would go to an exclusive "paradise" for martyrs in the afterlife, KS dismissed it with a dramatic toss of the hand and suppressed giggles. She insisted that her "brain was frozen," and all she wanted was to go to heaven.

"I didn't care. That was my second personality in control," KS continued whimsically, lunging closer to me. "I am thankful I didn't."

With a dizzying change of mood, the aging woman tugged her frayed hijab and burst into tired tears again. If it were any other woman, I would have reached for her hand or offered words of consolation. I certainly could not overture notes of sympathy to a convicted terrorist, but I could still feel silently sad for her. Was she evil? Was she mad? Was she sick and dying?

"I was going to hell if I did that," KS added, lost in a trance over how close she had come to ending it all. "And hell is a dark, cold place. It's wrong to die that way. It's not in the Islam."

Soon, a small-framed, weathered woman with a tiny tribal tattoo on the tip of her nose entered. I scrutinized her features: thin black eyebrows, high cheekbones, and a few missing teeth. She wore a grey sweater, black pants, and a loose black hijab. She was timid at first, but quickly gained a skittish momentum to share her narrative with the outside world.

A thirty-five-year-old mother of six children, AH — as I must reference her — was handed a life sentence for her ISIS membership on March 8. It was later reduced to twenty years, and then fifteen because the judge felt sympathetic toward her plight of motherhood. Her children were being looked after by the second of her husband's four wives.

Her husband was also in jail, AH said with a shrug, glancing down at her simple wedding band. But she didn't know where or why he was behind bars.

"He wasn't ISIS," AH, who hailed from the town of Qayarra, declared. "But

I got jail for being ISIS. They accused me of being a nurse to the militiamen."

AH claimed that she had worked at a civilian hospital controlled by ISIS. Despite the conviction against her — tending to cracked and crippled fighters — she swore she never did such a thing.

"People know I was only working there to get money," AH went on. "I was scared for my children's future. We were poor before and poorer when ISIS came."

Prior to the terrorist invasion, AH explained, she worked in a bakery setting up the mud ovens to make the traditional naan bread. But ISIS shut it down.

I let her waffle on uninterrupted. My technique in these types of situations was to listen — to observe every shift of intonation and every shift of the body. Eventually, something akin to the truth would emerge through the tall tales.

After talking, with the prison official paying little attention and wandering in and out of the room, AH let her guard down. She seemed to forget her previous denials of being a willing participant in the terrorist organization.

"I went to ISIS myself and said I will do anything — clean hospitals — if they give me a salary," AH divulged. "So, I was setting up IVs and injections for the fighters."

She collected a wage of $260 a month from the black-garbed jihadist outfit. Then, in the latter part of last year, she formally swore her allegiance.

Yet AH showed no guilt for her actions. She believed she was doing the world a favor, and she justified her ISIS membership by vowing that she was working as a secret spy for Iraqi intelligence.

"I was giving them crucial information about the ISIS wounds in the hospital, the nearby brick factory that became a bomb-making facility, and the places where chemical weapons were being made," AH pressed on.

However, fearing ISIS might catch her spying, she escaped earlier that year to join other family members who had fled to a KRG displacement camp. She claimed that she passed through an Iraqi army checkpoint first, where they confiscated her phone and all her evidence of working for their intel, and when she reached the KRG border she "surrendered" herself.

Zhino later told me that it was not uncommon for ISIS members to take money "from all sides, wherever they can get it." Nonetheless, the prison official told me she had no reason to doubt AH's proclamation that she had a financial agreement with external intelligence.

"Of course, I regret joining ISIS. But my family was hungry. My husband was old," she parlayed, her eyes awash with desperation. She clutched her chest as if trying to rip out her heart. "And it's not fair. I feel betrayed. They took my phone, my proof I was helping them."

As the interview drew to a close, AH looked through me like I had betrayed her, too. I think, somehow, she thought by telling her story to a foreigner that she would be saved and validated. People often think Americans will come to their rescue; that we have the power to free them from the wanton webs.

When my hands came up empty, AH scuttled out of the room like a little girl who was in big trouble.

It was Sunday, the first day of the Middle East working week, one of two days in the week that visitors — family members only — were permitted to see the incarcerated between 9 and 11 A.M. While men were allowed to visit, I only saw women wrapped in black abayas and a few well-dressed young children streaming in and out of the waiting room at the front. Hardened female guards patrolled the grounds, while the males were regulated to administrative roles and manning the exterior.

I took a quick glimpse into one of the prison "cells" which revealed a stack of ailing bunk beds and women sitting inside — some chatting and some sleeping — untouched by the bright sunshine outside. A large, weather-worn tennis court sat empty beside the cell.

While the facility was designed to hold 150 inmates, it teemed with more than double that — some 325 women and children. One hundred-fifty-three detainees awaited trial, which I learned typically began three to six months after their initial arrest — though some cases took up to a year before the accused was granted their day in court. The rest of the inhabitants had already been sentenced.

Forty-one children lived there with their mothers, who had been accused or convicted of crimes. However, some of the inmates were young girls with criminal misgivings of their own. The case files for them varied — there was a girl jailed for prostitution, another for murder, and even one alleged ISIS terrorist, only thirteen years old, in the company of thirteen adult female ISIS members of different ages. KS, at fifty-four, was the oldest.

"We do have problems, especially with the new ones radicalizing others," acknowledged the manager, Diman. "So we try to keep the terrorists separate from the rest, but they — the terrorists — are together."

She highlighted that they were starting a "deradicalization" program that coming week, complete with social activities and recreational programs.

"They all say they aren't guilty, they plead not guilty, but we know otherwise," Diman said, tapping a manicured nail on her desk. "We have to try to bring them back into the community."

Typically, Diman pointed out, the ISIS members were handed jail terms of one to fifteen years for their crimes.

In addition to the two visitor days, the inmates were permitted phone calls twice per week and could receive emergency calls through their social workers. Those not yet sentenced were allowed one hour a day of outside recreation, while those already convicted were granted an hour and a half. School, optional but encouraged, was provided for all ages inside the facility five days of the week.

For Diman — who had been at the helm for two years and previously worked as the director of a local autism center and as the manager of a women's shelter — it was a job that brought both fulfillment and frustration.

"It is rewarding to help those who are in deep trouble, to be part of a process that brings them back to normal life," she added. "But the downside — everyone has a problem — and some cases just cannot be fixed."

WESTERNERS AMONG THE RANKS
November, 2016

The town had been so obliterated that it was hard to imagine how it would ever be fixed. It was hard to fathom enough patience or a deep enough pocket to glue it back together. It was a sight that shocked you every time you opened your eyes.

Plumes of greasy smoke rose over a distant ISIS-controlled road with the first rays of daylight. The stench of rubber and burning oil got heavier as outgoing rockets cracked through the air from behind the obscured soot wall towards the Peshmerga-held posts in front.

"The smoke is designed to dampen our vision. But this is more than normal, which means they are moving around the ISIS leaders," one Kurdish Lieutenant Commander explained from the frontline wrapping around Sinjar. "And perhaps, their key western fighters too."

Within the ranks of the brutal terrorist organization, western fighters — especially those pocketing U.S. passports — held something of an esteemed position, if only for propaganda purposes. Especially in the early days of ISIS's territorial dominance, the westerners were routinely issued the most beautiful homes, the prime market pick of Yazidi sex slaves, and the freshest food.

While thousands of westerners — mostly from Europe — were estimated to have fled their homes in the last few years to join ISIS, it was unknown how many successfully made it out of the United States and into the swaths of Iraq and Syria.

According to a national representative for the Federal Bureau of Investigation in late 2016, some 250 Americans had "traveled or attempted to travel" to these conflict-encumbered countries. However, it was not clear specifically which group they left to fight with, nor did the FBI have explicit numbers on American jihadist deaths or those missing in action.

The FBI spokesperson also noted in an email that, in recent months, they had seen a slight decrease of those traveling to Iraq and Syria with jihadist intentions.

The slowing of foreign recruits, from a pinnacle of two thousand per month in the first two years to now less than fifty, came as a result of stricter border controls in neighboring countries. It was also symbolic of ISIS battlefield losses, which hindered their resolve and enlistment efforts.

But the slowing didn't necessarily mean America was any safer.

"This coincides with some of the ISIS rhetoric in which they have urged followers to attack where they are with what they can," the FBI official wrote.

ISIS leaders had shifted tactics. Through their media wing, the terrorists called for followers to attack in their native nations rather than risk coming in from abroad.

So as the rope around Mosul — and soon Raqqa — tightened, U.S. intelligence officials stood by to apprehend any potential American jihadists from returning undetected to the homeland. As it stood, around 8,000 total ISIS fighters, one-fifth of who were foreign, were believed to still be inside Mosul alone.

Colonel Marwan Sabri, of the Yazidi Peshmerga battalion, recalled that in March 2017, a disillusioned American surrendered himself to the Peshmerga. He had begged them not to shoot him. That fighter turned out to be twenty-six-year-old Mohamad Jamal Khweis from Virginia, who was later deported to Virginia's Eastern District for indictment. A twenty-year jail sentence handed down in October of 2017 awaited him.

According to the U.S. Department of Justice, Khweis left the United States in mid-December 2015 and ultimately crossed into Syria through the Republic of Turkey later in the month. Before leaving, Khweis strategically planned his travel.

"Using a sophisticated scheme of tradecraft, Khweis purposefully traveled to other countries first before entering Turkey to conceal his final destination. During his travel to the Islamic State, he used numerous encrypted devices to conceal his activity, and downloaded several applications on his phone that featured secure messaging or anonymous web browsing," the DOJ stated. "He traveled with ISIS fighters to multiple safe houses, participated in ISIS-directed religious training, attended ISIS lectures, constantly watched military videos with his fellow ISIS members for inspiration, frequently gave money to ISIS members and was forward deployed to Tal Afar, Iraq, before he was captured."

But his seizure sent a shiver through the U.S. and raised questions of who else was lurking between the black flags and grenades.

"The Americans are in the ranks," Marwan assured me.

Another high-ranking Kurdish soldier affirmed that American accents, on the odd occasion, had been intercepted.

"Some Americans were working intel, and some were fighting. Some get to high positions; some have been killed," the source said. "And some we think are still alive."

According to Brigadier General Sarhad Qader Mohammad, director of the Kirkuk Province Police Department, forces had "killed many" ISIS fighters thought to be from the U.S. throughout the war's duration.

However, the U.S. also faced a national security threat in the way of European jihadists returning to their native lands and potentially making a smooth move across the pond.

Michael Pregent, a Middle Eastern analyst and former intelligence advisor to General David Petraeus, pointed out that western fighters could acquire new Muslim names with fresh passports. With that capability, ISIS could push its militants into the refugee ranks without immediate detection.

"These western fighters have the ability to go back home after their deadly training and blend in," Pregent wrote over email.

But beyond overstretched security agencies and an oft-cited lack of intel data and data coordination between European countries, there was frustration within the intelligence community over some of these countries' unwillingness to deal with the terrorists criminally. At least one high-ranking European government official, according to Iraqi-based sources, had been busy pleading on behalf of ISIS fighters from his country since the Mosul offensive started country.

What is war? Victims, fighters, fighters who were victims — depending on who was doing the defining.

The leader wanted assurances that any jihadists from his country — who I was requested not to name — would not be jailed in Iraq but instead returned to his EU homeland. There, he planned to grant the ISIS operatives some sort of amnesty, employment, housing, counseling, and assistance to return to the community without penitentiary punishments.

WHERE IN THE WORLD IS BAGHDADI?
November, 2016

One individual whose bloodied hands would not be given an amnesty pass on any world stage was the mastermind, the ultimate puppet master.

Just as U.S. intelligence operatives zeroed in on western terrorists, increased attention was also directed toward determining the whereabouts of the ISIS chieftain, Abu Bakr Baghdadi. In the dwindling days of 2016, the locale of the assumed forty-five-year-old was a swirl of speculation, stippled by a string of alleged sightings.

Official sources based in both Baghdad and the Kurdish capital of Erbil pinned the self-declared Caliph to be in hiding in or around the fast-falling city of Mosul. Police General Mohammad affirmed that Baghdadi had been seen around November in Mosul, discreetly visiting his troops to "boost morale" among the ailing organization.

Subsequently, in October, he released his first audio message in over a year addressing the Mosul operation and urging his eroding infantry to "stay and resist the apostates and unbelievers." Several analysts surmised that the recordings were made several weeks before the release, and Baghdadi's point of compass was unclear.

By November, authorities already concluded that — under the thick haze of burning tires — he had likely made a move from Mosul into the "caliphate capital" of Raqqa.

"He moves frequently and very carefully, with family, avoiding the use of any technical communication, using tunnels," one Iraqi intel source told me. "And he has very good personal protection, mostly foreign fighters, he doesn't trust anyone outside his close circle."

Since the caliphate declaration in 2014, Baghdadi's location had been a secret to even those within his terrorist organization. Details regarding his personal life or background were also muddied. What's more, any questions about the leader were strictly off-limits.

I remembered my meeting with ISIS bomb maker Jasim Mohammed Atti'ya almost one year earlier. He had held the mid-level leadership post of Amir before being captured by Kurdish authorities in late 2015. He was defiant in the way he assured me that it was "prohibited" for anyone to see Baghdadi. It was as if committing such a misdeed would see one banished to an immediate and eternal hell.

"It's very dangerous to meet him. I wouldn't want to meet him," Jasim had said, his eyes nervously twitching. To them, the self-styled Caliph was too mighty to meet on earth.

Jasim had then recited the seeming propaganda they were fed about their ruler — stressing that he was a "good leader," "a simple soldier," and "just like everyone else."

But according to multiple Iraqi intelligence sources, the "simple soldier" was, for the first time in his organization's history, grooming a deputy. Perhaps it was out of concern for his mortality and the ISIS future. I was told that an "Al Khalifa successor" was in the process of being appointed, and that week some Mosul civilians were informed that there was a "new" — albeit unknown — person controlling the city.

Only the name never surfaced, and Baghdadi's bloodletting reigned on.

"Baghdadi will escape to Afghanistan if he survives this, to be Caliph there," one Iraqi intel insider anticipated. "That's next. That is where they are all gathering to regroup."

RETREAT TO RAQQA
November, 2016

ISIS was regrouping before our eyes and western powers did not possess the ability to stop it immediately.

Late one November morning, as more bullets flew in Mosul amid the intensifying quest to liberate its surroundings, I sat with the Yazidi soldiers on the mountain. We watched the rural roads headed west become increasingly choked with traffic. We watched in broad daylight as ISIS fighters and their families fled Iraq, bound for their Syrian buttress of Raqqa 275 miles away. Hundreds of cars crawled along the thirsty roads linking the two once beautiful countries, now spattered with their own blood.

But the ISIS convoys were safe from coalition attack — after all, most of their vehicles were known to be carrying civilians or children. For all the slack the U.S. so often received when it came to kids being caught up as collateral damage, I had also seen firsthand how much the U.S. valued the life of a child. Wherever possible, it would not violate international law with a precision strike on a minor.

"I haven't seen anything like this. They are running away massively," a Kurdish military intelligence official said, shaking his head at the absurdity of it all.

He picked up his special cell phone and called an ISIS informant who traversed the road in our distant purview.

"Ten minutes ago, the airstrikes hit a bomb factory in Bulayj," the official explained, repeating verbatim the words of the ISIS insider. "ISIS fighters came to Bulayj and arrested all the tribal sheiks and accused them of spying. Families are both willingly and being forced to go to Raqqa."

You knew ISIS was dipping deep into the depraved when it resorted to taking the lives of the religious leaders who had long protected them.

ISIS loyalists and victims alike were using every means possible to flee — embarking on the bumpy ride stuffed in pickup trucks, tractor-trailers, and small vehicles. The jihadists often sought to conceal their escape routes with the old rubber-burning trick on the rims of the road. But as we uselessly watched that morning, only the dust from a dirt track provided a scant cover.

It was a taste of their own medicine — running from their homes and their lives with little to no time to collect all the important things. It was a gamble of trust. The terror army's escape now depended on a different cover.

Vehicles making the 275-mile trek from Mosul to Raqqa had to use back roads that weaved through Arab villages. They had to hope and pray that they were still inhabited by ISIS sympathizers who would provide them with safe passage and, if need be, safe harbor.

The journey was typically completed in three legs. First, travelling from Mosul to the Syrian ISIS-controlled city of Abu Kamal, with one more stop in the town of Shadiya before the journey to Raqqa was completed. An alternative route extended from Mosul to the Iraqi ISIS consolidation of Tel Afar, then along unpaved trails to the border town of Ba'aj, before reaching Raqqa.

More cars piled up, and the frustration girdled inside me. But we all knew nothing could be done to corner the cars and round up the faces of evil before they could take more lives and spread their stupor.

"ISIS often has many different things they do to block vision," another Peshmerga officer explained. "But even so, we can't attack them [when they are] loading cars with kids and women. How could we attack kids? They have no part in this fight."

Similarly, the U.S.-led coalition would not unleash airpower with civilians in harm's way, giving ISIS — and likely its leadership — free passage to its Syrian base.

"ISIS is moving more and more of its families to Raqqa, they are kicking civilians out of their homes and occupying them," one source connected to Iraqi Forces intelligence told me. "Then, only the men return to Mosul to keep fighting."

Kurdish officials predicted the path would only get busier in the coming weeks as ISIS prepared to surrender Mosul and retrench in its bastion of Raqqa. Pentagon officials had made it clear that a military move on Raqqa would come quickly in the aftermath of a successful operation in Mosul.

Brave activists from inside Raqqa told me that ISIS operatives were bolstering checkpoints throughout the city. They were madly searching houses, rooting out suspected spies execution-style, and sending a renewed wave of worry through the embattled city.

"ISIS is afraid, arresting people every day, raiding Internet cafes," one Raqqa activist I knew only as the nome de guerre of Tim Ramadan wrote from within the depths of hell.

ISIS was also disseminating fear about the Iranian-backed PMF militias, which were sworn enemies not only of ISIS but most Sunni Muslims.

"ISIS is telling the people that 'the popular crowd' is coming to fight you, not just us," Ramadan continued, referring to the PMFs.

Experts reiterated that the U.S. would have to follow through to help instill stability between the sects and ethnicities if and when Mosul and Raqqa fell and ISIS was territorially vanquished. Some blamed a premature pullout of U.S. troops in 2014 for giving rise to the caliphate aspirants now moving along the back roads spanning its twin garrisons.

"I don't think the U.S., after declaring itself the leader in the fight against ISIS, can now step back without being seen in a similar light as post-Iraq 2010," observed Clint Watts, Middle Eastern expert at the Foreign Policy Research Institute. "Clearing the fight, but not being able to restore governance, leaving behind a broken country."

But Iraq was already broken. Now it was a matter of how — and by who — it would be put together. That was the subject of debate.

In the solitude of that mountain, I thought about all the failures, the falling bombs, the frontlines, the governments, the guns, the politics, and the proxies. I thought of the brainwashed children and the Yazidi sex slaves. I thought about the abused wives and stolen lives that were forced into cars with those barbarians — crossing countries, across the lines of their so-called caliphate.

I thought of the ones who had no choice but to sit in those beaten-up vehicles, and I wondered how many would make it through to see the end of ISIS in Iraq and Syria.

What is war? It is developing an innate sense of who might make it, and who might not.

Over the coming months, I knew much of that land route would be blown to bits. I knew some of those cars would be turned into suicide vehicles, and the bodies of their victims would be mopped into mass graves.

As I walked back down the winding Sinjar mountain and into the armored vehicle, I turned one last time to take in all the cars — instinctively understanding that the dusty road would very soon cease to exist, as would many of the lives that had crossed it.

No one doubted that there would be many, many casualties to come.

LIFE IN BETWEEN
December, 2016

The wounds of the walking were everywhere. The casualty counts, death counts, and displacement counts piled up.

One cold afternoon I attempted to do some clothes washing using an old dryer in the basement of a home where I was staying. I watched it churn and churn, and something felt very wrong to me. I tried to yank open the dryer door, but it would not stop, and the door was sealed closed. I pulled and pulled. Then that dream surfaced in my mind: putting my hand into that old-fashioned letterbox, crying tears for my mother, getting zapped. Instinctively, I flipped to the back of my hand and kept tugging.

Bam. The door swung open and with it a crazy number of vaults, throwing me back a few feet along with my clothes, popping with electricity. Outside, the electricity board had melted down.

I lay confused on the tiles for a moment, alone. That dream — my mother, my protector — had looked out for me. I was certain of it and I never felt alone again. Being a writer can be a lonely profession; it's you and sadness and a lot of words to string together. But I was not alone that day, or in any of the days to come.

The days passed and nights grew colder, the bombings louder and more unabashed. I slept on stiff couches and roamed through little villages. Like Sinonwy, the hospital still functioned and there was a small school for the children who wore a mishmash of clothes as close to a uniform as possible — as close as possible to something normal, to something as it once was in the world before ISIS came. The girls giggled as any little girls do, and the boys played ball. Outside, there was the beautiful sound of something old and familiar. Donkey bells jingled, and the market sellers sang out.

What is war? Often it is very ordinary moments, even when the surrounding plains being blistered into bits. But you keep going — you must.

The teachers at the Sinonwy school of Nasir Khider taught English and Math, and Hadi Murad, a sixth grade teacher, invited me for tea in their empty office. They told me that although the school appeared normal on the outside, on the inside it was a profoundly hurting place. Before ISIS, the town had nine schools, but now had been only two.

Students came doused in chickenpox, their hair falling out from malnourishment. There was no food they could give them, no drinking water to fill the fountains, and no staff to clean the toilets.

Some students were lucky enough to attend class twice a week, while others — if fortunate enough to pay cab fare to travel down the mountain — came just once a week. The classrooms were the old-fashioned kind, with flip-up wooden desks and chalkboards pasted to the walls. For six hours a day, the children learned Arabic, English, Kurdish, Math, Science, Geography, and History.

"We used to teach them the history of the ancient Islamic period," Nasir said. "But now, after this, we are soon going to start teaching the Kurdish history instead."

FOURTH YEAR OF ISIS: 2017
Lord Come Soon

THE LAST STAND
May, 2017

If regional history was to teach us anything, it would be that snakes are killed and wars end. But snakes procreate, and wars are reborn. The reasons are the same variations of one another. But what will always be admirable is the willingness of the victims to fight back over and over again.

All tools in the war against ISIS had eventually pointed to Mosul. It was the ISIS bread and butter — the head of the snake.

Days grew both darker and lighter as the fight to expel ISIS intensified through the first half of 2017. Night after night, soldiers gathered their blankets for weary nights on frontline posts, where there was little sleep as the fighting grew fierce. More blood spattered Iraq's earth; more people fled burning homes. More mass graves were unearthed and many more lives were lost.

But at the same time, the light at the end of the tunnel grew more visible. The number of ISIS loyalists dwindled. And, most importantly, the number of their days controlling the territory became fewer. Suddenly, the defeat that had for years felt so far away neared.

The ISIS reign of terror would come to an end, but at a tremendous cost.

In those horrific first months of the year, a myriad of horror stories landed in my lap. I learned that the basement of a decimated church in eastern Mosul — the once glorious Syrian Orthodox Church of St. Ephraim — had at some point become a dungeon for Yazidi sex slaves. The underwear of Yazidi girls were discovered after the walls had caved in from fighting. But more than a dozen of the persecuted minority had already been burned alive, chastened for trying to escape.

In April, it was reported that more than two dozen Iraqis stationed with the U.S. and Australian military advisers in the Mosul vicinity required treatment after being hit by another chlorine gas attack. That same month, seven Iraqi soldiers were injured in a similar attack in the Anbar neighborhood of western Mosul.

U.S. military officials carefully downplayed all this. One closely-connected Iraqi intelligence source told me that what was of paramount importance during the heated battle was "maintaining the psychological state of the soldiers." Thus, illuminating such attacks in the press could be perceived as making ISIS appear powerful and playing into the group's propaganda.

Nonetheless, there was no denying that chemical weapons had become something of a staple in ISIS's devastating — though diminishing — arsenal.

According to IHS Conflict Monitor, a London-based intelligence and analysis service, ISIS had used chemical weapons — sulfur and chlorine — at least fifty-two times in Syria and Iraq since the ISIS battle began. Several U.S.-led airstrikes had also targeted the group's chemical weapons depots and manufacturing facilities.

I could not help but feel that chemical weapons seemed something of a side freak show when it came to this war. Scores more were killed by regular bombs and bullets and yet, there was something about the use of such prohibited substances that piqued an interest — or perhaps a morbid fear — and generated mass attention and struck at the heart of the international community.

I learned that many Mosul civilians — innocent souls who had managed to survive over three years of ISIS occupation — were slaughtered in retaliation as Iraqi forces slowly surrounded the city. To have made it this far just to be taken out in the twilight of the fight jarred me.

Their body parts were strewn across the dusty streets — tiny bodies cracked open, left to die after their fleeing parents were gunned down, some hiding underneath the bloodied corpses of their family members, orphaned and forever traumatized.

I remembered the howls of a broken woman. Her little daughter had been lost for days, until she was found with nothing but a gaping black hole where the back of her head used to be.

What is war? Everything you could imagine hell to be, only worse.

The terrorist outfit had increasingly resorted to using civilians as human shields — making the battles all the more challenging, frustrating, and ultimately leading to more deaths within the ranks of Iraqi troops.

"Suicide belts are strapped on to helpless civilians — including women and children — by ISIS," Karim Aljobory of the Iraqi Counter-Terrorism Forces conjectured. "This was a big dilemma. We didn't know who a bomber was and who was not. Many of our men died from these people forced to be bombers."

A high-ranking Iraqi military official confirmed numerous incidents of ISIS "using human shields and fighting from civilian homes, mosques, hospitals, and schools." However, launching attacks from civilian-centric locations was hardly the only way in which the jihadist army used human shields.

Sometimes, the gambit blatantly tied up locals and placed them in front of an ISIS fighter, who then attacked them from behind. ISIS continued to drug kidnapped boys as young as eight and place them at the very front of their frontlines as shields for the cowardly men behind them. Yazidi sex slaves were forced into underground ISIS prisons and draped over their captors as protection against coalition strikes.

Those who didn't play along were slaughtered on the spot.

Female ISIS members were said to have stooped to weaponizing their own babies. Seemingly harmless mothers carrying their babies had been trained to enter areas thick with Iraqi soldiers only to blow themselves, their young, and the liberators around them to bits.

ISIS, especially in urban combat zones such as Mosul and Raqqa, went on to hijack homes of civilians, booby trap the structures, and then secretly abandon the civilians inside, well aware that the location could become a target for an airstrike.

"Sometimes, they will even trigger a secondary explosion, so the military is left dealing with an investigation of women and kids killed," said Mubin Shaikh, a counterterrorism expert on ISIS for the U.S. military and nonmilitary agencies.

ISIS had also began to use human shields as financing apparatuses. They extorted money from civilians by threatening to deploy them as shields if they refused or could not pay up. While the tactic of using people as shields was hardly new in war, ISIS's rampant use of the practice was unprecedented.

As a result, it had already taken Iraqi and partner forces more than seven months to get closer to Mosul, despite the initial hopes that it would take only a few months. And the job was not yet complete. But it was in the waning weeks of that battle for the city when ISIS was in losing mode and such in desperation to hold on that the use of human shields became even more commonplace.

An enemy is most dangerous when on the defensive, or when they are fighting for survival. This was not an easy fight, and ISIS was not the "JV team." ISIS did not care for the Rules of Engagement by which the west was taught to fight. ISIS did whatever it would take to achieve its strategic objectives, regardless of the consequences.

One high-level Iraqi official, who requested anonymity as he was not authorized to speak to the media, explained that the issue of human shields had been at the forefront of their strategic planning. And, in the quest to prevent collateral damage of civilian life, a larger-than-anticipated number of Iraqi soldiers had been killed.

While officials did not release exact figures during the Mosul operation — to avoid a dip in morale — it was estimated that hundreds of losses incurred monthly, especially in the early months of the year.

"Using human shields has made things very difficult for the liberating forces, as it forced them to expose themselves to the enemy, especially in close quarters combat in Mosul's Old City," the official said. "The Iraqi forces, particularly the counterterrorism forces, have been under strict instructions from the commander-in-chief, Prime Minister Haider Abadi, to do their utmost to protect civilians, and as a result, they have sustained high casualty rates. Unfortunately, there have been civilian casualties too."

ISIS used shields not only to delay strikes on ISIS targets but also to endanger advancing troops by ensuring that they could only advance to the point that was "manageable" to the terrorist group, Mubin said.

In addition, ISIS used human shields to stir up anti-coalition sentiment for the times when civilians were caught in the crossfire. For example, media and activist reports of civilian deaths by the coalition surged in early 2017 — with one alleged U.S. strike killing as many as 200 people in March — and prompted international outcry and further terrorist propaganda.

"The media will then amplify the detrimental impact of civilian casualties. No one wants to see women and kids killed by our bombs," he said.

So how did Iraqi forces and their coalition partners try to avoid killing helpless civilian shields while still defeating the uncouth enemy?

"We have limited our use of airstrikes in the Old City of Mosul, because buildings are very old, and it could cause them to collapse and kill civilians, also an ISIS tactic. We attacked on foot when we could, accompanied by bomb squads to dismantle IEDs," Karim, the Iraqi Counter-Terrorism Forces leader, explained. "We use snipers and light, as well as mid-sized rather than large weapons, to avoid hitting civilians."

Karim pointed out that when several ISIS fighters were grouped together, they used hellfire missiles. These have a "controlled, limited destruction range," generally up to fifty feet, and it was their way of minimizing civilian casualties.

"When you look at how many civilians were able to escape this cruel occupation," added Brigadier General Hugh McAslan, deputy commanding general of Operation Inherent Resolve, "it becomes clear how careful Iraqi Forces have been when attacking."

Often, the Iraqi and partner coalition forces simply had to wait until a high-value target left the premise. Subsequently, they attempted a precision capture or kill, or waited until civilians fled before striking.

"The U.S.-supported coalition forces in Iraq are adhering to the rules of combat to the best extent possible, including not attacking human shields used by ISIS," said Amit Kumar, president of the counter-terrorism firm AAA International Security Consultants. "ISIS forces have used the hesitancy on the part of the U.S. as a ploy to save themselves from attacks. This makes the task of battling ISIS very difficult."

FILES OF THE DEAD
June, 2017

Battling ISIS was difficult, but how different was it to fighting the lengthy U.S.-led war on Iraqi land years earlier? Almost every commander and geopolitical expert likes to posture that the war they are in is the hardest of all, but what does the mirror say?

Since 2003, more than 4,500 American military personnel died fighting in Iraq. Moreover, over 180,000 Iraqi civilian deaths were documented between 2003 and 2016 as a direct result of the ongoing fight inside the battered walls of the war-ravaged country.

According to a report released by LiveStories based on data gathered and distributed by Iraq Body Count (IBC), the most Iraqi deaths occurred in March and April of 2003. Those were the first two months of President George W. Bush's Operation Iraqi Freedom and the "shock and awe" campaign to dismantle the Saddam Hussein regime. During those two months, there were an estimated 7,186 civilian deaths — some forty-three percent of all civilian deaths — caused directly by the U.S. or its coalition partners.

However, the most lethal twelve-month period for Iraqis was during 2006, when 30,000 civilians were killed. This deadliest year for civilians on record was caused not by a particular group or the U.S. military and its coalition partners, but in sectarian-driven Sunni-Shia clashes. Mosques were routinely bombed, and executions became commonplace.

"This was the most surprising finding — the scale of sectarian violence between 2006 and 2007. Those were the deadliest for Iraqi civilians by far," Adnan Mahmud, founder of LiveStories, explained to me. "We knew it was bad, but it was shocking to see the numbers put into perspective."

The stunningly high number of deaths in 2006 was followed by a U.S.-led troop surge that resulted in relative assuage over the ensuing years. By comparison, 2004 and 2005 saw 12,000 and 16,000 civilian deaths, respectively, and in 2008 and 2009, civilian deaths numbered 10,500 and 5,000, sequentially.

"The legacy of violence from 2006–2007 continues to haunt Iraq today," the report stated. "The conflict between the Shiite-led Iraqi government and ISIS — a Sunni extremist group that has targeted Shiites for genocide — is in some ways a continuation of the sectarian violence of 2006 and 2007."

The report noted that, of all the known actors operating in Iraq, ISIS had killed more civilians than any other labeled party, but the identities of most of the executioners were not known. It also asserted that June 2014 — when ISIS suddenly swarmed in and overtook Mosul — marked the deadliest single month for Iraqi civilians, with over 4,000 slaughtered.

"The deadliest single months in the data were periods of rapid territorial takeover: the American-led coalition's 'shock and awe' campaign in March/April 2003, which took control of the country, and ISIS's lightning advance through northern Iraq in the summer of 2014," Adnan affirmed.

However, as something of a silver lining amid all the bloodshed, Adnan surmised that the then-ongoing American and Iraqi strategy against ISIS appeared to be working "without directly causing civilian casualties on the same scale as the 2003 invasion."

"ISIS is slowly but surely being defeated; it has lost control of every major Iraqi city except Mosul, and its stronghold there shrinks more and more each month," he added. "While many civilians have died, so far, the U.S. and Iraqi governments have managed to avoid collateral damage on the same scale as the shock and awe campaign."

DEMANDING ANSWERS
June, 2017

For too many, the shock and awe bubbled inside with no answers and nowhere to go. With Mosul's fall on the horizon, anger over the unanswered questions — the chase for information from the highest levels — was rising.

It was known simply as the "Speicher Massacre." But three years on, hundreds of families whose loved ones had been mercilessly murdered called on the U.S. to help them find some closure.

"ISIS called me from my son's phone and humiliated me. They said: 'Your son is killed, and we threw his body in the river so come and get him,' then they hurled abuses at me," Um Hussein, the mother of a victim identified only as Hussein recalled from her home in a poor part of the southern Iraq city of Nasiriyah. "I didn't hang up. I held on. I held on with the small hope that they might tell me where to find my son's body."

Um didn't just cry. She released a curdling sob that depleted all her energy, and even when she thought she could sob no more, she kept crying. I could begin to understand that there was no pit in a mother's love for her son. She had brought in the miracle of life and sent him off to serve his country. And now his country had let him die and betrayed her with the throes of silence.

While dozens had been held responsible for the attack, the families said that was not good enough. They wanted high-ranking government officials — including the former prime minister, Malaki — to also be held responsible. They claimed the officials had abandoned and betrayed the mostly low-ranking military recruits killed in the attack.

Part of what made the massacre so shocking was that ISIS had yet to take official control of Tikrit. The ancient city of Tikrit lay 150 miles from Mosul, where the bulk of the ISIS fighters celebrated a fresh victory. But despite its distance from Mosul, ISIS was still able to slaughter hundreds of Tikrit's young men.

"ISIS supporters and sleeper cells were ready and came out, taking advantage of a security vacuum," high-ranking Iraqi military officer Colonel

Mohammad Abdullah explained. "What happened was a response to the hidden hatred that was buried inside those close to Saddam's personal guards. They found themselves without jobs or authority after 2003. Their hatred led them to act in revenge."

The fateful day began calmly enough. It was June 12, 2014, and the unarmed cadets were leaving their barracks to begin a small vacation period. They had been walking along a road to reach the transportation that would take them to their homes in Baghdad. Several buses — one driven by the son of Saddam Hussein's half-brother — pulled up. The men inside the buses told the young cadets that they were from local Tikrit tribes and that they would assist them in their travels home. Instead, the young men, mostly between ages nineteen and twenty-five, were lured in and trapped inside the rickety buses and trucks that would drive them to their death.

The assailants separated the Shiite and non-Muslim cadets. They were taken to the Al-Qusour Al-Re'asiya region. One by one, hundreds of young men carved from the group were murdered — somewhere between 1,600 and 1,700 of them — just like that. If genocide could be captured in a frozen frame in time, it would be that of those men, barely out of childhood with their matching military-style haircuts, piled next to each other, their frightened faces pushed into the earth and their hands tied behind their backs, ISIS fighters poised with guns pointed at the backs of their heads.

Every gunshot kicked up a plume of dust, creating an evil fog as the person beside had no choice but to wait for their turn to take their last breath.

ISIS released videos of the massacre, showing the long line of young recruits blindfolded, tied up, and marched to what would become their own mass graves in the desert. Photos of cadets being beheaded, having entire magazines emptied into their frightened young faces, or being strangled to the death against the backdrop of jubilant militants became fodder for online ISIS recruitment.

For ten months after the cold-blooded mass slaughter, families received no word of what happened to their sons, nephews, husbands, and cousins. Some loved ones, overcome with emotion and anger, even broke into Iraqi parliament and hit security guards in fits of grief. Iraqi forces finally recaptured the region in March 2015, and some relatives were able to give DNA samples to assist authorities in identifying the bodies. More than a year later, mass graves were still being discovered and ripped open to retrieve the remains.

But it was now 2017, and a substantial portion of families were left begging for answers; for anything that could bring some closure to their calamitic lives.

"I still see him in my sleep, my son tells me not to cry and that he is in a better place," Um Hussein noted softly, with the type of hoarseness that could only be felt by a mother who had lost her child to the unknown. "But I can't change his bed covers; nobody can sleep in his bed because maybe he will come back one day."

The Iraqi government eventually blamed both ISIS and members of Saddam's dismantled Iraqi Ba'ath Party for the killings. But by then, some accused perpetrators had fled beyond Iraq's borders. In late 2015, two suspects were arrested in Finland, having been identified from the propaganda videos. The Finnish government denied an extradition request from Iraq, and instead, the twin brothers were acquitted on all charges in May of 2017.

Last August, the Iraqi government — despite opposition from human rights groups — sent thirty-six people to the gallows for their role in the massacre. But that was far from justice for many left in anguish. According to one military official, to whom I can only refer by his first name, Abdullah, "The authority figures in charge have not been charged due to political reasons." He passionately mandated that to avoid having to go after "large figures," the investigation "barely touched the surface."

"There were huge political and administrative mistakes such as sending young military cadets to train in an area that was not safe and left them without weapons or commanders and communications," he continued. "What needs to happen now is a real investigation that is unbiased, with the help of foreign specialists. Without charging the terrorists and also the authority figures that were in charge, we will leave a huge gap among the Iraqi people and make the national reconciliation very hard."

On the third anniversary of the horror, demonstrators swarmed through Baghdad's Tahir Square. They called for the prosecution of former Prime Minister, Nouri al-Maliki, accusing him of failing in his leadership role. Their eyes wet with anger and tears, they vehemently demanded he take responsibility. Instead, Maliki was installed as one of three vice presidents and was busy building his support base to run for the premier post once again.

"These soldiers went to Tikrit to protect the people and were instead betrayed by the people there. They were sold out to ISIS by local tribes. They were told that they would be helped to get back to their families but instead were handed straight to ISIS," lamented Mohammed, who hailed from the south-eastern Iraqi town of Amarah and lost his brother in the Speicher massacre. "Every commander all the way up the chain to the prime minister's office bears some responsibility for this. We want legal charges against every party responsible."

He, too, called on the U.S. and international community to help them reopen the case.

"It has been three years, and the majority of families don't know what happened. We don't know who was working and coordinating this attack with the new (post-Saddam) Iraq government," Mohammad said. "This massacre has become a wound that won't close. We feel like our brothers and sons were sold out in a political bargain between corrupt officials, and that is why they are trying to hide and close it forever."

When I raised the issue with U.S. officials, a spokesman for Inherent Resolve responded in an email that the Speicher massacre was "an internal matter for the government of Iraq."

I relayed the message to some of the family members begging for answers. Some mothers still left their windows open through the cold winter nights just in case their sons came creeping back. Even if they had already created cemeteries in their memories, the mothers were not ready to admit it.

But deep down, they knew that they would spend their lives begging for answers that may never come.

MOSUL BURNS, HAWIJA STARVES
July, 2017

Sometimes there are answers, but the critical questions are not asked —

that was the curious case of Hawija. Why had it mostly disappeared from the world's radar? Why was no one making a faster push to save the people from their abyss? What was war? Answers without questions and questions without answers; confusion, chaos, and complexity.

In the early months of 2017, as the fight for Mosul waged, friends and acquaintances in other ISIS-held towns and cities like Hawija reached out on messenger apps in breathless desperation. They felt as though they had been forgotten. They were going out of their minds with malnutrition and heartache, wanting to know when their liberation operations would begin.

Sometimes those knotted in the war bubble assume journalists, especially those based in the United States, have all the answers that will untie them.

"The government of my country and the media of the world are only interested in Mosul," a twenty-three-year-old resident of Hawija named Ahmed wrote, poised 100 miles from Mosul. "But what is happening here is horrible. Everyone is suffering from shortages of food. There are people dying because of hunger."

ISIS had been in control of Hawija — an almost entirely Sunni Muslim, 100,000-person city south of Kirkuk — since the Iraqi Army withdrew on June 16, 2014. More than two and a half years later, the city was a horror-scape of waste, sickness, and starvation.

"ISIS started cutting off food supplies six months ago," Ahmed continued. "People eat only bread and eggplant. It's $40 for a kilo of sugar and $70 for tea, $20 for rice. People cannot afford this. There is no cooking gas. There are no cleaning materials; people clean using the ashes of fire."

The battle for Mosul had prompted besieged ISIS members to take their rage out on their Hawija captives. Clusters of civilians had been slain inside the city on suspicion of working as "spies" for Iraqi or Kurdish forces. Fighters were being sent on suicide missions to kill families suspected of fleeing the city.

It was genocide.

Bodies of those executed by ISIS were wrapped in bags and stacked on city streets. Mothers washed dishes in murky water while their children looked on.

The painstaking images were not hard to find, as they littered social media. But still, nothing changed.

The failure to clear Hawija, which was poised between Baghdad and Mosul— before taking on ISIS in its mainstay of Mosul — had been a strategic risk, as Hawija had emerged as a harbor for sleeper cells and a haven for militants escaping Mosul.

The governor of Kirkuk, Najmadin Karim, called on the Iraqi government to begin an offensive to rescue Hawija as soon as possible, asserting that it was a "mistake" that the Mosul operation commenced before Hawija was liberated.

"It was a huge mistake from the beginning. Mosul is getting all the attention, and it is in slow motion," one Iraqi intelligence source said, speaking on the condition of anonymity. "But officials were in a hurry to announce the Mosul operation before the U.S. election and direct attention there."

Colonel John Dorrian, the U.S. Air Force spokesman for Operation Inherent Resolve, said Mosul came first simply because it was "the biggest prize to the enemy."

"Mosul is the second-most populous city in Iraq, and it will deeply hurt the enemy when that is taken away," Dorrian resolved. "The longer we allow [ISIS's hold on Mosul] to exist, the longer the brutal ideology of the group will exist in the world. Hawija is important, but it is not anywhere near as important as Mosul."

I flipped back in my notebook to January 2017, when victory in Mosul was still many months away, remembering those in Hawija who languished without an end in sight.

"Hawija isn't a priority for the Iraqi government because it does not have a lot of strategic value," Michael Knights, an Iraq-focused military and security affairs strategist at the Washington Institute, conjectured. "You could run a functional Iraq even if ISIS controls Hawija. Once you take Mosul, ISIS is reduced to a normal-type terrorist movement."

The Iraqi government had decided that, although Mosul was the largest city held by ISIS and would no doubt be the most prolonged and challenging battle of all, it was essential to liberate that city first. From that purview, the strategy was to cut the head off the snake and destroy the morale. Many analysts, experts, and journalists questioned the approach, pontificating that it was easier to free the smaller places first.

Yet emails flooded my inbox, and my Facebook messenger pinged. Again, I was a vessel to almighty America for those inside. Ahmed wanted to know when their time would come. I could not give answers. I could only tell him that they were not forgotten — that their time would come.

I believed it would. But I did not know when or how many would die waiting. I could not imagine which was worse for Ahmed: the years of suffering or the wait in anticipation of suffering some more.

Almost everyone I talked to in Iraq and at home seemed to remember with great clarity how they felt and what they did on that early June day in 2014 as news trickled in that Mosul had been stunningly overrun. I remember being late for work that morning, sleeping through my alarm. I remember walking through the front door of the Los Angeles offices and glancing at the monitors depicting grainy footage of the feeble situation. I remember clutching an oversized gas station coffee in disillusionment and receiving a searing text from a retired U.S. military friend:

"All those lives, all that training, and weapons we gave them," he wrote. "And they ran away."

But would we remember with such clear vision when it was over? The moment it was over? Would there be a moment it was over? Would it ever be over?

Finally, in July, during the burning Iraqi summer — when only smoldering remains of the Old Mosul City were left — the city was officially declared ISIS-free by the Iraqi Prime Minister, although few of us, including myself, were able to recall with the same clarity how we felt when the announcement was made. It was not much of a standout moment, even for the many of us who had lived and breathed the enveloping tragedy and followed it with a wary eye.

Hawija was still coated in blood and black flags.

Perhaps we all instinctively knew that the problem of ISIS was far from over — the plague would live on and induce terror with or without land to declare its own, and with or without an official defeat.

ISIS STILL STEALING, SPILLING AND SMUGGLING OIL
September, 2017

By September of 2017, ISIS was officially declared defeated — not only from its major Iraq bastion of Mosul but from its second bastion of Tel Afar, which came next. But their menacing money-making stream still spluttered throughout the war-ravaged country.

It had been more than two years since the Iraqi forces specifically sought to retake oil-rich areas from the militant brigade and cut off its predominant financial supply. Yet its militants continued to steal, spill, and smuggle crude oil from Iraqi oil fields. It remained a means to wreak havoc and fund their splintered but surviving campaign of terror.

"While ISIS is steadily losing its hold on populated areas, it still controls a not-insignificant portion of territory that contains oil and oil infrastructure," Justin Dargin, global energy expert at the University of Oxford, told me. "As a result, ISIS is continuing at a frantic pace to produce and smuggle as much oil as possible in a bid to acquire its ever-declining revenue base."

According to Iraq's state-run North Oil Company (NOC), ISIS still controlled scores of wellheads in parts of the northern Ajil field, which was considered contested land between Iraq and Kurdish governments. The terror network still controlled seventy-five percent of the Alas Dome in the nearby and prominent Hamrin field, NOC added.

ISIS gained control of the two fields in June 2014 after its sudden assault on Mosul. While Iraqi forces took back much of the region in early 2015, the militants retained a foothold in the more remote parts, such as the provinces of Salahuddin and Diyala. The jihadists were able to access these areas from their last prominent Iraq bastion of Hawija near the oil-rich city of Kirkuk.

It was in these areas that the terrorists orchestrated a massive oil spill, spanning thousands of acres southbound from the Hamrin Mountains and into the emancipated territory. Oil flooded into the streets of villages just northeast of Tikrit, according to the Iraq Oil Report and satellite imagery of the area.

It seemed that wherever there was blood, there was oil. Oil mattered more than blood. Oil was money — blood and human life had little worth by comparison.

But beyond triggering severe environmental damages, ISIS was still making money from the trade. The group continued to exploit local, financially desperate workers to keep the production and delivery of the oil functional. The group relied heavily on the professional technicians and engineers previously working in the areas to maintain and administer wells and production.

"ISIS was able to utilize to a great degree the old smuggling networks established during the Saddam [Hussein] regime to evade the international sanctions regime," Justin Dargin said. "While there has been significant degradation of these networks due to the bombardment and global efforts against ISIS, they still exist. When one smuggling route is under threat, ISIS is able to switch to another route."

Of course, ISIS's capacity to extract, refine, and export oil had been markedly degraded over the last two years as it had lost ninety percent of the land it once dominated. But since the group's shocking rise to prominence in 2014, the terrorists managed to survive through their illicit oil and gas trade. At its pinnacle in 2014 and much of 2015, it was estimated ISIS made as much as $50 million per month from its contraband energy operations, a figure that had been reduced to a still notable $10 million, according to Dargin.

Lee Oughton, a longtime Iraq security expert and former global manager for executive protection at oil field service giant Halliburton, pointed out that smuggling and selling endeavors continued with the help of splinter cells. These small and secretive ISIS alcoves allowed illegal trafficking into Turkey, Syria, and Iran.

"ISIS and other militia groups often have state-of-the-art weapons systems and intelligence networks just as good as some of the best intel agencies in the world," he contended.

Oughton also pointed out that ISIS-originated oil was known to have been trafficked up through Iraq and into Turkey. He claimed that it was refined inside Turkey and then either utilized within the country or extended outside its borders. Furthermore, the U.S. State Department accused the Syrian government of making deals with the militants to buy the black-market oil, which Bashar al-Assad's regime denied.

But the reality was that, in the majority of sales, the recipients of the terror-financing oil often had no idea of its starting point. ISIS was no stranger to masking its action, and smuggling oil from all sorts of groups and individuals made it impossible to ever really put the finger on who, precisely, manipulated the system.

"That is why ISIS oil operations have been so successful," explained Joseph Fallon, Islamic extremism expert and U.K. Defense Forum research associate.

He said that the bootlegging was primarily undertaken by an ISIS network of "venture capitalists" who utilized smuggling routes across Syria, Iraq, and Turkey, where they bribed or threatened government officials to accept their oil and get paid market prices. It was then mixed with the oil in legitimate pipelines, thus reaffirming that it had primarily become untraceable, and buyers were often unaware of its terrorist origins.

"ISIS makes its money up front selling to smugglers who take the risk and, if successful, make a significant profit. In addition to trucks and tankers, smugglers use boats, horses, or go on foot," Fallon continued. "ISIS is unlike other terror groups, the Taliban or Al Qaeda because international energy companies also use the transportation routes for smuggling; this source of revenue cannot be eliminated by traditional sanctions on a terror group's banking network. Because of oil laundering, no one knows if the oil purchased is from ISIS."

But those who bought the cheaper oil knowing full well of its ISIS origins often wired payments to female ISIS members in countries like Turkey. This tactic was based on the belief that women would not be as suspicious as men upon receiving international transfers.

"The money would then be physically transported into Syria and Iraq [to the terrorists] by courier," Justin Dargin said.

Hussein Allawi, CEO of the Akkad Center for Strategic Affairs and Future Studies and a national security professor at Baghdad's Al Nahrain University, also underscored that ISIS continued to profit from "oil derivatives" within the communities it controlled. Civilians were left with little choice but to buy gasoline, diesel, and fuel to supply electricity from the militants reigning over them.

And, before being run out of an area by liberating forces, ISIS in its final blow notoriously set oil wells and tankers on fire to limit vision and prohibit coalition airplanes from striking the area. The terrorists also set about pouring oil into the streets and opening taps on pipelines. This was not only to damage towns but also to trigger significant pollution in the Tigris River, which emptied into the Persian Gulf.

In Allawi's view, only a solid partnership between Baghdad and locals would be the key to ensuring another terror faction like ISIS could not swoop in and imitate the financing-with-fuel model of militancy.

"The control of the land by Iraqi forces and people is the guarantor," he added. "But we need an economic program for development that makes communities work in the oil areas for a partnership to protect wealth from theft, smuggling, and financing of terrorist groups. This is the next era."

A CALIPHATE IN TATTERS
November, 2017

When you talk to the people of Iraq, they speak in eras. There was life before Saddam and life after. There was life before ISIS, life during ISIS, and then the life after. The life after, for some, was untouched, while others would never really live again.

When you had been engulfed by so many decades of war and terror as Iraqis had, every building, hotel, and monument became defined by those epochs. Even driving late at night with my friend Rusly through the dim campus of the University of Baghdad — the second largest tertiary institution in the Arab world, second only to Cairo University — was a tour of beginnings and endings. It was a tour of conjuring the befores and afters.

Rusly had been studying statistics at the nearby Mustansirya University in early 2007 when suicide bombers attacked, killing seventy and wounding almost two hundred more. They attacked the innocent; they attacked the idea of education; they attacked religion; they attacked the students after class, as they waited outside for cars to take them home.

He remembered that day, the way it felt and the way it smelled like it was yesterday. There was the life before, and then the life that came after — a stunted version of the before.

The stories stitched into the fabric of Iraq almost always involved bloodshed and bombings. But in one's next breath, there were often happy narratives too, like how universities were almost always the birthplace of lifelong love affairs.

"Down in the south they do arranged marriages," Rusly explained. "But we here in Baghdad, we love the story. The romance."

He spoke softly and poetically, reminding me of the timeless sentiments that tell us love conquers all. It is the only tangible thing that can extinguish the pain.

Rusly dropped me off at my modest resting place, the Baghdad Hotel on Al Saadoun Street. He pointed out that the hotel had been shaken by a deadly car bomb blast in October of 2003 that slaughtered at least six and injured dozens more.

It seemed no building in Baghdad had been left unscathed. It seemed every story Iraqi's told was wrought with romance and happiness and unhappiness and uncertainty. It was both gripping and exhausting at the same time. But this was just how they lived their lives — balanced on an imaginary edge.

In many ways, it was fear, fatigue, and wild hope for a different kind of life that had first let ISIS in — forages of Sunnis, out of work and oppressed by Iraq's Shiite leadership. And it was that same fear, fatigue, and wild hope for a different kind of life that had caused their ranks to rapidly diminish after the fall of Mosul that summer.

Iraqis were slowly, cautiously stepping into their post-ISIS era.

While the liberation of Mosul was slow and painful, carried out between two U.S. administrations, the aftereffect appeared to be a case of fast-falling dominoes. President Trump scrapped his predecessor's often laborious approach to battlefield bombing, which critics insisted hamstrung the military. He allowed the decisions to be made by the generals in the theater rather than the bureaucrats in Washington, the generals said.

At its peak, ISIS held land in Iraq and Syria that equaled the size of West Virginia, ruled over as many as eight million people, controlled oilfields and refineries, agriculture, smuggling routes, and vast arsenals. It ran a brutal, oppressive government, even purporting at one point to print its own currency.

By mid-November, when I touched down in Baghdad again, the terror organization controlled three percent of Iraq and just below five percent of Syria. Its self-styled "caliph," Abu Bakr al-Baghdadi, was believed to be injured and holed up somewhere along the lawless border of Syria and Iraq.

Nonetheless, ISIS as a loose faction remained a danger. Its members — who once ruled cities and villages like a quasi-government — now lived secretly among civilian populations in the region as well as abroad in sleeper cells. These cells would likely present a terrorist threat for years. In addition, the terrorist organization was attempting to regroup in places such as the Philippines, Libya, and the Sinai Peninsula.

The military's job — to take back the actual land ISIS claimed as its caliphate and liberate cities like Mosul in Iraq, and Raqqa in Syria, as well as countless small cities and villages — was mostly complete. From the start of the forage into Mosul, it had taken less than a year.

"The leadership team that is in place right now has certainly enabled us to succeed," Brigadier General Andrew Croft, the ranking U.S. Air Force officer in Iraq, told me. "I couldn't ask for a better leadership team to work for, to enable the military to do what it does best."

President Trump gave a free hand to his then-Defense Secretary Mattis, who in May stressed military commanders were no longer slowed by Washington "decision cycles," or by the White House micromanaging that existed with

President Obama. As a result of the new approach, the fall of ISIS in Iraq — at least in terms of territory — came even more swiftly than hardened U.S. military leaders expected.

"It moved more quickly than at least I had anticipated," Croft said. "We and the Iraqi Security Forces were able to hunt down and target ISIS leadership, target their command and control."

After the battle to liberate Mosul succeeded in July, the U.S.-led coalition retook Tel Afar in August, Hawija in early October, and Rawa in Anbar province in November.

Marine Colonel Seth Folsom, who oversaw fighting in Al Qaim near the Syrian border, agreed. He wasn't expecting his part of the campaign against ISIS to get going until next spring and figured even then it would "take six months or more."

Instead, ISIS was routed in Al Qaim in just a few days.

"We really had one mandate, and that was tenable for the Iraqi Security Forces to defeat ISIS militarily here in Anbar. I feel that we have achieved that mission," Folsom said. "I never felt constrained. In a lot of ways, I felt quite liberated because we had a clear mandate and there was no questioning that."

Brigadier General Robert "G-Man" Sofge, the top U.S. Marine in Iraq, noted his commanders "enjoyed not having to deal with too many distractions" and that "there was no question about what the mission here in Iraq was."

"We were able to focus on what our job was without distraction, and I think that goes a long way in what we are trying to accomplish here," he said.

Sofge explained that while some in the western media implied that there had been a "loosening of the rules" since Trump took office, he insisted that such a suggestion was "absolutely not true."

"We used precision strikes, and completely in accordance with international standards," he said. "We didn't lower that standard, not one little bit. But we were able to exercise that precision capability without distraction, and I think the results speak for themselves."

The U.S.-led coalition released a statement highlighting that the Coalition Civilian Casualty Assessment Team had given thirty new staffers permission to travel throughout the region, likely in response to the growing chorus of criticism over accidental civilian deaths. It said military leaders continued to "hold themselves accountable for actions that may have caused unintentional injury or death to civilians."

The coalition also pointed out that dozens of reports of civilian casualties had been determined "non-credible," and just 0.35 percent of the almost 57,000 separate air engagements carried out between August 2014 and October 2017 resulted in a credible report of a civilian casualty.

In addition to air support, the U.S.-led strategy also included training and equipping Iraqi troops on the ground.

At Camp Taji, a sprawling military complex just outside of Baghdad, I watched as Iraqi forces arrived in old white buses from their nearby base and bury their faces in the dirt. They climbed rooftops for simulated exercises under the discernible eye of coalition forces, whose goal was to get them into tip-top shape to fight and squash any future threats before they could mushroom into anything malicious.

These young men had already encountered real-life combat time and time again in recent months. It was hard not to admire their enthusiasm and fire to be the best that they could be. These were the lives of those who served. These were our tax dollars at work, and for all the political rhetoric, it still seemed a fight worth fighting for. They were the fine young men of their generation, yet their young lives were disposable. How many of them would go down and how many outside their circle of loved ones would care?

While the Trump administration's success in the physical land defeat was often underplayed in the U.S. media, it was obvious on the ground in Iraq, according to Brigadier General Yahya Rasool, spokesperson for the country's Ministry of Defense and Joint Operations Command.

"I was not optimistic when Trump first came to the office," Yahya confessed from his opulent office with its high ceilings and brass-trimmed chairs. "But after a while, I started to see a new approach, the way the U.S. was dealing with arming and training. I saw how the coalition forces were all moving faster to help the Iraq side more than before.

There seemed to be a lot of support; under Obama, we did not get this."

Yahya kept saying that he hated politics, hated politicians, and that he was not a political guy. But he kept going down that political path the longer we talked. It was evident he was eager to please the Americans, who were ultimately responsible for propelling him into his esteemed position.

Despite the victories in the war arena, U.S. officials cautioned that much work remained to be done.

"ISIS is very adaptive," noted Colonel Ryan Dillon, the U.S.-led coalition spokesman. "We are already seeing smaller cells and pockets that take more of an insurgent guerrilla type approach as opposed to an Islamic army or conventional type force. So, we have got to be prepared for that."

He said as a result, the coalition is "adjusting some training efforts" so the Iraqi forces — upwards of 150,000 who had already undergone training — were equipped to address such threats and ensure long-term stability.

Folsom said "the worst thing we could do" was to not finish the job.

"If a country becomes a failed state, if it becomes a lawless region, you begin to set the conditions for what happened in the years before 9/11," he said. "In those ungoverned spaces where we don't know what is going on, that is where those seeds of extremism begin to blossom."

IN THE SLUMS OF SADR CITY
November, 2017

Many will argue with the privilege of hindsight that the seeds of extremism were planted in 2003 with the U.S. invasion of Iraq and the ousting of Saddam.

And the calamity that followed.

For thousands of U.S. personnel who fought in the Iraq War, Baghdad's destitute Sadr City still held a pivotal place in their memories — not only the years spent dodging the endless flying bullets, but the years spent trying to clean up the squalor, to win the hearts and minds, to show that there was a humanitarian side to the war after all.

I wanted to know what became of Sadr City, commonly known as the Thawra District, once deemed the ultimate danger zone.

"For those of us that fought there, we revere the name of that city like a ghost that we have been forced to make friends with," explained Boone Cutler, U.S. Army veteran and author of Voodoo in Sadr City: The Rise of Shiaism in Iraq. "It's a part of us. The Sadr City smell never leaves us. We all left something there that we miss from time to time. It's a birthplace to the souls we have becoming separated from the bodies we have become."

In late fall of 2017, I stopped on the way to Sadr and bought a cheap black abaya from a side store before I reached the checkpoint. It was for my own safety, so I could seamlessly blend in with the devoutly religious Shia population. I waited under the midday smog at the infamous turn circle — plastered with massive billboards of Iraq's famed Ayatollah Sistani and the ruler of Sadr City, Moqtada al Sadr — for my contact from the Mahadi Army.

His name was Moslem Salik, a hardened but polite man. He took his task of safeguarding me through the trash-crawling streets and the narrow pathways of the Muraidi Market with considerable pride and seriousness.

I breathed through my mouth as we wandered through the bustling markets. The soundtrack of the impoverished Shia-dominant Sadr City was a chorus of constant car honks and the shrilling, infant-like screams of poultry being burned alive in the open slaughterhouses. The pavements were thick with animal blood and urine. But the faces that stared back were smiling, working, sweeping floors, selling spices and scarves, and slaughtering livestock.

"I have a normal life now, there are no problems," a beaming, fresh-faced twenty-five-year-old named Sadoon Aziz quipped from behind his bench, where he made cheese and yogurt like a sculptor perfecting his Madonna. "It is much better now than under the Americans. They were closing the streets, cutting the roads off, arresting people, now we are all living in the quiet."

In April 2003, the U.S. Army 2d Squadron, 2d Armored Cavalry Regiment set up their headquarters in an abandoned cigarette factory in Sadr City, formerly called Saddam City. The HQ was comprised of more than a thousand soldiers and military police, and their focus was on repairing and rebuilding civilian infrastructure.

Six months later, however, hearts and minds gave way to guts and anger as the Mahadi Army, the city's esteemed militia loyal to Moqtada al Sadr — the prominent Shia cleric who still holds the city's sway — ambushed the U.S. troops. The chaos that ensued quickly degenerated into what would later be dubbed "Black Sunday."

The sky and the lives underneath it went black that day.

The moments that defined the following years were made up of urban fights, city lockdowns, almost daily mortar rounds, RPGs crackling in the reeking air, unearthing of shallow graves, and the sound of car bombs popping in every direction. The Mahadi Army's will to defy foreign presence only gained momentum throughout the American troop surges of 2007 and 2008, when rockets relentlessly fired from Sadr City into the American-controlled Green Zone nearby.

I meandered through the markets and met Abbas, a forty-three-year-old selling seeds and nuts in the local market. His face and one side of his body were mangled by discoloration and deep scars, like tiny trenches dug into his rough skin. He proudly proclaimed that he was one of the many arrested by U.S. forces and held from 2003 to 2006 in the notorious Camp Bucca prison — the same prison that had once sheltered ISIS leader Abu al-Baghdadi, the most wanted man in the world.

"I was attacking the Americans here, so they arrested me," Abbas explained. "They found out my name and took me from my house to the jail and tortured me. You can see the signs of torture on my face and body."

Shocked, I pressed him further on the torture allegations. The story unraveled: he was not tortured, but had gotten into a fight with the correctional officer. An uprising had stirred, and he was shot in the chaos.

Then there was an elderly lady named Saami in the next stall, who had run her fabric shop single-handedly for thirty years.

"During the Americans, I could not open my shop. Every day there was weapons," she said, wisps of her grey hair falling from behind her black abaya and into her tired eyes. "But we are secure now; we live in peace now. We have the Iraqi Army, the Mahadi Army, the Popular Mobilization — all of them together give us peace."

While recollections of U.S. occupation were typically not ones doused with happiness, there were some — the intellectuals of Sadr City — who had nothing but hope and praise for that era of their lives.

"I am a secular person. Trump now and all the American presidents before him, they are good men who want us to have a free and open society," Ismik al-Baghdadi, a local political writer and journalist, said softly over a sip of tea. "But the U.S. dream for an open society did not work in a country like Afghanistan, but it did in Japan. Maybe it is not too late for it to work here."

Nonetheless, Ismik insisted that it was far from a place of loss. He smiled and tipped his feathered fedora as a token of appreciation for the conversation, then disappeared into the fouled streets where wild goats scampered through the overflowing trash bins like rabid dogs, having been let off by their owner for a daily meal as he could not afford the feed.

According to Boone, Sadr City was a classic example of the challenges posed in their U.S.-led quest to help the poor during the occupation. The U.S. created programs known as "SWET" (sewage, water, electricity, trash), but if the Mahadi Army saw residents using the trash cans or participating in American-led assistance, they might have paid with their lives.

"It was a rough time. That was the leverage of the Mahadi militia," he recalled. "That was their game, not to let the Americans take credit for helping. We even brought in water, but they went along breaking the nozzles."

Six years since withdrawal of the troops, I could say that Sadr City had not become a beacon of prosperity. It was not squeaky clean, nor was it dripping with diamond trades and high-end market goods. But it was a place that — for the vast part of Iraq's last eight terror-rocked years — had seen little internal violence and crime compared to many other parts of the terror-torn country.

"The tribes enforce the law, not the law of the government," explained my

327

knowledgeable friend Rusly, who just published a book about his country's rises and falls called The Collapse. "Other tribes will punish for hurting someone; people know this, and that is why the crimes have stopped in Sadr City."

I understood why some of my U.S. soldier friends still had something of an odd affection for the impoverished place. I felt strongly that there was something here that they all should know. In a strange way, their mission in Sadr City had been completed.

It was a poor but tame place that more than three million people were proud to call home. Its inhabitants did not object; they did not want more. In fact, members of the local council claimed that they had rebuffed a recent multi-billion-dollar housing project awarded to a Turkish contracting company because they did not want to live in little apartments stacked on top of each other. They did not want their family homes knocked down and replaced by something towering and unfamiliar.

Most days in Sadr City were now peaceful and prosperous, but the residents were still targets of ISIS's bloody reign of genocide.

An ISIS bomb blast had killed seventy-six residents inside their cavity in August 2015. The city's members quickly mobilized to seal their borders from another infiltration.

Since the U.S. occupation, their leader Sadr had slowly redefined himself from a religious hardliner to a national patriot, a constant preacher of accord and harmony — even changing his army's name to the Peace Brigades — and brought his many die-hard followers on that journey to lay down arms.

"Sadr orders everyone not to talk about their own party and their own tribe, but all of us, we listen to him. We go to Friday prayers; we teach lessons of peace in the school," said Moslem Salik, Mahadi Army leader and my local guide and protector. "We are not scared from terrorists. Some of the simple people still worry about their businesses, but we will protect them with peace. ISIS will never come here."

Moslem invited me to his home for lunch, where his wife had prepared a Middle Eastern spread for me and the Mahadi peacekeepers, but I had to keep moving on. I texted a photo of Moslem to Boone along with updated pictures of the age-old area. Soon Boone texted back a photo of a younger and trimmer Moslem, snapped back in the early Iraq occupation days.

"Same guy? He was one of the ones turning off the taps and ruining the projects we were doing," Boone said, and I sensed his anger through the phone.

I shook my head in the coincidence of it all. Moslem, it seemed, had come far in his perception of westerners too. "Fuck that guy," Boone added for good measure.

ISIS CURSED, MOCKED IN MOSUL'S HAUNTED WASTELAND
November, 2017

"Fuck ISIS."

That was the message scrawled across what remained of the demolished buildings of Mosul's Old City, a now-apocalyptic wasteland destroyed by two and a half years of ISIS occupation and the battle that led to the city's liberation.

What is war? A victory that resembled an apocalypse.

After Iraqi checkpoint police had refused to let me cross the blown-up bridge connecting the new and old parts of Mosul, I made my way between security headquarters pleading my case. It was a goose chase for permissions, with every official passing me off to another. One general, after eyeing my business card, finally made a phone call to the federal police. I was ushered through more checkpoints and eventually into their disabled headquarters.

Inside the Federal Police Building, which teetered on the edge of the Old City by the Tigris River, a few young male civilians hoping to return to the city lined up. They were almost all amputees, holding each other's hands as they swayed in the freezing cold. Electricity and warm water belonged to a lifetime long gone. They had meandered into the hollowed place with broken faces and missing body parts, looking for answers about their loved ones.

I tried to talk to an old, frail man without hands, who stood like a ghost in the shadow of the door. He started to speak in a staccato dialect, but his husky words gave way to breathless pants — the kind of pants that come when you are trying so hard not to cry that it hurts like a throbbing fire at the pit of the throat. He stumbled back into the streets, his pallid body vanishing into the wreckage. For a moment, I wondered if I had even seen a real person at all.

The police chief pulled my interpreter aside and gave him a nudge that we should not have arrived without "a gift." I snapped back to reality. Bribery would always be next to godliness.

Nonetheless, after pleading my case all over again, I was given the green light to venture into the bowels of scorched earth. The remnants of the Old Mosul City were worse than even the most creative, evil Hollywood minds could have importuned with CG side effects.

There were parts of the Old City where the only scent was that of human flesh putrefying under the fierce sun. Dead bodies still rotted under the rubble of booby-trapped buildings, the stench of which morphed into the soot and sawdust. Iraqi officials claimed the corpses could not be removed until the area had been sufficiently secured. It could take months, maybe years.

Shrapnel, grenade launchers, and shell casings were like seashells dipped into the sandy and once densely populated neighborhood streets. The skeletons of vehicles used in suicide attacks piled up along closed or bombed-out roads. The remaining palm trees, which I imagined were once jewels in the historic landscape, now boasted mostly blackened leaves, wilting beneath the near-winter sun.

My feet crunched over the debris as I made my way to what was once the ISIS mosque — the infamous Grand al-Nuri mosque.

ISIS fighters bombed their own holy site in June as Iraqi forces closed in on the city. The front gate of the sacred site survived the bombardment, as did the pulpit where ISIS leader Abu Bakr al-Baghdadi once stood. The very spot where Baghdadi had made his public appearance in 2014 to announce himself the "caliph" of the so-called "Islamic State" was crushed into a dwarfed version of itself.

That was where the words of bitter revenge were immortalized.

The "Fuck ISIS" graffiti was tagged with a "Mein Ali" pseudonym, a reference to the first imam of Shiite Islam, one of the two major branches of Islam and one that frequently clashes with the other major branch of Sunni Islam. ISIS fighters were mainly Sunni Muslims.

Local officials seemed proud of the graffiti. The expletive had not only made it to the walls of the decimated Grand al-Nuri mosque but smaller renditions also stained the half-chopped walls and cracked ceiling.

Unlike the scene on Mosul's east side — busy streets choked with traffic and children swerving through the roadside markets on broken bicycles — life in the Old City was a long way from returning to anything that even remotely resembled normal.

In many areas of the Old City, not a single dwelling had survived the devastation.

"There was no way to get ISIS out without doing it this way," one Iraqi police officer said haplessly, explaining that every time they attempted to enter a house, ISIS fighters would slaughter a civilian in retaliation.

The Old City was unlivable, though a few families had trickled back despite the dangers of unexploded bombs and the absence of water or basic services. Police guarded the eerie streets and workers attempted to sweep out the hazards. Out of nowhere, ceilings still suddenly crashed to the ground.

For some, it was not even worth the cost of repair. It was the same argument I had heard a year earlier in Sinjar.

"The best way forward is to build a new city. Find some more land close by and just start again," Raghib Kawaji, a fifty-seven-year-old retired engineer said as he stared numbly at the guttered storefronts of the local market where he owned three trading businesses. "How can this city ever be what it once was?"

Mosul was poisoned by revulsion.

What is war? It was a surge of ruination and rubble; exhilaration and victory. It was different shades of gray. Color had been drained from every dead thing left languishing. The mountains of wreckage were drab, ash, powder, pasty, destroyed.

Only it felt as though the victory was hollow. Of course, the triumph was rimmed with a deserving sense of pride for all who had fought relentlessly against the enemy, and there was genuine cause for celebration. But inside all of that, waiting to burst out, was a sense of something else, something colder — a war of sorts still simmering, leaving so many unknowns to become knowns.

WHERE IN THE WORLD IS BAGHDADI? 2.0
November, 2017

But would the biggest unknown ever become known? Where in the world was the eponymous ISIS leader?

As the winter of 2017 dawned, Abu Bakr al-Baghdadi was believed to have been in retreat — alive, albeit wounded — and hiding near the Iraqi-Syrian border, according to intelligence gathered by Iraq's Ministry of Defense (MOD).

"We have a lot of information. He is alive, moving between the Iraq and Syria border in desert areas," Brigadier General Yahya Rasool, the spokesperson for the MOD and Joint Operations Command, in partnership with the U.S.-led coalition, told me from his lavish Baghdad office, where his underlings tapped away on computers and Iraqi Security Forces division flags flapped gently beneath the fan. "There is still ISIS sleeper cells scattered in these desert areas."

More specifically, MOD intelligence indicated the self-styled caliph was skulking between the border city of Al-Qaim in the Anbar governorate in Iraq and Abu Kamal in Syria's Deir Ezzor governorate, on the bank of the Euphrates River.

Yahya could not provide an exact number of militant operatives left but estimated that "tens" — Baghdadi among them — were still "living like rats" in remote underground shelters, with some using disguises like farmers or women's coverings to evade detection.

"ISIS as an organization still exists," Yahya cautioned. "We still expect terrorists and cells to attack."

The newly disclosed intelligence marked the latest in a series of statements and speculations from various groups about the terrorist leader's location and wellbeing.

A representative for Operation Inherent Resolve told me there was no valid information on Baghdadi's health or whereabouts, but U.S. forces were aware that members are still alive and "that includes some of its leaders who are in hiding."

The spokesperson also said Baghdadi sustained "severe injuries" on February 11th from an F-16 bomber strike in the al-Qaim area, which killed several of his guards. His condition, according to Yahya, meant that his movement between the two countries had become increasingly limited.

"The target was accurate. We hit the right place," he insisted. "But he is a clever man. He has been doing this a long time. He knows how to move to protect himself."

Simultaneous offensives to squash ISIS from both sides were launched earlier in the month. Al-Qaim was successfully secured by Iraqi forces with the support of the U.S.-led coalition on November 3, while control of Abu Kamal went back and forth between Syrian soldiers and ISIS, with Syrian officials declaring that it had again seized the city on the following Saturday. But pockets of ISIS fighters remained.

Yahya's assertions also threw into question the Russian claim that its forces had killed Baghdadi in an airstrike at a gathering of ISIS leaders in Raqqa, Syria, in late May.

Baghdadi, born Ibrahim Awwad Ibrahim Ali al-Badri al-Samarrai, who was then around forty-six years old, had made his last public appearance at the now-destroyed Grand al-Nuri mosque in June 2014, shortly after ISIS invaded Mosul. He had since released a spattering of undated audio recordings from undisclosed locations. In early September, ISIS released a forty-six-minute-long tape of Baghdadi speaking.

The vicious leader, who had a $25 million bounty on his head, referenced several then-current events, including the "nearly ten-month-long fight for Mosul," which began some eleven months before the recording's release, as well as North Korea's nuclear threats and Russia "taking control" of Syrian peace talks, indicating he had survived the ongoing ISIS offensives at least until then.

While it was not clear how much control Baghdadi still had over the group's operations, his death would ultimately serve as a blow to the remaining loyalists.

"We will get him," Yahya said casually, sipping tea.

If Baghdadi were to be killed by Iraqi forces, Yahya continued, they planned to present the DNA evidence just as they did after the 2006 death of his predecessor, the leader of what was then called Al Qaeda, Abu Musab al-Zarqawi.

"But personally, I would prefer if this criminal was arrested. And we could get a lot of information from him," the general said. "Baghdadi should be put in public and face the courts."

INSIDE IRAQ'S BIGGEST POTENTIAL WEAPON OF MASS DESTRUCTION
November, 2017

The threat was public and one which scores of officials all over were trying to combat. Tackling it was far from a cheap or easy task.

One of the country's most prized possessions looked magical from the outset, but below its surface was a stage set for catastrophe. For too long, next to nothing had been done to turn off the ticking time bomb slowly splintering below where the eye could see.

From the crack of dawn until the starry dusk, hundreds of technicians from all over the world could be seen against a backdrop of dun-colored mountains and a tranquil, sapphire lake. It appeared serene and picturesque, but the workers were desperately salvaging Iraq's Mosul Dam — which was once under ISIS's control and stood just forty miles from the former terror stronghold of the same name. The beautiful vision was long feared as a potential weapon of mass destruction.

"When we started, the risk assessment regarding the potential fate of the dam was very high. And ISIS had stolen everything that was here," Carlos Morales, Deputy Project Manager for Trevi — the Italian company awarded the repair and maintenance contract to frantically revert catastrophes — informed me. "The logistics have been challenging, especially in the beginning being so close to ISIS."

What is war? It was cities and landmarks tossed between palms of control. It was winning battles only to find other conflicts snaking beneath them.

That is what it felt like to return to Mosul Dam. I remembered what the place had felt like in the fall of 2014 when it was a gouged and dangerous place, with dogs eating fighters' faces in the distance. It had since become a race against time to secure the ailing structure from a much different, brutal force.

Since the emergency work commenced just over a year earlier, some 15,000 metric tons of cement had been poured into the infrastructure and more than 150 miles of electrical grids had been installed. Furthermore, "critical grouting"— the pumping of a mixture of clay, water, and cement — had been mainly executed using computer technology to quickly reinforce the dam's dangerously soft foundation of gypsum, which dissolved easily in water.

The dam, which had been a cause for construction concern ever since it was built in 1984 as the "Saddam Dam," triggered a renewed level of panic after ISIS captured it in August 2014. Although the terror group only controlled the area for ten days before being run out by Peshmerga and Iraqi forces, it was long enough to do severe damage. Not only was the daily, mandatory maintenance not performed during that time, but it did not resume following the heavy fighting as priorities shifted to the immediate war.

"The interruption of grouting efforts during the period of ISIS control was the most damaging effect of the occupation, and engineering and technical advice to reestablish grouting has been our main activity in support of the Government of Iraq," a spokesperson for the U.S. Army Corps of Engineers (USACE) — which served as the engineer and technical advisor to the Iraqi Ministry of Water Resources for its contract with Trevi — said. "Dams like Mosul provide immense benefits for clean power, clean water, and protection from flooding for the people of Iraq. They come with an equally critical responsibility for the dam owner, the Ministry of Water Resources, to provide for continued safe and secure operations."

The dam, the largest in the country with the capacity to hold three trillion gallons of water, administered the flow of the Tigris River north of Mosul and supplied electricity to more than a million residents. The USACE estimated that a burst of the 370-foot structure would send floodwaters tearing more than 200 miles downstream — swallowing up villages and much of Mosul City with up to eighty-foot waves, reaching as far as Baghdad and potentially resulting in the loss and displacement of millions of lives and up to $20 billion in fiscal damages.

A 2015 study from the European Commission's Science Center further concluded that even a partial fissure — just one-quarter of its full capacity — would have clamorous consequences. The concern even prompted a pressing memo from the U.S. Embassy in Baghdad in March 2016, cautioning Americans to "avoid areas within three miles of the river and have a plan in case of emergency."

The Trevi Group was calling its work to date a "success," yet the maintenance had to be rigorously maintained for the sake of those who lived in the dam's surroundings.

That onus, soon enough, needed to fall back to Baghdad.

"Some grouting results look promising, but uncertainty will remain until grouting efforts have progressed across the full length of the dam," the U.S. Army Corps of Engineers representative said. "The Ministry of Water Resources has concluded that the second year of grouting and training is necessary."

The extra year's work would complete the initial two rows of grouting and would continue the training of Iraqi personnel.

The Trevi contract also came with the Italian government's bonus caveat to deploy 450 troops to guard the vulnerable area while the repairs were underway. Along with protecting the workers, the soldiers — led by the Praesidium Task Force of the 3rd Alpine Regiment of the Italian Army, which was also part of the U.S-led coalition to defeat ISIS — had been training Iraq's Counter-Terrorism forces and had implemented initiatives to support the local hospitals, schools, and families inside the small villages of the Mosul Dam community.

Wars always had wars inside. And whenever there were wars, there were hearts somewhere, too. I watched with a silent smile as the passionate Italians sashayed from one town meeting to another clinic to a local child, taking notes and bearing supplies. Even with their armored vehicles, rifles, military fatigues, and plated vests, they wanted to prove to the townsfolk that they were there not to hurt but to help.

"We've been cooperating with the Italian task force with the objective of protecting the dam and the people around it," explained an Iraqi Counter-Terrorism leader, Major Ahmed, as he instructed his unit to guard a local clinic. "But the idea long-term is for us not only to help in a military way, but in a humanitarian way too."

TO STAY, OR TO GO AGAIN
December, 2017

When military missions become humanitarian missions, is it a given that they are helping and not hurting? Is a road often paved with good intentions a road that should have been paved in the first place? Every person has their own view of what constitutes good and evil.

Perhaps the American leadership intended only to do good with its 2003 infiltration — bombing and then building. Maybe the twisted leadership of ISIS also rationalized that they were only saving the lands for themselves.

Throughout the long history of what is now the Republic of Iraq, the nation was routinely invaded, occupied, and hacked open by both foreigners and despotic domestic regimes — the most recent being ISIS. War was nothing new. But with this latest breed of extremists defeated — if only in a territorial sense — would the nation be able to stand on its own? Or was a continued U.S. military presence a security necessity?

"We are here at the request of the government of Iraq to aid in the defeat of ISIS," a U.S. military spokesperson for Operation Inherent Resolve stated. "Future operations will be dependent upon the needs of the government of Iraq."

However, Defense Secretary Jim Mattis took a more affirmative stance when he testified before a Senate Appropriations subcommittee earlier in 2017, stating that it would be an error to cite victory and leave, as was the case in 2011, and then "find the same lesson." Similarly, Secretary of State Rex Tillerson had voiced the importance of retaining U.S. troops to avoid an ISIS-type re-emergence.

While U.S. voices agreed, the matter deeply divided the Iraqi people. Iraqis were tough and proud, and most did not want to acknowledge the need for outside support. But at the same time, most feared the responsibility that came with the handing back of independence.

Nseeif Al-Khattabi, governor of the Holy Karbala Province Council, explained that he was for political and diplomatic relations with the U.S. rather than military ones.

"Let us pick our destiny," he said, noting that it would be better for Iraq to reject outside interference.

Muoaed al Bahadely, a thirty-year-old from Baghdad, told me that he too was against U.S. presence because it was a "clear game to create terrorist groups that say they are Muslim, but it is orchestrated to destroy Islam" — citing the American backing of the 1980s' Mujahedeen to fight the Soviets in Afghanistan.

However, the majority of Iraqis I spoke to across the country seemed to be in favor of the U.S. remaining for the long haul.

"If America had stayed after 2011, nothing like ISIS coming in would have happened," lamented Baghdad native Ahmed Naeem. "Let's stop the cheap talk and agree that the American withdrawal cost us heavily, and the blood of our kids."

Moreover, Mazan Obedi, a twenty-eight-year-old from Baghdad, advocated for U.S. troops remaining in the "style of Japan, Germany, and Korea" after WWll and the Korean War, respectively. "Not only so ISIS cannot come back," he explained, but also to "put pressure on Saudi Arabia, Turkey, and Qatar" to not sponsor terrorists. Masereen Saed also conjectured that those who "tried to sell heroism against America" — like Cuba — ultimately fared far worse than the likes of other countries that aligned with the U.S.

Yahiya Akbar, a twenty-four-year-old university student, cited monetary reasons for supporting the U.S. staying. Meanwhile, Ahmed Naeem lamented the 2011 withdrawal of U.S. troops from Iraq, insisting that it cost the people of his country heavily.

"Without America, we will suffer economically," he stressed. "We should use America to train our soldiers and our army."

Others, such as twenty-five-year-old Marwa Alzede, a recent university graduate who studied geography, supported the U.S. military lingering, but not in a "continuous, forever way" — just until their own army was strong and unified enough to "answer to all the challenges that surround the country."

"We don't want to be part of the threats that come to America from our neighboring countries," she explained. "Then we have to pay the price."

On a visit to the U.S. in late March, Iraqi Prime Minister Haider al-Abadi said that he supported keeping a U.S. foothold for the longer term.

"The fight against ISIS's presence in the country will require a longer-term, sustained effort that goes beyond the major combat operations currently underway," Tom Basile, political commentator and author of Tough Sell: Fighting the Media War in Iraq concurred. "We need a sustained, supportive presence in the country to protect the Iraqis and our interests in the region."

One high-ranking Iraqi intelligence official, who was not authorized to speak on the record, pointed out that even if the U.S. did stay, it was uncertain what its role would be.

"We want a strong DOD strategy to help the Iraqi Army," said the source, adding that Iraqi officials also wanted assistance with greater "emotional" impact, such as assistance with hospitals.

The U.S. government had given $58.8 million to Iraq in 2016, designated to assist with everything from peace, security, and humanitarian and social services to education and governance.

Nonetheless, a continued American military involvement could potentially come with a high price for U.S. military personnel.

One young professional named al-Haidery, who identified himself as a "technocrat" and was aligned with the movement championed by prominent Iraqi Shi'ite Muslim cleric Moqtada al-Sadr, warned that U.S. troops would "of course" face steep violent resistance.

"America is interested only in oil and control of the region. It considers Iraq as a barrel of oil and strategic location to build its military bases," the technocrat said. "The great danger facing U.S. forces in Iraq if they remain, is the armed groups supported by Iran. These groups have evolved a lot."

Al-Haidery emphasized that they had evolved from even the post-2003 war days, in which the Tehran-backed militias were responsible for 500 U.S. service member deaths.

Danger from Iranian-sponsored PMF militias was recognized by people outside al-Sadr's circle.

What is war? It may be as old as time, but there is no template on how to fix it, stop it, or contain it. There are no firm answers, other than the distrust it perpetuates.

"Troops should stay," Loag Husain, author of the Iraqi political history book Dozens of Years of Chaos added. "But how can they deal with Iranian militia in Iraq? That will be the question."

IRAN-BACKED FIGHTERS VOW TO DRIVE OUT U.S. TROOPS
December, 2017

From the meniscus of the Iranian-backed militias, the answer to the next round of quagmires was to push out the Americans, whatever that would take.

The Popular Mobilization Forces had helped vanquish ISIS from much of Iraq. A battle-hardened mob of around 100,000 militiamen with close ties to Tehran, the PMF set its sights on the remaining U.S.-led coalition troops scattered across the country.

"America should only be here for an embassy — any military presence and we will target them," said Saif Ali, a thirty-seven-year-old member of the PMF's Harakat Hezbollah al-Nujaba paramilitary based in the southern Iraq governorate of Basra. "I fought the Americans after 2003, and the British in southern Iraq, and I am happy about that. I don't hate the American people, only hate the U.S. military, and I have killed many of them."

Ali was one of the thousands of PMF members who also took advantage of Iran-supplied weapons and ammunition to take the lives of hundreds of U.S. troops during the insurgency that followed the invasion of Iraq. They viewed themselves not only as the enemy of ISIS but the enemy of the United States too.

How ironic, I thought. If not for the 2003 U.S. invasion, none of these people would have any power. They would still be under the repressive fist of Saddam and his cronies, or they would be dead for attempting to rise up. How fickle memory and alliances can be.

Rayan al-Kildani, the thirty-two-year-old leader of the PMF's Babylon Brigades, an Iraqi Christian militia, also noted that he got his start fighting the Americans post-2003 — allegedly after learning how to use weapons from action-oriented TV shows and movies. Although he had relatives in the U.S. and even visited a few years ago, he boasted that he had threatened to attack U.S. intelligence personnel he encountered after the Mosul battle, and ultimately wanted to see American forces gone.

He then showed off battlefield selfies with the notorious spymaster General Qasim Soleimani. Anytime I wanted to go there, he said, he would take me on a private plane.

We sat for hours in Rayan's glossy militia headquarters one chilly Baghdad afternoon. More and more militiamen piled in as the afternoon turned to night, a line of AK-47s stacked around the door like trees bursting up in the woods. The shisha charcoals were lit, and the fruit and nut bowls replenished over and over again. Soft Iraqi music hummed in the background and, interwoven between all the talk of war and weapons and blood and guts, were conversations of the country's sumptuous culture and wisdom.

I listened to little lectures about the rich Assyrian history and the lost cities from ancient times, now buried beneath Baghdad's roads. Some complained that the U.S. invasion had unlocked the doors to the rabid looting of their national museum. They saw it as deliberate vandalism by the Americans, designed to wipe away their cultural bequeathal. From that horizon, to them, the United States was just like ISIS.

One suited militia man lamented that he had assembled a team to troll the local markets in the endless search to buy back and restore their national antiquities.

What is war? War left an orphaned past — a history with gaps and missing generations — because greed and death had taken away large chunks. War wandered the earth trying to stick it all back together again.

The PMF had been brought into existence soon after the June 2014 ISIS invasion in response to a fatwa — an edict issued by an Islamic leader — from Shiite cleric Ayatollah Sayyed Ali Hosseini Sistani. He called on all able-bodied males to fight the brutal Sunni insurgency. The PMF was initially an unofficial umbrella organization comprising some forty-odd militia groups. But, given their strong fighting skills and popularity among locals for their prominent role in combating ISIS, Iraqi Prime Minister Haider al-Abadi folded them into the Baghdad government's security forces in November 2016.

Only I had come to believe that heroism is always filled with flaws; there is no purity in heroism. One's hero is another's nemesis.

Most PMF fighters drew salaries from the Baghdad government. But Mohand al-Eqqaby, the PMF spokesman, informed me that at least 50,000 unpaid fighters were on the ground and — for now, at least — had no intention of fighting U.S. troops.

But he still wanted the Americans gone.

"Our stand is clear," Mohand asserted. "America was not there at the beginning of this ISIS crisis when we needed them most. We are strong now, and as long as we are fighting, Iraq does not need Americans on our land."

The PMF had also expanded its influence beyond the battlefield and into the political sphere ahead of Iraq's approaching parliamentary elections. Many militia leaders were expected to win crucial seats and challenge Abadi, a reliable U.S. partner agreeable to keeping Iranian influence at somewhat of a distance.

Anxieties grew over the PMF's increasing influence and the notion that many took their orders not from Iraq's commander in chief, but rather from Iran's leadership.

"Our goal is not to be employers of the Iraqi government, but to fight in Syria and al-Quds (Arabic for Jerusalem), and we will await orders from our religious men," said Hashim al-Maihi, a forty-four-year-old former policeman who was now a leader in the "League of the Righteous People" battalion, or Asa'ib Ahl al-Haq, in the PMF. He said that he did not draw a Baghdad salary and that it was his duty to fight American occupation in Iraq during the Bush-signaled war and later to fight ISIS.

"My rifle is standing up, and I am ready to protect any city," he said. "In my house, I raise pigeons as a symbol of peace in Iraq, but my dream is not to see Americans in Iraq."

The PMF's objective to disperse its military across the Middle East — as scores defied Baghdad's orders and fought for Iranian interests alongside Syria's army and Lebanon's Hezbollah — was troubling to some U.S. officials.

In November, CIA chief Mike Pompeo revealed he had sent a letter to Iranian Major General Qasim Soleimani, warning that forces under Iran's tutelage may attack U.S. troops. Pompeo added that the U.S. would hold him and his country accountable for "any attacks on American interests."

"Now that ISIS is not much of a threat, the PMF is likely to plan attacks against U.S. personnel in Iraq that would be carried out as soon as Tehran gives the orders," surmised James Phillips, a senior research fellow for Middle Eastern affairs at the Heritage Foundation. "This is a major concern, given that tensions between Iran and the U.S. are likely to grow in the future."

An American spokesperson for Operation Inherent Resolve, however, told me that officials "did not anticipate a PMF aggression toward coalition troops."

"There are certain factions within the PMF that may cause concern, but the PMF as a whole is not considered a threat to coalition forces," the representative noted.

While concerns had been routinely raised that the PMF could access U.S. weapons issued to the Iraqi Army—several fighters claimed to have "borrowed" Iraqi Federal Police uniforms to participate in battles that they were prohibited from joining — American military leaders said they continued to work with the Iraqi leadership to "maintain accountability of all equipment."

That, of course, had been their way into the Mosul fight. I thought back to that time over a year earlier when the militiamen assured me that they would be on that frontline, whether technically permitted or not.

Yet there were some PMF members who vowed to never fight the Americans.

"On the contrary, I stand with them because at that time we were liberated, and they removed the tyranny of Saddam Hussein's regime," said Abbas Naji, a twenty-three-year-old member of the PMF's Asa'ib Ahl al-Haq. He had left the Iraqi army to join the PMF after the ISIS blitz in 2014, disgusted that members of his army "ran away" and allowed ISIS in. The war has left him partially blind.

"I hope that Americans stay in Iraq and we can learn from them on how to make sure Iraq moves forward to be a prosperous nation," he opined. "I want us to join the developed countries. And fast."

THE KURDISH QUESTION
December, 2017

The flight from Baghdad to Erbil on Iraqi Airways was a fast one, just under an hour; one I had always found serene.

Even in the dense darkness, you can just make out the mountains climbing toward the dim stars. And when you rise above the clouds, the tapestry of stars goes on forever. I touched down again in November, less than two months after the federal government had reasserted control of the airport, rendering the Kurds no longer able to operate as an international facility but only as a small, domestic service. Every analyst and expert kept saying the matter would be resolved in days. But it had not been solved. Erbil had been an accessible hub for western journalists and aid workers to get to during the ISIS fight, as it did not require a visa.

Now, the backlog and difficulty of obtaining visas and having to go through Baghdad had proven to be an unwinnable challenge for many journalists and photographers. Many had left, and few were able to return. It had descended into a quiet, strange place. The Kurdish flag still hung loosely and signs encouraging people to "VOTE YES!" in the referendum still trimmed the entrance, flapping whimsically in the frosty air. They were like the Christmas decorations that were never taken down months after the occasion had come and gone, leaving a sad longing for a happier time that seemed so far away.

The defeat of ISIS was not a victory being celebrated in Erbil. They were already headfirst into their next war, a much more protracted war: the fight for their freedom.

But that overwhelming yes vote — the Kurds' long-running dream to form their own country unaffiliated with Iraq — had come back to haunt. The dream now seemed a lifetime away as Baghdad cracked down harder than anyone anticipated. The upset central government had retaken contested territory and exerted authority with an iron fist.

Almost the entire international community had warned the KRG against taking the non-binding referendum at a time when the ISIS threat had not yet been obliterated, fearing it would hurt the final phase of the fight.

The U.S. government had also issued warnings, doubling down on its longstanding policy of a united Iraq. Despite the State Department not mincing words, the Kurds had gone ahead with their reverie vote in late September. But with repercussions in full force, some people turned their frustration into a narrative of betrayal by the U.S., a country they had once looked at with great reverie.

The KRG top brass, however, knew too well that the American friendship was vital for their survival even as a semi-autonomous enclave.

While Washington opposed the September 2017 referendum for independence, Kurdish Prime Minister Nechirvan Barzani insisted that the people of Kurdistan still saw America as their number one partner and hoped the U.S. would come to endorse their ongoing dream of independence.

"There was disappointment among the Kurdish people; the people of Kurdistan have had high expectations from the United States, and they believe that the values the U.S. cherishes, we also cherish," Nechirvan told me over tea in his gilded office. "But the people of Kurdistan, they still love the United States. Kurds consider themselves a friend and partner to the United States. We want this to continue long term."

The U.S. — joined by most of the international community — backed the Baghdad Central Government in opposing the referendum in fear that the push toward independence would have potentially "catastrophic consequences" on the fight against ISIS and the region as a whole. The fear was that its neighbors, Iran, Syria, and Turkey, were already gripped with worry that their significant Kurdish populations would attempt to rise up and carve out land for themselves.

Those governments made no secret of the notion that they were willing to go to war over it. Images of civil wars sprouting like popcorn in the microwave were enough to make most of the broader community shudder. Wars had left everyone's head hurting.

Nechirvan noted that his people's disappointment stemmed not only from the U.S. policy to oppose their self- government quest, but what happened next.

After the Kurds refused Baghdad's insistence that the vote be canceled as unconstitutional and an antagonizing act aimed at weakening the Iraqi government, Iraqi Prime Minister Haider al-Abadi ordered the army to retake "disputed territories" — which the Kurdish Peshmerga had been guarding since the ISIS invasion. Iran-backed Popular Mobilization Units assisted the effort.

Most notably, violent tensions had arisen around the strategic oil-rich city of Kirkuk. Several casualties were reported on both the Peshmerga and Iraqi sides in the October 16 clashes, which ended when the Peshmerga withdrew.

"Over 1,846 Peshmerga soldiers have sacrificed their lives, and more than 10,000 were wounded fighting ISIS," Nechiravan said. "ISIS was a threat not only to Kurdistan, but to Europe, the U.S., to humanity. Therefore, the Kurdish people were expecting that when a threat comes in, the U.S. would stand by them. They were not expecting that American tanks given to the Iraq government would be used against them by the Popular Mobilization Units."

Iraqi officials denied that the Iranian-backed forces had possession over any U.S.-issued tanks or weaponry or that they were used against the Kurds.

Nechirvan also contended that it was never his government's intention to "control" or grab Kirkuk or the disputed territories from the Iraqi government. He said the Peshmerga forces went there in 2014 as the ISIS threat loomed at the behest of Abadi's predecessor, Nouri al-Malaki.

"The fact is neither Baghdad nor Erbil had full control over these areas," Nechirvan continued, accentuating that the issues should have been "addressed in accordance with the constitution" and not by military pressure.

The prime minister vowed that Iraq's military action in response to the referendum — which included shutting down the region's two international airports — was never anticipated.

"What we saw was a very peaceful experience of people to express their right to self-determination by putting their finger in the ink and voting, while the reaction from Baghdad was to use force," Nechiravan said. "We have made it clear we want to address all these issues through dialogue with Baghdad, but they have not yet shown their readiness for this."

Nechirvan — who had just taken the helm of the autonomous region after his uncle Masoud Barzani stepped down as president in the weeks after the referendum — welcomed a deeper involvement by the U.S. to resolve the issue. But he maintained that they had no regrets about holding the referendum.

"I don't believe anyone here, any political party, thinks that they made a mistake, or they did something wrong. What we have seen was a democratic process," he said. "It was an expression of will, not less, not more."

The long-awaited September 25th vote — in which more than ninety-two percent of eight million Iraqi Kurds voted "yes" to part ways with the Baghdad government — was non-binding in that unilateral succession would not immediately take place. Iraqi Kurds hoped it would prompt negotiations for eventual separation.

While it remained to be seen when and how Kurdish aspirations for an independent state would move forward — some analysts suggested it was in tatters and U.S. officials doubled down on the long-held policy to "support a federal, prosperous, unified, and democratic Iraq" — Nechirvan said they remained committed to the process and were still hopeful for American backing.

"We have to look at Iraq very realistically," he said. "For those who talk about a strong, centralized Iraq, we have seen that doesn't work. The most important point for Iraq and what the international community wants to see in Iraq is stability, which means we should find a model that all communities in Iraq can agree upon and can be sustained."

The Prime Minister emphasized that their position after the referendum was to address their ballooned problems with Baghdad "on the basis of the constitution."

"But our right to self-determination will remain as it is. This is a new era, and we hope the American people will come to support our cause," Nechirvan added.

The cause was a noble — if not a complex — one filled with many pros and cons. The Kurds were not going to give up their dream and were used to fighting alone. They had done it for centuries. Both physical and metaphorical fighting were built into the womb that brought them into life.

However, despite the many generations it was going to take them, I had little doubt that the Kurds were ever going to give up. They would be murdered and martyred as they stood before they ever dropped to their knees in defeat.

On Thanksgiving morning, I hitched a ride with a logistics convoy bound for a newly-established U.S. base in Kirkuk, which had recently been a site of fighting between the Kurds and Iran-backed militias. Peshmerga officials had likened the militias to being "worse than ISIS" and assured me that they surrendered and withdrew to avoid further carnage and conflict.

One of the trucks had broken down in the small town of Chamchamal, so I found an old, rusted motorcycle to ride, its clutch barely functioning and its pipes far too grating. After weaving through the wide streets and up and down the checkered hills, I played with some small Kurdish children in an empty land block. They raced around with their toy guns, imitating a scene from an apocalyptic action movie, pretending to slaughter each other.

"War is in their DNA," one of the interpreters said with a smile, as if reading my mind.

When I tried to take his photo, one of the little boys suddenly threw his toy rifle on the ground and dropped his eyes to the crusty earth. Even at this tender age—no older than five or six —I felt his hesitation, his shame, of what such an image would look like to those far away.

THE OTHER SLAVES OF ISIS
December, 2017

To those both close and far away, Fawzi carried his shame with heavy bags below his eyes. He carried the sorrow for his fractured family. He and his family were Turkmen, Iraq's third-largest ethnic group after Arabs and Kurds. Yet their plight of slavery had been largely underreported. Abbas was one of very few in his community speaking out.

The human voice is a powerful armament that can rise above all others. Fawzi had heard from the small grapevine entwining Baghdad that I was in town, and he had wanted to share his secret with me, so that his secret would become not so secret.

While much of the world had looked on in horror as tales of Yazidi girls and women emerged — held captive as ISIS sex slaves — Iraqi officials revealed that the tragedy had likely afflicted females belonging to other minorities, too. And even though numerous girls were still missing, many in these communities did not want it to be documented. In this case, the human voice was an armament they had come to fear.

"Six hundred forty of our girls — some younger than twelve — are missing by ISIS. But we aren't talking about it," lamented Fawzi Akram, a former Iraqi Parliament member representing the Turkmen and now a prominent aid and community leader.

He did not hesitate to explain why.

"We are very conservative," Fawzi continued. "If our wife or sister was raped, we cannot talk about it."

It was as though these communities believed that if they told themselves enough little lies of denials, it would come true and the nightmare they were experiencing would simply disappear. But the cracks in their communal texture had become too deep to ignore.

What was worse, Fawzi acknowledged, was that families were so deeply ashamed that they often didn't want their abducted girls to come back for fear they were violated. If they did escape and return, they faced being honor-killed.

"I am telling the families that the girls are not guilty, they have suffered, and the families must forgive them and take care of them according to the human rights," he said.

Iraqi Turkmen share close cultural and linguistic connections to Turkey and identify with either Shiite or Sunni Muslim traditions.

"Many girls won't return," Hasan Turan, an Iraqi Parliament member for the Turkmen Front party, said. "Many girls were held as slaves... I can only hope families accept them if they return. They are the victims. They have been attacked."

The scale of sexual violence extended far broader than many Iraqis previously documented. The minority Shabak — who resided mostly in villages east of Mosul, their faith and rituals centered on Christian, Yazidi, and Islamic adherence — also suffered in silence.

Hunien Kaddo, an Iraqi Parliament member and representative of the Shabak community — which numbers fewer than 35,000 in Iraq — conceded that the females in his minority were also swept into the sexual brutality.

Hunien said they had received information and eyewitness accounts that at least twenty-eight Shabak women were raped and had gasoline poured on them while locked in cages. Subsequently, they were burned alive in Mosul throughout the ISIS reign in a clear case of religious persecution.

Adding to the nightmare, as the Mosul liberation gained steam in late 2016 and Iraqi forces started to further advance on surrounding areas, ISIS kidnapped another fifty-nine Shabak women and children before being run out of the villages in December, he said.

"I have been visiting displaced and devastated families in recent weeks," Hunien said. "Their daughters are missing. Sadly, there is a lot of shame."

He also pointed out that several Christian females remained unaccounted for, their lives amounting only to hidden pieces of paper in files swept beneath the rug.

"People won't say much about it as they are petrified what will happen to them," concurred Canon Andrew White, known as the Vicar of Baghdad.

According to a Kurdistan Regional Government representative in the country's north, unlike that of the Yazidi community, other affected minorities had not come forward for help.

"The Yazidis came to us, and they needed our help, and we helped pay for rescues," explained the representative, who did not want to be named given the sensitivity of the matter. "But many in these other groups stayed quiet. They didn't want help."

It chilled me to think about those girls and women, writhing in agony with nobody to turn to, unable even to reach for those who were supposed to love them unconditionally. How different my world was from theirs; these women could not run away from themselves forever, and it seemed death was the only way out of their pain.

Vian Dakhil, the female representative for Yazidis in the Iraqi Parliament, told me one morning that 2,900 of their women and children were missing, even after the almost-complete ISIS liberation. But she said they would wait in the hopes that they came home. They would also tell the world what had happened to their girls as the long-standing cultural tradition of shame began to wane.

"For us, it was very good to talk about it. At the beginning many were afraid," Dakhil added, her eyes cast down, an imaginary shadow clouding her soft presence in a large, almost entirely white room. "But it was what we had to do."

LIFE AFTER: CHRISTIANS FEAR HOME
December, 2017

It should have been something they wanted to talk about. It should have been a narrative swathed in triumph. It should have been a positive, uplifting story: Christian residents of a small, newly liberated town in northern Iraq returning home after fleeing ISIS in 2014.

But now that Peshmerga forces had freed the town, many of the Christians who had trickled back — their livelihoods and homes in ruins, their sense of safety and security shattered — were again desperate to leave.

"The reality is we cannot stay without the U.S. or the U.N. helping to protect Nineveh directly," Father Afram al- Khoury Benyamen told me after Sunday Mass at St. George Cathedral, a 133-year-old stone church. "With international protection, maybe we can remain, but if it doesn't come soon... we go."

Bahzani, which means "House of Treasure" in ancient Syriac, was considered a contested area between the Baghdad Central Government and the Kurdistan Regional Government that Kurdish Peshmerga soldiers protected after ISIS was defeated. But Baghdad had ordered its troops to take over the area amid the fallout of the September Kurdish referendum for independence.

For Bahzani's Christians, the unknown faces at the town's checkpoints and the fear that something could erupt at any time had worn many of them to the depths of despair.

"ISIS is not finished in Mosul, and still they can come straight here," the priest said, looking through me as if to question how all of us outside could leave them to be sacrificed. "We expect more attacks. It is like staring into the darkness."

In addition to a plea for international protection, Father Afram yearned for financial aid that would enable him and others to piece their lives back together.

"We are the original people, the indigenous people here in Iraq, and the government should want us to stay. Instead, there is nothing. The village is dirty, and there is no electricity. No water is coming, no markets. All of our people are thinking to immigrate and leave."

Scores of Iraqi Christians in the region, who earlier fled in fear to neighboring countries such as Jordan, Lebanon, and Turkey, weren't much better off, Father Afram said. They had waited years for visas to western nations, only to be rejected. Now the refugees were stranded. They did not have money or the courage to resettle in other pockets of Iraq. Those fortunate enough to have been granted visas had to watch their families be split apart. Some members lived in the U.S., others in Europe, and still, others were strewn across the Middle East.

What is war? It was options — almost all bad. Does war ever bring about options that could be considered good? That sense of helplessness hung in the air.

During Sunday's service, women in aphotic mantillas sang and prayed, and the men struck candles to illume the darkened space while tiny children played outside in the cold sunshine.

"ISIS destroyed all the crosses — crosses that had been made 150 years ago," Father Afram said. "But I said to my people, 'Make new crosses.'"

Before ISIS, roughly 400 Christian families lived in Bahzani. The number had dwindled to about 130.

"There is no stability. Our homes are destroyed," said Mariam Ishaq, a fifty-eight-year-old born and raised in Bahzani. Despite the persecution the Christians had faced for generations, she could never have imagined wanting to leave her homeland so fiercely.

She held hands with Faiza Yaaqoub, sixty-eight, as she stopped to talk with me after the Mass. Faiza was also born and raised in Bahzani. She had spent her life near the Cathedral, which had been made of earth and brought to life with stunning archways that let in just enough light to touch the cindered floors.

"I don't want to leave," Ishaq said. "But what else can we do?"

St. George deacon Benian Abdullah echoed the frustration.

"We are always worried about who will be our future government. Who will be the next to control us?" he asked.

They worried about what they lost, and they constantly worried about what was left to lose.

After the church emptied, the priest made his way to the church hall, which had been looted and suffered severe damage when ISIS seized the town. ISIS fighters left behind bullseye targets painted on the walls for shooting practice. Dots of crusted blood made me think the room had also been punctuated by a succession of grisly massacres.

Ironically, the terrorists also used the building as a makeshift hospital to heal their wounded.

Father Afram then walked into town and pointed at the crooked streets where 350 houses had been bombed and burned in the battle with ISIS. He promised me that it had been a beautiful place before ISIS came. He still could not fathom how anyone could trash a place of worship, a place he cherished so profoundly.

The few residents who still lived in those homes were made to cook on antique stoves and fetch water from old wells as they continue to mourn loved ones lost both directly and indirectly in the ISIS assault.

What is war? War left no way out; it was a slow death, sometimes being an ancillary casualty.

Inside a small, faded scarlet home on a narrow street, I learned the story of Rimon.

Rimon was born in their small Christian village outside of Mosul. Shortly after ISIS invaded and he and his family fled, he got sick with cancer. Unable to leave or get medical help, he was left with little but to die slowly and painfully. These were the indirect casualties of such terrorists. Rimon had lived long enough to see his tiny town liberated, to find an ancient manuscript that ISIS had not discovered hidden below that beloved cathedral, to see that the crosses ISIS destroyed resurrected.

In all the photos his family shared, he seemed a gentle man, with a pale face and hair turned white from the depths of his suffering.

His mother, Silvia, wept for her thirty-three-year-old son, who had passed that February and was laid to rest at the church.

"Because of this crisis, we could not find him medicine. We could not get help for him to leave," she sobbed. "And so, he lost his life."

I was guttered with uselessness. As I had written in my notebook a year ago in Sinjar, when the Yazidi father told me he could not find more money to save his wife, there was always that one story that breaks you.

I cried. I cried with the family and for the family, for Rimon, for myself. For Iraq.

Rimon's family had welcomed me, a stranger, into their humble living room and served me tea. They shared their love and grief and only asked for one thing in return.

His mother — still cloaked in the color of mourning — asked me to light a candle for her departed son if it wasn't too much trouble. And so, we diffused illumination into a blackened world. She talked about her gentle Rimon, and I did not want to leave that little rubble house — because to have her talk was to keep alive her memory. It was her means of never forgetting her only son. It was her means of holding close the threads of lost humanity. Those were the sorts of exploits that could only arise at that fragile brink separating the living from the dead; the ones that arise during the moments when you have to hold on and move on all at once.

A large photo of a young Rimon, filled with warmth and the picture of health, hung like a shrine on the wall. Rimon's little sister stared at it with wide eyes only of sadness, and his father touched my shoulder, insisting that their country had once been a place of strength under Saddam's reign.

He wanted to leave their village, but his wife wanted to stay so she could be close to her son's resting body. Sylvia had given way to an obsession with memory, of holding on to everything she could remember of her eldest child. The longing that this mother felt for her son was so deep that I wondered how she managed to close her eyes and fall asleep night after night.

How she missed her child of light, and how hard it was for her to accept in blind faith that he had returned to the beauty he was before earth. She prayed and prayed.

But somehow, despite it all, there they were — still living.

FAREWELL TO THE OLIVE GROVES
December, 2017

The haunting signs of ISIS's brutality were everywhere, around every corner — reminders to a traumatized mind that to go on living would be to suffer.

"The bomb fell down from the mountains at this place, and you can see the effect," Father Afram said, staring up at the town's ISIS-ravaged wedding hall.

He was not openly angry, but I could tell the anger was still there — swelling deep down, suppressed just enough to get through the day. Sometimes even the most devoted of us could not forgive. Father Afram sought justice before he could forgive.

The priest and other locals had pooled what little money they had to pay for repairs to the banquet hall so that the residents would at least have a place for celebrations. But those meager funds ran out before the project could be finished. Their parties would wait.

The priest said there were other treasures in the town that he feared were beyond the point of restoring. Among them were Bahzani's famous olive trees, which once coated much of the plains of Nineveh to the banks of the Tigris River.

"Before ISIS, everything was green," he said poignantly. "Now everything is finished, nobody gave the olive trees water."

Bahzani had been a charming alcove with its grassy terrain, and untamed greenery up until the medieval siege had laid it to waste. Father Afram looked out into the shadow of what felt like a new place, a new reality to which he no longer belonged. It had been molested by evil. He was partly mad, partly sad, and very lost.

"And when I see the village like this," he added solemnly. "I feel there is no life here. We used to have 150 doves come to our church, too. But after ISIS, even they have not come back."

When no one was listening or watching, Father Afram pulled me aside and whispered in desperation.

He wanted to know if there was anything I could do — visas, sponsors, scholarships — that would serve as his one-way ticket out of a dwindling life. Like the olive groves he loved, the love he had for his land had been sickened by hatred. That bottomless cup of hatred that the Ancient Greek Euripides, the last of the three great tragedians of classical Athens spoke of — the bottomless cup he would pour and pour.

He was a resilient man of God, but if he once had any hope of a rebirth rising from the ashes of destruction, it was now gone.

Father Afram wrote me a letter weeks after my visit. He wanted me to learn the story of his life. I wanted to publish it here, untouched.

I grow up in Bahzani an Idyllic hamlet at the foot of a mountain with may water springs and embraced by the only evergreen Olive Grove in Iraq. The only townlet which was inhabited for centuries by only Syrian Orthodox Christian and Yazidis. We enjoyed a tranquil co-existent and reciprocal relations.

Bahzani located about 30 KM to the East of the Tigris river at it pass through the ancient city of Mosul the main urban center of our region a central location in the Fertile Crescent which served since time immemorial as the breadbasket of the Assyrian Empire and all other Emperies that follows and used our region as their musical chair. They came and went but we stayed. We loved our life and were eager to maintain our enjoyment of the fraternal and peaceful relations of our rustic milieu, busy with eternal cycle of planting and harvesting, our Olive, Onion, sesame many other different produces for human consumption and forage group for our farm's animal. We monitored the metrological fluctuations to ensure that our harvest is plentiful.

On Sunday, we went to the church under the watchful eyes of a swarm of snow-white Doves and heard of lamb and cows grazing in different lush and tranquil farms of Bahzani. The gathered faithful joined in prayer wearing their Sunday their joyful melodic voices echoing and reflecting in chamber our 200 years old Church of St. George built by a special local alabaster known as the blue marble of Mosul. That was the cycle of our life punctuated with work and joyful occasions share our neighbors in their happy and sad occasions and going holidays.

Suddenly on a moonless and wicked night in June 2014 we heard that the defense of city of Mosul had collapsed and the city of two million inhabitants had fallen the inhabitants were terrorized creating a biblical scale mass exodus in front of to the advancing merciless bandits of ruthless reputations coming from the west. We were taken by surprise and had not enough notice and no choice but to embark in a hurry of a mass exodus from our houses leaving everything behind rendering our idyllic hamlet o become a ghost town.

The only safe option for us is to head to the Kurdish region. Luckily, it was summer, we spent the first couple of weeks in the streets, in building sites, the lucky among us will be housed in Churches halls and gardens tormenting with worries all day due to the fact that not knowing what to do and what the future hold for us, nursing a great fear and phobia that these bandits will advance deep into the Kurdish region. At night gazing at the stars for a clue. We had no house no address later on humanitarian organization manage to provide us with tents or caravan and housed the ethno-religiously cleansed people in what became known as Internally Displaced Person; IDP camps.

The lowest status of human existence under the UN charter. We spent three years as aliens in our own country in this drastically reduced situation. We waited for an early liberation of our towns and villages; I use to go to watch through binocular our village from an overlook mountain. After long awaited liberation we were anxious to know the state of damaged to our house, church, farms village.

One day after another, I wanted to go to my house, but I could not get out soon for a few kilometers, but I could not After liberation, I was very eager to see our Church our housed our farms sadly they were all pillaged, burned and the village distracted beyond recognition as it became a real ghost town. After the village were made safe of mine and explosives. I quickly tried to have a collective campaign to clean up the church, so we can have thanks given mass. Sadly, many people could not come back to their houses, some, especially the youth had already immigrated to Europe, we are left with the old and infirm people to rebuild our life.

They killed our joy they destroyed our way of living, burned our orchids and olive grove. Those bandits who annexed our village and the entire province of Mosul had no value for life, meaning for humanity, appreciation for culture and respect for the tradition of others. They terrorized the Living Stones and forced them deserted the village, waged a systematic campaign of cultural genocide and urbicide — violence against the city — leaving the dead stones to tell the story of this once ancient village.

Now we are going through a stage of drastic demographic changes, our communities were uprooted and ethno- religiously cleansed and subjected to a collective annihilation and became endangered in their homeland which amount to a genocide. Even the dove had to fly away not a single one to give us the hope for peace. Our house used to be the center of the village extending hospitalities to Patriarchs, Bishops and other religious and temporal leaders. We have lost everything, but we did not understand what is all that about?

Who are these bandits and what did they want from us? The burning question which remain unanswered is that: Were they after the Christians, the Yazidis, the Muslims or to wipe out these ancient and historical villages, towns and the *cities for what they represent? Till now we have had no explanation neither from the government which failed to protect its citizen and its sovereignty nor from the international community who are even unable to provide the minimum humanitarian's aid or minimum reparation to those IDPs who lost everything without any fault of their own.*

History is a potent force, and nothing will be kept untold forever.

The threat for Christian communities, I quickly realized, had become so much more than ISIS alone.

IRAN'S QUIET INFILTRATION OF IRAQI CHRISTIAN COMMUNITIES
December, 2017

The threat — or, at least, how it felt to them — was all around. And it was far from mere paranoia.

Christians who had called northern Iraq their homeland since the first century were recovering from ISIS' carnage while at the same time facing an emerging threat that they feared would be just as challenging: the growing influence from Iran.

That influence came from outside in an array of shapes and forms — and from inside, from within the Christian community.

Most flagrantly, it included the direct arming and funding of a prominent PMF militia of Iraqi Christians. Christians were naturally grateful for the sacrifice the militias had made in driving out ISIS, but they knew that the remaining vacuum would suck them into someone else's agenda.

The real intentions of the militia — known as the Babylon Brigade — worried some Christians who remained in or wanted to return to their ancient homeland, known as the Nineveh Plains.

"We had ISIS, and now we are struggling with this increasing Iranian rule, the changing demographics," lamented Dr. Salem Hana, a thirty-three-year-old Iraqi Christian dentist. "The Nineveh Plains is an important part of their Crescent to link Iran with Syria, but this will have a negative impact on the survival of Iraqi Christians in their original areas."

The Babylon Brigade, which was led by Rayan al-Kildani, who I had recently met at his headquarters in Baghdad, was closely aligned to the Badr Organization. The militia began in Tehran decades ago, with both political and armed wings. It was now headed by the former Iraqi transportation minister, Hadi Al-Ameri. Badr officially vowed that "any violation to Babylon means a violation to Badr."

To some Christians, there was comfort in such protection. To others, it instilled pure fear — they said that they were concerned that Iran, the home of Shiite Islam, was not funding and equipping the Babylon Brigade solely out of a religious impulse.

"Iran is directly funding a Christian militia, so it can extend its authority in the Nineveh Plains," claimed Ano Jawhar Abdoka, an Erbil-based Christian activist and international relations analyst.

And it was not just Iraqi Christians who were concerned about Iran's generosity to the Christian militia.

"This is a real problem, and the world is looking the other way," former congressman Frank Wolf, R-Va., who had personally tracked the issue in Iraq, opined over the phone one afternoon. "The land bridge enables Iranian trucks and weapons to casually go all the way through to the Mediterranean. Iran is on the move."

For the land bridge known as the Shiite Crescent — which crossed from Tehran through northern Iraq, Syria, and then into Lebanon — to be realized, Iran required territory from the shrinking Christian communities of the Nineveh Plains. Many members of those communities remained displaced and thus could not protect their homes. And, over the past couple of months, the land route had quickly come closer to completion.

One reason for concern was the close friendship between Rayan, the Babylon Brigade's leader, and Iran's most powerful military figure, Major

General Qasim Soleimani.

"Without Soleimani, much more of Iraq would have fallen into ISIS hands," Rayan said from his Baghdad office.

The Christian militia leader also said that Soleimani was now a "top adviser in the Iraqi government," and that he advised on battles to take back Christian areas from ISIS in Iraq. Rayan said that the Iranian General even took things one step further over the border in Syria where he "personally led the battles to free Christian areas."

"He wanted to play a lead role in liberating these lands," Rayan had assured me, with a tough guy cock of the head. "He wanted to protect the holy places."

Aside from the troubling connections between the Babylon Brigade and the Iranian military, Christian civilians claimed that Iran's Islamic influence was creeping into their daily lives.

That influence inside the Nineveh Plains, according to many Christians, was becoming more blatant with each passing day. They had been injected with a new strain of unease, something they hadn't quite experienced before. It came with the sensation that they would always feel in exile, no matter where they went, for the rest of their lives.

Residents said it was not uncommon for posters to spring up featuring Iran's former Supreme Leader, Ayatollah Khomeini. At a checkpoint near the entrance of the Syriac Christian town of Bartella, a poster of the Virgin Mary had been ripped down and replaced with images of Khomeini and his successor, Ayatollah Khamenei. And, in late September, a school named after Khomeini — his name hung over a large banner across the tallest building — even opened there, the ribbon-cutting ceremony attended by the Iranian Consul General in Erbil, Murtadha Abadi.

Romeo Hakari, who headed the Bait-al-Nahrain — an Assyrian Christian political party in Iraq — said that he routinely fielded complaints from Christians across the Nineveh Plains about the building of houses from outsiders. They presumed these outsiders were from Shia communities, including fellow minority Shia Shabak who adhered to many pillars of Shia Islam.

"There is clearly a larger plan for demographic change," Romeo opined, asserting that Christians felt increasingly pressured to sell their land out of financial desperation, having lost everything post-ISIS, and out of fear their land may eventually be taken from them by Iranian dominion.

In Iraq's largest Christian town of Qarakosh in the Al-Hamdania district of the Nineveh Governorate, Christian activists bemoaned that their small university — Al-Hamdania University — had been directed by the federal government education ministry to accept upwards of 180 students from central and southern Iraq, most of which were Shia. This had prompted dramatic protest from locals, who panicked that they would have to give over their properties to the new influx of residents.

The protests withered over time. The passion waned into exhaustion. Many no longer had it in them to keep rattling the cage and biting back. They could only be brave and stand up for themselves when they were not drained to the bone.

Many Christians found solutions in doing whatever they could to leave their country, with no desire to ever return.

THE LAST CHRISTMAS
December, 2017

For those who decided to stay a little longer, or had nowhere to go, church was their paradise — but it would forever be a paradise dipped in fear.

Just days shy of Christmas, dozens of Iraqi children filled the stage at Baghdad's Alliance Evangelical Church to practice "Jingle Bells" and rehearse their Nativity play. I sat at a pew in the far back as the shrilling web of voices sang out; defiant, raucous, unabashed. For many, this would be the last Christmas in their indigenous homeland.

"The majority of Christians have left, and we are leaving too," one of the small children told me after the choir had finished, his mouth an endearing popsicle blue.

Those words had become a broken record to Reverend Joseph Francis

Joseph, president of Alliance churches in Iraq. There was little he could do but watch as his country's Christian population plunged — from 1.5 million before the U.S.-led invasion in 2003 to about 200,000 today. It was the result of systematic persecution, coupled with the genocidal storm of ISIS in 2014.

"I tell these families I wish for them to fight and stay, but it is their decision. We Christians feel we have no rights here," Joseph explained from his dimly-lit office. "How to save our people?"

Joseph didn't have the answer and no longer tried to come up with one. Fatigue and disappointment had engulfed Baghdad's Christian community, accentuated by the dragging acceptance that not even their faith would keep them safe and shield them from violence.

"All of us priests and pastors have been talking to the U.N. and international community, but I feel there is no solution to our problems," Joseph said. "When the Saddam regime fell down, we all thought it would get better, but it only became worse."

After Hussein's government toppled in 2003, eight new evangelical churches quickly sprang up in Baghdad — including Reverend Joseph's Alliance Evangelical.

But years passed, and the Shia forces of Baghdad grew. Sectarian schisms proliferated. Some of those new evangelical churches closed their doors due to low attendance and a lack of financial resources. Joseph had seen the attendance of his own Sunday Mass drop from 400 to less than 300, and the number of children attending Sunday School dwindled from 150 to just fifty. To him, each number mattered. Each was human life in the endangered minority.

Eight Baghdad churches had closed in just one month earlier in the year, according to Jeff King, president of International Christian Concern.

At Our Lady of Deliverance Syriac Catholic Church, memories remained raw of a 2010 al-Qaeda attack during Sunday evening mass. Six jihadists, strapped in suicide attire, stormed the Assyrian church and meticulously and individually gunned down every terrified worshipper. The haunting executions continued until finally, hours later, Iraqi commandos could not wait out the siege any longer and assailed the church. Their entrance triggered the six jihadists to pull their vests, blowing up themselves and dozens deep in silent prayer. In the end, fifty-eight worshipers, priests, policemen, and bystanders were killed. Seventy-eight more had been maimed in such a way that their lives would never be the same.

"Since then, all the churches must have these now," said Uday Samir Slawa, a soft-spoken, thirty-seven-year-old bodyguard, motioning to the high concrete walls that protected the church. "We are scared here. We are destroyed here. There is no future."

Moreover, there was little future for the inhabitants of Camp Virgin Mary, which housed more than one hundred displaced Christian families in the middle of Baghdad. The camp, just off one of the city's bowed dirt tracks, consisted of nearly 150 blue-and-white trailers.

The families there had all been driven from their homes when ISIS extremists seized Mosul.

"I have been asking myself, 'Should I leave Iraq?' The answer is yes, and I feel very sad for that," Fryal Abbo said in a whisper.

Fryal, in her forties, was dressed in all black. As she spoke, her eyes welled with tears, and she clutched the fingers of one of her children, seventeen-year-old Najma.

Her husband, Amir Abbo, had been one of several individuals killed two days before last Christmas in deadly attacks on Christian-owned shops that sold alcohol. He had been working at the shop less than a month, delighted to have found a job so far from his now ISIS-occupied home.

But since her husband's death, Fryal had no source of income — nor any sense of justice. She had begged for almost a year, wanting to know who was being held accountable, but nobody cared enough to answer.

What is war? It is waiting for justice that too often never comes.

"We have no information which insurgency did this," Fryal whimpered, opening her hands and raising them to the sky. "We Christians didn't want anything. Only peace."

Others at Camp Virgin Mary told comparable stories of death and persecution.

Seventy-seven-year-old Ena Kromy clasped a cross in one hand and a photograph of her son in the other as she sat wistfully in the sunshine. She, too, was dressed all in black. Ena's son was shot in the head at a restaurant where he worked eight years ago. The restaurant had also been targeted for serving alcohol.

That day, Ena learned that belief in God was not enough. She learned that they needed someone or something in the human form to hold their hands and guard their lives.

Ena said the shock of her child's death proceeded to take the life of her husband a few months later.

"My son died from his head," she said, not bothering to wipe the tears. "And my husband from his heart."

Recently, Ena packed up and returned to Mosul, Iraq's second-largest city, after it was recaptured from ISIS militants. But when she got there, only a pile of bricks were left — her family's house had been destroyed in the fighting. So she trudged back to the bus stop with her life in plastic bags and returned to Camp Virgin Mary. Life chugged on in a colorless cloud of dust and dank perfume. They suffered because they had to, not because they wanted to. War is a menu of options — terrible options.

"The government tells us to go back, but I will never go back to that home," said Nehla Kheder, who had fled Mosul on foot with her family. All they had were the clothes on their backs and their identification cards.

"We can't go there, and we can't stay here," she pressed on, her throat catching with a paralyzed yelp. "There is no such thing as home anywhere here for us."

I arrived home to New York just in time for the first snowfall of the 2017 season to dust Central Park; for mulled wine to be served at the markets; for the carols to fill the subway stations; for windows of Fifth Avenue to fill with graceful strings of golden lights contouring the long, lean window mannequins.

"They call me Father Afram at the Church, but I didn't tell you my birth name is Maran Atha," the priest wrote to me in a message, which arrived the dawn of Christmas morning.

I stood alone, staring out the window of my tiny pre-war, walkup Manhattan apartment.

"It means 'Lord come soon,'" he added.

FIFTH YEAR OF ISIS: 2018
The Dead Can't Hurt You

VICTIM OR THREAT?
February, 2018

While the ISIS fight across the Euphrates in Syria carried on, the dust settling in other parts gave rise to a new dilemma: what to do with the ISIS wives and children. Their fathers and husbands belonged to one of the most brutal militant forces on the planet, yet they had committed no known crime.

But were they national security dangers? Were they victims? Were they criminals by association?

After years of avoiding the issue, followed by months of debate, Iraqi officials finally assembled a plan on how to deal with captured foreign ISIS wives and children of the crumbled caliphate. They believed it would balance security concerns with international law and due process.

"We are holding 500 wives of ISIS — all foreigners — and their children, which makes 1,500 in total," said Mohammed Shia al-Sudani, the Iraqi Minister for Labor and Social Affairs, who presided over childcare issues. "And some of the ISIS wives are pregnant."

Mohammed told me that there had been "many communications through our ministry and the court system" over what to do with the children since the collapse of Mosul in July. That was followed by the fall of other major ISIS mainstays across the country.

Iraqi authorities now mandated that children three and under would remain with their mothers in detention facilities. Those between the age of four and fourteen years old would be placed in state-run orphanages until agreements with embassies were established when the families could be "handed off" to their home countries.

The plan required a hasty amendment to Iraq's legal code, as a Saddam-era 1980 law stipulated that only minors of Iraqi or Palestinian origin were permitted into the country's orphanages. Authorities now contended with children of more than twenty different nationalities.

"We deal with the kids as victims. They had no fault in what happened," Mohammed insisted. "They will be taken care of and not blamed. And we have prepared an integrated program to de-radicalize the kids away from the extremist mindset and ideology."

The spouses would not be viewed under such a lens.

The foreign wives of ISIS fighters were to be tried in Iraq, and not in their country of citizenship, to determine what — if any — level of involvement they had in the caliphate.

"They will be given a fair trial in the court system," Mohammed assured me.

Human rights groups were particularly worried about the fate and fair treatment of adolescent males over the age of fourteen who were being held separately from their mothers in multiple facilities across the country. These were boys of fighting age, and authorities could not be sure they had not joined — or at the very least sympathized — with the brutal ISIS ideology.

Again, Iraqi officials stressed that they were complying scrupulously with international guidelines on the detainments.

"We are concerned that torture may be utilized in coercing confessions from these adolescents," noted Dr. Homer Venters, director of programs at the Physicians for Human Rights. "Captured children forced into fighting with ISIS are also victims of human rights violations, including physical and mental trauma and should be treated as such."

The majority of the foreign wives and children were documented to be from Turkey and Russia, with significant numbers from the Caucasus region. There were smaller percentages of fighters from numerous other nations, including many in Europe.

Mohammed also underscored that Iraqis were still in the process of trying to determine the nationality of many detainees who were languishing behind bars without proper documentation. This was most challenging for children, who were born and or raised under the governance of black flags that operated by its own rules. The truth was in many cases that the identity of the father was unknown. And sometimes the wives, who were often widowed and hastily snatched up by another fighter, did not even know with whom they had conceived their young.

Even for those whose nationalities had been verified, there were still unsolved diplomatic snags. I learned that Baghdad was in the process of negotiating with their countries of origin to have most of them repatriated, but there was a lot of resistance. Most of their countries simply did not want them back.

At this point in the ISIS war, the wives and babies were enclosed in a camp in al-Rusafa, one of the oldest quarters of Baghdad. Mohammed, the Iraqi Minister for Labor and Social Affairs, explained that they had to be held in an area separate from non-ISIS, displaced families on the grounds. Aid workers and officials routinely expressed concern that the ISIS families would be subject to retaliation from those who had been deeply afflicted by the insurgent group.

But the street ran two ways. I also heard from guards — whose job it was to preside over the ISIS families section — that they frequently dealt with being spat on, hit, and verbally abused by the ISIS wives. Maybe it was post-traumatic stress, grief, homesickness, or just twisted ISIS thinking.

At the request of the government, the International Committee of the Red Cross (ICRC) had provided the mothers and children in camps and orphanages with baby formula and hygiene items, as well as helping to "restore the links" with relatives in their country of origin, mostly by facilitating the exchange of Red Cross messages, Mohammad said.

In addition to the 1,500 ISIS wives and families, more than 7,000 foreign

ISIS males were being detained across the country, waiting to stand trial. More than ninety had already been executed for their terrorist membership.

Over the ensuing months, the central government was subject to more upset and outcry as the trials began under the guise of an opaque judicial system. Baghdad was taking no chances. If an ISIS advocate was allowed to live, he had the potential to radicalize others, to harm, and to ignite a terror tenure all over again. There was no sympathy for alleged ISIS cohorts on the streets of Iraq.

The nation's legal powers sentenced thousands of convicted Iraqi nationals and foreign fighters — accused of membership to the brutal terrorist group — to the gallows. But speedy trials and shadowy evidence had international watchdogs concerned that the quest for swift justice was not only in violation of human rights law but that it would serve as a precursor to further violence among factions in the near future.

In mass trials that often lasted just a few minutes, even foreign fighters were handed sentences of capital punishment, as were dozens of ISIS women.

The ISIS aftermath had ushered in a different mess of concerns and abuses.

"It is critical to remember that, even when someone is proven to be a member of a terrorist organization, their family members are not guilty by association," added Tuva Raanes Bogsnes, a spokesperson for The Norwegian Refugee Council (NRC).

ISIS WIVES: INFIGHTING, JEALOUSY - AND REGRETS
April, 2018

If there was a common thread, it was that every ISIS wife I met pleaded for the world to understand that they were innocent — that they were not guilty by association. One might also assume that they had much more in common than that thread, given their special status as foreign wives and widows of ISIS fighters.

Such assumptions would be wrong.

Many of the women held in this Syrian displacement camp — abandoned by home countries that didn't want them back — led lives marred by infighting, jealousy, and spiteful theft.

"They have a lot of internal conflicts between them. At least twice a week there is physical punching, and fighting breaks out," said an official for the camp, which was operated by the U.S.-backed Syrian Democratic Forces (SDF).

In Syria, the scenario was much different from its neighboring Iraq. ISIS families were held in a legal gray zone, with no trial in sight and no path to return home. Iraq was mapping out plans and churning through case files while Syria, still in disarray with its civil war and an assortment of fighting factions, had no such solutions.

It was a cool April morning when I crossed the Euphrates in a small boat, clutching just my body armor and a backpack. When I reached the Syrian side, families immediately started to haul small coffins onto the boat for transport to the other side. Those families clung to each other and wailed, bathed in bereavement. It was a shrilling symbol of the world I had wandered into, encapsulated by suffering in every direction.

Days later, I made my way to meet the wives cornered off in the Ain Essa displacement camp, poised on the road to Raqqa in the northeast of Syria. The women all had questions. It was as if, in their minds, the vision of a foreigner was their vessel back to the world. The camp guards bemoaned the behavior of many who were known to lash their frustrations out on one another with the odd fist throw and tongue-lashing.

Most of the altercations, I was told, stemmed from arguments involving their children, as well as accusations of theft.

The 123 women held in the camp were tended to like any other group in need at the Ain Essa facility, some fifty miles from former ISIS "caliphate" capital of Raqqa. Ranging in age from eighteen to seventy years old, most of the women also had an average of three to four young children fathered by ISIS fighters.

The women were kept in a heavily guarded section away from the rest of the camp for fear of retaliation by angry locals who suffered at the hands of the terrorist group — and for fear that they would spread their poisonous ideology into the hurting minds of other displaced persons.

"The civilians do not accept these women," the official said flatly. "But we deal with them as we deal with any civilians, not as ISIS members or wives."

Such civilized treatment was wearing thin. The official complained that many of the women were resentful and ungrateful, often throwing the food they had been given on the ground, swearing and disrespecting those on guard duty.

Then there was the problem of their radicalization. Officials estimated only twenty percent of the women had "changed their extremist minds," making the strong majority a continuing security peril.

I sat with some of the ISIS women in the dusty camp confines one afternoon. They agreed to tell their story, in the belief that someone from home would read it and somehow come to their rescue.

Lena Frizler was a twenty-eight-year-old, blue-eyed blonde with milky pale skin from Hamburg, Germany. She was once an aspiring business student with the European Dream of money, travel, family, and success.

In 2012, she had married, converted to Islam, and left the comforts of her home for Turkey. She said that she had made the abrupt decision after being courted and encouraged by a known radical Salafist in the Hamburg area — she called him Pierre Vogel — who urged others to rise up and fight against the Bashar al-Assad Syrian regime.

Her husband had also come under Pierre's spell.

"One day my husband came home and told me he wants to go to Syria and fight," Lena told me matter-of-factly as she nursed her one-year-old son — her second child with an ISIS fighter.

Lena's husband, who had renamed himself Abu Bilal, joined Syria's al Qaeda affiliate, al-Nusra. After being captured and released in a prisoner exchange with the Free Syrian Army (FSA), Bilal was shot down in a friendly fire incident in 2013.

A distraught Lena, pregnant with her first child at the time, had appealed to a prominent ISIS leader in Raqqa. She asked for permission to go back to Turkey so that she could find her way back to Europe. Instead, the ISIS patriarch sent Lena off to a desert area for intensive Islamic religious training.

"There was a special place where they sent all the widows," she said.

After giving birth and attempting — and failing — to be smuggled out, Lena ended up in an ISIS prison for her rebellion. After her release, she was married off to an Afghan ISIS man, who called her "a bitch" with almost every breath and physically abused her.

However, it seemed her greatest nightmare was that she did not want to stay in the camp, but she did not want to go, either.

"Even if I go home now from this camp, I am scared that they will take my children from me," she said, her face falling with a flood of tears. "But I want to send them to a good school and have a good life like I had... from the moment I got to Syria, I just wanted to go home."

Lena wanted to be forgiven, but it was clear her country — and the world — was not ready to forgive her. And maybe they never would be. Nobody from the German government had reached out to her; there was radio silence when it came to the issue of getting her home.

She patted her sleeping child, still and coiled on her lap. He did not yet know of the world out there nor what awaited him. I wondered if the world would forgive those children. Their lives were hard, and would always be hard given how they had been conceived.

Another German native, a stunning, raven-haired twenty-six-year-old named Heida Raufi, told me that she spent most of her days alone in her tent. She explained that she wanted to avoid gossip and distrust among the other women. She waved her hand dismissively, signifying that such pettiness surely was beneath her.

Then, Heida leaned in, moving closer beside me on the office couch.

"I'm writing a book," she said, attempting to bond writer-to-writer. "I want to protect other women from making the same mistake I did."

Heida told her story like she was narrating a summer romance novel that would ascend to a gut-wrenching climax, speaking in crisp and almost sensual overtones.

She said that she had fallen in love with an older boy in 2009. Then, several years into their relationship, he informed her that he was going to "help" the people of Syria that were suffering as a result of the war and Bashar al-Assad. Lovestruck, Heida ditched her social work studies for the life of a jihadi wife in 2014. Her beloved, Kareem, later died on the battlefield.

Over the next eighteen months, the grieving widow spent some $8,000 that her family had wired in three failed attempts to be smuggled out of the terrorist den. The smuggling operations, she scoffed, were all scams. The fighters took the money and then drove them around the desert, only to return them home. If they were unlucky, the fighter also told on them to superiors, and they were punished with beatings and prison time.

In frustration, Heida configured that all she could do to make ends meet was remarry.

"It was an easy process. There was an ISIS man we all knew with a laptop, and he would just ask us what we wanted and bring us guys to choose," Heida recalled nonchalantly. "I met three, but I chose a man from Kosovo blinded by shrapnel because he wanted to go to Turkey for an operation."

Then she smiled.

"That was my out," Heida quipped. "Going to Turkey with him. I hoped I could get out that way."

She never made it across the border. Months dragged by and she just wanted to return home to Germany. Heida had lost count of the days she had been far from home. Yet, she seemed to be at peace with whatever would become of her life if she reached her native land.

"I was in love. It was a mistake," Heida confessed. "But I'm ready to go home, I am ready to go to prison. I just cannot stay a minute longer here."

Her eyes pivoted to the guard in the corner. Her voice dropped to a slightly huskier notch.

"But if I cannot leave," Heida continued, "then at least let me work, volunteer, or tutor school students like I used to."

Other foreign wives held at the dun place seemed more committed to the ISIS cause than Heida, who acted like she had gotten caught up in a Danielle Steele novel that accidentally got mixed with some Stephen King-like horrors.

Khala Ahmed, a forty-three-year-old, departed Karachi, Pakistan, with her husband and children to "fight for the Syrian people."

"My husband was distraught after seeing a UNICEF documentary about the war in Syria," explained Khala, who had six children ranging in age from two to fourteen years old. "He wanted to fight Bashar. My husband sold our house and all our things for us to leave."

She paused, looking puzzled for a moment.

"He used to be a normal man, worked in telecommunications," Khala said. "But he saw that documentary, and he made a mind change."

She hoped that her husband, missing in action, was in prison somewhere. But in the meantime, she remained hopeful that the ISIS "caliphate" would resurge.

"I still think it might come back," she said. "We are waiting."

I just shook my head.

All the women I spoke to said they were prepared to receive visits from representatives from their home governments. Those SDF appointees tasked with running the resource-sapped camp were just as anxious for a solution.

"Most countries don't want them, and most of them are too scared to go back," bemoaned the official, who added that the women's children were being sent to a "deradicalization" school in the camp for good measure.

"But we can't keep them here forever," he said with a shrug. "Someone needs to help here."

U.S. FOR THE LONG HAUL?
April, 2018

The U.S. and other foreign forces could walk away from the conflict at any given moment. Technically, they could pull the rug from their help on the ground the second that the orders came down. The Syrians stuck inside the war bubble were awash with anxiety over what would become of them if the great America decamped. They knew too well that their fight would only intensify — that they were trapped in a war which would never leave them, even though they had not started it.

A military convoy rolled down a rubble road outside the northern Syrian city of Manbij on a Saturday afternoon in early April, just hours after U.S. and allied forces struck several Syrian regime chemical facilities in and around Damascus.

Gule, a young female soldier with the 5,000-strong Manbij Military Council (MMC), stopped and stared in awe for a moment as they passed.

"It is beautiful," she declared to no one in particular.

Gule's sentiment reverberated throughout the city that not so long ago had been hammered under ISIS. A much quieter version of Manbij existed now, a peppering of U.S. military installations supported by the Syrian Democratic Forces (SDF) who had seized control over much of the region.

After weeks of questions and concerns from locals over the U.S. commitment to the region — fueled by President Trump's earlier statement that the boots-on-the-ground would be withdrawn — many saw the U.S. strikes against the authoritarian regime as a hopeful sign. Not only was America willing to take the lead against blatant violations committed, but that the great power was here to stay.

While much of Syria remained scourged by ever-changing checkpoints and intermittent bombing, Manbij had bounced back from its ISIS hold, morphing back into a bustling city. The streets were filled with markets and motorcycles. Women and men roamed freely through the bazaars and sipped tea along the sidewalk. All a testament to resilience.

"We are so happy the U.S. troops are here. The most important thing is we know we won't be bombed when the U.S. is here," said Khalid, a thirty-one-year-old mobile phone seller and graduate of Homs University. "If they leave, we worry Russians will be the first to come in and bomb us. Right now, we are calm and comfortable."

Mahmoud, a sixty-year-old purveyor of sweets, also expressed gratitude over being spared the aerial bombardment that had ravaged much of his country.

"Of all the players in Syria, America is better than the others," he surmised. "Seven years of this war and no one else has come to take care of us. I'm happy for this strike. This gives me hope."

Mahmoud described Trump's hardline approach as "heroic."

"He said he would hit, so he did," he continued.

Others sitting in the streets having cigarettes and tea said they weren't familiar with all the political ins and outs, but recognized their environment as far more stable than others.

"The most important thing is we have some stability," stressed Raheem, a forty-five-year-old tradesman. "We just want to keep this peace. We want anyone who will help us keep this peace."

But the peace — whereby Kurds, Arabs, Turks, and other minorities lived together with Majority Muslims of all sects — was fragile.

"ISIS can't control Manbij again, but there are sleeper cells here," cautioned Abu Adel, the thirty-nine-year-old head of Manbij Military Council.

He had first joined the Syrian Revolution in 2011 as a fighter with the Free Syrian Army (FSA), and he had not lost that rebellious spirit to fight and keep fighting.

"This is a big country, and we liberated this city alongside the U.S.," Abu explained. "We still have threats; we still need their expertise."

While ISIS and Turkey remained the most immediate concerns for the council, Adel would not discount the impending menace that the regime brought. If Assad's forces found a way in, they could lose their newfound liberty.

"When we started with the revolution, it was not about wanting Assad to leave," Abu recollected. "We just wanted changes, we wanted a chance to speak freely, and we waited for the changes to happen. But those changes did not happen. And the protests moved from peaceful to the military."

By that, he meant that the opposition was pummeled with bombs and blasts by Assad's security forces — so they took up arms wherever they could find them and fired back.

Out in the pastures, overlooking a traditionally sandbagged frontline, one Manbij Military Council soldier, Laurence, reiterated his desire for the U.S. to stay engaged.

"I was so happy for this bombing. Innocent children should not be killed with chemicals. Fighting military troops is one thing, civilians is another," Laurence said before eagerly detailing his "life-saving" medic training under U.S. forces. "We can defend ourselves, but having the U.S. morale behind us has been important. We hope they stay."

There was a growing concern that the Turkish forces posted nearby would encroach farther into Manbij. President Erdogan made no secret of the fact he would stop at nothing to "neutralize" hideouts occupied by their designated terrorist group, the Kurdistan Workers Party (PKK). In his eyes, all the Kurdish fighting factions amounted to one and the same under the PKK brolly.

The future of Manbij — for all its vitality, spices, souks, and smiles — was still marred by uncertainty, prompting locals to crave a time before the uprisings of 2011, which later developed into a bloody and protracted conflict. They craved the stability, if even if it meant towing the dictator's line.

What is war? It is feeling utter loss of control; it is pining for a time of constancy. Better the devil you know.

"We don't know what Islamic rule could come in and whether we will be allowed still to be Yazidi," lamented Tahsin, a displaced Yazidi from Afrin who had been left to live in a forsaken building in the Kurdish city of Kobane. "We don't know what will happen tomorrow."

TARGETING THE LAST STRONGHOLD
April, 2018

Tomorrow came soon enough and, once again, the young soldiers of the U.S.-backed, Kurdish-led Syrian Democratic Forces (SDF) rose from half-slumbers. They scattered themselves around their makeshift checkpoints ahead of the full slant of spring sunshine.

Young men manned many of the checkpoints, veiled only by a ripped sheet — often alone, staring out at what was left of the vicious Islamic rule. While ISIS had been reduced to holding just a few hamlets of desert territory, the fight still occupied every waking move.

For hours I spluttered down a snaking vein of unpaved roads and through broken oil refineries destroyed by ISIS and then by airstrikes. These were refineries where children still played in the fractured equipment like it was the only play park they had left for leisure.

Finally, I made it to the quiet frontline, positioned half a mile from the village of Hajin in Eastern Syria. It was one of the few remaining areas that a beaten-back ISIS force still occupied.

"They still attack us every day, any time of the day," said twenty-one-year-old Hassan, the senior SDF soldier at the post. "Sometimes mortar, sometimes rockets. Always lots of bullets."

He spoke casually, like he was ordering a McDonald's Happy Meal. You knew you were going to get a surprise, but you just did not know which one. Most twenty-one-year-old men I knew from home relished their new-fangled adult freedom with college parties, clubs, football, and part-time jobs. Hassan had the seeming weight of the world on his shoulders, but he took it all in his composed stride.

Although ISIS had been defeated in more than ninety percent of the territory it once controlled in Iraq and Syria, removing this final pocket along the Iraqi-Syrian border — including Hajin, on the eastern side of the Euphrates River, north of Abu Kamal, and Dashisha, west of Deir ez-Zor — was proving to be a frustratingly slow process.

"This is their last territory, and thousands of them came here after Mosul and Raqqa," Hassan explained. "They are digging tunnels and planting mines all over."

The push against ISIS came to a sudden halt in January, when Turkey launched "Operation Olive Branch" on the primarily Kurdish city of Afrin, 250 miles northwest and close to Turkey's rugged border.

"We didn't want to fight here and lose Afrin," observed fellow SDF fighter Mihdi Khalil. "The coalition wanted us to stay here, but Afrin was just as important to us to fight for; we decided to send many of our troops from here to there."

The mission to defeat ISIS subsequently slowed and gave rise to a diplomatic quagmire for the United States.

While the U.S. has backed the SDF as the primary and most trustworthy ground force against ISIS, NATO-ally Turkey viewed the group as an extension of the outlawed Kurdistan Workers Party (PKK), which for more than thirty years waged a campaign specifically against the Turkish state.

U.S. officials stepped back from the Afrin battle, which disappointed the SDF — and, more so, left them heartsick.

Turkish forces as well as their fighting partners, the Free Syrian Army (FSA), went on to seize Afrin from SDF control in March, dealing a massive blow to the SDF. Some impassioned fighters dumped their U.S. weapons and the ISIS mission and strode over to the battle for Afrin. The chaos left the ISIS fight in a paralyzed limbo.

U.S. officials were the first to admit that the Afrin campaign cost valuable

SDF forces, with as many as 1,700 SDF troops choosing to fight the Turks. That fight had more sentimental value to them than a bunch of ISIS jihadists creeping around in the desert.

"Since that departure, the SDF has been limited," acknowledged Colonel Ryan Dillon, spokesman for Operation Inherent Resolve (OIR), the name given to the U.S.-led coalition against ISIS. "When SDF was constantly putting pressure on ISIS in the two remaining locations, they were achieving success through ground forces/attacks."

Colonel Dillon pointed out that the U.S.-led coalition had launched airstrikes against ISIS forces, but relied mainly on the SDF to provide the ground pressure.

"Example: SDF attacks, we see ISIS react/move, we strike."

With fewer SDF forces in action, Dillon said, U.S. military planners couldn't effectively target ISIS as they had before Afrin.

But new efforts were underway to get the mission back on track. Assets had been reallocated to gather more information on ISIS targets, and the pace of coalition strikes quickened.

"This has allowed for the coalition to deliberately plan targets — targets that can take days to weeks to develop — before actually conducting the strikes," said Dillon.

"ISIS remains an adaptive and savvy enemy that still poses a threat," he continued. "They are largely in hiding, attempting to reconsolidate, and are planning what to do next: either fight, surrender, or try to flee."

ISIS increased attacks in other areas of Syria, Dillon said, and had even retaken some neighborhoods south of Damascus.

For civilians still struggling to survive under the repressive rule of the Islamic State more than four years after its fall, the waiting game — and the suffering — lugged on.

"They are frightening the people, they behead people, explode bombs in markets," exclaimed Mustafa Bali, an SDF spokesman. "They still create an atmosphere where it is impossible for people to escape from them."

The smell of death was the cologne that defined their lives. Civilians who tried to escape ISIS-controlled territory did so in the face of death.

The SDF medic on hand, stationed at the closest "emergency" clinic — a room with limited supplies — was thirty-five-year-old Akif. He sat slumped against a brick wall behind the firing line, behind the row of loaded rockets and RPGs. He stopped wearing body armor long ago, he said. If it was his time to go, a thin layer of high-tensile strength plastic was not going to save him.

Akif said that the slowing of the offensive amid the Afrin distraction had meant he was tending to fewer battlefield casualties. But dozens of civilians in recent weeks had been killed and mutilated by ISIS-planted landmines.

A few days earlier, a six-year-old girl lost a leg to a landmine, he said, and a few days before her a young woman had her left foot blown off.

I examined the wincing photographs of the victims Akif kept on his phone. I studied the anguish that crossed their blood-freckled faces — a synthesis of shock, pain, regret, and fear. For the first time, I did not flinch. I felt nothing. I had always told myself that I would never get to that point. I would never become so jaded by the pain of others that my first reaction was no reaction.

What is war? War is a vision of agony that becomes normal. That's what war does to people.

The numbness passed into the familiar jolt of helplessness, and I slowly reached for my legs and arms, a strange reflex to show gratitude that they were still there.

"Half of Hajin is under ISIS and the other half SDF," Akif explained. "So, ISIS plants a line of mines to protect themselves, and even if people just want to go to visit family or friends on the other side, it could be deadly."

The SDF recognized that Syrian government forces, distracted elsewhere, were not doing much to help clear out ISIS.

"The Syrian regime all these years has been too busy fighting people in Ghouta, they haven't bothered with ISIS," Akif continued. "It's up to us."

The burden had been a heavy one for the 100,000 SDF members. Exhaustion was engraved on young, sun-creased faces as the fighters shuffled between the front and the nearby Tanak oil fields. Some troops stayed half a day on the firing line; others stayed for days on end. Almost all positioned there told me that they were no older than twenty-one.

Akif's clinic was located in the mangled Tanak oil facility. The field was once one of the most prominent in Syria and boasted approximately 150 wells and the capacity to produce up to 40,000 BPD. It became a significant funding center for ISIS operations until the group was run out by the SDF five months earlier.

But Tanak, along with several other prominent oil refineries clustered in the area, was decimated the previous year by Syrian and Russian regime warplanes. Only one well currently worked, SDF soldiers said.

The ISIS danger still prowled. Suicide bombers hit the area intermittently, and concerns over sleeper cells prompted a curfew of 3:00 P.M. on the immediate area. The surrounding stretch, reaching to the village of Shadadi seventy-five miles away, had a curfew of 7:00 P.M.

"Any cars moving through after that," one soldier said cryptically, "we shoot."

Hassan insisted the SDF was "very well equipped" for the much-anticipated final takedown against ISIS — with U.S.- supplied rifles, rocket-propelled grenades, and Russian machine guns and missiles at the ready.

"We are waiting our orders," he observed leisurely, priming a rocket-propelled grenade.

We were on a rooftop, our stomachs flat against the ground, as low as we could go so that ISIS could not spot us across the no-man's-land.

"When they tell us to move in," Hassan added. "We will destroy them."

ANCIENT CHRISTIAN RUINS DISCOVERED UNDER ISIS-HELD TERRITORY
April, 2018

The patch of urban land had been destroyed and gnawed at by the terrorist reign. But far below what met the eye was a magical world touched only by the passage of time.

For more than two years, ISIS forces occupying the northern Syrian city of Manbij paid little attention to the tip of an old gate, barely visible through the hardened dust. Instead, they used the empty mound of land as a waste dumping ground. Little did they know that the gate ran several feet into the earth, down to something they might well have destroyed: the ruins of an ancient Christian refuge or early church, possibly dating back to the first centuries of Christendom's existence under the Roman Empire.

"I was so excited; I can't describe it. I was holding everything in my hands," Abdulwahab Sheko, head of the Exploration Committee at the Ruins Council in Manbij, exclaimed giddily as he led me into the folds of antiquity.

Among the artifacts found — which indicated it was a significant Christian site — were several versions of crosses etched into columns and walls, and writings carved into stone.

"This place is so special. Here is where I think the security guard would stand at the gate watching for any movement outside," Abdulwahab explained, working his way through what he called the "first location" of the newly-discovered site. "Here, he could warn the others to exit through the other passage if they needed to flee."

The ancient space was carved with narrow tunnels, complete with grooved shelves to offer light. These were believed to provide passage for worshippers. There was a myriad of escape routes tucked into the tunnels as well, featuring large stones that may have served as hidden doors. Also visible were three jagged steps leading up to what Abdulwahab believed was something of an altar.

The discovery of a so-called "secret church," dating as far back as the third or fourth century, A.D., could be an extraordinary find, according to a leading American archaeologist I spoke with after my tour.

"They indicate that there was a significant Christian population in the area which felt they needed to hide their activities," said John Wineland, professor of history and archaeology at Southeastern University, upon examining the plethora of photographs and video I sent him. "This is probably an indication of the persecution by the Roman government, which was common in the period."

John said Christians were persecuted "sporadically at first, and later more systematically by the Roman government." Christianity was illegal in the Roman Empire until Emperor Constantine decriminalized its worship in 313 A.D.

Christians of the time "met in secret, underground, to avoid trouble. But the Romans were fearful of any group that met in secret," the professor said.

"The Romans misunderstood many Christian practices and would often charge them with crimes, such as cannibalism," John explained.

He said such charges stemmed from the "Roman misunderstanding of Christian communion where Christ said to take and eat His body and drink His blood."

It is not yet clear just how important a find these new ruins might be.

Abdulwahab told me that he had reached out to international archeologists and organizations since his team began cleaning up the site last fall. He needed help identifying artifacts and wanted to "test the bones" of the human remains found. But the response from abroad so far, he lamented, was that it was too dangerous to send archaeological teams to this part of the country.

Abdulwahab was hopeful the Vatican would "become aware of these discoveries," and would not wait too long to send someone to inspect the ruins.

The site was fortunate to escape ISIS's attention. He believed it was divine intervention.

Abdulwahab had already been studying the neighborhood when the infamously Christian-hostile group invaded in 2014. He knew something was there, but he did not know what. He kept his studies quiet until ISIS was driven out in a bloody offensive by the U.S.-backed Syrian Democratic Forces (SDF) in 2016.

Due to the area being riddled with mines and booby traps, extensive cleanup and digging at the site couldn't begin until late August of last year. Enough excavation had taken place by March for Abdulwahab to go in with curious locals making up his team of assistants.

It was the locals who had paved the way to another, very recently discovered "second location." We walked to it — a block littered with insects, trash, and even a stray dog sleeping inside. The young guard, who had gone down first, came running up in a panic with the frightened animal hurtling behind him.

I followed Abdulwahab down eleven steep stone steps and into a cave that opened into a multitude of rooms. Overt Christian symbols had been chiseled all over, etched into the stone walls, and drawn across the arched ceilings.

"We think this place after Christianity was no longer a secret anymore," explained Abdulwahab, gesturing to the abundance of emblems.

John agreed and said he believed that — based on the photographs — the crosses in the walls, along with geometric designs consistent with the Roman era, appeared to have been added later— after a wider acceptance of the Christian faith had been sewn into the social fabric.

"That is what we would call a secondary use of the tomb," he explained. "And it might well have been a Christian place of meeting or worship."

Further into the subterranean maze was a "graveyard," likely reserved for the church clergy. Each tomb displayed an elevated "stone cushion" for the head.

Human remains laid inside the tombs, remnants from centuries long, long ago. One resident told me sheepishly that once he came to see the ruins on his own and upon touching the human bones watched them "disintegrate" before his eyes.

The cleanout process for the "second location" was set to start in September

2017, five months away. It would require seven men, digging tools, and a forklift.

Many more potential ruins had yet to be unearthed, Abdulwahab said, but residential buildings hoisted above them had made excavation even more complicated.

For now, those two sacred sites were guarded by a young, plain-clothed twenty-one-year-old and his AK-47. Outside the nondescript Ruins Council office, precious artifacts were simply left on the street due to lack of resources for safeguarding and "no museum to put it in," Abdulwahab announced.

Those precious pieces included a Roman-era effigy grooved into a limestone building block, grave markers, arch fragments, and column bases, one of which had a Greek inscription on an architectural block.

"Greek was the common language of the Eastern Roman Empire," John Wineland later told me. "Which explains why the New Testament is written in Greek during the Roman period."

Hassan Darwish, the council's field monitor responsible for archiving and topography, had managed to salvage some key historical pieces discovered by ISIS and sold off in local markets. Among the rescued were old mosaics whose faces had been destroyed by ISIS before being pawned off for quick funds.

Manbij, located in northeastern Aleppo Governorate near the Turkish border, eighteen miles west of the Euphrates, had long been considered one of Syria's most ancient and prized townships. Given the area's prominence in the centuries following Christianity's founding, archaeologists believed more Christian sites could be brought to light in the areas liberated from ISIS.

If there was any type of silver lining to the tragedy, perhaps this was it.

Most of the land encompassing modern-day Syria was annexed in 64 B.C. by the Roman Republic. For centuries it was an important center for trade and commerce in the Eastern — or Byzantine —empire.

By the seventh century, however, Islam began to expand through the Arab conquests. Syria eventually became majority Muslim.

At the start of the civil war seven years earlier, Christians made up about ten percent of Syria's population. It was not clear how many were left. Numerous houses of worship had been razed, and the continuous threats far and wide had prompted many in the minority to flee, fight, convert, or die.

John observed that these recent discoveries reminded him of the intense persecution of Christians in modern-day Syria and Iraq.

"This has led to a significant decline of Christians in the region. Some have been killed, others have fled, and still others have been coerced into converting to Islam," he added.

What is war? It was a coming together of people from all stripes, with the common goal of wanting to right a wrong.

Despite Christianity's difficult history in Syria, however, Abdulwahab wanted to make clear his commitment to protecting whatever ruins he and his team might find.

"We are Muslim, but we are not like ISIS Muslims," he said slowly, looking me dead in the eye as if to plead his case to the unconvinced world. "We take care of these Christian ruins. We respect them. We respect humanity."

ISIS FIGHTER'S WARNING TO THE WORLD
May, 2018

And then there were the fighters themselves. Whether they had been captured or had surrendered, they were squished into cells and left waiting.

On a humid afternoon in an old building ringed by thickets and security guards, I sat with Belgium native Hamza Nmeie — likely a last name he had made up.

He had just turned twenty-seven and confessed to being one of few foreign fighters to have seen the barbaric and bloody surge of ISIS in Syria long before the group was known to the world. It was easy to hate someone like Hamza, to perceive him in the one-dimensional sense as a wretched and unlovable killer. But as a journalist, I never go into an interview hostile or with the intent to stick it to the bad guy.

Why would someone want to open up to you or trust you if they thought your only objective was to have a go at or interrogate them? The benefit of being a print journalist was that I didn't need to make good television. What I needed was a raw conversation without the lights and cameras and crews and fanfare.

In the hour that passed, I held back any type of judgment and simply talked. I asked Hamza questions, and he asked me ones in return. I started to tie the pieces of his life as an ISIS member together in a truncated narrative of events.

Hamza had arrived in Syria as a fresh-faced recruit in June 2013. He had signed up for what was then the Syrian al-Qaeda affiliate, known as al-Nusra. However, he went on to become one of the first to pledge his way into ISIS, he said, after in-fighting had triggered a rupture between the two terrorist outfits.

These men had no respect for humanity. They had burned people and the land alive, and yet the SDF — and, by default, the U.S. taxpayer — was coughing up money to keep them behind bars. It was a frustrating avocation in waiting for all involved. The SDF bewailed the lack of help they had in sorting out the mess of ISIS fighters filling up their makeshift detention centers. Washington had not squashed the ISIS threat territorially, so it was not yet consumed with handling the matter.

Born to Moroccan parents in the idyllic countryside just outside Brussels, Hamza was well known in his community, revered for his soccer and boxing skills. His last job was with the DHL delivery service, he claimed, before he set off for Syria.

Hamza admitted that in 2011 he became more militant in his ideological views after being introduced to a Salafist group called Sharia4Belgium. The group called for the overthrow of democracy, and it urged young people to join ISIS abroad. Almost two years after he heeded the call and set out for the battlefield, the organization would be formally designated as a terrorist group by the Belgian state.

How many more minds had been infected in those twenty-four months? I thought to myself.

"There, we learned this ideology of jihad; we were told that there was no country in the world that was properly ruled by Sharia. This was all new for me," he said, referring to his involvement with Sharia4Belgium. "But in Syria, I saw and heard even more extreme things than I had heard in Belgium."

Hamza acknowledged that his "extremist" tendencies at home had even caught the attention of local law enforcement. One day, police even came to question him, confiscating his passport.

"But then I learned I could travel just with my ID," Hamza said with a wry smile.

A few weeks after the authorities had knocked on his door, the aspiring jihadist packed a bag and left. He flew to Düsseldorf, Germany and then to Istanbul, Turkey, before meeting up other Belgian recruits in the southern province of Adana. From there, they crossed into Syria with the permission of Turkish border guards, he claimed.

It was a time when Syria's civil war had reached the point of inferno, and Turkey — which opposed the Syrian regime— had not yet shuttered its borders. Rebel fighters and refugees floated freely through the porous delineation between nations.

Hamza was first placed at an "immigrants' location" in the opposition bastion of Idlib, where he was housed alongside several Western fighters. After two weeks, he was sent for forty days of training — weapons, fitness, religious doctrine — in the desert of Deir ez-Zor. After that, he was deployed to the northern Syrian city of Aleppo to fight.

It was there, in the summer of 2013, that he first learned of the self-professed "caliph," Abu al-Baghdadi. And it was ISIS's governor for the Syrian province of Aleppo, Amr al-Absi, who coerced him to declare his allegiance to the "son of the Prophet."

Hamza said the shadowy leader, who remained the most wanted man in the world, even visited the "immigrants' location" at the time he was training. Baghdadi personally swore in the other ISIS recruits who had broken away from al-Nusra. Hamza recalled that the newly-established group initially fought alongside the Free Syrian Army (FSA) against the regime. But relations soured later in 2013 after photographs of commanders alongside U.S. Senator John McCain in Turkey started circulating.

They were then instructed to turn their weapons on those who were once their "friends."

Hamza also insisted that after 2014, FSA members set up black-market weapons deals in which they would sell arms— including those issued by the U.S. and abandoned by the Iraqi Army — to the highest bidder, even if they were the FSA's own "enemies."

"They have no honor. They just want money," Hamza said.

When he talked about the ISIS betrayal, he spoke about it in such a way that made me think that the real tragedy in all of this was that he had betrayed himself, and there was no longer a way out.

Hamza particularly remembered the ISIS celebrations after the 2014 beheading of American journalist James Foley, and how leaders used the gruesome event as "motivation."

"It was to say, 'Look how we are fighting the Americans,'" he continued, underscoring that ISIS initially gained momentum after the formation of a coalition of over sixty allied nations designed to defeat them. The coalition's creation was spun by the ISIS propaganda machine to show how "strong" the militant group was against such a massive force.

Hamza repeatedly emphasized in the interview that the ideology driving ISIS was "not going to stop," and had permeated some circles so profoundly that it would be next to impossible to defeat. He also said each new incarnation of the group brought a school of thought even more rigid than that of its predecessor.

A central tenet of ISIS's brainwashing of new followers was its singular focus on the United States, Hamza said, in what he described as an "obsession" with

America.

"It was the big enemy," he said.

During his terrorist tenure, Hamza also set out to find an ISIS bride, also from Belgium, and claimed he received a $50 per month salary for himself, another $50 for his wife, and $35 for each child — they had two. He said his family was now living in a displacement camp in Ain Essa, outside Raqqa. They had no contact.

But Hamza stayed on for years, witnessing the group's rise and decline as the "caliphate" crumbled under a U.S.-led coalition effort in Iraq and Syria. He jostled from hotspot to hotspot until his luck ran out. Hamza had surrendered to the U.S.-backed Syrian Democratic Forces (SDF) in Raqqa last September.

While the Belgians sought to downplay his role as a frontline soldier, refusing to admit he had killed anyone, an SDF intelligence official overseeing the prison contended to me later that he was "so active," and had played a leading role among the fighters.

Hamza claimed he had not received any visits or official correspondence from Belgian officials.

"Now," he said, sitting back in his chair. "Can I ask you a question?"

He did not wait for my response. Hamza wanted to know if I had heard anything out in the functioning world that indicated whether his country intended to allow ISIS fighters back. I answered as honestly as I could, explaining that so far it appeared that Belgium — and other Western countries with ISIS fighters held by the SDF — did not want the headache of having to bring them home.

He nodded, and his face dropped to the ground. It was the first glimmer of him losing composure, slumped in momentary disappointment that he tried to conceal. Of all the ISIS collaborators I had met until that point, Hamza struck me as the most educated, well-spoken, and devoted. He pulled himself together just as quickly as he had slipped apart.

For now, Hamza and others like him existed in legal limbo. He had not been criminally charged, faced no trial to date, and was being held by captors who lived on hope that representatives from the prisoners' home countries would just come and take them away.

As it stood, he was confined to a solitary cell to avoid attempts to radicalize the prisoners. Other ISIS members held there — spanning a multitude of nationalities — were given three meals a day, a weekly checkup by a doctor, and an hour of daily "recreation" time, which included outdoor access, soccer games, television, and reading sessions.

Suddenly, Hamza warned of more plots and vowed that splinter groups were likely to creep out from under the carcass of ISIS.

"Another group will come," he cautioned, noting that fighters disgruntled with ISIS commanders were already in the process of planning breakaway terror groups before the fall of Raqqa, the so-called caliphate capital.

Hamza said he was wrong to join ISIS. He declared that he was "not an ISIS Muslim" anymore. He denounced the group's brand as being full of lies and dubbed Baghdadi "an evil guy."

But he also seemed aware that shaking his association with the universally reviled group had left him in a tight spot. What he said next had a chilling effect, and it came as dank rain started to fall outside and through the open window.

"ISIS is like the Mafia," he added. "Once you get in... you never come out."

This time, Hamza's eyes fell to the floor and remained fixed there, lost in thought. I made my way to the door, and I never saw Hamza look up again.

U.S. FORCES LURKING IN SYRIA
May, 2018

When I looked up from my notebook after scrawling viciously in the back of the car, the red, white, and blue caught my eye in the starkness of the dun desert terrain. Even though the SDF were the front men leading the charge, the quiet, low-profile U.S. military presence in Syria wasn't quite so low-profile up close. Strings were being pulled from behind the iron curtain.

The American flag flew high from a dozen or so positions the United States military had established. It could also be spotted from afar on that bright spring day as convoys rumbled along the dusty village roads of northern Syria, near the Turkish border. Most of the 2,000 troops the Pentagon had deployed here were confined to their bases —which were occupied by Islamic State militants not long ago — but the U.S. footprint did not go unnoticed.

The Americans visited local shops and restaurants from time to time, and local civilians excitedly pointed them out. Small groups of U.S. soldiers were also noticed in the former ISIS "caliphate" of Raqqa, often alongside Syrian Democratic Forces (SDF).

There was no denying the familiarity of the U.S.-SDF partnership: the shared offices, meals, cigarettes, family stories.

U.S. foot soldiers trained their SDF partners in everything from media and camera use to weapons training.

What is war? It is big militaries coming to train the smaller, doctored-up militias.

That was the new Pentagon model — advise and assist others to do the bloody work. But that certainly did not mean that the U.S. was not embroiled in the combat, nor did it mean the U.S. was immune to casualties within its ranks.

While President Donald Trump had spoken earlier of a pullout from Syria, he qualified his statement this time with the provision that the withdrawal would happen when the mission was complete.

That was still a cause for concern from the SDF's point of view, as they had hoped the United States would stay beyond the time it took to clean out what was left of ISIS resistance in the region.

They felt as though they had been burned alive too many times by too many different enemies — from Assad to Turkey to ISIS and other hardline Islamic factions. They worried they would be sitting ducks when their security blanket was taken away.

But for now, all eyes remained transfixed on the widely-touted mission: to decimate ISIS once and for all. And it was kicking back into high gear.

A renewed offensive against ISIS in Deir-ez-Zor by the SDF was set to resume in the coming days. The end game was nearing.

"It will likely take two to three months for the operations to be completed," said Keno Gabriel, an SDF spokesperson, with a weary smile. "But after that, about another three to six months to clean up the cells and other threats."

That was wishful thinking. ISIS was so furiously entrenched in its last territorial hold that it was not going to fall easily, nor quickly.

Our politicians at home wanted us — a largely battle-tired American public — to believe that the war was not our war; we were merely accessories to aid locals in a necessary fight that was in our national security interests. But the U.S. had already invested more in the fight than most Americans realized. Since the stunning rise of ISIS across Iraq and Syria in 2014, the United States had spent a daily average of more than $13 million, according to Defense Department figures. At least 8,000 troops were in the broader Iraq-Syria region at any given moment, and more than sixty members of the U.S. military had already been killed in both combat and non-combat-related deaths.

Yet the effort was already being touted as having paid off. ISIS had been compelled from more than ninety percent of the terrain it once controlled and had then been diminished to land pockets along the Iraq-Syria border. While still far from finished, the anxiety of what would come next clung like nervous energy in the arid air.

An American exit could be disastrous, cautioned those who had come to view the U.S. flag as a beacon of peace in the war-ravaged region, as was the case when America withdrew from Iraq in 2011 after removing Saddam Hussein from power.

"A complete U.S. withdrawal is a lesson that should be learned from Iraq; the U.S. is a major player and a major stabilizing force in the Middle East," Keno warned.

Despite talk of withdrawal, the U.S. presence had expanded over the past year.

"The Americans started with just one base, and now there are two more just in Manbij, bigger than before," said Abu Adel, head of the Manbij Military Council. "Of course, we want them to stay. They said they will protect us."

But like the smaller-scale troop surge that had preceded the end to the war in Iraq, it felt for many on the ground like the calm before the storm.

What Syrian Kurds feared more than ISIS or the return of Syrian government control was the power of Turkish forces who perceived the SDF as an offshoot of the Kurdistan Workers' Party, better known as the PKK. That militia had waged a separatist military campaign against Turkey for more than thirty years, prompting Turkey to take control of the nearby Kurdish-dominant town of Afrin. Erdogan had moved to threaten that he would next cleanse Manbij of "terrorists."

"Having the U.S. gives us hope and stability, not just for Kurdish people, but for all of us living together here in Syria," Anwar Moslim — a forty-five-year-old official in the presidency of the Euphrates Region Office in Kobane — passionately appealed to me as we sipped tea from a bullet-pocked office. "We have concern about what might happen if they go. Who will invade us? Who will attack us?"

Without wasting a breath, he went on to highlight that Americans were also critical to the continued presence of non-governmental organizations that had come from abroad to help Syrians. Without them, he stressed, the humanitarian outfits would likely disappear too, citing security woes.

However, Trump, who had recently affirmed that America "does not seek an indefinite presence in Syria," also said that he had looked to other nations to step up their contributions. Other critics concurred that it was time for other allies to step up, that the U.S. had done more than its share in the fight.

"The United States did the heavy lifting in defeating ISIS in Syria by working closely with the Syrian Democratic Forces on the ground and providing the bulk of the air support that enabled the SDF to roll back ISIS forces," said James Phillips, a senior research fellow for Middle Eastern affairs at the Heritage Foundation. "It is time for U.S. allies to step forward to assume a greater role in stabilization efforts in eastern Syria, and free up American Special Forces for other missions."

Layla Mustafa, who co-chaired the newly formed Raqqa Civilian Council, emphasized that the notion of the U.S. pulling out was "more than just a worry," but agreed that the onus should be on international partners, too.

"We fought ISIS here on behalf of the whole world, and we should receive support from all countries," she told me. "Not just the U.S."

There was that classic line again. The armies across Iraq and Syria saw their endeavors as being on behalf of the world's national security.

But while the role of coalition partners in Syria might seem nonexistent from the outset, they were there contributing to the effort.

General Mazloum, the rarely-seen head of the SDF forces, told me that while the U.S. was provided them with the bulk of the assistance, the U.K. and France also had troops in Syria. They, too, were focused on the anti-ISIS campaign and on training his SDF protection forces. General Mazloum stressed that the coalition forces had been working alongside the SDF since late 2015 and that they "have taken part in all the campaigns against ISIS."

But there were no flags, no uniform patches, and no public presence by British or French troops. The French, though, "recently played the main role in defending Manbij," whispered Farooq Al Mashi, co-chair of the Legal Counsel of Manbij.

Keno, too, praised the role of the British and the French and predicted they would step up their involvement.

"The U.K. and the French have been very effective. I think France will take a bigger role, and they will increase if the U.S. leaves," he said. "The French have a long history with Syria; they really understand the dynamics."

According to a statement sent by the French Armed Forces, 1,100 personnel had been committed to the anti-ISIS effort in two types of missions: advising and training missions in Iraq, and operational support to allied forces fighting ISIS.

"The French military operates in Syria against ISIS but does not own any facility on Syrian soil," the statement read. *"Its missions in Syria are conducted by air capacities based in Jordan and the United Arab Emirates."*

The SDF begged to differ, and the denials confused me. Was it a PR problem for the countries? A diplomatic dilemma? Or was it just more comfortable for the U.S. to bear the brunt of it, for better or for worse?

Keno asserted that both the French and Brits had roughly 200 pairs of boots on the ground, although I could not independently confirm such figures.

The British denied the presence of troops, even though one of their soldiers was killed alongside an American near Manbij last month.

Another British official, speaking on the condition of anonymity, said that the U.K. contribution was strictly air support— that it had the assets at RAF Akrotiri, their base in Cyprus, and remained "engaged in Operation Shader," the British codeword for the intervention against ISIS. But the Brits and their highest caliber top-tier troops were well-known to the SDF by undertaking roles far removed from just air backing.

What is war? It is myths and policy, and myths about policy. There is a reason we all distrust in the theater of battles.

Moreover, some doubted the ability of any coalition effort that didn't include a prominent American presence.

"Other NATO and coalition forces can, of course, assist in the continued fight against ISIS and violent jihadists," said Alan Mendoza, executive director of the Henry Jackson Society, a British conservative foreign policy think tank. "But only the U.S. has the capacity to manage a joined-up military campaign at every level, so its continued engagement is essential."

Nonetheless, Trump's reported plan to support an "Arab force" to maintain security after a U.S. pullout had some support in the SDF.

"As we know, Jordan, Saudi Arabia, United Arab Emirates, have been part of the coalition. Maybe not on the ground, but they have been part of this," General Mazloum said. "We see it as a positive step if they come here — they are welcome."

But the looming question of how Turkey would respond in the waning days of the ISIS operation remained a huge issue. In a bid to ease mounting tensions, one high-ranking U.S. official explained to me on a quick trip into Ankara — the Turkish capital — that America had continued to tell its NATO ally, Turkey, that the SDF "is not an ally" in the same sense. The official underscored that the U.S.-SDF agreement had always been to "shake hands and move on" once ISIS was defeated.

What did that mean for the Syrian Kurds? Had they been fooled into being foot soldiers for the west? Many could not understand why dozens of countries had descended to help Iraq with its ISIS battle over the border, making firm long- term commitments when nobody would offer them the same kind of agreement.

In Iraq, at least seventy countries publicly participated in the anti-ISIS fight.

"We are here for as long as the Iraq government needs us to help then defeat ISIS," U.S. General Eifler told me. "The people do not want to go through this [ISIS invasion] again. Iraqis have spent a lot of blood and treasure. And they have come a long way."

The Kurds faced an unknown commitment and an unknown future. But, as they often pointed out, betrayal was not new to them, and they were preparing for the worst.

General Mazloum told me that he had already requested that a no-fly zone be implemented over the region should the U.S. withdraw, in hopes of avoiding bombardment by the Syrian and Russian forces.

But he hoped it would not come to that.

"We have been partners with the U.S. and the coalition against terrorism, and of course we hope this partnership will stay for a long time to defeat all of this terrorism," he said with a kind of stoicism that reminded me that he had seen the playbook before. "Still, we are waiting for the final decision."

WHERE IN THE WORLD IS BAGHDADI? 3.0
May, 2018

The waiting game dragged on. The wait to strike down ISIS leader Abu Bakr al-Baghdadi — still the world's most wanted man, with a $25 million bounty on his head — was, as of May 2018, ongoing. The terrorist was believed to be alive, concealed in the vast desert terrain of Syria.

That was the assessment of multiple officials who said Baghdadi — whose real name is Ibrahim Awwad Ibrahim al-Basri — was likely sheltering in a remaining ISIS bastion in the Euphrates River Valley, barren terrain with vast open plains on the Syrian side of the porous border of Iraq.

"The last information we have is he is in Al-Hajin in Syria, eighteen miles from the border in Deir ez-Zor province," said Abu Ali al-Basri, director-general of the intelligence and counter-terrorism office at the Iraqi Ministry of Interior. Al-Basri said fresh information about Baghdadi's whereabouts had come as recently as the last couple of days and was being used to conduct a "multi-force raid" with Russian, Syrian, and Iranian troops.

Brigadier General Yahya Rasool, spokesperson for the Iraqi Ministry of Defense and the Joint Operations Command, concurred that Baghdadi likely survived on the border east of the Euphrates River — with Syria's Al Shadaddi in the al-Hasakh province being another possible location.

"It is not difficult for him to hide in the Syrian desert," Yahya said.

That was also the estimation of the U.S.-backed Syrian Democratic Forces (SDF), who believed Baghdadi was in one of the "tens of villages" along the Iraqi-Syrian border, according to SDF spokesperson Mustafa Bali.

While ISIS had been primarily defeated across Syria and Iraq, the U.S.-led coalition continued for one week in May to carry out twenty-seven airstrikes against remaining targets near Abu Kamal, Deir ez-Zor, and Al Shadaddi on the Syrian side, as well as near Mosul, Ar Rutbah, and Al Huwayjah on the Iraq side.

Hisham al-Hishami, a member of the National Reconciliation Commission and a researcher in extremism and terrorism affairs — who advised Iraq and several foreign governments on ISIS activity — told me that the land where Baghdadi may have been hiding out "is very large, and he can hide in thousands of square miles between Iraq and Syria."

Hisham said the last reliable sighting of the ISIS honcho was in the summer of 2017, in Iraq's Ninawa province near Mosul.

"I met with people and some of Baghdadi's assistants who were captured, and they said he is able to hide because he moves without a convoy or bodyguards," he claimed. "There are just three people with him, his son, his son-in-law, and his friend and driver."

Sadeq al-Husseini, head of the security committee of eastern Iraq's Diyala provincial council — which in recent months had endured several ISIS attacks amid Iraqi forces' successful efforts to routinely kill and capture many of the group's remaining chiefdoms — also noted that Baghdadi left Iraq for Syria at some point during the liberation of Mosul.

"Baghdadi himself is a coward and ran away like a rat," Sadeq quipped. "He is alive but outside Iraqi lands. If he stayed in Mosul, he would be very easy haunting Iraqi forces, or killed in Mosul."

Sadeq said that in Syria, Baghdadi was able to use an array of "disguises," such as dressing as a woman. Abu Ali Basri also asserted that Baghdadi donned "modern clothes," and lived without any electronic devices to avoid detection.

Experts also surmised that Baghdadi had minimal contact with other ISIS members, and never stayed in areas when the fighting or strikes became too intense.

As I pored over documents and undertook as many interviews on the matter as I could, I learned that Baghdadi was known to "move around a lot" between Syria and Iraq. The intel officials working on his case believed that he was protected not only by his devoted circle of pledgers but by trusted local Arab tribes around the areas under ISIS control. However, the mythical murderer was severely wounded on multiple occasions, intelligence indicated, which had significantly hampered his ability to move frequently.

Russian officials had earlier claimed that Baghdadi had been killed in one of their strikes outside of Raqqa, Syria. But such claims were never proven. Reports later surfaced that he may have been badly lacerated in the Russian attack, but survived.

I remembered what Yahya had told me some five months earlier, highlighting that Baghdadi almost certainly had sustained "severe injuries" from an F-16 bomber strike in Iraq's al-Qaim area, which killed several of his guards. And earlier, in March 2015 in the Iraqi town of Sharqat near the Tigris River, just under 200 miles northwest of Baghdad, authorities were said to have accurately targeted him. But again, he presumably survived.

"He has been injured at least three times, twice in Iraq and once in Syria," said Abu Ali. "He has severe injuries to his legs, and his health is not good."

Evil can last a long time. But Baghdadi wasn't just evil; he was battle-hardened and knew how to stay in front of the game. Chillingly, he also still had a stream of strong and steady supporters who would shield him at any cost.

A U.S.-based intelligence source told me that they operated on the premise that Baghdadi was still alive until conclusively proven otherwise. Another well-placed American intelligence insider affirmed that there had been robust markers suggesting "he is very much alive."

With all the high-powered military technology afforded to the United States and its allies, human intelligence remained at the forefront of the search for Baghdadi and the protracted endeavor to bring him to justice.

Sightings and voice interceptions of the shadowy figure — who was assumed to be around forty-seven years old — emerged from time to time throughout his reign. But the only known public appearance of Baghdadi came in June 2014, when he appeared at the now-razed Grand al-Nuri mosque in the old city of Mosul to declare himself the so-called "caliph."

In September 2017, eight months earlier, Baghdadi's alleged voice surfaced on a recording. He urged his followers to "fan the flames of war on your enemies" and to continue fighting in Iraq and pursuing attacks on foreign lands. While the audio was undated, the voice referred to several then-current issues — including the escalating threats between the U.S. and North Korea and the recapture of Mosul.

In March, the media wing of ISIS released a video via the encrypted messenger app Telegram glorifying the attack in Niger last October — in which four U.S. Green Berets and five Nigerien troops were killed — while at the same time paying tribute to Baghdadi.

The so-called caliphate had withered into dying days, but the propaganda push had not.

INSIDE RAQQA: FROM ISIS "CALIPHATE" TO CRUMPLED CITY LITTERED WITH LANDMINES AND LOSS
May, 2018

More than seven months since ISIS was defeated in their once "caliphate" capital of Raqqa, Syria and the city remained an apocalyptic wasteland. The ramifications of four years of ISIS occupation — followed by four months of intense liberation fighting led by the U.S.-backed Syrian Democratic Forces (SDF) — continued to take a toll.

The city and its people were still bleeding, and lingering fears gnawed at the minds of everyone who wanted to get on with life again. One misstep could cost you your life or a limb. Broken bodies festered below the surface. History was a monster that still watched over them.

"The situation is very bad; the mines continue to explode almost daily. Mass graves are exposed almost weekly," opined Sarmad al Jilane, founder and former CEO of activist group Raqqa is Being Slaughtered Silently. "But the most difficult moments are the memories — the murders in the public squares, and the scenes of people having to watch will always be stuck in our minds."

It wasn't that Raqqa had been slaughtered in silence. For years, Raqqa was slaughtered with the eyes of the world watching from afar, reading news article after news article. Images of screaming souls in cages and blindfolded men tossed from rooftops under murmurs about their sexuality filled social media. It wasn't that there was no will to root out ISIS; every foreign government universally detested the terrorist outfit, but there were limits to our collective power to stop it. When a nasty insurgency is left to muscle its way into the terrain for too long, the cement dries, and its foundations are set.

That was the most frustrating thing about the ISIS war. For years, we were powerless to stop it, so we sympathized from the other side of the stained-glass window. And then the only path forward was to lay waste to history.

The United Nations estimated that eighty percent of the buildings in Raqqa had been razed or damaged. Bodies were still buried deep beneath the rubble, sleeper cells still lurked, and occasional car bombs claimed more lives. There was next to no electricity or water, and phone lines remained down. From where I stood, examining an ancient city almost wiped from the map, it did not look nor feel as though the war was over...

And maybe it never was.

Raqqa was once heralded by the Hellenistic, Roman, and Byzantine rulers — and it had been brought to his bloody knees several times before. The first time was by the Persians in the early sixth century when it was called Callinicum and was then rebuilt by the Byzantine emperor, Justinian. Then the Mongols laid it to waste in the mid-thirteenth century. The devastation was so widespread that it took centuries for the city to be brought back to life, plagued by political and intellectual in-fighting. Raqqa's reign as the Islamic caliphate, its religious heartbeat, was over. ... until ISIS stormed in with its delusional quest to return to history and restore the world to the time of antiquity. That era came and went and, in the process, Raqqa was again left a steaming pile of waste. In their absence, tokens of their time there shadowed us as we moved through.

ISIS was infamous for planting homemade landmines and setting booby traps everywhere from homes and streets to sewage pipes. They even harnessed hidden bombs onto corpses and inside children's toys to ensure their legacy permeated long after they were squeezed out.

According to Human Rights Watch, between October 21, 2017, and January 20, 2018, mines injured or killed at least 491 people, including 157 children.

Residents sometimes erected small skull signs near places where they had spotted an unexploded mine to warn people to stay away until an expert could come and clear it. It was just one of the many wincing reminders of the years of ISIS occupation.

The landmines would taunt them for years to come, that was a given. Everywhere the people went, they would find them in their cupboards and gutters and market trolleys. They would fear them with every step during the day, and dream of them in their sleep every night. Was it possible for anyone here to sleep properly?

Dust roiled along the crooked Raqqa roads, many lined with small shacks set up as makeshift checkpoints manned by SDF forces. Giant black holes gouged the city's roads, grimly exposing the underground tunnel system ISIS operatives built to evade detection and to shield their weapons and spoils of war.

Around 150,000 residents were estimated to have returned to Raqqa, which had a pre-war population of almost 300,000. Tiny children pattered through the destruction, many having stood witness to beheadings and crucifixions. The city center's al-Naeem traffic circle still exhibited hallmarks of blood and dents from where dissected heads were showcased.

There were small, moral wins for civilians facing their skeleton city. In late April, locals made their mark by holding the first soccer match since the liberation in their mortar-wracked soccer stadium.

But beneath what had long been called the Black Stadium — due to its dark design palette — some of the greatest ISIS-inflicted miscarriages of justice took place.

As I walked through, I imagined the suffering and the heartache that filled this painful place. It was easy to imagine; the vestiges of horror were laid bare for all to see.

The terrorists converted the rambling array of locker rooms, showers, and board rooms into a prison rife with torture cells and execution chambers. Blood still stained the walls, scrawls of graffiti still indicating the names and dates of inmates' deaths, and iron straps used to hold victims down or hang them upside down still swung from the bullet- cracked roof.

It was a place that the light barely touched, and a place that made one realize that if evil is not fought, then all of us far away and ignorant act as its accomplices.

My good Kurdish-Syrian friend, Mazloum, who had stood by my side as my fierce protector, had been captured at a checkpoint in the early days of the ISIS invasion before anyone knew who or what the terrorist group was all about. One moment he was driving along an open road, and the next, he had disappeared. For days, his family did not know where he was or what had happened. Trapped in a dark ISIS jail, he remembered how the sound of a mother's cry outside would sift through the cracks during the witching hour.

Over and over, the mother would call her son's name. Sometimes, a frightened male voice would cry back. It reminded me of my favorite childhood book, Love You Forever by Robert Munsch. It was about a mother's love for her son, who she brought into the world and watched grow.

"He grew and he grew and he grew. He grew until he was a grown-up man. He left home and got a house across town. But sometimes on dark nights the mother got into her car and drove across town," the book delineated. "If all the lights in her son's house were out, she opened his bedroom window, crawled across the floor, and looked up over the side of his bed. If that great big man was really asleep she picked him up and rocked him back and forth, back and forth, back and forth. And while she rocked him she sang:

I'll love you forever,
I'll like you for always,
As long as I'm living
my baby you'll be."

The mother, risking her own life to slither around the jail in the darkness, would never give up on her baby.

Then the mother's voice disappeared.

Thankfully, Mazloum was released, and he rushed home to his family in Kobane, but their lives were never the same. He walked beside me through the thickets of the prison, and I was angry that anyone could hurt this kind young man who had risked his own life to be my fixer and guide me through the web of Syria's heartache. For most foreign journalists, our fixers become like family. They treasured and protected us in an environment that sought to target and maim those who try to be a vessel for the voiceless.

From Raqqa's city center, seventy-eight-year-old Omar Ibrahim explained that he had lived in the city for fifty years — including under ISIS rule — and that he and his son Yousif had reopened their local store. But business was hard to come by. Who wanted to risk their life by stepping out in Raqqa? Who wanted to be reminded of all that had transpired?

"Our houses were destroyed; this is all we have. It is too expensive for people to buy anything here, we are all poor," Omar lamented. "We can only hope good things might come to us. The most important thing is safety. We want to just live in peace."

Roaming through the mortar-whipped, befouled city center, I thought of all the public executions that had occurred near where I was standing. I thought about the men in black, patrolling and arresting, and I thought about the women, too. They were not always placid bystanders to the hate.

In ISIS's endeavor to subvert to the Dark Ages, a group of burka-clad women was dispatched into the heart of Raqqa. Their task was to terrorize other women who fell short of their Shariah standards. The group was known as the Al- Khansa brigade and was made up of sixty armed women in their twenties who hunted down, arrested, beat, and lashed those who committed infractions such as allowing their ankles to be exposed or stepping out without a male chaperone.

Formed early in the ISIS "caliphate" days, the small militia was named after seventh century female Arab poet Al- Khansa, a contemporary of the Prophet Mohammed. The brigade expanded its role into overseeing brothels where thousands of kidnapped Yazidi women were forced to service Islamic State jihadists, as well as assisting at military checkpoints. Their purpose at the posts was to catch infiltrators disguised in female clothing because men were forbidden from searching women.

There was no sign of the brigade now, but everything in Raqqa was ripped and haunted.

Others expressed extreme upset over something that, on the surface, seemed small considering all they had endured — but was a symbol of the desire to return to a life and place with dignity.

"Every day we bring our own tank of water to clean the streets, but someone late at night keeps coming and dropping their trash here. We need someone to come and punish them for this, we need a government, and we need rules," said exasperated Abu Mohammad, a thirty-eight-year-old shopkeeper. "We are used the destruction here now, but there is no need to put trash in the streets. Summer is coming — and we don't want the smell to get worse."

For those tasked with such municipal chores and putting the pieces of the broken city back together, cleaning and rebuilding still seemed a faraway fantasy — security and stabilization stood at the forefront.

"We are faced with big minefields, the background of the city is destroyed totally, and people's psychology and morale are very wounded," said Layla Mustafa, once a civil engineering professional and now co-chair of the Raqqa Civil Council (RCC). "But we have achieved some good things."

Layla and I sat at an old wooden desk and locals wandered in and out, desperate for answers. She smiled and responded calmly, unruffled by the weight of her job. Dressed in jeans and a short-sleeved black t-shirt, Layla lit a thin cigarette and puffed away as she engaged with locals and rummaged through files.

Victory could not be declared in Raqqa overnight. It could not even be irrefutably declared months later. But perhaps this was her moral victory— her big F-you following the hardline barbarity of the ISIS rule that forbade everyone from smoking and reduced women to black burkas inside the house.

Layla stressed that they had reopened more than two hundred schools and seventy bakeries. She said that over two million tons of trash and debris — as well as some six hundred bodies — had been erased from the streets. She was collected and calm, and where most people wallowed in the gloom of the situation, she was confident it would all come to an end.

Yet the future of Raqqa and how it would ever return to the place it once was hung in question. Even though the U.S. was reported to have spent over $60 million on helping resurrect critical infrastructure post-ISIS, the Pentagon said that the United States had no defined role in reconstruction efforts. And in late March, the Trump administration froze a $200 million fund earmarked for aiding northwestern Syria. Furthermore, the President vowed to withdraw all the American troops — of which there were around 2000 — from the region.

Many Raqqa locals feared not only an ISIS resurgence should their U.S. security blanket be removed, but that the Assad regime would return to reign with bombs and a dictatorial rule. The tension between some of the population and its liberators was unmistakable.

While the SDF was a mixture of ethnicities and religions, it was primarily led by the Kurds. The schism lies in that Raqqa was an almost entirely Arab city. Adding to all the anxiety was the notion that many of Raqqa's young male population under the age of thirty-two were now obligated to join the SDF military conscription — even if they already did their mandatory time in the Syrian Army. Thus, many hid to avoid being hauled off to the barracks.

Havrin Khalaf, Secretary-General of the new "Future Syria Party," headquartered in Raqqa and officially formed on November 30. 2017, stressed that their goal was to mitigate any hostilities to ensure the ouster of the Assad regime and to prepare not just Raqqa but all of Syria for those who fled to return.

"We wanted our base in Raqqa because these people have lived under the black flag, they know what it is to lose a life and still want to live again," she said.

Havrin noted that they had been working with Syrians across the country, including in secret regime-dominant areas to establish councils as well as the diaspora abroad to gain support to rebuild their devastated homeland and open a fresh chapter.

"In the past, everything that was related to Syria was directed from one center in Damascus," Havrin emphasized. "The majority of the Syrian people do not accept this regime; the regime must fall down. But the problem isn't only in one person — the entire system must be replaced."

Her words stayed with me through the long and bumpy ride back to the abandoned Kobane school I was staying in. ISIS was one fight in the fabric of a much larger, complicated fight. Could it be solved?

Mazloum and I, along with our driver, brushed off the day at a dark restaurant on the roadside with bootlegged beer, hookah, and fish from the Euphrates. Even when people had no money or there was little to celebrate, they found a reason. If their lives could come to an end in an instant, then while they were here, they would live. It was not enough for them to simply survive.

What is war? It gives way to the personal defeat of surviving another day. It was acceptance of life and acceptance of death — the kind of acceptance that those who don't live in that zone, thankfully, will never really understand.

With the first hints of sun the next morning, I ran up and down the quiet, bombed street near the school. One-by-one, children from the neighborhood joined me like it was some kind of hilarious game of cat-and-mouse. I waited for Mazloum and the driver, but they did not come. I grew anxious. Finally, their drawn faces emerged in the dead garden where I waited outside.

Mazloum's tiny nephew, Hamode — after only a few years on earth — had been killed in a freak accident when a gas canister exploded as his mother made tea   that morning. The mother and her baby girl, Maryam, who she was cradling when the eruption happened, were rushed to the hospital. Just a few months within her time on earth and Maryam's eyesight was gone.

"What can we do?" Mazloum asked, comforting me. "This is the life here."

They solemnly faced death in a way that struck me as tragic. If people here had once been idealistic about their future, the protracted civil war in Syria and the ISIS hurricane had shattered it into a million pieces.

ISIS hurricane had shattered it into a million pieces.

UNDER THREAT AND HOMELESS, VICTIMS RETURN TO THE CAMPS
May, 2018

Across the other side of the Euphrates, any semblance of idealism was shattered day-by-day. Any idealism that came with displaced people returning home — of watching their fallen township come back to life — was usually crushed upon arrival.

Families who returned to little more than decimated homes and towns following the defeat of ISIS forces across Northern Iraq were coming to the realization that living in a tent city or a ramshackle housing camp was better than the alternative of homelessness and uncertainty. The unexpected reverse migration flow had authorities in an exasperated bind.

"We heard Mosul was safe, so we went back in October, but when we returned, our house was destroyed. We had no money to rent," Basma Aiden, a forty-year-old mother of nine, told me from the Baharka camp outside of Erbil after I had arrived back on the Iraq side. "There were no jobs. We decided it was better to live in a tent. At least we can be comfortable here. There is safety and security."

Officials with the Kurdistan Regional Government (KRG) said they had hoped to close the camps after ISIS was driven out of the area last year, but that hadn't happened. I was reminded once again that the war was not over.

"Since the end of last year, we have been experiencing a reverse flow," Hoshang Mohamed, Director of the Joint Crisis Center in the Kurdistan Regional Government (KRG), said with desperation. "The numbers at the camps are accumulatively increasing again. We have waiting lists."

Hoshang explained that between January and April alone, more than 4,500 people who had left for Mosul or other formerly ISIS-held areas had returned to their region. An average of forty families a day had been registering at the camp as returnees.

"They are coming barefoot because of lack of services, and many are being threatened by militia groups," he continued. "This is a real concern for us. We want to encourage people to go back, but to go back with dignity. If you look at the west side of Mosul, how can anyone survive that?"

The west side — also known as the Old City — was largely destroyed when ISIS was driven out in July 2017 after three years of ISIS occupation. Booby traps, bodies, and bruised memories remained awash across the once historical paradise.

What is war? It was wondering how to sew up the tears and ruins.

Even the east side of the city — which was freed earlier in 2017 with significantly less destruction — offered little in the way of livelihood.

A few officials expressed private concerns that many internally displaced persons (IDPs) had perhaps become "too dependent" on the camp system. But most insisted such cases were rare and argued that those displaced genuinely wanted to put their broken lives back together.

"Some people are even going home to dozens of waiting electricity and water bills," Hoshang went on. "Despite the fact that they were in camps and it was ISIS living in their homes."

I sat with families who had returned to camps after trying to go home, documenting their dark reality. After two months of moving between relatives' homes, Basma said she and her family had retreated north in December to the same camp they had lived in since the summer of 2014.

Her children played at her feet as she wept a little. Basma did not want to be dependent on anyone for anything, but the alternatives were not survivable. Even if she wanted to break down right there, I knew she would not. Mothers of wars didn't have time to fall apart.

"If I could unlearn being sad," she said, squaring her shoulders.

I am not sure why, but I felt more at home sitting with women like Basma — who had pushed through decades of hardship and stood resilient in the face of uncertainty — than I ever would at a Hollywood party or a highbrow

Manhattan club. Perhaps it was the authenticity and the strength that I most admired — the loss of everything and the resolve to build it back once again.

And for Khatar Khalaf Rashid, a fifty-three-year-old father of fourteen from Salahuddin — which was freed from ISIS control in October 2016 — the decision to return was a matter of life or death. Rashid, after hearing his village "was safe," went back in February 2017. But the place he had called home for all his life had been tempered into a place he no longer recognized.

His family rebuilt their obliterated home, but the sectarian threats from what he claimed to be unofficial Shia militias intensified.

What is war? It was living in a state of anxiety that became the norm.

"Every family has its own militias, these are not organized, these are gangs, and they want the Sunnis out," Khatar avowed.

Around 8:00 P.M. one day last June, he recalled, gunmen attacked his new home. His brother and nephew were killed. His family then received threatening phone calls warning that they had just three days to leave.

"When the time was up, we went. We left everything, all our new furniture," Khatar lamented from his small but cozy tent complete with a television, mini-refrigerator, and air-conditioning unit. "We will spend our entire lives at their camp; otherwise, we will leave Iraq."

At the height of the ISIS invasion between 2014 and 2015, the KRG hosted some 1.8 million displaced Iraqis. Most of those — around 1.2 million — were still in the Kurdish north. Just nine of the many camps set up after ISIS's invasion had already been closed, Mohamed said, with the future of the rest now in limbo.

Several of the returning families at the camps said schooling was a deciding factor in their return. Yet for many, the possibility of returning anytime soon seemed an impossibility.

Months earlier, the Iraqi government had asked its affluent allies — including the United States — for more money to address the problem. Four billion dollars were offered at a fundraising conference in Kuwait to discuss the matter, which wasn't enough.

"It is not just the buildings and the houses, but the morale of people has been demoralized," KRG spokesperson Safeen Dizayee said. "What will be the future for them?"

Safeen vowed they would not force any displaced person to return to whatever was left of their homes and neighborhoods. However, the dwindling of ISIS militarily also meant less aid money and donations, leading to deteriorating conditions at already dire displacement camps and concern over how long they could remain open.

"There is donation fatigue. And there is a heavy burden on the hospitals in the region too," Safeen acknowledged, adding that many travelled north, even from Baghdad, for free medical services.

Sattar Norroz, a spokesperson from the Ministry of Immigration in Baghdad, concurred that "reverse flow" had indeed become a growing problem.

"Some families come back and find their houses damaged or exploded and that there is no infrastructure," he explained, denying allegations that families were being forced out of camps in Baghdad's bid to resume life in the post-ISIS era. "We only want to encourage people to go back and help them."

A spokesperson for the UN High Commissioner for Refugees also affirmed that while returnees are "in the minority," they included highly vulnerable families. It was a situation several officials at the camp took very seriously.

"We take details from people registering in our camps, and the most common reasons given by people returning to camps are economic: a shortage of employment opportunities and inability to pay rent," the representative added.

IRAN AIMS TO BE KING OF THE HILL
May, 2018

Everything was in shortage on the mountaintop where the Yazidi minority faced slaughter and extermination under a savage ISIS siege almost four years earlier.

Although that danger had been trampled, a new weed threatened to extend into their precious parcel. Just as the Christians worried about the extended arm of Tehran, the Yazidis also expressed fear about Iran establishing a critical strategic foothold that could leave much of the region — reaching as far as Israel — in the crosshairs of an attack.

What is war? It is never-ending concerns, like poisoned weeds in a field whose roots never die.

Worries infected the minds of victims every day, forming pillows of paranoia that then poisoned their sleep.

When war is unleashed, it cannot be put back.

Doused in springtime sweat, I squished into a barely-functioning old car filled with Yazidi mothers and children. We chugged through more than fifty checkpoints, mostly operated by the Iran-backed PMF militias. Each time they stopped to question us, I put my head down and held my breath.

The plan worked. Assumed to be a Yazidi, I whooshed past the flutes of grass contrasting with the dead fields and reached my destination.

The tip of the 4,800-foot Sinjar Mountain, known locally as Chilmera, was a mostly quiet place. But this ostensibly picturesque setting — featuring a small, chalk-white temple dedicated to Sharfuddin, a holy Yazidi figure — belied its potential strategic importance.

A lookout spot atop the mountain offered a clear view miles in all directions. The patchwork rug of color below, every shade of green and brown blending into the aperitif that was the beauty of the land where time began. But that clear view was a double-edged sword, and some believed it could serve as a useful missile site against Israel, more than 500 miles away.

"This point is the closest point to Israel in which Iran can do harm. And the view is clear, the plain is wide, there are no mountains in the way," explained Abdulrazaq Ali, an Erbil-based analyst who had long studied the issue. "It is also possible for Hezbollah to enter from Syria and get to this position."

The importance of the spot didn't go unnoticed by former Iraqi dictator Saddam Hussein. He was said to have used the mountain as the launch site for the thirty-nine Scud missiles he fired into Israel during the Gulf War of 1991. Nestled beside the Yazidi temple, there was a structure featuring a slab of six-foot-wide concrete steps that appeared to lead thirty feet up into nowhere. It was from there, some locals believed, that Saddam launched his Scuds.

This special Sinjar peak may also have been a testing site for Saddam's much-hyped plan to develop a "supergun" in the late 1980s. Dubbed "Big Babylon," the weapon would have had a potential range of more than 600 miles. But it was never built.

Whatever its potential as a missile site, Sinjar also served as a vital piece of territory connecting Iraq and Syria and was part of a larger Shia "land corridor" that took shape in recent years in the war against ISIS.

The emergence of an Iranian-backed, Iraqi paramilitary force to fight ISIS allowed more than 100,000 fighters to secure control of a ground supply route that enabled free passage from Tehran through Iraq, to its allies in the Syrian regime, and then directly into Hezbollah groups in Lebanon — and, thus, Israel's doorstep.

Outsiders visiting Chilmera were welcomed, not turned away. While there were logistical challenges in getting there, Qassim Osman, Chilmera's caretaker, emphasized there were no restrictions.

"We want this to be open to everyone. We won't close our doors for those who are not Yazidi," he said. "Christians, Muslims — anyone can come to visit."

Tehran's top brass, too, I thought to myself.

An Iraqi flag flew high above the lookout point, but it was the forces of the People's Protection Units (YPG) — a Kurdish-dominated Syria opposition group that locals referred to as the PKK, the Kurdish force that waged a separatist war against Turkey for more than thirty years — standing guard there.

But that, too, had come to arouse suspicion.

The PKK/YPG's quiet presence in Chilmera had long attracted the ire of Turkey. The group allegedly withdrew and removed its flags in recent weeks, but locals still considered it one of their most stringent protectors. It was not historically known as a particularly pro-Iranian group, and some analysts observed a drift toward Tehran as the convenient allies pursued common goals.

A Washington Institute policy paper last year wrote that the two groups shared the commonality of "weakening Turkey's influence," and suggested that the PKK was "distracted by their rivalry" and allowed itself to be used as a proxy by Iran and regional powers.

While the Turkish government reviled the PKK, the outfit was widely credited by the Yazidi community with saving many lives by coming to their aid after ISIS overran the region in August 2014.

Further down the mountain, however, the roads and towns were controlled by a variety of militias influenced or entirely controlled by Iran. With that influence, military analysts fear, came the power for Iran to create trouble for its enemies far beyond what Saddam Hussein attempted.

"Iran's present arsenal is more diverse and more capable than Saddam's arsenal," said Behnam Ben Taleblu, a research fellow at the Foundation for Defense of Democracies (FDD). "Iran's missiles can function as both a tool of deterrence and coercion."

Iranian-backed militias had gained uncontested control of not just Sinjar, but also the larger region. After all, the checkpoints I had navigated to reach the mountain were like none that I had ever seen on previous trips, and they were all under the thumb of the PMFs.

I thought back to a phone conversation I had just a couple of months earlier with former U.S. diplomat Paul Bremer. In Iraq, he remained a household name mostly for worse. It was Bremer, as head of the Coalition Provincial Authority, who led Iraq for just over a year in the early stages of the U.S. occupation in 2003. Over the years, critics of the U.S. invasion had faulted Bremer-led policies for the chaos and instability that followed for more than a decade.

He may have gotten a lot wrong throughout his tenure, but there seemed little doubt in his mind that the Iranian threat was only burgeoning.

"The significant Iranian involvement, particularly through the Popular Mobilization Units (PMU), poses a real challenge for Baghdad. The question now that the job of defeating ISIS is largely done, what do we do with them? There are more than 100,000," he cautioned. "It raises the issue of reconciliation, and that goes in two dimensions — there is the ethnic dimension of Kurds and Arabs, and the sectarian dimension of Shia and Sunnis. The large-scale Iranian presence, particularly through the security forces, complicates that problem for the Prime Minister."

I looked out at the smashed villages of Sinjar at the hoof of the mountain.

The villages were filled with Iraqi flags flapping above burned and bombed-out streets. The Iranian presence felt oddly electrified as I studied the smattering of flags from militia groups, all of which had carved out areas of control in the ISIS aftermath.

One of those groups was the PMF's "Lalish Forces." Named after the holy Yazidi temple, the group relied on support from Badr, which had long been seen as Iran's oldest proxy group in Iraq.

According to twenty-four-year-old Lalish Forces leader Hamo Sherkani, of the 400-person forces, half were volunteers and the other half received salaries — around $400 monthly — directly from the Badr organization.

"We get all our support from Badr. Our food, trucks, oil, weapons," he said, pointing out that the group received shipments of everything from AK-47s to heavier weapons.

Other pro-Iranian groups were also active in Sinjar. There was the Imam Ali Combat Division, reportedly tightly linked with Iran's religious leadership. There was also the Êzîdxan Protection Force, a local Yazidi militia that was said to get its money from Baghdad.

The various groups operating in Sinjar were — for now at least — getting along. Qasim Shesho, a top Yazidi commander who I had met for the first time in 2016, said his forces saw groups of Persian speakers routinely moving through. They usde the mountainous terrain to cross into Syria, he asserted.

Some U.S. officials and experts in the northern region seemed less concerned about the possibility of attacks on Israel from Mount Sinjar. Defense experts I later spoke to said that they did not think that Tehran, at least in the short-term, would risk moving a medium-range ballistic missile into Iraq to fire at Israel. But the biggest concern was how the region would be used if another round of skirmishes erupted.

"The risk of potential Israeli strikes in Iraq's Sinjar go up if a next war breaks out, Israel shuts down or significantly hampers Iran's bridge to Syria," said Amir Toumaj, an Iran research analyst at Foundation for the Defense of Democracies. "Any government in Baghdad would be opposed, and potential Israeli strikes would be more way to pressure if that comes to pass."

But to Israelis themselves, the Iranian threat was not one to be easily dismissed.

"The takeover of this strategic point in the region is a part of their successful strategy to control every possible point in the region, to fill every vacuum, and to use it for the next aggression and subversion," General Ephraim Sneh, former deputy defense minister of Israel, wrote to me in an email. "Since their aim is to control Iraq entirely, it gives them a huge advantage."

ENSLAVED IN TURKEY
May, 2018

Despite all the advantages that came with being liberated from ISIS, when it came to the embattled and dissipated Yazidi community, liberated lands had not brought back thousands of their still-missing people.

The mystery deepened, and souls were crushed.

According to families and rescue groups, at least a piece of the puzzle could be solved by scouring Turkey. Many believed that some of the enslaved were being disguised in various locations across the neighboring nation.

"We are finding many of our women, our girls, our kids in Turkey," said my old friend Hussein Al-Qaidi, Director of the Office of Kidnapped and Rescue Affairs. "What happens is most are given fake IDs or marriage certificates. Their names are changed to Muslim names, and they become part of another family. And then they are smuggled over the border from Syria."

Data provided by the KRG prime minister's office showed that roughly half of the 6,417 taken captive by ISIS remained unaccounted for. Among those rescued were 1,151 teenage girls and women, 336 boys and men, and 858 children under fifteen.

That left 3,132 Yazidis still missing. And, while Hussein anticipated many of those missing had likely been killed, he said a "significant number" were believed to be enslaved across Syria and Turkey.

Among those rescued was twenty-one-year-old Shaza, who returned home from Ankara, Turkey on January 9th — more than three years after being taken and forced into marriage as a "second wife" to an ISIS fighter.

Shaza, a slight and whimsical young beauty, was smuggled into Turkey last fall along a "secret way" with family members of the ISIS husband who stayed behind to fight in Syria as Iraqi troops closed in.

For the next few months, Shaza said, she remained bound to an Ankara apartment as a slave before being salvaged in a rescue operation involving smugglers and middlemen.

"Thanks to God I am alive," she whispered.

Over and over she whispered thanks to God that she was still here.

Ten-year-old Jaqueline was just seven when she was whisked from her village and transferred to what was then an ISIS parapet of Tel Afar. She was subsequently sold to the family of an ISIS leader, Waleed, and his wife, Zena.

The family moved to Syria in early 2017, and Jaqueline said she was then smuggled with their extended family over the border into Turkey, where she spent another six months in Ankara. She recalled the family referring to her as "our daughter" when questioned at checkpoints by officials.

Jacqueline said she was forced to work long hours for the family, essentially functioning as a domestic servant.

"They treated me very badly," the small girl said. "Making me clean for them all day and all night, while the wife did nothing."

Her words were crushing. Surely there is a place in hell for those who hurt children.

One day last July, Jacqueline continued, she was informed out of the blue that she was "going home." She was put on a plane to Baghdad, where one of her captive's brothers had flown weeks earlier. As it turned out, he was stopped by a member of the PMFs and questioned, leading to some sort of deal that secured Jacqueline's release, with the forced assistance of the ISIS member's sibling.

Most rescue cases were coordinated by Hussein's office, funded by the KRG Prime Minister's office. Complicated cross-border rescue missions, such as the one involving Jacqueline, also required liaising with Iraqi and Turkish security agencies to secure her family reunifications.

A spokesperson for the Turkish Embassy in Baghdad told me that Turkish authorities "have worked with Iraqi counterparts, especially with the Iraqi Ministry of Migration and Displacement, as well as Iraqi Border Authority, in a cooperative manner to ensure the safe return of refugees, including Yazidis."

It was not just one or two isolated cases. Nobody knew how many Yazidis were stranded with families that were not their own in Turkey, and nobody knew how many had been brainwashed and manipulated into not wanting to come home. Or worse, many were so young when they were abducted that they may not even remember.

The first Yazidi rescue from Turkish territory took place in December 2016. It was a twenty-three-year-old woman named Watha. Fifteen other rescue operations had since been carried out successfully all over Turkey — most recently on April 4. But Hussein said he knew it would take many more rescues, particularly because most of those being held were "very young."

One of the challenges of international rescues was, first of all, being able to prove that the subject was indeed a Yazidi being held against their will — that required DNA proof.

My attention turned to a small boy with big, dark eyes and a little twitch when he smiled. On the surface, he seemed light and playful. But when I went to touch his shoulder, I felt him immediately cower into his pod of memories.

Lazem, now six years old, had been just three when he was bought by a woman to be an "ISIS son." He was forced to convert to Islam, renamed "Abdullah," issued a new identity card to match that of his ISIS family, and spirited away to Turkey.

But after his real father, Kassim, received credible information that Lazem was in Turkey, a trip was coordinated for him to travel there and provide a DNA sample personally.

Forty-five days later, on September 9 of 2017, Lazem and his father were reunited. The moment was beautifully tragic. Because of the little boy's tender age and because of the many years he was gone, Lazem did not recognize his father. The boy had also forgotten his native language, the Kurdish dialect of Kurmanji. He could speak only Turkmen and Turkish.

The more we talked, the more I noticed how the trauma still seemed to weigh on Lazem. He rarely made eye contact and spoke only to ask when his mother and three brothers — also taken by ISIS — were coming home.

The chances of that reunification depended on where his mother and brothers were being held — if they had made it this far. Yazidis captive in Turkey likely stood a better chance of returning home compared to those who were trapped with remaining ISIS families in Iraq and Syria.

Then I met Enas. The cheerful eight-year-old girl had been found in Syria late last summer, after the ISIS family that took her needed money and sold back her freedom. The effort to get enough money to return her took months, but it paid off. Enas was quietly moved out of Syria — first to Turkey, then home to Iraq.

The "buyback" rescue was the most common. More often than not, the families of the missing were contacted or used their networks to determine the location of their loved ones. They then worked through Hussein Al-Qaidi's office to establish a plan to collect and deliver the money through middlemen and women.

Enas was still smiling and sweet, as a child should be. She spoke about her ordeal — being shuffled about by a fake family as if she had pulled herself up and was looking down on a chapter of life that was her, but not the real her. The girl below was the version ISIS had created in its warped perceptions.

I watched from a slight distance as the Yazidi families mingled in the doorway. They shared a survivor's collective memory, exchanging pleasantries and names of their missing loved ones. I noticed how Yazidis mourned for those they had lost, but there was nothing more aching than mourning those who they thought were still out there — alive and hurting.

Hussein sipped his tea, deep in thought, and lamented that the defeat of ISIS had produced a sharp rise in the cost of ongoing rescues. Yazidi children could be anywhere, and he hoped that Turkey would be the farthest place they would have to search.

"There are many cases still in Turkey we know of, and we want them home," he added defiantly. "We will continue this process until the last of our people is brought home."

ONLY THE LIVING
May, 2018

Many would never again go home. Instead, their lifeless remains would be wrapped in thick, black, plastic bags, piece by piece, and laid to rest deep in the earth.

Many more would never be found.

I spent a restless night on a cot surrounded by dozens of strange men inside the headquarters of the Mosul Civil Defense Unit. In the minutes between dark and daylight, we boarded trucks to make the drive to Tel Afar. The unit had received information that two mass graves containing at least twenty bodies were submerged beneath slabs of concrete and decomposing in the sewage system of the former ISIS bulwark — a sickening reminder of the lasting devastation caused by the group's three-year occupation of northern Iraq.

We reached the residential neighborhood of Ayadia, one of many nearly empty neighborhoods in the cryptic city. It looked like any war-wracked Iraqi neighborhood, stuffed with an extra kind of sadness. The team of roughly a dozen men in bright red suits immediately got to work plowing through the earth, a painful job that had become all too commonplace in the post-ISIS cleanup.

They began by cutting a four-foot square above a portion of the sewer, which was then drained. One person entered in a hazardous-materials suit and oxygen mask to survey the situation. The recovery then commenced with a few hooks, a ladder, and gloved hands.

The first wasted life to be wretched up from the sewage was that of an Iraqi soldier. His bones, a blood-drenched uniform, and a pair of handcuffs were exhumed. Then came seven more, all dragged from beneath a home that had once served as the local headquarters of ISIS. Local officials who had been tipped off to the presence of the remains just a couple of days earlier said the victims were likely held in the basement.

Across the street at a second location, another twelve decomposed civilian bodies were exhumed. Among the remains found were those of at least two children, and dismembered heads without bodies.

Each skeleton bore a thick black blindfold. Most of the victims appeared to have been slain execution-style, bullets showered into the backs of their heads.

"It was a massacre. More and more of the same," one police official told me stoically.

A police official always accompanied the recovery workers through their day's work, a standard practice.

"It is never-ending," the official continued, staring out into the yellow fog which lifted into bright sunshine as the day passed on.

Officials had become all too familiar with the discovery of ISIS victims.

"Our duty is to the innocent people under the rubble," Saad Hamadi al-Hussein, commander of the Nineveh Civil Defense Corps "Emergency Convoy" unit, had explained to me over cold tea the night before. "ISIS kills them and throws them into the sewage one by one and covers it over with cement. This is their way."

Over supper in the unit's Mosul base, our meals were illuminated by candles as the generator flicked on and off until going dead. I had watched the men pack their bags of tools, hazmat suits, and face masks. We had all crammed close to the only working fan on Saad's office cots.

After several grueling hours, with small children watching from low-lying rooftops above, twenty body bags were sealed and handed over to the Iraqi Federal Police. Law enforcement took them to a specialized committee established for examining the bodies. Whenever possible, surviving family members of the victims were notified.

I had wanted to cover the eyes of those few children who looked on as the endeavor unfolded. I had wanted to run over to them and usher them inside to play games and tell jokes. But it was too late. Their innocence had already been taken from them, and I had no idea of the number of horrors that had already been encrusted into their tiny bodies.

Tel Afar, forty miles west of Mosul, had a population of about 100,000 before being captured by ISIS in June of 2014. The city was liberated in October of 2017. Remnants of war were everywhere. Bodies found around and under homes, I learned, were not uncommon. Neither was the smell of putrefied flesh.

Saad said that in many cases, families living under ISIS rule were forced to bury bodies in their own homes and backyards, as well as in local public squares. Sometimes victims were made to dig their own shallow graves. Once remains were identified, the victim's family could then lay them to rest with a proper, dignified goodbye.

The forty-three-person Emergency Division was tasked only with removing civilian remains from mass graves. The larger, 700-person Nineveh Civil Defense Corps was in charge of sweeping up bodies from the streets and collecting them from within individual homes.

The corps was established in 2003 under the U.S.-led Coalition Provincial Authority (CPA), and many received training from Americans in Bahrain. Members now lamented that they did not have adequate tools to do their jobs effectively, as the post-ISIS undertaking had overwhelmed their resources. They claimed that their requests for help, directed to both the Baghdad Central Government and international humanitarian organizations, had gone unanswered.

But the corps' situation had been easier since the territorial defeat of the barbaric terrorist group. When ISIS still retained control, the men bravely tried to unearth mass graves and collect the dead, but their efforts were routinely sabotaged.

"Sometimes ISIS would make us go away after an attack, and they knew it was only civilians killed," Saad recalled. "Or if they knew their fighters were there, they would let us go in. Other times, they would come and force us to recover their dead fighters for them."

For Daoud Salem Mahmood Ali, a forty-four-year-old rescue worker from Mosul — considered something of a "hero" among his peers for excavating bodies for twenty-seven years — it was a job that never got easier.

"Sometimes, it's five or six entire families all buried in one house," he told me after hosing himself off behind the fire truck at the end of a shift in Tel Afar. "As a father, especially when I see women and children, it hurts. I have had to pull out many pregnant women, too."

Daoud said he and his team had recovered 2,400 bodies since Mosul was liberated last July, with more than 2,000 of those coming from the Old City on the west side. In Tel Afar, they had recovered 640 bodies, many of whom were still unidentified. Another 500 bodies were discovered last year in a mass grave between the two strongholds, at the Badush prison.

The men were all well-built, hardened, and brave. But even the ever-burly Daoud seemed lost for a split second, sometimes speaking to my eyes and sometimes to the clouds.

It wasn't just human recovery required of the dedicated team. Ali was also burdened with "de-mining" bodies — sometimes those of ISIS fighters.

"I can tell straight away if they are ISIS. They are usually booby-trapped and often have foreign passports strapped to them," Daoud explained. "We don't remove them. Our command after de-mining is then to leave them, and authorities take those."

With an Iraqi federal election looming that coming Saturday, the cleanup and recovery effort in the blasted city temporarily took a back seat to politics. A large poster of the head of an Iran-backed group striking battlefield poses with the leader of the Iranian Revolutionary Guard's Quds Force adorned the gates at the city entrance. Other candidate posters were taped everywhere, even on bombed-out buildings.

"If it is our intention to put a poster in the street, cleaning will take at least another two years," Daoud said, his voice grating. "But if our intention is a humanitarian one, we can remove all the remains in a year."

I stood alone as the last of the lives were swathed in those big black bags, their brains bursting through empty eye sockets. I tore off my surgical mask, heaving at the smell of rotting corpses in the unbearable heat. Iraq still stood at the fork between a potential future of death and one that would value life. It was a place that resembled a fractured mosaic that could only be put back together by a young generation who knew little of a life not maimed by brutality.

It was supposed to be a time after the war; it was supposed to be a time of peace. Only, all it felt like was strange and sorrowful. I thought about that tried-and-true expression we all tend to offer one another during hardships: everything happens for a reason.

No, I internally argued. There was no reason these young men and women had to die alone, their bodies left to decay in the literal bowels of their country. There was no great lesson to come from that, no sense in that they had completed their mission on earth, and no reason that it was their time to be taken by God. That is the lie we tell ourselves.

A child from the neighborhood, who had watched without flinching as the bodies were brought up, peered over what was left of the bombed-out fence. He looked through the gaping hole and into my tearful eyes.

"Soon we stop crying for the dead," he whispered. "But all we can do is cry for the living."

That, too, was war.

EPILOGUE

While ISIS was officially expelled from its territorial control in early 2019, the brutal terrorist outfit has steadily continued its bloodletting across the plains it once considered its "caliphate."

As the year stretched on, the U.S.-led Combined Joint Taskforce's Operation Inherent Resolve, in conjunction with Iraqi troops and the Syrian Democratic Forces, has had to execute dozens of strikes to take out ISIS cells and weapons stockpiles. It has obliterated caves and vehicles used by the jihadists. When one hotspot is rooted out, it seems a dozen more spring up from the barren landscape. It's an exhausting example of a terrorist army morphed into a still dangerous and unpredictable insurgency.

ISIS has, furthermore, developed more "creative" techniques of instilling fear in communities and destroying the livelihoods of those who long only to get back on their feet.

Along with the 2019 summer sunshine, ISIS brought with it a rash of violent heat. Its members took to setting fire to more than 120,000 acres of agricultural crops – an act they claimed was retaliation against those refusing to pay the group taxes. For those clinging to those last strips of land and livlihoods, as well as those who had just resumed living, seeing the inferno swallow it all up again was nothing short of heartbreaking.

ISIS still possess the remarkable ability to dip into its still plentiful and steady monetary supply. The group has diversified its revenue streams through such methods as oil extortion, taxing hapless villagers and running slick black-market operations.

In late October, 2019 the group's shadowy leader Abu Bakr al-Baghdadi – the world's most wanted man with a $25 million bounty on his head – was finally brought to a bitter end. As U.S. forces closed in on his compound in the al-Qaeda terrain of Idlib, Syria the terrorist chiefdom detonated a suicide vest and took three of his young children out with him. The following day, his newly installed successor was taken out in a targeted campaign, living the group scrambling for another unknown to take the reins.

Baghdadi's death was indeed a victory in the fight against such brutality, but it would be foolish for anyone to think that cutting the head off a snake with take with it all the young that swarm in the bushes.

Globally, ISIS has remained a cause for concern. They orchestrated a series of horrific attacks over Easter weekend in Sri Lanka – stealing the lives of hundreds and cemented a new milestone by claiming their first-ever attacks in Mozambique and the Congo – in addition to beefing up their ranks across much of Africa, Yemen and Afghanistan.

Moreover, how to deal with tens of thousands of alleged ISIS prisoners clogging the jails across Iraq and Syria has become a cause of contention. While Baghdad is refusing to take any chances, often sentencing accused members to death by hanging or life behind bars in mass trials that last anywhere between one to ten minutes and in doing so igniting the ire of humanitarian watchdogs across the globe, the SDF in Syria did not have the authority to impose the death penalty and continued to plead for international help to deal with the ailing prisoners.

Many of them are foreigners, yet most foreign governments have refused to take back citizens who went abroad to join or marry into the ISIS calamity – often times the children born under the caliphate reign are left languishing in the grey, stateless area of the law.

The desperation of the situation heightened dramatically in early October, 2019 when President Trump – followed by an phone call with Turkish President Erdogan – decided to abruptly pull U.S. troops from Syria, leaving the SDF raw and exposed to an immediate Turkish incursion that spiraled into havoc. ISIS prisoners and families in camps ran free, scores of fighters went down in a fresh round of fighting of a different kind.

Perhaps the most hear-rending and personal for me was the morning a video was splashed across YouTube of a vehicle on the periphery of Raqqa being ambushed by masked gunmen and a young woman dragged out. Her porcelain face was baked into the dirt and her frightened body riddled with bullets.

That victim was Hevrin, the beautiful and calm politician I had met in Raqqa who wanted nothing more than a serene Syria inclusive to all walks of life. It was one of those moments where I ran out into the soggy streets of Manhattan, guttered with such a helpless sadness.

At the same time in Iraq, thousands were flooding the Baghdad streets calling for an end to the PMF and Iranian influence rocking their country, calling for the government to take care of its people and give the jobs and future. Hundreds paid with their lives as government forces fired back. Hauntingly reminiscent of the early Arab Spring uprisings, yet with little attention of the world's media that seemed filled to the brim with chaos and collapse.

Both Iraq and Syria are struggling with severe infrastructure shortages and to raise the funds needed to rebuild as the dust of the ISIS war settles, yet not really over and under a canvas far from calm, prompting concerns are of revived recruitment drives among the disaffected and frustrated civilian population.

But amid all the policy concerns, the protracted terrorist threat, the academic predictions – the long, quiet search for the missing still slices at the heart of thousands. Shallow mass graves, mostly cloaked with the remains of Yazidis, are still being wretched open. Christians are left with tattered churches, tiny children are forced to work rather than seek an education.

The victims of all those years of depravity have been left with life sentences too – their loved ones gone forever, their ancient lands decimated, a fear and a distrust that will forever taint their psyche as life moves forward.

On a bitter day in the dead of winter, as 2017 was drawing to a close, Shatha Salim Bashar was rescued from hell. The Yazidi made it home after almost three-and-a-half years as an ISIS sex slave in Iraq and Syria.

"I can't forget the first time I was raped," Shatha, a 28-year-old survivor told me. "I was traded fourteen times among the jihadists."

She was kidnapped alongside her mother, her sister, and two younger brothers. In the beginning, the fear-filled woman pretended to be the mother of her youngest brother – who was just three years old – in the hopes she would be spared violation if ISIS militants believed she was not a virgin.

But Shatha was brutally violated by every one of her 14 enslavers. Moreover, the tiny young woman was used as a human shield by ISIS, thrust onto the frontlines in Syria and forced to watch her best Yazidi friend die on the battlefield. Her reunification months later should have been one of jubilation – but her friend's family also arrived with smiles, thinking the women were rescued together. Shatha was the one to break the shattering news.

In spite of all she has endured since ISIS suddenly stormed her village of Kocho, in the foothills of Iraq's Sinjar Mountain on August 15, 2014, Shatha's scars – inside and out – have become her stories.

Next month, a representative for the Kurdish President's Office told Fox News, Shatha will travel to Germany and face one of her alleged rapists in the court of law as stands trial for ISIS membership in his European home of origin. She intends to testify against him.

It has been more than five years since ISIS ravished the villages of Iraq's Sinjar Mountain – slaughtering thousands of Yazidi boys and men and abducting thousands of girls and women into their horrific ranks of sex slavery.

And Shatha wants to be a voice for the voiceless. She wants to remind the world not to forget their fractured community who are left languishing with little in the way of help.

According to statistics issued to Fox News from the Office of Kidnapped Affairs – established in 2014 by the former Prime Minister and now President of the semi-autonomous Kurdistan Regional Government, Nechirvan Barzani, to rescue kidnapped Yazidis – 550,000 Yazidis remain in war-ravaged Iraq. Some 360,000 of them are still in displacement.

1,293 Yazidis were killed on August 3 and over the following few days at the beginning of the ISIS invasion. A total of 6,417 Yazidi were kidnapped at that time – 3,548 females and 2,869 males. Some 3509 Yazidis are documented as having survived the ordeal: 1192 women, 337 men, 1033 girls, and 947 boys. Chillingly, 2908 Yazidis are deemed still missing – 1323 females and 1585 males.

The number of orphans produced by the invasion stands at 2,745 and the number of Yazidis who have emigrated out of Iraq, their ancestral homeland, is documented to be more than 100,000.

Moreover, 80 mass graves have been discovered in the Sinjar region, and the Islamic terrorist outfit blitzed 68 of their religious temples throughout the four-year war.

While the Office of Kidnapped Affairs rescued Shatha, along with her mother and sister, her brothers – who were just three and eight when they were captured, remain unaccounted for. The last she saw of the small boys; they were carted off to ISIS training camps.

"We need help to rescue the rest of the people that are still missing," Shatha said.

That's a slow and wincing process. The Office of Kidnapped Affairs made its most recent rescue last week – two Yazidi girls were brought back from the rebel-stronghold of Idlib, Syria. Since the "Caliphate" formally crumbled earlier this year, the Office has spread its resources into locating the lost girls and boys across Syria and Turkey. Many of them are believed to be disguised as Muslim wives; still entangled in their terrorist purgatory.

Moreover, Shatha's brothers are two of thousands of Yazidi boys yanked into the ISIS lair of forced conversion, indoctrination, and violence. While their fate is not known, the boys who are rescued, face another kind of enduring nightmare amid a crisis of psychological help.

"Yazidi boys who are forced into Cubs of the Caliphate training often are the amongst the most courageous fighters and volunteer for suicide missions, believing they will go the 'The Paradise," said Anne Speckhard, director of the Study of Violent Extremism (ICSVE) and Adjunct Associate Professor of Psychiatry at Georgetown University, "These boys were separated from their older male relatives by ISIS who shot them dead and from their mothers and sisters. Of course, they would opt for any escape offered to them – a palatable escape from overwhelming psychic pain and unbearable traumatic grief."

Subsequently, Hussein al-Qaedi, the Yazidi Director of the Office for Kidnapped Affairs, is calling for permission from the central government to conduct DNA testing inside the detainment facilities where foreign ISIS fighters and their families are held.

"We believe Yazidis are among them. If countries take back foreign fighters, they might take Yazidi kids with them," he stressed. "And then they will be disappeared forever."

The tight-knit Yazidi faith, which prohibits interfaith marriage and conversion into the religion, is also grappling with integrating babies conceived-out-of-rape to ISIS fathers. Community leaders have called for the infants to be embraced, but the notion is a strange and unsettling one for the ethnicity who have long lived reserved lives dotted across quiet farmlands.

It's unclear exactly how many babies have been born from the tragedy, but official estimates hover between one and two hundred. While Yazidi's religious authorities have announced that they will subvert their ancient traditions and accept the babies as Yazidis, the matter is further complicated by Baghdad's law that children must take the paternal religion.

It's a decree many hope will be formally changed.

As it stands now, most Yazidis live in tattered tents in displacement camps, and in ravished and abandoned dwellings across the Nineveh Plains. Funds are fast falling, and the despair is searing.

"Infrastructure is disintegrating. Public washrooms need to be renovated. There is an ongoing lack of electricity and water in the camp and in local areas. Some Yazidis are still struggling for food," Lisa Miara, Founder of Springs of Hope Foundation Inc., lamented. "Some women suffer from a kind of Stockholm Syndrome and (want to) return to their captors. There are still women being held as ISIS wives."

Speckhard also noted that the trauma for some Yazidi women runs so deep that they are known to "re-enact their rape," which she referred to as "pseudo-seizures."

"The young girl woke up out of it tearful and disorientated," Speckhard said of one case. "Her sisters say it is the reason they avoid talking about ISIS and their rape experiences, to avoid triggering one of these seizures and that it happens multiple times a day to their sister."

Shatha and her family are among the tens of thousands left languishing in a displacement camp on the outskirts of the Kurdish city of Duhok. They have little in the way of help when it comes to gluing together what is left of their lives, but she said her camp – called Rwanga – at least has prefabricated caravans.

Many other camps are stuffed with tethered tents from 2014, and she wants to see that small but pivotal improvement.

"Yazidis need not only boxes of food; we need a guarantee that we can survive. We can't spend our whole lives in camps. We want to go home. But we cannot go home without security," Shatha underscored. "There is still a lot of armed conflict and illegal groups there. If we can feel safe, we can start rebuilding our areas."

Safety, for now, feels something of an illusion. The black flags of ISIS still wave in the shadows.

"Insurgent-style attacks by ISIS still happen regularly, with some of those attacks targeted specifically at Yazidis. The Yazidi community knows these realities," added Ian Bradbury, CEO of 1st NAEF, a non-profit focused on humanitarian aid and assisting victims of all gender-based violence. "After five years, there is little hope of a return to any semblance of their former lives living off the mountain and the valley lands around Sinjar."

And in the words of the small Iraq child, who played around dead bodies pulled up from the sewerage depths as if were the most ordinary thing in the world, only the living can hurt you.

For too many, they will go to the grave with the never knowing.

ABOUT THE AUTHOR

Australian-born journalist **Hollie S. McKay** has been an investigative and international affairs/war reporter with a specialized focus on terrorism, and crimes against humanity.

Hollie has worked on the frontlines of several major war zones and covered humanitarian and diplomatic crises in Iraq, Afghanistan, Pakistan, Syria, Iran, Turkey, Yemen, Saudi Arabia, Burma, Russia, East Africa and Latin America, and other areas.

Her globally-spanned coverage has included exclusive and detailed interviews with numerous captured terrorists, as well as high-ranking government, military, and intelligence officials from all sides. She has spent time embedded with US and foreign troops, conducted extensive interviews with survivors of torture, sex slavery and forced child jihadist training recruits, refugees, and internally-displaced people to communicate the complexities of such catastrophes on local populations.

@holliesmckay

Hollie McKay

www.holliemckay.com